Corporate Power and Human Rights

There is ample evidence about the negative effects business activity of all types can have on the provision of human rights. Equally, there can be little doubt economic development, usually driven through business activity and trade, is necessary for any state to provide the institutions and infrastructure necessary to secure and provide human rights for their citizens. The United Nations and businesses recognise this tension and are collaborating to effect change in business behaviours through voluntary initiatives such as the Global Compact and John Ruggie's Guiding Principles. Yet voluntary approaches are evidently failing to prevent human rights violations and there are few alternatives in law for affected communities to seek justice. This book seeks to robustly challenge the current status quo of business approaches to human rights in order to develop meaningful alternatives in an attempt to breech the gap between the realities of business and human rights and its discourse.

This book was previously published as a special issue of *The International Journal of Human Rights*.

Manette Kaisershot is a researcher and lecturer at the Human Rights Consortium, School of Advanced Study, University of London, UK. Her research primarily concentrates on issues in business and human rights, but also encompasses cultural studies, politics, sociology and economics.

Nicholas Connolly is a doctoral researcher at the Institute of Commonwealth Studies, School of Advanced Study, University of London, UK.

Corporate Power and Human Rights

Edited by
Manette Kaisershot and Nicholas Connolly

LONDON AND NEW YORK

First published 2016 by Routledge

2 Park Square, Milton Park, Abingdon, Oxfordshire OX14 4RN
711 Third Avenue, New York, NY 10017

Routledge is an imprint of the Taylor & Francis Group, an informa business

First issued in paperback 2018

British Library Cataloguing in Publication Data
A catalogue record for this book is available from the British Library

ISBN 13: 978-1-138-65502-7 (hbk)
ISBN 13: 978-1-138-39177-2 (pbk)

Typeset in Times New Roman
by RefineCatch Limited, Bungay, Suffolk

Publisher's Note
The publisher accepts responsibility for any inconsistencies that may have arisen during the conversion of this book from journal articles to book chapters, namely the possible inclusion of journal terminology.

Contents

Citation Information

The chapters in this book were originally published in *The International Journal of Human Rights*, volume 19, issue 6 (August 2015). When citing this material, please use the original page numbering for each article, as follows:

Chapter 1
Introduction: Corporate power and human rights
Nicholas Connolly and Manette Kaisershot
The International Journal of Human Rights, volume 19, issue 6 (August 2015)
pp. 663–672

Chapter 2
Corporate human rights commitments and the psychology of business acceptance of human rights duties: a multi-industry analysis
Kendyl Salcito, Chris Wielga and Burton H. Singer
The International Journal of Human Rights, volume 19, issue 6 (August 2015)
pp. 673–696

Chapter 3
Extreme energy, 'fracking' and human rights: a new field for human rights impact assessments?
Damien Short, Jessica Elliot, Kadin Norder, Edward Lloyd-Davies and Joanna Morley
The International Journal of Human Rights, volume 19, issue 6 (August 2015)
pp. 697–736

Chapter 4
'From naming and shaming to knowing and showing': human rights and the power of corporate practice
Christian Scheper
The International Journal of Human Rights, volume 19, issue 6 (August 2015)
pp. 737–756

Chapter 5
Global production, CSR and human rights: the courts of public opinion and the social licence to operate
Sally Wheeler
The International Journal of Human Rights, volume 19, issue 6 (August 2015)
pp. 757–778

Chapter 6
These are financial times: a human rights perspective on the UK financial services sector
Manctte Kaisershot and Samuel Prout
The International Journal of Human Rights, volume 19, issue 6 (August 2015) pp. 779–800

Chapter 7
Company-created remedy mechanisms for serious human rights abuses: a promising new frontier for the right to remedy?
Sarah Knuckey and Eleanor Jenkin
The International Journal of Human Rights, volume 19, issue 6 (August 2015) pp. 801–827

Chapter 8
Beyond the 100 Acre Wood: in which international human rights law finds new ways to tame global corporate power
Daniel Augenstein and David Kinley
The International Journal of Human Rights, volume 19, issue 6 (August 2015) pp. 828–848

Chapter 9
CSR is dead: long live Pigouvian taxation
Nicholas Connolly
The International Journal of Human Rights, volume 19, issue 6 (August 2015) pp. 849–866

Chapter 10
Defending corporate social responsibility: Myanmar and the lesser evil
Andrew Fagan
The International Journal of Human Rights, volume 19, issue 6 (August 2015) pp. 867–882

Notes on Contributors

Daniel Augenstein is associate professor in the Department of European and International Law at Tilburg University, The Netherlands. In 2015 he worked as a Humboldt senior research fellow at the Wissenschaftszentrum Berlin. His main research interests are in the areas of business and human rights, and transnational and global law.

Nicholas Connolly is a doctoral researcher at the Institute of Commonwealth Studies, School of Advanced Study, University of London, UK. He is also Head of Corporate Development for the London based youth homeless charity Centrepoint. He previously worked for a global bank outsourcing back-office functions to India.

Jessica Elliot is a research associate of the Human Rights Consortium, and has co-authored articles with Damien Short for *The Ecologist* and *The Conversation* on the impact of fracking on civil and political rights. Her research interests lie primarily with the impact of extractive industries upon human rights and the environment. She currently works as part of the British Red Cross Refugee Support team.

Andrew Fagan is based within the Human Rights Centre and the School of Law at the University of Essex, UK. He is currently Director of Undergraduate Studies in Human Rights.

Eleanor Jenkin is a consultant to the UN Office of the High Commissioner for Human Rights, and is the former senior advisor to the Initiative on Human Rights Fact-Finding, Center for Human Rights and Global Justice, and Arthur Helton Global Human Rights Fellow, New York University School of Law, USA.

Manette Kaisershot is a researcher and lecturer at the Human Rights Consortium, School of Advanced Study, University of London, UK. Her research primarily concentrates on business and human rights but also encompasses cultural studies, politics, sociology and law. She is a member of the editorial team for *The International Journal of Human Rights* and is on the steering committee for the Institute of Commonwealth Studies' Corporate Power and Human Rights working group.

David Kinley holds the chair in Human Rights Law at the University of Sydney, Australia. He is also an Academic Panel member of Doughty Street Chambers in London. He works and writes principally in the area of human rights and the global economy.

Sarah Knuckey is associate clinical professor of Law, director of the Human Rights Clinic, and Faculty co-director at the Human Rights Institute, Columbia Law School, USA.

Edward Lloyd-Davies is a research associate of the Human Rights Consortium, UK. He trained as an astrophysicist at the University of Birmingham and has worked for over

10 years as a postdoctoral fellow at the University of Michigan and the University of Sussex. He has been involved in writing over 20 papers on extragalactic astrophysics and cosmology. He now works as a freelance researcher, focusing on environmental issues, particularly extreme energy.

Joanna Morley is a research associate at the Human Rights Consortium, UK, with interests in the connections between human rights, development, business and international governance. She is currently completing an MA in Understanding and Securing Human Rights at the Institute of Commonwealth Studies in London, England.

Kadin Norder is a research associate at the Human Rights Consortium, UK, with interests in the connections between human rights, economics, governance and the environment. She previously conducted research for the Commonwealth Human Rights Initiative and the US White House. She works for the Rights of Nature European Citizen's Initiative in Sweden.

Samuel Prout is a guest lecturer at the University of London, a student barrister at BPP Law School (London), and works in Public and Social Work Law.

Kendyl Salcito has an MA in Journalism and a PhD in Epidemiology. She is interested in the development, validation and application of methodologies for assessing human rights impacts of corporate development projects. This line of scientific inquiry commenced in 2008 at NomoGaia, a US-based non-profit think tank dedicated to clarifying human rights responsibilities of corporations. Salcito is also a consultant of NewFields, a consulting firm in the impact assessment field for the extractive and energy industries.

Christian Scheper is a research fellow at the Institute for Development and Peace at the University of Duisburg-Essen and a PhD candidate at the University of Kassel, Germany. He holds an MA in International Relations (with distinction) from the University of Exeter, UK. His current work focuses on human rights and transnational corporations, international political economy and contemporary political theory.

Damien Short is reader in Human Rights and Director of the Human Rights Consortium and the Extreme Energy Initiative (http://extremeenergy.org) at the School of Advanced Study, University of London. He has published extensively on indigenous peoples' rights, reconciliation projects, colonialism and genocide studies. His more recent work concerns the genocide ecocide nexus and the role of extreme energy.

Burton H. Singer is trained in statistics (PhD). He is adjunct professor at the Emerging Pathogens Institute, University of Florida and a member of the National Academy of Sciences of the USA. Burton's research interests centre on integrated control of infectious diseases and the human health risks of corporate development projects, including the biological, environmental and social risks associated with vector-borne diseases.

Sally Wheeler is professor of Law at Queen's University Belfast, UK.

Chris Wielga holds an MA in Economics from the University of Colorado Denver, USA. He has six years of experience conducting qualitative and quantitative data analysis of corporate social responsibility policies and practices.

INTRODUCTION

Corporate power and human rights

Nicholas Connolly and Manette Kaisershot

Human Rights Consortium, School of Advanced Study, University of London, UK

> The rise of the modern corporation has brought a concentration of economic power which can compete on equal terms with the modern state – economic power versus political power, each strong in its own field. The state seeks in some aspects to regulate the corporation, while the corporation, steadily becoming more powerful, makes every effort to avoid such regulation. Where its own interests are concerned, it even attempts to dominate the state. The future may see the economic organism, now typified by the corporation, not only on an equal plane with the state, but possibly even superseding it as the dominant form of social organisation. The law of corporations, accordingly, might well be considered as a potential constitutional law for the new economic state, while business practice is increasingly assuming the aspect of economic statesmanship.[1]

The pervasive influence of the corporation and its ever-increasing effects on human rights globally 'is now the two hours' traffic of our stage'.[2] Though there are doubtless many ideologies, theories or polemics that may argue that capitalism is inherently flawed in such a way that it will always inhibit the human rights cause (hence the emergence of conflicting ideologies of communism, Marxism, Mao-ism, Leninism, etc.), in this instance (and for the means of this special issue and introduction) the assumption is being held that capitalism is an immutable fact of life that we will not attempt to try and dismantle.[3]

Following the 'Great Crash' and the ensuing 'Great Depression', the increasingly dominant role of the corporation as a means of organising production became apparent.[4] Sensing the zeitgeist, Berle and Means (a lawyer and a historian of economics respectively), sought to reformulate the corporation. By highlighting the effect the publicly owned and traded corporation had on the reality of property rights – the separation of control and passive property rights (or, benefit without effort or responsibility) – they justified reconceptualising the corporation or the 'reorientation of enterprise' so they embed responsible behaviour and work for the benefit of humanity.

By the 1950s and 1960s, the New Deal of the United States and the welfare state principles of the 'great' European powers had shifted the debate to an extent. Galbraith[5] described a world of giant privately and state-owned corporations that cooperated with the instruments of the nation state and organised labour to create a planned economy, which apparently protected ordinary people from the pernicious greed of shareholders. They collaborated to create a veneer of manufactured economic demand, false consumer choice, administered prices and faux employee power intrinsically linked to grinding obsession with economic growth and efficient productivity, the economic success of which, ultimately, was driven by military expenditure through World War II and into the Cold War.[6]

The 'good life', so created, distracted people from a trend that accumulated power in the hands of a few corporations, not the democratically elected representatives of the people.[7] Berle and Means were correct – the nation state did become dominated by the corporation – but whether these corporations had, or should have been, 'reoriented' to benefit communities, is a different matter.[8] As highlighted by the influential and often quoted economist, Milton Friedman, in his 1962 publication *Capitalism and Freedom*[9]:

> Few trends could so thoroughly undermine the very foundations of our free society as the acceptance by corporate officials of a social responsibility other than to make as much money for their stockholders as possible. This is a fundamentally subversive doctrine. If businessmen do have a social responsibility [...], how are they to know what it is? Can self-selected private individuals decide what the social interest is? Can they decide how great a burden they are justified in placing on their stockholders to serve that social interest? Is it tolerable that these public functions of taxation, expenditure, and control be exercised by the people who happen at the moment to be in charge of particular enterprises, chosen for these groups by strictly private groups?

While Berle and Means would, no doubt, both disagree with Friedman's analysis,[10] the reality of corporate behaviour in the globalised era, as illustrated by numerous books and hundreds of articles by investigative journalists and regular human catastrophes reported in the mainstream news, would suggest attempts to 'socialise' the corporation have failed. We are no closer to taming the corporation in 2014 than we were in 1933.

The debate

Frequently, discussions regarding corporate behaviour and the state – be that through international trade compromises and agreements, or domestic application of regulations – are reduced to philosophical disagreements which pitch big state socialist-style ideology[11] against neoliberal free market principles[12] that are equally ideological. Yet there are no examples of entirely successful planned economies just as there are no examples of governments that permit the unalloyed application of free market principles.[13]

In practice, contemporary human society, through the function of government, treads an uncertain path between serendipity and misfortune, arbitrary foresight and risk-aversion,[14] towards poorly defined objectives with few meaningful comparative measures of success.[15] For many seeking potential solutions to gigantic human problems this false dichotomy[16] undermines the ability of academics and policymakers to address the nub of many key issues.[17]

The corporation – in contrast – suffers from no such opacity of purpose. Although Berle and Means argued this should not be the case and adherents to stakeholder theory[18] might object[19] that it is not the case; the weight of evidence is that business leaders and managers believe they are employed by corporations to maximise shareholder value.[20] This obligation is rooted in the concept of a fiduciary duty that exists between the business's employees and its shareholders where success is gauged through decontextualised competition, which occurs on stock exchanges throughout the world.

The negative implications of this myopic focus on reliable maximal shareholder returns are evidenced in various industries through regional, national and transnational activism, investigative journalism and, occasionally, whistle-blowing. They are frequently the cause of substantial public outrage worldwide (as in the case of Rana Plaza, where well over 1000 garment factory workers were killed when a building that was known to be unsafe collapsed in Bangladesh in 2013), but often they are left in relative obscurity. Many of these negative implications are summarised in, for example, *The Corporation*[21] or *No Logo*[22], and characterised as a 'race-to-the-bottom'. Its positive implications, such as the reliable supply of cheap and safe goods and services ranging from food to pensions for public consumption and the mitigation of regional or temporal economic challenges through the global aggregation of risk, are frequently overlooked or taken for granted, but are no less real.[23] In short, this is not a binary debate that can meaningfully argue entirely for or against the corporation.

Purpose and scope

The intent of this special issue is to provide an interdisciplinary approach to identifying potential solutions to the negative impacts, as gauged against international human rights obligations on states, of corporate activity in the globalised era.[24] It assumes that no single academic discipline is capable of drawing together a sufficiently broad evidence base or range of theoretical constructs to address a human challenge that unquestionably spans economic, sociological, psychological, human rights, legal and political disciplines. Consequently, one purpose of this introduction is to illustrate the paucity of constructive academic investigation into the reality of corporate activity and decision-making as regards human rights and the resultant need to develop alternative methodologies for harnessing corporate activity for the good of humanity.

It takes as given the assertion that human rights represent the only meaningful attempt at a universally applicable a-religious 'moral' code – a blueprint to define reasonable regulation of human life through government – and that the corporation, in the globalised era, is the most influential and dominant form of economic activity.[25] Moreover, it takes as proven that corporations, despite their key role in the undoubted positive effects of globalisation did and do inhibit the provision of and on occasion violate human rights.[26]

In a previous journal article[27] it is argued that CSR is currently the dominant response to the tension outlined above, but that CSR is doomed to fail because no matter how thorough and well-intentioned a CSR policy is, from a shareholders perspective, the commercial value of globalisation is cost reduction, while more humane operational practice will, almost universally, increase costs.[28] Importantly, individuals employed by the business are socialised to think from a 'corporate perspective' which precludes them from making business decisions that ignore business logic which identifies shareholder value as the business's paramount concern.

There is an enormous quantity and rich history of literature exploring the personality of the corporation and the fiduciary duties of its employees.[29] Equally, scores of academics, activists and journalists have written reams surveying and analysing the nature and purpose, the positives and negatives, of industrialisation, the corporation, globalisation, CSR and business ethics, the role of the United Nations and the Bretton-Woods organisations, and the application of national and international law in relation to trade and corporate activity. This journal is not intended to supplement this work.

Neither is this journal intended to contribute to the existing vein of work undertaken by human rights professionals and academics. This is because the editors of this journal have not in their research to-date identified any books or journal articles by human rights scholars that attempt to move the discussion around human rights and the corporation beyond assessing the measurable effectiveness of CSR or asserting the need for better, or the better application of, regulations.

This paucity of creative thought is well illustrated by Ann Zammit in *Development at Risk: Rethinking UN – Business Partnerships*[30] which summarises the inherent weaknesses of the existing approach but only offers solutions that evolve the existing consensus by arguing for more specific CSR commitments or the creation of regional rather than global 'business partnerships' rather than recognising the need for a revolutionary idea.

Since the 1930s there have been two primary approaches to managing the corporation from a human perspective. One argument that is essentially rooted in the thinking of Berle and Means, which has since been updated to some extent by the thinking of Edward Freeman and is popular amongst the CSR community, is that corporations can, or at least should, act with conscience. The other asserts that, whether or not you think CSR is a positive trend, the only way to control the corporation is through behavioural regulation. We argue that this bifurcation of thinking essentially sums up the entire debate and has not moved on significantly in a century.

The majority of respected commentators agree that regulation is the only solution but that such regulation is impossible unless there is a world parliament of some description. Given the world parliament approach seems phenomenally unlikely, CSR is the only option available. Yet CSR is a false option because it most likely cannot achieve the goal of taming business and may actually prevent humanity from collectively understanding that business has been designed by humans to facilitate the production and transfer of the goods necessary for life and enjoyment.[31] This journal is an attempt to address this quandary.

The special issue

The range and quality of the contributions to this special issue reflect the growing body of academic literature that seeks to dissolve the tension between the ever-pervasive influences of global business on human rights. Though each article explores different themes, disciplines and approaches, each of the papers has relevance to the others; they serve to illuminate each other and, as a group, present incredibly interesting conversation on the theme of corporate power and human rights. The contributions to this special issue reflect upon gaps in current scholarship, many use a multidisciplinary approach to their subjects, and they all offer an original insight to the conversation on the issue of human rights in the financial age.

The original research and quantitative analysis found in 'Corporate Human Rights Commitments and the Psychology of Business Acceptance of Human Rights Duties: A Multi-Industry Analysis' by Kendyl Salcito, Mark Wielga, Burton H. Singer and Chris Wielga[32] seeks, amongst other things, to demonstrate the degree to which companies have adopted human rights in their company policies. The article highlights the disparities in the adoption of human rights language amongst global corporations. The authors find that 55% of companies included in their analysis have not fully accepted the responsibilities set for them in the UN Guiding Principles on Business and Human Rights, which – for better or for worse – seems to have become the yardstick by which corporate responsibility is measured, into company CSR reports. The research presented in the article shows European-based oil and gas companies scoring the highest in the adoption of human rights responsibility (as set forth in the Guiding Principles), with 80 % acceptance of those responsibilities found in their company policies.

The aforementioned findings of Salcito et al. present an interesting comparison to the issues described in 'Extreme Energy, "Fracking" and Human Rights: A New Field for Human Rights Impact Assessments?' by Short et al.,[33] namely in the mishandling of human rights in the context of energy extraction. The implications that can be interpreted from the findings in the article by Short et al., based on the gathered information from anti-fracking protesters in the United Kingdom, Europe and elsewhere, is that despite the inclusion of human rights language or objectives in company policy or CSR statements, human rights continue to be maligned in the pursuit of big business interests. Short et al. discover in their research an alarmingly high rate of 'interaction' between the police and protesters involved in the anti-fracking protests, which hints at government involvement, as well as business, in a lack of human rights compliance. The findings of Short et al . further support the reputation that (especially) the United Kingdom has for mishandling protest situations and the tension between those who wish to protest and the police.[34]

Many conventional oil and gas companies have pursued fracking or other forms of unconventional energy – and the high percentage of oil and gas companies who include Guiding Principles' responsibilities in their policies (as found by Salcito et al.) begs us to consider why, if the companies are engaging with human rights, do gross violations of human rights persist? A potential explanation may be found in Christian Scheper's article 'From Naming and Shaming to Knowing and Showing: Human Rights and the Power of Corporate Practice'.[35] Scheper posits that international business and corporations appropriate the language and concepts of international human rights and remake them to fit the business world. Businesses manipulate the normative language and concepts of human rights to their own advantage rather than adjusting business practice to meet normative standards. The practice of moulding rights language and objectives to meet the needs of businesses as defined by Scheper could erode the efficacy of human rights in the business context and perhaps explains why, despite the increase in human rights policies enacted by businesses, the relationship between business and human rights at ground level remains fraught. Looking at this dilemma through the lens of the sociology of critique, Scheper presents an insightful and unique position on the much-debated CSR topic and offers yet another explanation of why CSR is failing to effect any real change.

Social licence is an increasingly popular concept for protesters and communities that wish to make a human rights claim and who have no alternative (or conventional) route to access their rights. The social licence claim has been effective. In New South Wales, for example, the 'lock the gate'[36] campaign used the idea of social licence to refuse community consent to fracking operations; a refusal that has resulted in many changes in that community and many others like it in Australia. However, as Sally Wheeler suggests in 'Global Production, CSR and Human Rights: The Courts of Public Opinion and the Social License to Operate',[37] social licence or 'the courts of public opinion' may yet be another confusion to add to the gamut of CSR-type strategies that companies employ to gain the trust of investors, stakeholders, and the general public. Wheeler echoes the finding of Salcito et al. that only about half of corporations include any human rights-specific language or obligations in their company polices. This seems to suggest that a CSR policy does not necessarily include any human rights-specific intentions; further illustrating the irony that, for many corporations, being socially responsible does not mean engaging with human rights. The discussion of the failure of CSR to appropriately address public concerns lays in the foreground of Wheeler's discussion of the concept of social licence.

As Wheeler so aptly summarises, social licence is 'what is left in the absence of a structure of legal enforcement'. Wheeler takes a close and pragmatic look at Ruggie's Guiding Principles; amongst other insightful criticisms of the Guiding Principles is the observation of a lack of methodology for the production of accurate company reporting on human rights and the danger that all the hard work put into business and human rights dilemmas (i.e.

Ruggie's Guiding Principles, etc.) will be left to the chaos of a system with no set rules. The Guiding Principles make an assumption that corporations will comply with their duty to respect as they would be subjected to the 'courts of public opinion', but with no standards by which to set what a social licence entails it leaves itself open for misuse. Given that international law is still problematic, the Guiding Principles have no discernible guidance on the reporting requirement of companies, and that most corporate activity does not generate media interest which means the 'public' are unaware of issues, the concept of social licences as a way to ensure that companies comply with international standards (as set by the Guiding Principles) is, as Wheeler points out, unlikely.

Wheeler also discusses the conflated nature of global supply chains (or 'global value chains') and how these chains make tracking human rights abuses impossible and, incidentally, presents an almost insurmountable challenge when it comes to company reporting. A similar dilemma is posed with financial supply chains in 'The Government Does Nothing: A Human Rights Perspective on the (UK) Financial Industry'.[38] Samuel Prout and Manette Kaisershot, in exploring the relationship between the financial industry, the state and human rights, suggest the activities of businesses, especially financial firms, are too complex in many cases to empirically link them with human rights violations. The intricacies involved in tracing the activities of financial business to human rights violations does not, of course, mean the link does not exist, but the result has been that the legislation and regulation have remained largely unchanged and unchallenged for financial firms since the crisis of 2008 despite ongoing public scrutiny of bad corporate behaviour.

Prout and Kaisershot point out that through funding or direct involvement in various business activities, the financial industry does much to malign human rights worldwide. The government, meanwhile, seems to have no policy in place for those who feel their rights have been or continue to be put at risk by the behaviour of large corporations and financial firms; these individuals have little state protection for their rights or agency through which to access their rights. Though Ruggie's Guiding Principles have put state responsibility at the heart of the business and human rights problem it seems many states have yet to acknowledge the role that these financial behemoths play in the maintaining of global inequalities and the part they play in human rights issues worldwide.

Sarah Knuckey and Eleanor Jenkin also address the lack of remedy available to victims in their article 'Privatizing (in)justice?: Using Corporate Grievance Mechanisms to Remedy Grave Human Rights Violations'.[39] Knuckey and Jenkin investigate the efficacy of 'operational grievance mechanisms' (OGMs) as a potential remedy for human rights violations. OGMs are not a state-sponsored mechanism and they were not intended to remedy human rights violations, but they have been used to function as such. Knuckey and Jenkin have fashioned a new term for OGMs discussed in their article, calling them an 'operational-level reparations mechanism' (ORM) to distinguish them from traditional OGMs. The ORM is 'new form of transnational privatised justice', which throws up some interesting questions about the role of the private company occupying human rights functions that conventionally (and according to the Guiding Principles) are reserved by the state. Primary amongst these questions are: should companies be in charge of paving the way in transnational justice? Is it appropriate to put the rights of people in the hands of an industry whose main objective is to maximise profit? It is a worrying proposition.

As Wheeler's criticism effectively demonstrates, criticism of the Guiding Principles is that they are voluntary and provide no set enforcement mechanisms; the same criticism is levelled at the ORM process by Knuckey and Jenkin with the additional concern of allowing business to be the standard setter in transnational justice. The possibility of a global, legally enforceable human rights regime seems beyond the realm of possibility, but the alternatives are not appealing. The Guiding Principles, which left the responsibility of business and human rights to the state, enforced a problematic power dynamic between the state, business and human rights. In this ménage a trois the state is limited in its legal reach by finite boundaries (both physical and theoretical), business is able to transcend most state boundaries, and human rights violations caused by business occur in most states, which creates a legal jurisdictional grey area (or governance gaps). The governance dilemma seemed a circular quandary with no practicable solution. However, Daniel Augenstein and David Kinley posit a convincing argument that dissolves the issue of limitations of state power versus the far-reaching effects of global business in 'Beyond the 100 Acre Wood: In Which International Human Rights Law Finds New Ways to Tame Global Corporate Power'.[40]

There is a dilemma or perceived dilemma that transnational business and the concept of state responsibility inherently clash which makes transnational justice a Sisyphean task. Augenstein and Kinley dissect this argument and find that nothing about a state's responsibility means that states cannot or should not take responsibility outside their boundaries. A state's boundaries are as much a theoretical perception as they are a physical or legal boundary and the concept of the state's limitations are changing. Rulings of the European Court of Human Rights support extraterritorial responsibilities of the state, or, rather, decisions on cases recently have suggested that the distinctions between 'extraterritorial' and 'territorial' are beginning to be less important, relevant or considered in rulings. The central point of the article is best summed up in the authors' own words: '[…] there is nothing preordained or immutable about a state's jurisdictional territory and all the way in which it structures relationships between spaces, events, and people, including the allocation of rights and responsibilities'. The authors quite expertly and convincingly shatter the argument that the responsibility of the state is such that it excuses a state's responsibility for human rights violations in any situation. The case law that Augenstein and Kinley draw upon to support their argument hints at the possibility there is a real future for international human rights law.

While Augenstein and Kinley provide a useful solution to the problem on transnational justice, Nicholas Connolly in 'CSR is Dead: Long Live Pigouvian Taxation'[41] presents another approach to dissolving the tensions between global corporate regimes and human rights. By revitalising the much overlooked ideas of economist Arthur Pigou, Connolly proposes an entirely realistic solution that may be useful in bringing big business into compliance with human rights standards that exists outside 'traditional' human rights agencies (i.e. the law). Connolly's proposition is centred on the idea of taxes that recognise the human rights impact of the underlying product; in Connolly's proposal tax would be applied to businesses in a sliding scale that is calibrated on the human rights impact of that company or its products.

According to the analysis done by Salcito et al., consumers are not driving corporate change. As established earlier in this introduction, CSR has been largely ineffective in curtailing human rights abuses. Alternative mechanisms lack structure and enforceability. The state cannot be relied upon to properly address or recognise human rights concerns arising from business practice. A transnational human rights regime, though possible, is still a way off. Perhaps a Pigouvian tax scheme could be an effective way for states to recognise their human rights responsibility? A Pigouvian tax structure also might have the potential for recalibrating the underlying social understanding of consumer demands and their associated human rights costs. If two seemingly similar products vary greatly in price due to ethically imposed tax then consumers will be able to recognise that x product or service does y human rights harm. Connolly presents a very interesting proposal with potential for real impact that is worthy of further exploration.

Lastly, and perhaps most controversially, is another proposed solution to the problem presented by business and human rights. In 'Defending Corporate Social Responsibility: Myanmar and the Lesser Evil' Andrew Fagan[42] presents an argument for the use of CSR in developing a human rights dialogue with businesses in Myanmar. CSR has, in this special issue alone, undergone a fire of criticism from lack of enforceability to lack of methodology and everywhere in between, but just when CSR seemed fully, entirely discredited Fagan presents an argument that CSR can be useful in establishing some semblance of human rights consideration in regimes that previously have had no human rights understanding. Fagan looks closely at Myanmar and how the use of CSR on Myanmar at least introduces human rights concepts into a space that otherwise would be completely devoid of human rights considerations. Fagan takes all the criticisms of CSR into consideration when he considers it as the 'lesser of two evils'; where CSR is providing however minimal protection or, at the very least, consideration of human rights ideas where they might otherwise be given no consideration.

Disclosure statement

No potential conflict of interest was reported by the author.

Notes

1. Adolf Berle and Gardiner Means, *The Modern Corporation & Private Property* (Harcourt, Brace & World Inc., 1932; Transaction Publishers, 2007), 313.
2. William Shakespeare, *Romeo and Juliet* (1.1. Prologue).
3. This despite, of course, the acknowledgement that a society/state built on a growth model (i.e. economic growth that is always expanding) is unsustainable and presents its own theoretical and practical problems.
4. John Galbraith, *The Great Crash 1929* (Hamish Hamilton, 1955 ; Penguin, 2009).
5. In his books *The Affluent Society* (Houghton Mifflin Company, 1957; Penguin, 1999); and *The New Industrial State* (Houghton Mifflin Company [1967] (1985)).
6. Galbraith, *The Affluent Society*; and Galbraith, *The New Industrial State*; and Gardiner Means, 'Collective Capitalism and Economic Theory', in *The Corporation Take-over*, ed. Andrew Hacker (Anchor Books, 1965).
7. Andrew Hacker, 'The Elected and the Anointed: Two American Elites', *The American Political Science Review* 55, no. 3 (1961): 539–49.
8. See Paddy Ireland's 'Corporate Governance, Stakeholding, and the Company – Towards a Less Degenerate Capitalism', *Journal of Law and Society* 23, no. 3 (1996): 287–320, for a summary of the rise of managerialism and the 'socialised business, its fall in the 1980s and an assessment of Stakeholder Theory in the globalised world'.
9. Milton Friedman, *Capitalism and Freedom* (The University of Chicago Press [1962] (2002)), 133–4.
10. See: Means, 'Collective Capitalism and Economic Theory'.
11. Karl Polanyi, *The Great Transformation* (Beacon Press [1944] (2001)).
12. Fredrich Hayek, *The Road to Serfdom* (Routledge [1944] (2001)).
13. Joseph Stiglitz, *Globalization and its Discontents* (Princeton, NJ: Princeton University Press, 2002); Dani Rodrick, *One Economics, Many Recipes* (Princeton, NJ: Princeton University Press, 2007); Amartya Sen, *Development as Freedom* (Oxford: Oxford University Press, 2001).
14. Nassim Nicholas Taleb, *The Black Swan* (London: Penguin, 2007).

15. Amartya Sen, *Development as Freedom* (Oxford: Oxford University Press, 1999); Richard G Wilkinson and Kate Pickett, *The Spirit Level* (London: Penguin, 2009).
16. Consider the 'aid debate' characterised by the disagreement between William Easterly, *The White Man's Burden*, Oxford University Press, 2006 and Jeffrey Sachs, *The End of Poverty: Economic Possibilities for Our Time*, Penguin, 2005.
17. Abhijit Banerjee and Esther Duflo, *Poor Economics* (London: Penguin, 2011).
18. Stakeholder theory is often referenced within the corporate social responsibility (CSR) literature as evidence that business management can profitably take various 'social stakeholder' views into account and can therefore be manoeuvred to act ethically. In fact, Freeman argues that business leaders cannot separate CSR from economic results because CSR can affect economic results, which is very different from proposing that CSR should determine what economic objectives a business should pursue or how a business can best pursue its economic objectives.
19. Edward Freeman, *Strategic Management: A Stakeholder Approach* (Pitman, 1984; Cambridge University Press, 2010).
20. Joseph Stiglitz, *Making Globalization Work* (London: Penguin, 2007); Robert Reich, *Supercapitalism: The Battle for Democracy in an Age of Big Business* (Icon Books, 2007); Joel Bakan, *The Corporation* (Constable, 2004); Milton Friedman, *Capitalism and Freedom* (1962); Thomas Friedman, *The World is Flat: A Brief History of the Globalized World in the 21st Century* (London: Penguin, 2005); David Vogel, *The Market for Virtue* (Brookings Institution Press, 2005); John Kenneth Galbraith, *The Economics of Innocent Fraud* (Houghton Mifflin Books, 2004; Penguin, 2009).
21. Bakan, *The Corporation*.
22. Naomi Klein, *No Logo* (Flamingo, 2001).
23. See William Meyer, *Human Rights and International Political Economy in Third World Nations* (Praeger, 1998); and Robert Shiller, *Finance and the Good Society* (Princeton, NJ: Princeton University Press, 2012), for a discussion of why the globalised finance system benefits humanity and how it can be improved.
24. Sen, *Development as Freedom*, 240–2, sees human rights as an antidote to the remorseless social and cultural change initiated by globalisation .
25. As opposed to the informal economy, which for most people globally is the dominant form of economic interaction (Sen, *Development as Freedom*).
26. Evidence to support this statement can be found in Marie-Monique Robin, *The World According to Monsanto*, English ed. (The New Press, 2010); Gary Greenberg, *Manufacturing Depression* (London: Bloomsbury Publishing, 2010); John Ghazvinian, *Untapped: The Struggle for Africa's Oil* (Harcourt, 2007); Ed Vulliamy, *Amexica* (Bodley Head, 2010); Eric Schlosser, *Fast Food Nation* (Penguin, 2001); Klein, *No Logo*; Bakan, *The Corporation*, and countless news stories.
27. Nicholas Connolly, 'Corporate Social Responsibility: A Duplicitous Distraction?', *International Journal of Human Rights* 16, no. 8 (2012): 1228–49.
28. There is extensive debate about whether managers *should* assume short-term profit-oriented decisions provide optimal value for the shareholder (John Hutton, *The State We're In* (Vintage, 1996)) and it has been argued the Anglo-American shareholder-focussed interpretation of capitalism should be replaced by a more 'social' interpretation of capitalism such as that operated by German or Japanese businesses (John Kay and Aubrey Silberston, *Corporate Governance* (National Institute of Economic Review, 1995)). For the purposes of this review, however, this debate is irrelevant because corporate managers – with their decisions shaped by the rigours of globalised production – appear to substantially ignore this interpretation of their responsibilities.
29. Adolf Berle, 'Corporate Powers as Powers in Trust', *Harvard Law Review* 44 (1931): I049; Dodd, E. Merrick, 'For Whom Are Corporate Managers Trustees?', *Harvard Law Review* 45, no. 7 (1932): 1145–63.
30. Ann Zammit, *Development at Risk: Rethinking UN - Business Partnerships* (South Centre and the United Nations Research Institute for Social Development, 2003).
31. Connolly, 'Corporate Social Responsibility'.
32. Kendyl Salcito, Mark Wielga, Burton H. Singer and Chris Wielga, 'Corporate Human Rights Commitments and the Psychology of Business Acceptance of Human Rights Duties: A Multi-Industry Analysis', *The International Journal of Human Rights* 19, no. 6 (2015): 637–696.

33. Short et al., 'Extreme Energy, "Fracking" and Human Rights: A New Field for Human Rights Impact Assessments?', *The International Journal of Human Rights* 19, no. 6 (2015): 697–736.
34. See, for example, the Equality and Human Right Commission (EHRC) report 'Human Rights Review 2012: Article 11: Freedom of Assembly and Association', http://www.equalityhumanrights.com/sites/default/files/documents/humanrights/hrr_article_11.pdf (accessed 1 November 2014), where the EHRC highlight several issues with United Kingdom policy on protest that may have the consequence of eroding the European Convention on Human Rights, Article 11, right to peaceful protest. Continued media coverage suggests that the tension between police and protesters has not been effectively dealt with (see, for example, http://www.theguardian.com/uk-news/2013/dec/05/three-arrests-student-protest-university-of-london). The statement by Mr Maina Kiai, United Nations Special Rapporteur on the Rights to Freedom of Peaceful Assembly and of Association at the conclusion of his visit to the United Kingdom on 23rd January 2013 highlights, again, further problems with protests in the United Kingdom and, especially, the role of the police (who continue to use the controversial practice of 'kettling') See more at: http://www.ohchr.org/EN/NewsEvents/Pages/DisplayNews.aspx?NewsID=12945&LangID=E#sthash.bx82zNV4.dpuf (accessed 1 November 2014).
35. Christian Scheper, 'From Naming and Shaming to Knowing and Showing: Human Rights and the Power of Corporate Practice', *The International Journal of Human Rights* 19, no. 6 (2015): 737–754.
36. http://www.lockthegate.org.au/
37. Sally Wheeler, 'Global Production, CSR and Human Rights: The Courts of Public Opinion and the Social License to Operate', *The International Journal of Human Rights* 19, no. 6 (2015): 757–778.
38. Samuel Prout and Manette Kaisershot, 'These Are Financial Times: A Human Rights Perspective on the (UK) Financial Industry', *The International Journal of Human Rights* 19, no. 6 (2015): 779–800.
39. Sarah Knuckey and Eleanor Jenkin, 'Company-created Remedy Mechanisms for Serious Human Rights Abuses: A Promising New Frontier for the Right to Remedy?', *The International Journal of Human Rights* 19, no. 6 (2015): 801–827.
40. Daniel Augenstein and David Kinley, 'Beyond the 100 Acre Wood: In Which International Human Rights Law Finds New Ways to Tame Global Corporate Power', *The International Journal of Human Rights* 19, no. 6 (2015): 828–848.
41. Nicholas Connolly, 'CSR is Dead: Long Live Pigouvian Taxation', *The International Journal of Human Rights* 19, no. 6 (2015): 849–866.
42. Andrew Fagan, 'Defending Corporate Social Responsibility: Myanmar and the Lesser Evil', *The International Journal of Human Rights* 19, no. 6 (2015): 867–882.

Corporate human rights commitments and the psychology of business acceptance of human rights duties: a multi-industry analysis

Kendyl Salcito[a,b], Chris Wielga[b,c] and Burton H. Singer[d]

[a]*NomoGaia, Denver, USA;* [b]*NewFields, Denver, USA;* [c]*University of Colorado Denver, USA;* [d]*Emerging Pathogens Institute, University of Florida, Gainesville, USA*

Between 2012 and 2013, we analysed and coded the human rights policies of the largest corporations in six of the world's most globalised industries: finance, mining, oil and gas, food and beverage, apparel and agribusiness. Using the language of the UN Guiding Principles on Business and Human Rights as benchmarks, we developed a scoring mechanism to evaluate the level of responsibility companies had accepted to (1) respect human rights, (2) conduct human rights due diligence, and (3) provide remedies for human rights violations associated with their activities. Statistical analysis using both standard regression and ordinal logistic regression revealed that companies domiciled in the United States score poorly, nearly on par with sub-Saharan Africa, while companies based in Europe and Commonwealth countries demonstrate the highest adoption rate of human rights duties. Additionally, extractive industries produce, overall, the strongest human rights policies, while apparel companies are laggards. Furthermore, membership in socially responsible industry groups may not correlate with higher human rights scores. These findings are analysed in the context of the external influences that align most closely with shifts in corporate policies. The article considers explanations for the disparities, which have policy implications for home states and industry associations.

Human rights and business

'Human rights' is a term that has created confusion in the corporate sector. It can be an emotional or political epithet to refer to fundamental human values. It is also used in a precise sense as a term of art referring to a set of rights explicitly recognised in international instruments. There is a select group of human rights instruments understood to be directly applicable to companies. These documents are the Universal Declaration of Human Rights, the International Covenant on Civil and Political Rights, the International Covenant on Economic, Social and Cultural Rights and the eight Fundamental Conventions of the International Labour Organization (ILO).[1] Taken together, these documents represent an expansive list of rights, ranging from freedom of expression to the right to a fair trial, from the right to health to the right to education, from non-discrimination to the right to a clean environment. They are tabulated, along with their source articles, in Appendix A.

The already strong focus on voluntary initiatives governing business and human rights has intensified in the wake of a series of judicial restrictions on tort procedures for hearing complaints against companies.[2] The most effective such initiative, the United Nations Guiding Principles on Business and Human Rights (the Guiding Principles), is currently at the core of corporate human rights management. The Guiding Principles were established after six years of multi-stakeholder consultation to achieve consensus on corporate duties towards human rights.

The ascendancy of the Guiding Principles was not entirely foreseeable. Their development followed on the heels of several weaker United Nations (UN) initiatives to incorporate businesses into the human rights framework. Between the late 1970s and early 2000s the UN established a series of sub-commissions to examine corporate abuses of human rights. The final such effort developed a normative framework for placing human rights obligations on private businesses wherever those businesses were powerful enough to shoulder the burden. The 'Draft Norms on the Responsibilities of Transnational Corporations and Other Business Enterprises with Regard to Human Rights', as the 2004 effort was named, were decried by business and governments, and roundly rejected by the UN Human Rights Commission (now replaced by the Human Rights Council) in 2005.[3] Businesses, which had been excluded from the drafting process, argued that the norms were an unwelcome imposition. The Human Rights Commission put forth that the creation of a new normative mechanism for allocating the duty to protect, promote and fulfil human rights was outside of the mandate of the working group and the authority of the commission.[4]

The same year of the norms' demise, then-UN Secretary General Kofi Annan appointed Professor John Ruggie of Harvard's Kennedy School as Special Representative to the Secretary General for Human Rights and Transnational Corporations. Consultative deliberation and careful, conservative diction characterised Ruggie's work. The language in his 2008 preliminary report was deliberately noncontroversial, ensuring corporate buy-in to a conversation that governments and civil society had historically dominated. The primary duty allocated to business was to 'respect' human rights. Ruggie clarified this duty three years later with the submission of his Guiding Principles. The Guiding Principles were unanimously approved by the UN Human Rights Council in July 2011.

The UN consensus was validated by resounding support from governments, companies, and non-government organisations. Businesses readily endorsed the responsibilities allocated to them in the Guiding Principles, a fact Ruggie attributed to the consultative process that empowered them to help define their role.[5] Because the Guiding Principles enjoy such strong and broad backing, they have become the de facto tool for advancing corporate respect for human rights worldwide. However, the mere voicing of support is not the same as proactive adoption of the Guiding Principles. On the contrary, the Guiding Principles themselves make clear what governments and companies need to do to demonstrate their acceptance of human rights duties. In monitoring corporate uptake of the Guiding Principles, important trends become apparent, with implications for regional and industry-level human rights outcomes. Investigating how businesses are (and are not) adopting the principles enabled us to identify conditions that correlate to improved uptake of human rights responsibilities. Our statistical analysis examined the assumptions that endorsement of the Guiding Principles would be strongest in Western countries and extractive industries – regions where Ruggie's consultations were concentrated, in industries where he engaged most directly. The aim of statistical analysis was to control for confounding variables and ensure the robustness of the findings identified in raw data.

Background: the UN Guiding Principles

The Guiding Principles begin by distinguishing the human rights duties of corporations from those of governments. Governments retain the duty to *protect*, *promote* and *fulfil* human rights. These duties include provision of access to 'positive' rights, such as education and health care, and the protection from infringement of 'negative' rights, such as freedom of expression or tenure of property.[6] Additionally, governments must refrain from violating the rights of their own citizens by, for example, ensuring due process of law and controlling police brutality.

Under the Guiding Principles, corporations, by contrast, have only the duty to *respect* human rights. This means that corporations may not 'cause, profit from, or be complicit in' the violation of human rights.[7] To ensure that operations respect human rights, corporations have three specific responsibilities: (1) to publicly state a commitment to the duty to respect, (2) to conduct human rights due diligence and (3) to provide access to remedy when rights are violated as a direct or indirect result of company activities.

Accepting the Guiding Principles is voluntary, and so companies in practice accept those responsibilities separately, picking and choosing among them. While the supporters of the Guiding Principles may, rightly, claim that they are an integrated whole, they are not always adopted as a whole. We take the position that a partial commitment is not a nullity, but is a meaningful step which should be noted and considered. It represents a movement, if not a full-scale shift, in corporate psychology. As such, clear definitions are needed to effectively measure, monitor and analyse adoption that extends beyond a basic binary categorisation. The definitions proposed below evaluate a company's separate commitments to respect human rights, to conduct due diligence and to provide access to remedy. The categorisation and definitions proposed could potentially be employed for broader application across businesses as they implement human rights standards. This is important for researchers who might pursue investigations analogous to this one, but beyond the suite of 220 companies evaluated in this study. These ratings include a scoring mechanism, linked to the significance and enforceability of each component, with duty to respect weighted most heavily (60/100) followed by due diligence (30/100) and access to remedy (10/100). Reasons for this scoring are elaborated in later sections of the article. Careful diction analysis was employed to issue scores, as described below.

Public commitment to the duty to respect

The duty to respect is the main theoretical advance in the Guiding Principles. It articulates a corporate role within the human rights regime, separate and distinct from the role of states. Corporate human rights policies that employ clear language of respect reflect an understanding of the allocation of human rights responsibilities among duty bearers. Not all corporate human rights policies are clear however. Here is the language of Mexico's Femsa:

> We guarantee that all of our operations are undertaken with full respect and compliance with the principles of human rights, for our employees and for the communities and groups with whom we interact.[8]

Operations are undertaken with respect, but are they carried out with respect? The principles of human rights are not the same as the rights listed in key human rights instruments. The specification of employees and communities may exclude contractors. With this diction, the company has not committed to respect the full suite of human rights, as applicable to all potentially impacted rights holders. The policy does not fulfil the duty to respect.

In contrast, Repsol, an integrated oil and gas company based in Spain and operating worldwide, articulates its duty to respect as a direct commitment to the Guiding Principles:

> … because it is our responsibility, Repsol's commitment to respecting human rights is present throughout our organization. We joined the United Nations 'Protect, Respect and Remedy' framework on human rights and companies. At Repsol, we understand that the responsibility of respecting human rights should be our rule of conduct in every country where we are present and for all our operations.[9]

Although the duty to respect may be considered voluntary, once the duty has been accepted, a company can be held to that duty by interested stakeholders. Because due diligence and remedy processes flow from a commitment to respect rights, it is the fundamental element from which due diligence and remedy derive their meaning.

Due diligence

To know and show that they respect human rights, businesses have a duty of investigation and knowledge. They must take affirmative steps to find out how their operations affect human rights. This is called 'human rights due diligence'.[10] Due diligence is intended to support the duty to respect. It involves the ongoing assessment and monitoring of the impacts resulting from corporate action.[11] This includes direct impacts of a company's operations and personnel and the indirect effects in its supply and value chains. While it is theoretically possible that the duty to respect may be fulfilled without due diligence, in practice it is very unlikely. Also, without due diligence, there would be no way to know that the duty to respect is being carried out.[12]

Microsoft's human rights policy clearly states a commitment to conduct due diligence:

> We assess the human rights impacts of all our operations on an ongoing basis. To best respect human rights, we regularly review and update our relevant policies, processes and management systems.[13]

This due diligence process examines operations, policies and systems in an ongoing manner. In contrast, PVH Corp commits only to assess labour impacts through its statement:

> PVH is a member of the FLA and adheres to its due diligence process and to our requirements to establish effective grievance procedures. PVH has country risk policies and assessment mechanisms in place.[14]

This commitment is partial and avoids the use of a human rights lens to examine operations and policies. However, PVH also committed to a wholesale 'commitment to and alignment with the United Nations Guiding Principles for Business and Human Rights'. As such, though it excludes mention of due diligence, it is credited for covering all elements of the Guiding Principles.

Due diligence informs action and is a necessary component of the duty to respect. It also begins the process of formally analysing a corporation's interactions with human rights, impelling the company to confront the effects of is actions. It creates a knowledge base that can be used to inform decision-making and value judgements.

Access to remedy

Where impacts are negative, businesses have a duty to mitigate them using means acceptable to rights holders. Companies are expected to create and promote systems of private complaint and redress that provide an alternative to legal redress. Such systems, often known as 'grievance procedures', can include resolution by agreement or, if both parties consent, by an outside arbitrator. If negative impacts are significant enough to result in human rights *violations*, companies are required to provide and participate in non-judicial grievance mechanisms which potentially result in rulings *against themselves.* As a corollary, the mechanisms must also be authorised to require remediation of whatever violations the company is found to have committed, which may affect business activities and revenues. This is called 'access to remedy'. Companies have found the development of holistic grievance mechanisms challenging.[15] Coca-Cola has begun the process of establishing access to remedy through its bottlers, stating that,

> … all are required to implement a process for remediation of any adverse human rights impacts they cause or contribute to. Our efforts to promote respect for human rights across the Coca-Cola system and throughout our supply chain are being recognized.[16]

This is a firm statement that remediation will apply to all human rights impacts, and that the full supply chain will be included in the process. Nordstrom issues a much more limited commitment: 'Our team has addressed a broad range of remediation projects, including production and efficiency, wage improvement, overtime reduction, management systems and worker retention and safety.'[17] The exclusion of non-employee grievances as well as a variety of human rights pertinent to the workforce renders this a non-commitment to access to remedy.

Access to remedy is an important element of the Guiding Principles and of any human rights regime; a right without a remedy is a practical nullity. However, the Guiding Principles' description of access to remedy is neither specific nor robust. It is soft, aspirational and general, and its suggestions would be difficult to police and rate in practice. Furthermore, a commitment to provide remedies for human rights impacts without any extant process for identifying those impacts is inherently weak; unidentified human rights impacts are very difficult to remedy. A corporate grievance mechanism that is constructed in the absence of a human rights framework cannot easily be employed to address human rights grievances, and, as such, cannot easily be seen to meet the standard for access to remedy set in the Guiding Principles.

Problems in evaluating human rights commitments

The Guiding Principles recognise the importance of a company's human rights policy as a first step in accepting the duty to respect.[18] Taken together, due diligence and access to remedy ensure the ultimate effectiveness of the duty to respect. However, the Guiding Principles themselves do not create a mechanism or procedure by which a company can be formally considered to have accepted them.[19] There is no document to sign or group to join; there is no separate body or method that definitively determines if a particular company has actually adopted the Guiding Principles. This makes it difficult to accurately track trends in adoption. If we wish to understand corporate acceptance of the responsibilities outlined in the Guiding Principles, a method must be created for determining whether, and to what extent, a particular company has adopted the Guiding Principles.

To fairly represent a company's adoption of the Guiding Principles, categories of commitment must be established, and benchmarks for the completeness of a company's commitment to that category need to be set forth. The benchmarking process is important, because corporate language addressing human rights is often vague and legalistic. Once the company's level of commitment has been established, its human rights policy can be scored using a weighted system elaborated below.

Categories of commitment

We categorised commitments into the following: (1) complete acceptance of the Guiding Principles, (2) acceptance of the duty to respect, (3) acceptance of the commitment to conduct human rights due diligence and (4) acceptance of the duty to provide access to remedy for human rights violations. Companies can commit to none, some or all of these. Commitment to all three latter categories is treated as the equivalent of complete acceptance of the Guiding Principles. Anything less represents a partial or incomplete commitment to the Guiding Principles.

Benchmarks

A corporate commitment to each component of the Guiding Principles is binary. Either a company accepts the duty to respect, or it does not. While some ambiguity is unavoidable, it is reduced if the standard for acceptance is clear and applied uniformly. In considering corporate policies, the simplest case is when the Guiding Principles are referred to by name and adopted as a whole. By 'adoption' we mean a public statement agreeing with the values stated in, and the commitment to act in accordance with, the Guiding Principles.[20]

Where adoption is less clear, we employ a combination of word usage analysis and close reading to differentiate firm commitments from vague references. For example, 'commitment' and 'responsibility' in direct reference to 'respect' are among the key terms. Close reading is employed to check for overly limiting caveats, for example where a company 'commits to respect the rights of employees', but no mention is made of other rights holders. Terms that overlook distinctions between government and corporate human rights duties are taken as an indication that a corporation has not adopted core elements of the Guiding Principles. Such terms include commitments to 'uphold', 'subscribe to' and 'support' human rights, which have no clear meaning in the business and human rights field. Public statements embracing voluntary duties must be clear to be effective. Companies that desire to accept some or all the elements of the Guiding Principles, but do so in overly vague or defensive language, do not adequately express acceptance. The companies were provided with opportunities to react to our ratings. Where appropriate, scores were revised upward as a result, in accordance with guidelines presented below. The commitments to elements of the Guiding Principles reported below were recorded with confidence.

Methodology

Data

Our statistical data set was composed of 220 companies from 48 countries in six major, global industries: finance, petroleum, mining, food and beverage, apparel, and information and communications technology (ICT).[21] These are the world's most global industries and also the ones that have faced the most significant human rights scrutiny in recent years and decades. The Forbes 2000 list provided corporate size information in the fields of apparel, technology, and food and beverage, mining, oil and gas and finance.[22]

To validate the use of the Forbes 2000 list, we also used revenue as a measure of company size, gathered from annual reports and other sources. This is because not all Forbes 2000 companies published revenue data (some were subsidiaries, some were government-owned, and some were listed with no explanation for the lack of data). Five companies that had no public revenue data were excluded from analysis. We augmented our data set with member companies of leading, socially responsible industry associations, adding some smaller but socially engaged companies to our analysis. Most of the companies analysed (60.6%) are members of one of four industry groups: Equator Principles (banks), Thun Group (banks), the International Petroleum Industry Environmental Conservation Association (oil and gas) and the International Council on Mining and Minerals (mining). These associations represent the finance, mining and oil and gas industries. These groups were chosen because of their corporate social responsibility influence in sectors that have potentially large human rights impacts. No equivalent groups exist for apparel and food/beverage industries.[23] The ICT sector's Electronic Industry Citizenship Coalition (EICC) or Global Network Initiative (GNI) may be considered in future research but were excluded from this analysis. GNI is limited to telecommunications companies, which is too narrow for our ICT category; EICC membership limits human rights commitments to the workforce, rather than the full suite of rightsholders, and thus was excluded.[24]

In addition to industry type, association affiliation, size and acceptance criterion, data was sorted into eight regional categories modified from World Bank regions (US, Canada, Asia, Australia, Europe, Latin America, Middle East and North Africa, and sub-Saharan Africa). World Bank regions were modified because disaggregation revealed that geography in both North America and Oceania was less pertinent than cultural and political ties to Europe. Specifically, Australia and Canada aligned more closely with the United Kingdom (UK) than with their respective geographies. Owing to the concentration of corporate wealth in the northern hemisphere, 63% of companies analysed were based in Europe and North America.

Scoring individual companies

Ordinal and numeric scoring has established value in combined qualitative and quantitative analysis for documenting patterns.[25] In this context, it is helpful to compare companies' commitments, to correlate level of commitment to external factors and to track commitment of individual companies or groups over time. A simple, intuitive and meaningful scoring system has been built out of the elements and the definitions of acceptance described above. Our scoring system categorises levels of acceptance of the Guiding Principles as complete, absent or partial. Partial acceptance is further categorised according to which components of respect (i.e. duty to respect, due diligence, access to remedy) are accepted.

Scoring partial acceptance of the Guiding Principles poses methodological challenges. There is no basis to assume that the three parts of the Guiding Principles are of equal weight; however, weighting components in a scoring system carries risks of arbitrariness. Justification for the scale employed is supplied by the necessity of the component and its specificity of definition. The duty to respect is the foundational principle of the corporate role in human rights,[26] and is also the most firmly established of the components. Without it, the additional components lack meaning and thus merit lower weighting. As such, we weigh it heavily. Due diligence is the process by which a company demonstrates its respect for human rights. It contributes to the company's ability to remedy violations (by identifying them) and to demonstrate respect. While practically and theoretically important, Access to remedy is only broadly defined in the Guiding Principles, with no real clarity on what commitments need to be made.

We tested a variety of weightings, valuing respect, due diligence and access to remedy at, respectively, 80/10/10, 70/20/10, and 50/30/20. A sensitivity analysis (elaborated below under 'Results' and Appendix B) revealed that these variations ultimately had little impact on final company ratings, so a moderate weighting was employed. This is partly because uptake of respect was highest in companies, followed by due diligence, followed by remedy. Our weighting is as follows: duty to respect (60 points), due diligence (30 points), access to remedy (10 points), and Guiding Principles as a whole (100 points).

Any weighting of the elements will be inexact. The ratings show comparative level of acceptance so that comparisons among groups of companies can be made. Each company's policy was scrutinised by a minimum of two independent researchers who separately determined which of the three components of the Guiding Principles were covered (see 'Background' section for clarification of this process). Where there was disagreement, a third researcher was called in and consensus was sought. Policy scores ranged from 0 to 100 as a numeric sum of the components of the Guiding Principles included. No partial scores were possible within any category – for example, a company either earned 10 points for an access to remedy policy, or zero. Two sample scores are provided in Table 1 to demonstrate the process.

Verification and validation

Every effort was made to clarify the expressed meaning of each company's human rights policy. On numerous occasions, researchers discussed specific policy statements to determine their sufficiency against the standard of acceptance. Professional judgement has limitations as a benchmarking process, but it is appropriate for early-stage, exploratory research. Consensus among three independent researchers was required for all contested cases. This is an accepted means for establishing rigor.[27]

Professional judgement was supplemented with direct validation by the companies under analysis. All companies were contacted to allow them to comment on the scores issued on their policy statements. Companies that objected to our scoring were asked for documents that could change their scores. Companies that requested alternative means of communication (telephone, hard-copy mail) were contacted via these media. Because public statements were the source of acceptance or non-acceptance, private communications to us, even ones emphatically claiming acceptance of the Guiding Principles, were not considered adequate to override public statements.

Table 1. Sample scoring process for two companies.

Component of Guiding Principles	Coca Cola	Femsa
Duty to respect (60)	**60**	**60**
Due diligence (30)	30	0
Access to remedy (10)	**10**	**10**
Guiding Principles as a whole (100)	0	0
Total	100	70

Data analysis

Raw scores for industries and regions

In analysing our data, we contrasted company policy commitments across industries and geographic regions. We also examined the rates of non-, partial and full adoption of responsibilities across the whole data set. Over half of analysed companies (55%) have taken no action to accept the Guiding Principles (see Figure 1). Companies that fully accept the duty to respect represent 12% of the sample. There is a wide range of partial adopters – 20% have established a policy commitment consistent with the duty to respect, and an additional 8% supplement that commitment with a requirement for due diligence. Only two companies (representing less than 1% of the sample) commit to provide access to remedy without committing to the duty to respect. A slightly higher number commit to due diligence without formally committing to other components (7, or 3%).

There were noticeable scoring differences between different groupings of companies. Table 2 shows summary statistics by subcategories of industry, region and group.

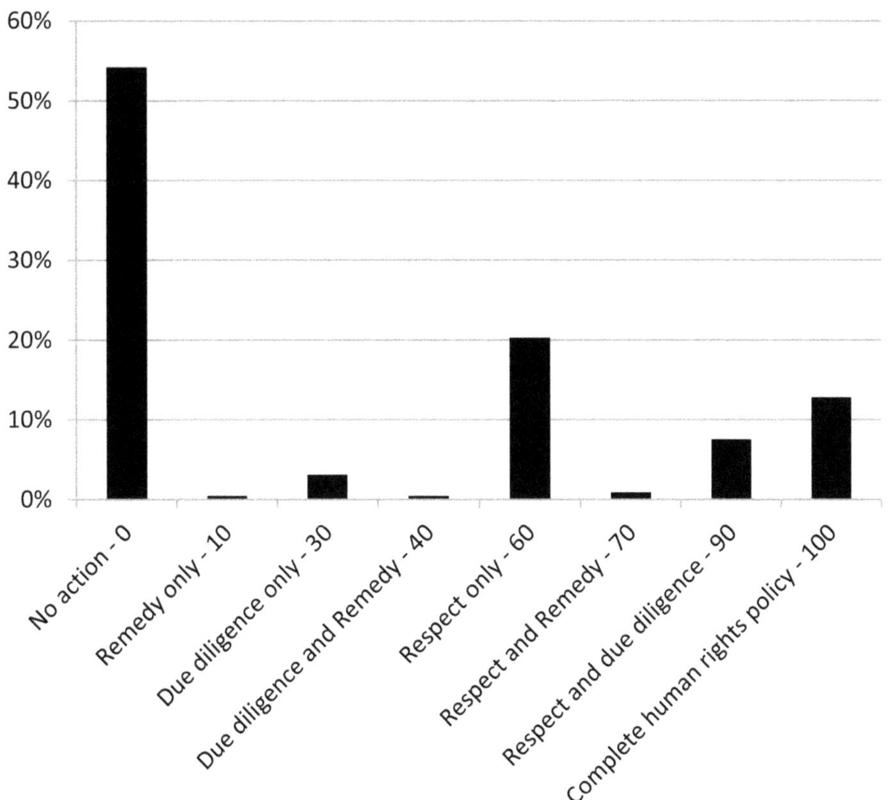

Figure 1. Nil, partial and complete corporate human rights policy commitments.

Table 2. Summary of scores.

Summary of scores by industry region group					
Industry	*Mean*	*sd*	*min*	*max*	*n*
Mining	43.87	37.74	0	100	31
Technology	30.00	38.73	0	100	21
Apparel	16.25	37.16	0	100	24
Food and Beverage	40.00	39.64	0	100	22
Oil and Natural Gas	45.90	43.69	0	100	39
Finance	29.40	37.78	0	100	83
Region	*Mean*	*sd*	*min*	*max*	*n*
Europe and Central Asia	49.86	40.74	0	100	73
United States	28.82	41.12	0	100	51
East Asia and Pacific	20.57	31.52	0	90	35
Canada	48.00	39.50	0	100	15
Sub-Saharan Africa	20.91	32.70	0	100	11
Middle East and North Africa	7.50	21.21	0	60	8
Australia and New Zealand	45.00	39.28	0	90	8
Latin America and Caribbean	15.26	31.33	0	100	19
Group	*Mean*	*sd*	*min*	*max*	*n*
None	28.79	39.49	0	100	91
Equator Principle	27.36	35.72	0	100	72
ICMM	49.09	36.89	0	100	22
IPIECA	46.45	43.25	0	100	31
Thun	95.00	5.77	90	100	4

Raw scores show Europe, Canada and Australia as leaders in Guiding Principles uptake. Sub-Saharan Africa, the Middle East North Africa Region (MENA), Latin America and the East Asia Pacific region all score below 21 (see Figure 2).

Figure 3 depicts an industry-level breakdown that makes plain the disparity between the US and European and Commonwealth countries: the US is outperformed in every industry. The only industry where US companies appear comparable to their European

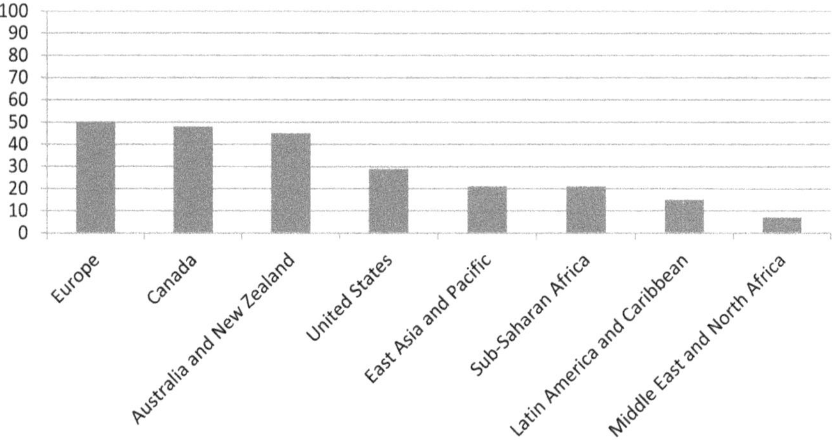

Figure 2. Corporate human rights responsibility adoption scores, disaggregated by geographical location.

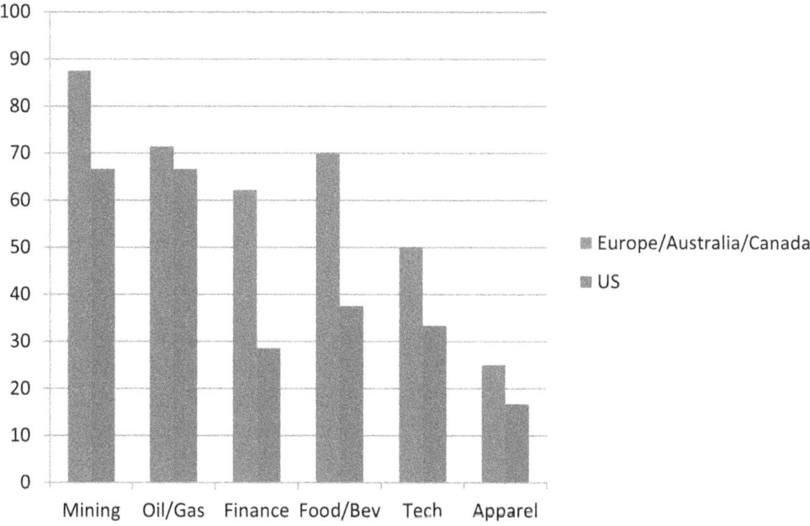

Figure 3. Comparison of US business and human rights scores compared to European and Commonwealth countries.

counterparts is oil and gas. However, three Russian oil majors, all of which have scores of zero, are included in Europe's score. If they were excluded, uptake of human rights duties in the European oil and gas sector would set the sector score above 80. The disparity is most glaring in the finance sector, where European banks outscore their US counterparts by more than two to one (28 to 62, respectively).

Figure 4 presents the overall industry-level breakdown, aggregating all countries. While there is still a range of policy commitments across industries, variations are less severe than at the regional level.

Statistical analysis

The relationships between policy adoption and company location, size and industry were investigated using both ordinary least squares (OLS) and ordered logit regression.

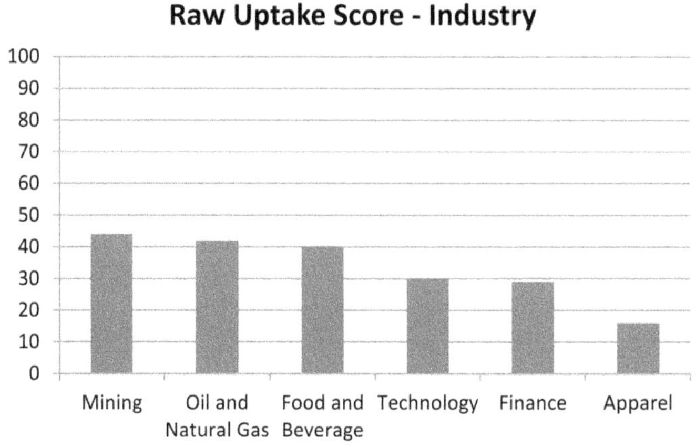

Figure 4. Corporate human rights responsibility adoption scores, disaggregated by industry.

Because results were comparable and OLS results are easier to interpret in narrative form, the OLS results are presented below. The ordered logit results are available in Appendix B.

Results

The policy adoption score served as the dependent variable in the base OLS model employed. Independent variables were: geographical location (the region in which the company is domiciled), industry, and size of company as expressed by the natural log of its sales. Additional specifications in supplemental regressions included a measure for membership in an industry group.

The basic specifications for analysis are shown in Column 1 of Table 3. Companies domiciled in Asia, the Americas and the MENA region performed significantly lower than companies from Europe ($P < 0.05$) when controlling for revenue and industry. Companies based in the Middle East and North Africa scored, on average, 41 points worse than European companies of the same size and industry. Companies domiciled in both Asia and Latin American had similar coefficients of −32 and −31 respectively. Companies domiciled in the US scored 21 points lower than their European counterparts. This is similar to the score for companies based in sub-Saharan Africa (−21), although the estimate for sub-Saharan Africa is less precise ($p = 0.09$), partially owing to its small sample size ($n = 11$). Companies from Canada and Australia had coefficients of −3.3 and −3.8, which are not statistically significant. The small magnitude of these coefficients provides evidence that the lack of a significant difference is due to true similarities, not just imprecise estimates.

Among industries, apparel and finance performed significantly lower than the reference category of mining (p-values of 0.012 and 0.036, respectively). Holding location and size constant, apparel companies scored on average 26 points lower than mining companies, while finance companies scored 16 points lower.

The effect that membership in an industry group has on policy adoption scores was subtler. Using a single dummy variable to indicate membership in any of the industry groups (ICMM, IPIECA, Equator Principal, Thun) produced a positive but not statistically significant coefficient for member companies. However, we also analysed the effect of industry association on each industry individually. This allowed for flexibility to consider that different industry groups might have different effects. Under this specification, only Thun Group membership correlated to a statistically significant difference from non-member companies. This relationship was strong, with a coefficient of 64 (p-value of 0.007).

We considered the possibility that the results may have been partially driven by our weighting of policy scores. To test this, we re-ran our base model with different scoring weights. Our results proved mostly insensitive to these changes. These results are presented in Appendix B.

Discussion

When we evaluated the human rights policies of companies, there were clear trends by region and industry. The aim of running regressions was to evaluate whether the impressions drawn from the raw scores were robust when simultaneously controlling for location, size and industry. The regressions showed that indeed they were. All of our model specifications reinforced the finding that where the company was domiciled was a stronger predictor of policy adaptation than the company's industry. The best evidence

Table 3. OLS regression analysis.

	Dependent variable: Total Score		
		TotalScore	
	(1)	(2)	(3)
lnsales	3.871**	4.235***	3.861**
	(1.603)	(1.622)	(1.632)
Technology	−11.711	−4.359	−4.264
	(11.003)	(12.267)	(14.690)
Apparel	−26.484**	−17.994	−17.865
	(10.524)	(12.255)	(14.589)
Food and Beverage	−8.213	0.040	0.777
	(10.533)	(12.172)	(14.588)
Oil and Natural Gas	−3.059	−4.264	0.967
	(9.236)	(9.261)	(17.785)
Finance	−16.428**	−18.349**	−23.163
	(7.808)	(7.923)	(18.447)
United States	−21.091***	−20.097***	−17.748**
	(7.175)	(7.199)	(7.257)
East Asia and Pacific	−32.416***	−29.337***	−26.729***
	(7.760)	(8.077)	(8.157)
Canada	−3.377	−4.054	−1.521
	(10.547)	(10.539)	(10.534)
Sub-Saharan Africa	−21.014*	−21.755*	−19.061
	(12.419)	(12.407)	(12.373)
Middle East and North Africa	−41.096***	−42.092***	−39.159***
	(13.961)	(13.953)	(13.910)
Australia and New Zealand	−3.884	−3.692	−0.219
	(13.736)	(13.710)	(13.769)
Latin America and Caribbean	−31.236***	−30.723***	−28.291***
	(9.666)	(9.655)	(9.611)
Group		12.090	
		(8.990)	
Equator Principle			14.994
			(15.505)
ICMM			11.978
			(14.834)
IPIECA			6.314
			(14.466)
Thun			64.080***
			(23.525)
Constant	50.215***	39.920***	38.999***
	(9.031)	(11.826)	(14.161)
Observations	220	220	220
R^2	0.210	0.217	0.243
Adjusted R^2	0.160	0.164	0.180
F Statistic	4.219***	4.062***	3.823***

Note: *p<0.1; **p < 0.05; ***p < 0.01.

for this is the large-magnitude coefficients for regional variables, paired with p-values below 0.05. In general, companies from Europe, Canada and Australia outperformed the rest of the world. The lowest performing companies were based in the Middle East/North Africa and Asia. Companies based in the US and sub-Saharan Africa formed the middle group, although due to a lack of certainty about the estimate for sub-Saharan

Africa it is difficult to place it exactly.[28] Across all model specifications larger company size (as measured in the natural log of total sales) was associated with a higher level of policy adoption.

Verification of scores

When verifying our scoring with company personnel, the non-response rate was high, with fewer than 10 companies providing commentary on our scoring. No company claimed our analysis overstated its commitment to human rights. In three cases companies pointed us to a relevant public statement that we had not already considered, resulting in amended scoring. In a small number of cases companies rejected our scoring as too low but provided no additional documentation to demonstrate acceptance of the Guiding Principles. Of the companies included in our analysis, none overtly rejected the legitimacy of the Guiding Principles as a framework for analysing human rights policies. Frankental has argued that this may be a result of the strong evidential basis bolstering the framework, in effect that a corporate duty to respect human rights is not only intuitive but also based on the way past corporate complicity in human rights violations (or disrespect for human rights) has been perceived and rejected by the public sphere.[29] This may indicate that there is a reputational risk associated with openly opposing the corporate duty to respect human rights. Some company responses indicated that the absence or timidity of a policy reflected internal conflict over acceptance and implementation of the Guiding Principles. Banks, in particular, expressed confusion about the applicability of the access to remedy responsibilities; given their distance from rightsholders, they may have fewer responsibilities for providing remedy than the borrowers whose actions actively and directly affect human rights.

Data analysis

Our initial regional categorisation used World Bank boundaries. Australia and New Zealand were included in a Southeast Asia and Pacific category. North America was consolidated. However, country-level data revealed that Canada performed more like Europe than the US. Likewise, Australian uptake of the Guiding Principles more closely resembled Europe than any Asian country. Both Canada and Australia retain strong political ties to the UK and develop policy recommendations that align with British common law. This helps to explain why companies domiciled in these countries expressed more policy ties to Europe than to their local geographies. As a result, we modified these groupings in our analysis.

In all statistical analyses, US industries demonstrate an overall low adherence to international human rights standards. We think this would surprise many Americans, who believe that the country's founding values embody human rights.[30] The assumption that human rights are embedded in American culture may result in diffidence towards international human rights treaties. In essence, American businesses may be saying 'we already do this'.[31] Ruggie has theorised that American exceptionalism transforms into 'exemptionalism' when there is a possibility of outside influences affecting US institutions such as the Constitution or Bill of Rights. A comparable 'exemptionalism' may apply to US businesses. Along this line of thought, operating according to US laws, with accountability to US courts, is American companies' highest and most appropriate standard for action.[32]

The correlation between industry sector and adoption of the Guiding Principles merits further investigation. The high rates of uptake in the oil and gas and mining sectors may reflect the high level of engagement these companies have had with human rights complaints from project area inhabitants in recent years. Another factor may be the in-depth involvement these companies had with the UN Special Representative on Business and Human Rights in the development of the Guiding Principles, a factor which may also explain the low uptake of the Guiding Principles among technology companies.

The low uptake in the apparel sector is noteworthy, as many public human rights violations in apparel industry sweatshops appeared as early as the 1990s. The Rana Plaza factory collapse in Bangladesh in April 2013 exposed ongoing human rights violations in the supply chains of dozens of European and US brands, but at this early stage it has had no impact on uptake of human rights standards.[33] Hamm has argued that the complexity of value change in the apparel industry undercuts the effectiveness of voluntary codes of conduct.[34] The opacity of the chain of responsibility may result in governance gaps that obscure the points of entry for duty-bearers to conduct due diligence and provide remedies. Islam and McPhail, in contrast, tracked major increases in the uptake of human rights language in the apparel industry in the years after the ILO Fundamental Conventions were ratified (1990–2007).[35] Indeed, many apparel companies *do* have human right policies specific to the labour rights enumerated by the ILO (e.g. freedom from child labour). However, it seems that this carly action has resulted in an industry-wide sense that the apparel sector's work is done and that new initiatives and mechanisms are not applicable. At the time research was conducted (2013), no apparel company had published a formalised human rights due diligence procedure.

Policy implications

The conduct of global business enterprises is shaped by three forces: law, public pressure and corporate governance.[36] The adoption of policy statements, which is the centrepiece of this article falls into the third sphere. Procedures for implementing policy statements also fall under corporate governance. Such procedures were not analysed in this article but are vital for ensuring follow-through on stated commitments. A major reason for omitting procedures is the extreme opacity of these processes. Of companies that profess to conduct human rights due diligence, 2% (Nestle, Coca-Cola, Rio Tinto and Anglo American) state how. Likewise, 2% (Nestle, Rio Tinto, Goldcorp and BP) have actually published documentation of human rights impact assessments. In the wake of the UN Guiding Principles' endorsement, the lack of an accepted methodology for human rights impact assessment provided justification for companies' slow action on policy statements. Such methodologies now exist and have been peer reviewed and field validated.[37] Corporate governance now lags of its own accord.

Law and public pressure represent other forms of governance, which also have important roles to play in the promotion of human rights standards within business operations. Our data analysis sheds light on some of the strengths and weaknesses of these governance systems as they are currently employed. Where they have been effective, these processes can be replicated.

Governments must lead the way

Government signals of interest, including those that fall well short of regulation, offer promising opportunities for increasing corporate responsibility for human rights. Geography serves as the primary predictor of Guiding Principles adherence, and governments in the highest-performing regions have instituted rights-respectful policy initiatives that correlate to human rights policy uptake. The EU and UK, where corporate policies present the strongest commitment to the Guiding Principles, have both passed national guidance and action plans in recent years to manage corporate impacts on human rights. The EU has also developed specific guidance for the oil and gas sector. In turn, European oil and gas companies demonstrate the world's highest rates of adherence to the Guiding Principles. In Canada, where in 2009 the government developed a strategy for improving the human rights performance of mining companies operating abroad, all of the country's largest and ICMM-member companies meet, at a minimum, the duty to respect standard in their policy language. In the wake of the global financial crisis, political pressure mounted on the European financial sector and several European banks (the Thun Group) voluntarily expanded their human rights commitments. The European Investment Bank issued a 2011 commitment not to invest in projects that negatively impact human rights. In February 2013, the European parliament proposed a resolution on the impact of the financial and economic crisis on human rights, and the banks are already prepared for any outcome of this resolution.

Meanwhile, such policy shifts are slower at the government or corporate level in the US. The most apparent discrepancy between US and European approaches is in the financial sector, where the US lags in human rights uptake. The US government has taken no position on the impacts of financial sector activities on human rights, and in turn, US bank policies have remained largely unmodified. The vocal criticisms by academics and activists have had little effect. Yet the US government is not powerless to modify corporate or public behaviours, even in the absence of regulatory change. For example, in managing CO_2 emissions, states within the US that have adopted energy efficiencies at the state and city level (financial incentives, government greening and eco-friendly research and development) have spinoff effects on the energy efficiency approaches of their constituents and constituent businesses. Evidence suggests that stronger engagement with the corporate sector by the governments of lagging regions can facilitate adoption of corporate human rights duties for companies domiciled in these regions. In 2015 the US government will begin hosting dialogues in the development of a national action plan on business and human rights.

Consumers are not driving corporate change

The strong correlation between home-state human rights approaches and corporate policies provides strong impetus for governments to help companies respect rights. The much weaker correlation between industry and corporate human rights policy has more nuanced implications. Extractive industries, a highly regulated sector but one often considered by activists to be the most egregious corporate violator of human rights, have demonstrated the highest uptake of international human rights language. Apparel industries, which have the longest track record of facing public scrutiny for alienating workforces, remain reluctant to embrace human rights duties. It appears that public opinion neither drives an industry to change nor changes as an industry's human rights approach evolves. This finding should not undermine the importance of public opinion. Fisman, Heal and Nair have found that companies in competitive industries where general uptake of corporate social responsibility standards are low use social and environmental stewardship to differentiate themselves. In turn, they profit significantly compared to competitors.[38] The implication may, instead, be that the public sphere is sufficiently acquainted with the business and human rights framework as a guide for corporate practice.

A key conclusion, which aligns with a large body of existing literature,[39] is that consumers cannot be expected to drive the human rights agenda for companies or industries. Although consumers can be educated on human rights concerns in the supply chains of supplier goods, and this can sometimes affect buying choice, there are other factors involved in purchasing that outweigh socially responsible consuming. Additionally, King and Soule have found that consumer activism pertaining to non-core business activities (i.e. issues beyond labour and product quality), tends to have significantly less effect on share price and business performance.[40] Consumers' buying behaviours do not necessarily align with their attitudes towards responsible corporate behaviours. Consumer product industries, it appears, have internalised this, as demonstrated by the low level of human rights policy uptake.

An opportunity for industry associations

When we ran analyses to isolate the effect of membership in industry associations, our findings were nuanced. Though there was some correlation between higher policy scores and membership in industry associations, it is not possible to make a causal connection. For example, mining companies belonging to ICMM outscored mining companies that did not, but is this because ICMM sets a higher bar for its members, or that socially responsible mining companies self-select into ICMM? ICMM certainly has standards to which its members are held, including reporting standards on social and environmental performance. Such standards are not enforced in the IPIECA framework. Human rights were only very recently added to Equator Principles standards, so it may be too early to evaluate whether they will benefit from the existing enforcement mechanisms of the association. Causal relationships in industry associations and corporate human rights performance provide a rich topic for future research. A next level of investigation might consider what elements of membership foment good practice, in contrast to what associations attract high-performing companies.

Conclusion

The differentiation between laggard and leader regions and industries is not as clear as the data set suggests, because only the biggest, leading companies were selected for analysis. That within this group over half of companies had taken no action to incorporate the UN Guiding Principles into policies and management systems suggests that movement towards improved human rights consideration and practice remains slow. Interest has increased – for example, over 2000 participants attended the UN Forum on Business and Human Rights in Geneva in December 2014, roughly double the meeting's attendance in 2012 – however, turning interest into action will involve further effort.

This research investigated policy statements, but it did not address the actions companies are, and are not, taking to back up policies. Of the 220 companies evaluated, over 20% profess to conduct human rights due diligence, yet only two companies (less than 1%) have actually published any documentation of human rights impact assessment. Some policy statements would actually be impossible to meet, such as Microsoft's statement that the company conducts assessments on 'all our operations' in an ongoing manner. Such due diligence would be prohibitively costly and time consuming.

A significant opportunity for encouraging the adoption of corporate human rights standards arises in the ongoing World Bank review of its social and environmental safeguard mechanisms. The World Bank funds development projects and programmes implemented by states and by private contractors. If World Bank funding were tied to human rights standards, governments and companies would experience an increased prerogative to accept human rights duties.

Ongoing monitoring will be important to track the continuing trajectory of the Guiding Principles as the foundational principle of the corporate duty to respect human rights. Stated commitments are the first step in a long process of assessing, understanding, mitigating and reporting on human rights impacts. Additionally, a broader sample size would be of value, extending beyond the largest companies and the most committed industry associations. The methods applied to score these 220 companies could equally be applied to smaller companies as well. Such research would allow scholars and human rights practitioners to come to conclusions about business and human rights in general, as opposed to the more limited sphere of mega-business and human rights. Indeed, a new initiative has been announced to do just that. The 'Corporate Human Rights Benchmark' initiative, a multi-stakeholder collaboration, aims to benchmark and rank the human rights policies and practices of 500 companies. This initiative merits attention.[41]

Acknowledgements

Mark Wielga contributed significant insights to this article, for which we are deeply grateful. Profound thanks are due to the companies who took time to correspond with the authors while the database was under construction. Their candour and time were invaluable.

Disclosure statement

No potential conflict of interest was reported by the authors.

Funding

This research was paid for in full by the individual donors who support NomoGaia.

Notes

1. Office of the High Commissioner for Human Rights (OHCHR), 'Guiding Principles for Business and Human Rights: Implementing the UN "Protect, Respect and Remedy" Framework' (Irvine CA: OHCHR, 2011).
2. Michael D. Goldhaber, 'Corporate Human Rights Litigation in Non-U.S. Courts: A Comparative Scorecard', *UC Irvine Law Review* 3 (2013): 127–49, http://www.law.uci.edu/lawreview/vol3/no1/goldhaber.pdf.

3. UN Sub-Commission on the Promotion and Protection of Human Rights, 'Draft Norms on the Responsibilities of Transnational Corporations and Other Business Enterprises with Regard to Human Rights, E/Cn.4/Sub.2/2003/12' (Washington, DC: United Nations, 2003).
4. John Girard Ruggie, 'Business and Human Rights – The Evolving International Agenda', *American Journal of International Law* 101 (2007): 819–840.
5. John Girard Ruggie, *Just Business: Multinational Corporations and Human Rights,* Vol. 1, Amnesty International Global Ethics Series (New York: WW Norton, 2013).
6. Henry Shue, *Basic Rights: Subsistence, Affluence and U.S. Foreign Policy*, 2nd ed. (Princeton NJ: Princeton University Press, 1996).
7. OHCHR, 'Guiding Principles for Business and Human Rights'.
8. Femsa, *Sustainability Report 2010* (Monterrey, Nuevo Leon, Mexico: Femsa, 2010).
9. Repsol, 'Repsol and Human Rights', http://www.repsol.com/es_en/corporacion/responsabilidad-corporativa/como-lo-hacemos/modelo-rc/compromisos-adquiridos/politica-respeto-derechos-humanos.aspx (accessed 17 April 2014).
10. OHCHR, 'Guiding Principles for Business and Human Rights'.
11. J. Harrison, 'Human Rights Measurement: Reflections on the Current Practice and Future Potential of Human Rights Impact Assessment', *Journal of Human Rights Practice* 3, no. 2 (2011): 162–87.
12. J. Harrison, 'An Evaluation of the Institutionalisation of Corporate Human Rights Due Diligence', *Warwick School of Law Research Paper* 18 (2012): 16, http://ssrn.com/abstract=2117924 (accessed 28 July 2012).
13. Microsoft, 'Global Human Rights Statement' (Redmond WA: Microsoft, 2013).
14. PVH, 'Corporate Social Responsibility' (New York NY: PVH, 2011).
15. Caroline Rees, 'Piloting Principles for Effective Company-Stakeholder Grievance Mechanisms: A Report of Lessons Learned' (Cambridge MA: Harvard Kennedy School, 2011).
16. Coca-Cola, 'Sustainability Report: Beyond Compliance' (Atlanta GA: Coca Cola, 2012).
17. Nordstrom, 'Nordstrom Cares' (Seattle WA: Nordstrom, 2012).
18. See, for example, Guiding Principle 16 (OHCHR, 'Guiding Principles for Business and Human Rights'). This policy commitment 'is the first essential step for embedding respect for human rights into the values of the enterprise'.
19. Peter Frankental, 'Business and Human Rights: Towards Global Standards', in *Corporate Social Responsibility: A Research Handbook*, ed. A. Murray, K. Haynes, and J. Dillard (New York: Routledge, 2012), Chap. 13.
20. Because the Guiding Principles are still relatively new, the policies often refer to the framework, which was the precursor to the Guiding Principles. It contained the respect, protect, remedy structure which is also the framework for the Guiding Principles.
21. Five companies from our data set of 225 were not included in our regression analysis due to a lack of revenue data.
22. There is significant, but not complete, overlap between industry affiliation and top-20 status. As such, the sample comprised the 20 largest companies in each industry *plus* industry association members; some small companies are association members, and some large companies are not.
23. The Fair Labor Association was considered for the apparel industry, and Fairtrade and Rainforest Alliance for food and beverage, but there is such a broad array of labour standards organisations for textiles and agriculture that selecting any of them could not be justified.
24. Electronic Industry Citizenship Coalition, 'Code of Conduct Version 4.0' (Alexandria VA: Electronic Industry Citizenship Coalition, 2012).
25. M. Sandelowski, 'Real Qualitative Researchers Do Not Count: The Use of Numbers in Qualitative Research', *Res Nurs Health* 24, no. 3 (2001): 230–40, http://www.ncbi.nlm.nih.gov/pubmed/11526621 (accessed June 2014).
26. Norman K. Denzin and Yvonna S. Lincoln, *Handbook of Qualitative Research*, 2nd ed. (Thousand Oaks, CA: Sage, 2000).
27. Michael Ignatieff, 'American Exceptionalism and Human Rights', in *American Exceptionalism and Human Rights*, ed. Michael Ignatieff (Princeton, NJ: Princeton University Press, 2005), 1–26.
28. Interaction regressions were run for European and Commonwealth countries as they interact with the oil and financial industries, as well as for the role of being domiciled in the US as it interacts with the oil and financial industries. Results were not interesting.

29. Paul Kahn, 'American Exceptionalism, Popular Sovereignty, and the Rule of Law', in *American Exceptionalism and Human Rights*, ed. Michael Ignatieff (Princeton, NJ: Princeton University, 2005), Chap. 7.
30. John Girard Ruggie, 'Exemptionalism and Global Governance', in *American Exceptionalism and Human Rights*, ed. Michael Ignatieff (Princeton, NJ: Princeton University, 2005), Chap. 11.
31. Brigitte Hamm, 'Challenges to Secure Human Rights through Voluntary Standards in the Textile and Clothing Industry', in *Business and Human Rights*, ed. Wesley Cragg (Northampton: Edward Elgar, 2012), Chap. 8.
32. Muhammad Azizul Islam and Ken McPhail, 'Regulating for Corporate Human Rights Abuses: The Emergence of Corporate Reporting on the ILO's Human Rights Standards within the Global Garment Manufacturing and Retail Industry', *Critical Perspectives on Accounting* 22, no. 8 (2011): 790–810.
33. There have, however, been corporate and government-level efforts to improve conditions for Bangladeshi textile workers, focusing on building and fire safety.
34. John Girard Ruggie, 'Global Governance and "New Governance Theory": Lessons from Business and Human Rights', *Global Governance* 20 (2014): 5–17.
35. Kendyl Salcito et al., 'Assessing Corporate Project Impacts in Changeable Contexts: A Human Rights Perspective', *Environmental Impact Assessment Review* 47 (2014): 36–46.
36. R. Fisman, G. Heal, and V.B. Nair, 'A Model of Corporate Philanthropy' (paper presented at the American Economic Association Annual Meeting, San Francisco, 4 January 2009).
37. Timothy M. Devinney, Pat Auger, and Giana M. Eckhart, *The Myth of the Ethical Consumer* (New York: Cambridge University, 2010).
38. Brayden G. King and Sarah A. Soule, 'Social Movements as Extra-Institutional Entrepreneurs: The Effect of Protests on Stock Price Returns', *Administrative Science Quarterly* 52 (2007): 413–42.
39. Institute for Business and Human Rights, 'Launch of the Corporate Human Rights Benchmark' (London: Institute for Human Rights and Business, 2014).
40. King and Soule, 'Social Movements as Extra-Institutional Entrepreneurs'.
41. Institute for Business and Human Rights, 'Launch of the Corporate Human Rights Benchmark'.

Appendix A – human rights, by article

		ILO	UD	ESC	CP
A. Working Conditions	1. Right to Favourable Working Conditions		23	7	
	2. Right to Work		23	6	
B. Child Labour	1. Freedom from Exploitive Child Labour	138, 182		10	
C. Non-Discrimination	1. Non-discrimination	100, 111	1,2,6	2,7	Var.
	2. Equal Pay for Equal Work	100	23, 7	7	
	3. Freedom of Religion		2	2	26
D. Unions	1. Freedom of Association	87, 98	20	8	22
	2. Right to Belong to a Trade Union	87, 98	23	8	22
	3. Right to Strike			8	
E. Fair pay	1. Right to Just Remuneration	100	23	7	
	2. Right to Holidays with Pay		24		
A. Freedom from violence and coercion	1. Life, Liberty, Security of Person		3		Var.
	2. Freedom from Degrading Treatment/Torture				
	3. Freedom from Forced Labour/ Slavery	29, 105	4, 5		7, 8
	4. Freedom from Arbitrary Arrest, Imprisonment		9		9
B. Free speech	1. Freedom of Thought		18		18
	2. Freedom of Expression		19		19, 25
	3. Freedom of Assembly, Movement		20		21
A. Environment	1. Right to Adequate Supply of Water		3	11, 12	
	2. Right to Clean Environment			12	
B. Health	1. Right to Health		26	12	
C. Housing	1. Freedom of Residence, Movement		13		
	2. Right to Housing		25	11	
D. Livelihood	1. Right to an Adequate Standard of Living		25	12	
E. Property	1. Right to Property		17		
F. Privacy	1. Right to Privacy (Non-interference)		12		17
G. Food	1. Right to Food, Freedom from Hunger		25	11	
A. Education	1. Right to Education		26	13	
B. Childhood	1. Rights of Children				24
C. Corruption	1. Right to Public and Political Participation				17
A. Informed consent	1. Right of Self Determination, Subsistence			1	1
B. Culture	1. Right to Cultural Participation		27		27

Notes: UD = Universal Declaration of Human Rights; ESC = Convention on Economic Social and Cultural Rights; CP = Convention on Civil and Political Rights; ILO = International Labour Organization Core Conventions.

Appendix B – regression results

Ordered Logit Regression

In addition to the two basic OLS regression models presented in the article, we also employed ordered logistic regression. This is because scoring was ordinal (the only possible scores are: 0, 10, 30, 40, 60, 70, 90 and 100), rather than continuous. These scores, generated for each company, should theoretically have implications for statistical analysis, which inspired the dual analysis. Regressions using both ordinal and continuous analysis revealed no relevant differences in analysis, a finding that shaped the content of this article, but the ordered logit processes and outcomes are supplied here for the interested.

The Raw scores were sorted into four groups, by the level of completeness of their commitment to these policies: minimal commitment (0–10, group 1), partial commitment without language of respect (30–40, group 2), partial commitment with respect language (60–70, group 3), and full commitment (90–100, group 4). The dependent variable was the logit of this score grouping. The independent variables for this regression were the same as those in our OLS model: *company size*, as measured by the natural log of company sales, *location*, with Europe as the reference category, and *industry*, with mining as the reference category. Some model specifications included a measure for *membership in an industry group*.

The results of this model are presented in Appendix Table 1.

Sensitivity tests

In order to test the sensitivity of our results to our choice of scoring weights, we re-ran our basic model with alternative scoring weights. The results of this test are presented in Appendix Table 2. The first column is our basic results with the weights of 60/30/10 where respect = 60, due diligence = 30 and access to remedy = 10.

Table A1.

	Dependent variable: Score Group		
	(1)	(2)	(3)
lnsales	0.296***	0.322***	0.304***
	(0.103)	(0.105)	(.130)
Technology	–0.497	–0.022	–0.233
	(0.584)	(0.678)	(0.796)
Apparel	–1.743**	–0.678**	–1.377
	(0.686)	(0.791)	(0.889)
Food and Beverage	–0.447	0.093	–0.006
	(0.545)	(0.667)	(0.785)
Oil and Natural Gas	–0.027	–0.122	–0.127
	(0.484)	(0.492)	(1.041)
Finance	–0.868**	–0.994**	–1.957**
	(0.408)	(0.420)	(1.316)
United States	–1.225***	–1.178***	–1.068***
	(0.406)	(0.406)	(0.411)
East Asia and Pacific	–1.744***	–1.564***	–1.432***
	(0.454)	(0.468)	(0.476)
Canada	–0.093	–0.127	–0.036
	(0.526)	(0.529)	(0.536)
Sub-Saharan Africa	–0.850	–0.894	–0.742
	(0.689)	(0.693)	(0.699)
Middle East and North Africa	–2.949**	–3.044***	–2.932***
	(1.177)	(1.185)	(1.191)
Australia and New Zealand	–0.125	–0.121	–0.117
	(0.690)	(0.689)	(0.706)
Latin America and Caribbean	–1.937***	–1.923***	–1.806***
	0.629)	(0.637)	(0.638))
Group	–	0.749	–
		(0.526)	
Equator Principle	–	–	1.400
			(1.189)
ICMM	–	–	0.453
			(0.782)
IPIECA	–	–	0.454
			(0.807)
Thun	–	–	16.536***
			(0.000)
1|2	–0.407	0.246	0.067
	(0.476)	(0.664)	(0.773)
2|3	–0.221	0.434	0.259
	(0.475)	(0.664)	(0.773)
3|4	1.049	1.714**	1.586**
	(0.482)	(0.675)	(2.031)
Observations	220	220	220

Note: *p < 0.1; **p < 0.05; ***p < 0.01.

Tablc A2.

	Dependent variable: Total Score			
	(Basic)	(80/10/10)	(50/30/20)	(70/20/10)
lnsales	3.871**	3.466**	3.324**	3.399**
	(1.603)	(1.742)	(1.434)	(1.621)
Technology	–11.711	–9.920	–6.902	–8.550
	(11.003)	(11.961)	(9.845)	(11.129)
Apparel	–26.484**	–29.257**	–19.514**	–25.650**
	(10.524)	(11.440)	(9.416)	(10.645)
Food and Beverage	–8.213	–3.777	–4.173	–3.661
	(10.533)	(11.450)	(9.424)	(10.654)
Oil and Natural Gas	–3.059	–4.722	–3.289	–3.888
	(9.236)	(10.040)	(8.263)	(9.342)
Finance	–16.428**	–17.579**	–14.482**	–16.148**
	(7.808)	(8.487)	(6.986)	(7.897)
United States	–21.091***	–25.486***	–18.358***	–23.083***
	(7.175)	(7.799)	(6.419)	(7.257)
East Asia and Pacific	–32.416***	–31.728***	–28.486***	–30.503***
	(7.760)	(8.436)	(6.943)	(7.849)
Canada	–3.377	–4.047	–5.400	–4.820
	(10.547)	(11.465)	(9.437)	(10.668)
Sub-Saharan Africa	–21.014*	–28.756**	–17.906	–25.360**
	(12.419)	(13.499)	(11.111)	(12.561)
Middle East and North Africa	–41.096***	–41.665***	–32.595***	–38.623***
	(13.961)	(15.176)	(12.491)	(14.121)
Australia and New Zealand	–3.884	–2.308	–8.044	–4.112
	(13.736)	(14.931)	(12.290)	(13.893)
Latin America and Caribbean	–31.236***	–32.195***	–23.334***	–29.339***
	(9.666)	(10.507)	(8.648)	(9.777)
Constant	50.215***	55.540***	40.754***	50.257***
	(9.031)	(9.817)	(8.080)	(9.135)
Observations	220	220	220	220
R^2	0.210	0.197	0.180	0.193
Adjusted R^2	0.160	0.146	0.129	0.143
F Statistic (df = 13; 206)	4.219***	3.891***	3.490***	3.800***

Note: *p < 0.1; **p < 0.05; ***p < 0.01.

Extreme energy, 'fracking' and human rights: a new field for human rights impact assessments?

Damien Short, Jessica Elliot, Kadin Norder, Edward Lloyd-Davies and Joanna Morley

Human Rights Consortium, School of Advanced Study, University of London, UK

This article explores the potential human rights impacts of the 'extreme energy' process, specifically focussing on the production of shale gas, coal-bed methane (CBM) and 'tight oil', known colloquially as 'fracking'. The article locates the discussion within a broader context of resource depletion, the 'limits to growth' and the process of extreme energy itself. Utilising recent secondary data from the United States and Australia, combined with the preliminary findings of our ethnographic fieldwork in the United Kingdom, the article outlines a *prima facie* case for investigating 'fracking' development through a human rights lens. Indeed, based on considerable emerging evidence we argue that 'fracking' development poses a significant risk to a range of key human rights and should thus form the subject of a multitude of comprehensive, interdisciplinary human rights impact assessments (HRIAs) as a matter of urgency. Finally, given the close relationships between government and extractive industries, we argue that these impact assessments must do more than bolster corporate social responsibility (CSR) statements and should be truly independent of either government or industry influence.

Introduction

Limits to growth, extreme energy and the 'minimally good life'

While the theory and practice of 'human rights' has produced many differing conceptions, justifications, formulations and relativistic exceptions,[1] for the purposes of this article we will principally utilise the relatively uncontentious, empirically grounded, 'minimalist'[2] conception articulated by legal scholar James Nickel. For Nickel, contemporary human rights standards are justified moral and legal claims 'universally held' by all persons vis-à-vis their governments, coupled with their corresponding moral and legal duties that governments, at all levels, owe their citizens in order for them to lead a 'minimally good life'.[3] National and international institutions bear the primary responsibility of securing human rights and the test for successfully fulfilling this responsibility is the creation of opportunities for all individuals to lead such a life. The realisation of human rights requires establishing the conditions, positive and negative, for all human beings to lead minimally good lives and thus should not be confused with attempts to promote the highest possible standards of living, or the best or most just form of economic system, or a morally perfect society. The impression that many have of human rights as being unduly utopian testifies less to the inherent demands of human rights and more to the extent to which the fairly modest aspiration of a 'minimally good life'[4] for all is so far from being realised in the world today. Here, we are not just talking about the seemingly infinite number of discrete human rights violations around the world, about which much has been written, but also the systemic denial of the 'minimally good life' for millions of people that seems to be the inevitable by-product of the capitalist mode of production[5] and about which much less has been written. Perhaps the most well-known debate in the human rights literature is the exchange between Rhoda Howard-Hassman and Admandiata Pollis. The debate highlighted contrasting interpretations of the pros and cons of the spread of global capitalism for human rights, but it is the former's[6] faith in capitalism's 'long term' prospects for the enhancement of human rights that is symptomatic of a distinct academic and popular denial of the two most important and unsavoury facts facing humanity today – the 'limits to growth' and anthropogenic climate change.

The 1972 Club of Rome report *The Limits to Growth*[7] utilised a system dynamics computer model to simulate the interactions of five global economic subsystems, namely: population, food production, industrial production, pollution and consumption of non-renewable natural resources, the results of which posed serious challenges for global sustainability. A recent study collated historical data for 1970–2000[8] and compared them with scenarios presented in *The Limits to Growth*. The analysis shows that 30 years of historical data compares favourably with key features of the 'standard run' scenario, which results in collapse of the global system midway through the twenty-first century. The key driver behind the Limits to Growth prediction – and arguably the one most poised to quickly cause global economic collapse – is the depletion of non-renewable energy sources, especially of oil and natural gas.[9] Despite the best efforts of the fossil fuel industry to propagate a paradigm of energy abundance, especially in the United States (US),[10] global production of conventional oil has already peaked and – barring incredibly unlikely huge new discoveries of easily extracted oil – must soon decline as predicted in *Limits to Growth*.[11] New discoveries of oil and natural gas liquids[12] have dropped dramatically since their peak in the 1960s, and the world now consumes four to five barrels of oil for every one discovered.[13] Because oil production from conventional fields drops globally by 5% each year, it is thus assured that such fields will eventually 'run out'.[14]

This downward global trend in oil discovery and supply has not gone unnoticed by the major international actors, namely states and multi- and trans-national corporations, who have taken various actions since the end of the Cold War to secure access to remaining conventional oil supplies. An examination of major international conflicts in the Persian Gulf region alone since 1990 demonstrates the determination of countries such as the US to maintain control of conventional energy resources.[15] Indeed, conventional energy supplies have become so precious to many states that 'energy security'[16] is now an overriding objective within which foreign and domestic policies situate the procurement of oil (and other energy sources) as a matter of national security. Such a discourse often elevates concern for the global fossil fuel market over other considerations such as the environment and human rights.[17]

This change in rhetoric to boost the perceived necessity of fossil fuels is furthered by the influence of major energy corporations upon state governments. As numerous internationally reaching corporations, such as Exxon Mobil and ConocoPhillips, have developed larger economies than many sizeable states,[18] their power has correspondingly grown. Since such companies' business models centre on fossil fuels, examples of corporate-state collaboration to further non-renewable energy use may be found in varying arenas, from the more than 50 million dollars Koch Industries spent on lobbying the US government between 1998 and 2010[19] and the formation of the American Legislative Exchange Council (which brings private corporations together with elected US state officials to draft new legislation),[20] to direct connections between advisors to the United Kingdom (UK) Cabinet Office and energy sector companies such as Centrica and Riverstone.[21] Because of the overly close, arguably corrupt and undemocratic relationships,[22] between politicians and corporate interests, it could be argued that the exclusion of 'the underground injection of natural gas for purposes of storage' and ' ... of fluids or propping agents ... pursuant to hydraulic fracturing operations related to oil, gas, or geothermal production activities' from the US Safe Drinking Water Act[23]; the British government's determination to make unconventional energy extraction through hydraulic fracturing an 'urgent national priority'[24]; the failure of the European Union to create legally binding environmental legislation for hydraulic fracturing[25]; and George W. Bush's administration's policy of attempting to 'refute the science of global warming and install in its place economic and environmental policies that not only ignore but deny the views of the scientific community on climate change'[26] are – at the very least in part – results of the wishes of the energy sector. As the 200 largest listed fossil fuel companies spent $674 billion on developing new energy reserves (five times as much as they spent returning money to shareholders) in 2012,[27] the energy industry remains invested in pushing the 'limits' as far as they can go.[28]

Though corporations may lobby otherwise,[29] resource limitations to growth are not the only significant, impending, ecological threats to human rights on a global scale. Carbon dioxide atmospheric concentrations 'have increased by 40% since pre-industrial times', with concentrations of carbon dioxide, methane and nitrous oxide at the highest in at least 800,000 years,[30] and the rate of carbon dioxide release is unprecedented, at least in the last 300 million years. The result of this level of pollution – inherently tied to an insistence on using and depleting non-renewable energy sources[31] – is the phenomenon of climate change, in this context represented by the anthropogenic increase in the earth's surface temperature. Since 1880, the average global temperature has increased by roughly 0.85 degrees Celsius, with most of the increase – 0.72 degrees Celsius – occurring in the past 50 years.[32] The effects of this global warming are diverse and range from shrinking glaciers and ice sheets, to the highest rate of sea level rise in the past 2000 years and increasingly frequent extreme weather events; all of which clearly result from 'human influence on the climate system'.[33]

Knowing that these two results of humanity's 'addiction' to fossil fuels are imminently approaching, it may be hoped that global use of oil, natural gas and coal are immediately curbed. At present, however, fossil fuels still remain the world's main source of energy, accounting for 81% of global primary energy use in 2010.[34] This is undoubtedly due, at least in part, to the current, Western propagated, largely fossil fuel dependent, neoliberal economic model, wherein corporations, being legally bound to pursue profit above all other considerations, continuously, and most often successfully, lobby for favourable legislation, deregulation and tax incentives. As Bakan noted in his seminal text, *The Corporation: The Pathological Pursuit of Profit and Power*,[35] under corporate law, the primary legal duty of the corporation is 'simply to make money for shareholders' and failing to pursue this end 'can leave directors and officers open to being sued.[36] Thus, the multitude of multi-billion dollar companies that depend upon the continued global use of fossil fuels have not only a vested interest in advocating for further non-renewable energy extraction, but arguably, in the current energy market, a legal duty to do so – and at the very least an obligation to continue pursuing oil, coal and natural gas extraction as long as it is profitable (and legal) to do so. Thus, while the use of renewable energy sources is growing,[37] they are forced to compete with an established and highly subsidised[38] non-renewable market, rather than be allowed to replace it.[39]

Furthermore, as conventional reserves are depleted[40] and demand for energy rises, there is increasing pressure to exploit unconventional energy sources.[41] Michael Klare[42] first coined the term 'extreme energy' to describe a range of relatively new, higher-risk, non-renewable resource extraction processes that have become more attractive to the conventional energy industry as the more easily accessible supplies dwindle. Edward Lloyd-Davies points out, however, that this definition of extreme energy as a category is highly problematic as it is dependent upon specific examples; it lacks 'explanatory or predictive power',[43] and leaves open the question of who decides which extractive techniques qualify. A conceptual understanding would suggest that extreme energy is a 'process whereby extraction methods grow more intense over time, as easier to extract resources are depleted'. The foundation of this conception is the simple fact that those energy sources which require the least amount of effort to extract will be used first, and only once those are dwindling will more effort be exerted to gain similar resources. Extreme energy, in this sense, is evident in the history of energy extraction – in the change from gathering 'sea coal' from British beaches and exploiting 'natural oil seeps', to opencast mining and deep-water oil drilling. Viewed in this light, the concept of extreme energy becomes a lens through which current energy extraction efforts can be explained and the future of the energy industry predicted. Using this extreme energy lens necessitates an understanding of 'the amount of energy which is needed to obtain energy', as in this process it is that value which is continually rising. This value may be calculated as either 'net energy' or 'energy return on investment' (EROI), whereby net energy is the available energy for use after subtracting the energy required for extraction, and EROI is the percentage of energy produced divided by the amount required for extraction. When charted together, the net energy available to society is seen to decrease along with EROI in a curved mathematical relationship which forms the 'energy cliff' – i.e. the point at which EROI becomes increasingly low and net energy drops to zero.[44]

In the extreme energy process the economic system can be conceptualised as consisting of two distinct segments, the part which is extracting, refining and producing energy (the energy industry) and everything else, which just consumes energy. What needs to be clearly understood is that the energy industry is in the rare position where the commodity which it produces is also the main resource it consumes. Therefore, as energy extraction becomes more extreme, while the rest of the economy will be squeezed by decreasing energy availability and rising prices,[45] the energy industry's rising costs will be offset by the rising revenues it receives. The net result will be a reallocation (through the market or otherwise) of resources from the rest of society to the energy industry, to allow the energy industry to target ever more difficult to extract resources. This process is ongoing as easier-to-extract resources are depleted, and data from recent extraction methods, such as hydraulic fracturing and tar sands extraction, show that industry is increasingly lurching towards the net energy cliff. Such action on the part of some of the largest and most commercially successful trans-national corporations may only be understood as the logical result of the extreme energy process[46] – there simply are not enough easier-to-extract resources available.[47]

Despite the obvious negative implications of these developments, the process shows no sign of stopping, but continues towards the precipice at an ever-increasing rate, fuelled by ever-increasing levels of energy consumption. Perpetuated by the global economic 'growth' fixation,[48] increasing amounts of energy are consumed each year,[49] driving the process over the edge. Of course, industry is not willing to halt the process[50] as intense demand further pushes up the price of energy,[51] allowing extraction to remain economical – as long as enough resource is extracted at each site and the price stays high. The result is that higher energy consumption leads to faster resource depletion, which in turn results in the acceleration of the extreme energy process. Within this neoliberal economic context of increasing demand and profit potential the results of extreme extraction techniques,[52] and the consequences of continuing the process, are easily trumped in the interest of short-term profiteering and 'energy security'. Indeed, as Stephanie Malin notes, neoliberal 'normalization' of unconventional energy extraction emerges most saliently regarding environmental outcomes and economic development.[53] Despite the prospective consequences of reaching our limits to growth, and with considerable evidence demonstrating a strong correlation between extraction effort and damage to both society and the environment, the extreme energy process continues to accelerate with potentially disastrous consequences.[54]

The depth of connections already established between the extreme energy process and the 'minimally good life' illustrates the otherwise overlooked insidious nature of this insistence upon striving towards the energy precipice. Human rights violations due to climate change and the release of pollutants are yet another side effect of humanity's dependence on fossil fuels that grows in magnitude with each decade. The tropics and subtropics have seen droughts increase in intensity and duration since the 1970s,[55] and diseases such as malaria are affecting larger portions of the population.[56] Two hundred thousand deaths in the US each year result from air pollution,[57] while a heat wave across Europe in 2003 (most likely resulting from global climate change)[58] left roughly 30,000 people dead.[59] There is strong evidence to suggest that the worst consequences of anthropogenic climate change on human rights have not yet been felt. As predicted in *The Limits to Growth*.[60] the effects of climate degradation will rapidly increase with temperature throughout the twenty-first century,[61] resulting in large-scale deaths across Europe due to heat stroke,[62] worsening droughts across continents,[63] further loss of food and water, and a potential, eventual, extinction-level event for humanity if global emissions are not reduced in accordance with the latest climate science modelling. Such events, along with resulting unrest, wars and mass migrations,[64] threaten people's rights to life and health worldwide.

The rush to scrape the bottom of the fossil fuel barrel is thus creating a veritable perfect storm for current and future human rights abuses. As resources become scarcer our scramble to use them grows, increasing the political prioritisation of fossil fuel extraction over ecosystems, human health and security; while increasing demand also ensures that such resources will run out sooner, which in turn will result in further human rights violations as food, health care and other basic needs are no longer met, to say nothing of the abuses to human security which would also necessarily increase. These violations will most likely increase exponentially as resources are depleted – at least, that is, until the sharp population decline predicted in *The Limits to Growth* occurs.[65]

'Fracking' as the latest step in the process

In addition to the infamous 'tar sands'[66] in Alberta Canada, the march towards the net energy cliff is arguably spearheaded in the West by the most recently developed family of extreme energy extraction methods known as 'fracking', a colloquial expression which usually refers to the extraction of shale gas, CBM (coal-bed methane) and 'tight oil'. The term, however, has become somewhat loaded, such that it is necessary to outline the contrasting uses and define the senses in which it is invoked in this article. In public discourse about 'fracking' different sides often talk past each other, due to very different understandings of what the issues are, and differing definitions of the term itself. These differences fall along a spectrum that can be understood in terms of the interests of the parties involved.

Exploitation of unconventional oil and gas is a new, more extreme form of fossil fuel extraction, targeting much less permeable rock formations than previous conventional oil and gas extraction. It is characterised by the drilling of dense patterns of, usually horizontal, wells (up to eight per square mile or more) in conjunction with other more intense processes such as hydraulic fracturing and de-watering. Different rock formations can be targeted, such as shale (shale gas and oil) and coal (CBM), but the negative impacts on the environment and society are very similar. For many local people affected, 'fracking' has come to mean petroleum extraction companies turning up where they live and coating the area in hundreds or thousands of well-pads, compressor stations and pipelines alongside large volumes of truck traffic with some likening it to an 'invasion' and 'occupation',[67] bringing with it a large variety of negative consequences for them and their environment.

The word 'fracking', however, is derived from 'fraccing', a much more narrowly defined industry slang for 'hydraulic fracturing', one particular stage of unconventional petroleum (oil or gas) extraction. A scaled-up form of hydraulic fracturing (high volume), involving injecting fluids under high pressure to crack the rock, is often used to release hydrocarbons during unconventional oil and gas extraction. The communities living with the consequences of unconventional oil and gas extraction are mainly concerned with the impact it has on them and their environment. Unconventional oil and gas extraction is a complex process, involving pad construction, well drilling, casing, stimulation (often including but not limited to hydraulic fracturing), extraction and transport, along with well plugging and abandonment (or failure to do so). All these stages have a consequent impact on their local environment and, due to the fact that fracking requires so many more wells covering much larger areas, these impacts mount up to a far greater extent than for conventional extraction and production.

In an era of peaked conventional supplies,[68] extractive industries are principally concerned with finding new fossil fuels to extract in order to ensure continued profits, the cumulative impacts of which are likely to be seen as little more than simple 'externalities' for the companies involved. Focused as they are on getting gas and oil out of the ground, regardless, the industry and their government supporters are concerned to utilise the technologies for just that. Moreover, they work on a drilling site by drilling site basis, and the cumulative impact of the whole process seems to be of little concern. It is also useful in their public relations to focus on micro details rather than the macro picture, and a narrow definition of 'fracking', as simply hydraulic fracturing, helps promote the impression that fracking is simply conventional extraction plus hydraulic fracturing, rather than an entirely different process with very different impacts. Quite possibly one of the reasons the term 'fracking' has become synonymous with unconventional oil and gas extraction more generally lies in the choices made by the industry in their early promotional pitches to investors. Indeed, in the early part of the last decade, it seems that to raise funds for exploration a simple technological explanation was preferred when pitching to non-experts. The industry chose to focus attention on hydraulic fracturing as the key ingredient out of a complex array of technological processes. It is not difficult to understand why the idea of a new, high-tech well completion method, 'massive slick-water hydraulic fracturing', which was going to single-handedly revolutionise the industry by allowing access to a wealth of previously untapped resources, was an attractive sales pitch to investors. A more accurate view of unconventional oil and gas, as requiring much more effort, drilling greater numbers of much more expensive wells in order to produce much less oil/gas, does not sound like such an attractive proposition in comparison. It is therefore unsurprising that the terminology used to describe the industry (and the understanding of the issues involved) has become somewhat skewed by this initial spin.

Given that this article deals with the impact of unconventional extraction on people and the environment from a human rights perspective, the issues raised are the wider ones surrounding the overall effects of the entire more-intense extraction process, rather than ones specific to particular technologies the industry may or may not use. For this reason it is far more appropriate to use this wider definition of 'fracking', rather than the more narrowly defined industry slang that has the effect of limiting discourse to just the narrow technical process of hydraulic fracturing itself, as if it could occur in an isolated vacuum without its necessary production infrastructure. Even so, it should still be acknowledged that since there are often significant levels of confusion surrounding the use of the term, the particular understanding being used should always be defined. Thus, to be clear, in this article 'fracking' is being used in its wider sense to include all of the required industrial elements of hydraulic fracturing, from huge quantities of water, to compressor stations, truck traffic and waste disposal.

In the countries where 'fracking' development has taken place it has been controversial and divisive. Supporters of unconventional gas development often claim that it reduces gas prices, creates employment opportunities and provides 'energy security', all the while producing lower carbon emissions than coal. Its detractors often contest all such claims, usually pointing to contrary data emerging from the US and Australia. Indeed, in numerous studies from both countries, local communities most affected by developments often cite considerable negative impacts on the environment and human health, including groundwater contamination, air pollution, radioactive and toxic waste, water usage, earthquakes, methane migration and the industrialisation of rural landscapes,[69] the cumulative effect of which has led to calls for the United Nations Human Rights Council (HRC)[70] to condemn fracking as a threat to basic human rights, particularly the rights to water and health. Fracking development is fast becoming a human rights issue.[71]

A need for human rights impact assessments

The United Nations Environment Programme (UNEP) has issued a 'Global Alert'[72] on the issue of fracking development, warning of significant environmental risks to the air, soil and water (contamination and usage competition); ecosystem damage; habitat and biodiversity impacts; and fugitive gas emissions – which will endanger carbon reduction targets. In terms of public health, UNEP[73] warned of risks of pipeline explosions; release of toxins into air, soil and water; and competition for land and water resources needed for food production and that unconventional gas would likely be used 'in addition to coal rather than being a substitute'[74] and would thus pose a threat to the development of sustainable economies.

Most of the academic papers on the impacts of fracking have focused on such issues as the macroeconomic benefits of a 'shale gas revolution', the 'green' credentials of shale gas,[75] and the levels of environmental impact and responsibility for it.[76] The few human impact investigations undertaken have come from investigative journalists,[77] small non-governmental organisations (NGOs)[78] and documentary filmmakers.[79] While valuable, such studies have been limited in scope and were not comparative. Recently anthropologists and sociologists have started to document the social and political discourses of fracking and the surrounding social conflicts in discreet Australian communities[80] and perceptions of risk and opportunity in American communities,[81] but they predominantly engage in discourse and perception analysis rather than invoking an impact-based analysis. A recent sociological study of the UK context takes a similar discourse analysis approach, albeit at an earlier stage of development, i.e. the exploration stage.[82] Though such studies highlight the relevant priorities – and possible weaknesses – of arguments for and against fracking, they do not utilise an interdisciplinary approach that would engage with scientific findings that speak to an empirical reality beyond individuals' 'perceptions', nor do they systematically interrogate how individual perceptions and behaviours are affected by wider social structures and institutionalised power.

Taking a broader, more structurally aware approach, a recent study has shown that 'neoliberal logic' has led stakeholders to self-regulate their behaviour in order to facilitate fracking, by seeing its current role in rural industrialisation, its potential environmental and health outcomes, and its economic outcomes as part of a 'new normal'.[83] The consequences of this normalisation of loss of agency therefore raises fundamental questions about the ability of communities to resist extractive operations and make informed choices about the sources of their energy. Green criminologists have also called for a more theoretically robust approach to the study of ecological harms and crimes.[84] A recent study by Shelley and Opsal[85] of the social and ecological impacts of energy extractive practices on local communities implies that green criminologists are starting to investigate this issue, documenting not only illegal actions but also processes and outcomes that are 'harmful' to humans, animals and the environment. In a recent paper de Rijke noted:

> the extraordinary expansion of the unconventional gas industry has … led to questions about social power and the rights of individuals and local communities, the role of multinational corporations in politics and rural service provision, as well as related questions regarding fundamental processes of democracy, capitalist economies and social justice[86]

while the

> close relationship between governments and powerful multinational corporations brings to the fore questions about political influence and human rights.[87]

Thus, to address these 'important conundrums', de Rijke advocated further academic research into fracking from multiple perspectives, including social impact assessments. Given the weight of evidence of human impacts that is emerging from countries with a mature fracking industry, such as the US and Australia, we suggest it is time to meet de Rijke's call through the human rights lens, i.e. the creation of comprehensive interdisciplinary human rights impact assessments (HRIAs) of fracking.

The last ten years has seen a growth in HRIAs that have been developed by a variety of actors as an extension of, or improvement on, social impact assessments (SIAs), which in turn developed from environmental impact assessments (EIAs). Recent academic literature on HRIAs[88] has identified a number of distinct advantages of such assessments over broader SIAs. With recent UN-based developments regarding the human rights due diligence obligations for companies,[89] particularly in the extractive industries, the HRIA methodology is valuable because it uses a set of norms and standards that are based on shared values and, therefore, represents a solid normative foundation on which to base impact assessments.[90] Second, human rights represent legal obligations of states, rather than simply aspirations, and so HRIAs may compel duty-bearers to act to protect the rights of rights-holders.[91] Third, HRIAs require a disaggregation of impacts to ensure that the effects on vulnerable groups are identified, such as women, children and indigenous groups. The human rights approach also encourages respect for stakeholder rights to information, participation, transparency and accountability[92] and a commitment to 'improving the quality of life of people and communities'[93] and a desire to influence policy and practice to that end. The methodological focus of a HRIA is an evidence-based evaluation of commitments made by a state and the actual ability of individuals, groups and communities in a country to enjoy these rights. HRIAs provide (intergovernmental) organisations, governments and companies with instruments to better focus their human rights efforts; and civil society, community activists and NGOs can use them as an analytical and lobbying tool. A HRIA can be done before the activity takes place (*ex ante*), or after the activity has taken place (*ex post*).

What is missing, both from academia and the world of public policy are impartial interdisciplinary human rights-based investigations of a range of effects, impacts and changes brought on by fracking projects and experienced by individuals, families and communities in countries with a developed industry, such as Australia and the US, so as to better understand actual and potential human rights impacts for future affected communities in those countries and in countries at pre-production stages. At the same time research must include data collected from sites with different levels of industry maturity as evidence from the US has shown that support for fracking reduces with experience of cumulative impacts.[94] It is vital that this research commences forthwith since many countries currently at various exploration stages (e.g. the UK, Poland, Romania, Botswana, South Africa and Argentina) are seeking to move to full production within the next five years and production is already beginning in some countries (e.g. China, India and Indonesia), while established producers will seek to expand when, and where, possible. This is all taking place without adequate research on the social and human rights impacts of such development and how these relate to the environmental impacts. Indeed, the next five years represent a crucial window of opportunity for stakeholder communities, civil society organisations and NGOs to meaningfully engage with those proposing fracking development; impartial, community-based HRIAs will greatly aid this endeavour.

In the balance of this article we demonstrate that there are at least ten areas of concern that would provide key 'indicator' data for such assessments due to their inherent connection with the fracking process and its social and political context. These areas are: water, air, land, health, freedom of peaceful assembly, freedom of expression, liberty and security of the person, right to a fair trial, right to respect for the private and family life, and anthropogenic climate change.

Many of the negative effects of fracking have revolved around these key issues, each of which has a legal basis in human rights and an obvious connection to Nickel's 'minimally good life'. Thus, an examination of each topic is essential to making the prima facie case for assessing fracking's human rights impacts in an interdisciplinary manner that goes beyond existing 'perception' studies to include additional empirical data, often from scientific sources.

Water

One of the most contentious and widely publicised environmental, and we would argue human rights, issues connected with fracking is the water impact: groundwater contamination, water use and contaminated water waste disposal. Shale gas production is a highly water-intensive process, with a typical single well requiring around five million gallons of water, and an average well-pad cluster up to 60 million gallons, to drill and fracture, depending on the basin and geological formation.[95] The vast majority of this water is used during the fracturing process, with large volumes of water pumped into the well with sand and chemicals to facilitate the extraction of the gas; the remainder is used in the drilling stage, with water being the major component of the drilling fluids. Once that water is used by the industry it is no longer a useful resource for society. While increasing quantities of water are being recycled and reused in the US, freshwater is still used in large quantities for the drilling operations as 'produced' water is more likely to damage the equipment and reduce the chance of a 'successful well'. The industry's requirements[96] for such quantities of freshwater are clearly a serious concern in water-scarce regions of the world and in places with high cumulative demand for water.

In the case of CBM extraction the major water use is the dewatering of the coal seams, in order to allow the gas to flow. This involves pumping large quantities (hundreds of thousands of litres per day) of water out of each well. The overall effect of pumping out such large amounts of water, when multiplied by potentially thousands of wells in any given region, is usually to dramatically lower water tables in the area, since freshwater aquifers nearer the surface tend to drain down into the coal seams when water is removed from them. For instance, the Queensland Water Commission predicts a massive water table drop of 700m in some areas due to CBM extraction.[97] So while the mechanisms are very different, the overall impacts of shale and CBM extraction on water availability are just as serious. Such demand pressures are already being felt in areas of the US and Australia, leading to pressure on water sources and competition for withdrawal permits.[98]

The large quantity of water used by the fracking industry is but one of many serious concerns. The contamination of groundwater sources,[99] from failure in the well casing over time,[100] what industry refers to as 'zonal isolation' failure, is a very serious issue across regions that have seen considerable fracking development to date, and has duly featured as a central public relations battleground for industry and pro-fracking governments. Even so, arguably the most concerning issue with fracking's use of water is the issue of produced/waste water treatment and disposal, often simply referred to as 'waste water management'. And yet, the risks in this regard go well beyond the concerns of corporate risk minimisation. Indeed, the whole process of dealing with fracking's waste water is a highly risky business for local populations and the environment, with considerable risks of water or soil contamination from surface leaks and spills.[101] But perhaps the most concerning issue with waste water is that it can contain significant amounts of radioactive material[102] due to the 'naturally occurring hypersaline brines associated with the formations targeted for natural gas production'.[103] For instance, radium has been found to be building up in rivers downstream of shale gas waste discharge points in Pennsylvania,[104] while a company has been fined for contaminating an aquifer with CBM (termed coal seam gas (CSG) in Australia) waste containing uranium in New South Wales, Australia.[105]

Summarising much of the data, a recent landmark US study by Vengosh et al. argues that the overall risks posed by fracking development for water are fourfold (a similar, though subtly different list could be produced for CBM[106] extraction)[107]:

- Contamination of shallow aquifers in areas adjacent to shale gas development through stray gas leaking from improperly constructed or failing gas wells.
- Contamination of water resources in areas of shale gas development and/or waste management by spills, leaks or disposal of hydraulic fracturing fluids and inadequately treated wastewaters.

- Accumulation of metals and radioactive elements on stream, river and lake sediments in wastewater disposal or spill sites, posing an additional long-term impact by slowly releasing toxic elements and radiation to the environment in the impacted areas.
- Reduction of water supply through withdrawals of valuable fresh water from dry areas and overexploitation of limited or diminished water resources for shale gas development.

The human right to water was first recognised within the UN system by the Committee on Economic, Social and Cultural Rights through their 2002 General Comment 15, which located it implicitly in the rights to an adequate standard of living and to the highest attainable standard of health set out in Articles 11 and 12 of the International Covenant on Economic, Social and Cultural Rights (ICESCR), respectively. In 2005, the Special Rapporteur of the Sub-Commission on the Promotion and Protection of Human Rights issued draft guidelines for a resolution on the right to drinking water and sanitation,[108] which were adopted by the Sub-Commission in 2006 as the Guidelines for the Realization of the Right to Drinking Water and Sanitation. The HRC followed the guidelines with a request for the High Commissioner for Human Rights to study the scope and content of human rights obligations related to access to safe drinking water and sanitation under current international human rights instruments.[109] The results of the study were presented to the HRC in 2007 and included the High Commissioner's recommendation that '... it is now time to consider access to safe drinking water and sanitation as a human right'.[110] An independent expert on the issue of human rights obligations related to access to safe drinking water and sanitation was established by the HRC in 2008, and in July 2010 the UN General Assembly adopted resolution 64/292 recognising the 'right to safe and clean drinking water and sanitation as a human right this is essential for the full enjoyment of life and all human rights'.[111] In March 2011 the independent expert's mandate was extended and the title altered to Special Rapporteur on the Human Right to Safe Drinking Water and Sanitation.[112]

Though the right to clean drinking water and sanitation has now been affirmed by the General Assembly and the HRC,[113] there is no explicit international instrument on the right. Rather, the HRC has defined the human right to water and sanitation to derive from the right to an adequate standard of living and found it inextricably related to the rights to health, life and human dignity. Additionally, numerous international instruments include the right to water and sanitation. The 1979 Convention on the Elimination of Discrimination Against Women (CEDAW)[114] is the earliest such example, stating the right of women to water and sanitation as elements of the right to adequate living conditions. Subsequently, International Labour Organization (ILO) Convention 161 of 1985[115] referred to the right of workers to sanitary installations, the 1989 Convention on the Rights of the Child (CRC) stated the right of children to clean drinking water,[116] both the 1990 African Charter on the Rights and Welfare of the Child and the Protocol to the African Charter on Human and Peoples' Rights (ACHPR) on the Rights of Women in Africa[117] include the rights to safe drinking water, and, most recently, the 2006 Convention on the Rights of Persons with Disabilities (CRPD) includes the rights to clean water services as a subset of the right to social protection.[118]

With such evidence of wide international acceptance of the human right to water and sanitation, and considering the place of this right within the context of a 'minimally good life', it is thus appropriate to consider access to clean water and sanitation a fundamental human right and necessary to consider the impact of the fracking industry on that right. Despite its widespread use in the US for over a decade, hydraulic fracturing has only recently been scrutinised to determine if and what its effects are on human rights. Under the special procedures of the HRC, the Special Rapporteur on the Human Right to Safe Drinking Water and Sanitation, Catarina de Albuquerque, concluded her 2011 mission to the US by outlining serious concerns over the effect of a range of polluting activities associated with the hydraulic fracturing process, observing a distinct: 'policy disconnect … between polluting activities and their ultimate impact on the safety of drinking water sources. The absence of integrated thinking has generated enormous burdens, including increased costs to public water systems to monitor and treat water to remove regulated contaminants and detrimental health outcomes for individuals and communities.'[119] While a comprehensive report on the effects of hydraulic fracturing on water quality is expected from the US Environmental Protection Agency late 2015,[120] there have recently been other, smaller-scale studies revealing water contamination due to fracking processes. Ingraffea et al.'s review of compliance reports from conventional and unconventional oil and gas wells drilled in Pennsylvania between 2000 and 2012[121] reveals that casing/cement impairment is six times more likely to occur in shale gas wells than in conventional wells. Such flaws may result in cases of subsurface gas migration into the water supply, as has already occurred in the state. Indeed, published data demonstrate evidence of 'contamination of shallow aquifers with hydrocarbon gases … contamination of surface water and shallow groundwater from spills, leaks, and/or the disposal of inadequately treated shale gas wastewater … [and] accumulation of toxic and radioactive elements in soil or stream sediments near disposal or spill sites … ' from hydraulic fracturing throughout the US.[122] Qualitative data from Colorado have further revealed complaints of water contamination from residents living near fracking sites that are often intentionally misunderstood, assigned a different cause, or diluted by state regulatory bodies.[123] Recently the Pennsylvania Department of Environmental Protection disclosed details of 243 cases in which fracking companies were found by state regulators to have contaminated private drinking water wells in the last four years.[124] Cumulatively, these reports indicate likely impairment of the right to water for residents living near fracking sites.

Air

A major, and often under-appreciated, impact of fracking is air pollution. Despite water issues gaining the majority of press and public attention, it is becoming clear that for most people reporting health problems associated with fracking, air pollution is far more likely to be the initial cause.[125] This is because air pollution will be present as soon as drilling begins and it is much harder to avoid exposure to it. In comparison, the effects of water pollution take much longer to emerge and it can take years for well casings to degrade causing the wells to leak. Also, in the West at least, using alternative sources once a problem is spotted can mitigate water contamination issues. A particularly serious air pollutant produced by fracking is ozone, a powerful lung irritant that contributes to asthma and other breathing disorders, and which can form as a result of reactions between leaking methane and nitrogen oxides emitted from exhausts of diesel-powered equipment. Areas with previous pristine air such as the Upper Green River Basin in Wyoming are now seeing ozone levels spiking higher than those seen in Los Angeles, with people complaining of watery eyes, shortness of breath and bloody noses.[126] Ground-level ozone is a component of smog and a costly, high-priority public health risk. Ozone exposure can cause irreversible damage to the lungs and significantly increase the chance of premature death.

In addition, numerous other chemicals present in natural gas at the well-head (including hydrogen sulphide, benzene[127] and other volatile hydrocarbons) can adversely, and seriously, affect air quality. Moreover, we need to consider the whole unconventional gas extraction and production process when considering the effects of such developments. In terms of impacts on localised air quality, emissions from trucks, compressors, pumps and other equipment used in the drilling and production process contain a complex mixture of benzene, toluene and xylene as well as other volatile organic compounds (VOCs).[128] Dust levels must also be considered: drilling activities and associated site traffic generate significant levels of dust while the small particle-size silica sand used in hydraulic fracturing can cause silicosis, an incurable lung disease, and increases the risk of lung cancer.[129]

Fracking operations release VOCs 'at each stage of production and delivery'[130] and while ozone is usually associated with automobile exhaust emissions, fracking generates it when VOCs in wastewater 'ponds' evaporate and come into contact with well site vehicle and generator diesel fumes.[131] VOCs and ozone pollution have been detected at dangerous levels at fracking sites in the US across Colorado, Wyoming and Utah. Indeed, a major study in North-Eastern Colorado[132] found exceptionally high levels of VOCs in the air and traced the chemical signature of around 55% of them directly back to gas and oil operations. Over significant periods in 2011, the level of ozone pollution in rural Wyoming's gas drilling areas exceeded that of Los Angeles and other major cities, and with an upper limit of 116 parts per billion, exceeded the US Environment Protection Agency's healthy limit of 75 parts per billion.[133] Uintah County, Utah, an area with some of the highest-producing oil and gas fields in the country, has experienced dangerously high levels of VOCs and resultant ozone for over five years: the amount of VOCs released in 2013 in Uintah County alone was calculated as the equivalent of emissions from 100 million automobiles.[134]

A University of Colorado Denver, School of Public Health study documented dangerous airborne levels of benzene[135] – known to cause multiple forms of leukaemia and other blood disorders – near hydraulic fracturing operations.[136] The study found elevated risks of cancer for residents within half a mile of a drilling site. In another study focussing on Northern Texas,[137] ambient air testing near gas drilling operations found excessive amounts of many toxic chemicals, including benzene and carbon disulphide, an extremely high-risk pollutant, possessing what the Texas Commission on Environmental Quality called 'disaster potential'.[138] These chemicals were traced back to the drilling operations, as the testing location had 'virtually no heavy industry other than the [natural gas] compression stations'.'[139] Another report identified significant amounts of over 40 health-harming chemicals in the air near drilling sites in Colorado and although none were detected at levels above United States Environmental Protection Agency (EPA) limits, that study and others have noted that the EPA's ambient air quality standards may not be strict enough.[140] Health standards often do not fully account for long-term health effects of chemicals and enhanced risks to vulnerable populations[141] such as pregnant women, young children and the elderly.[142]

A University at Albany Institute for Health and the Environment study[143] recently identified eight highly toxic chemicals in air samples collected near fracking and associated infrastructure sites across five states: Arkansas, Colorado, Pennsylvania, Ohio and Wyoming. Chemicals detected included two benzene and formaldehyde (proven human carcinogens) and hexane and hydrogen sulfide (two potent neurotoxins). The study found that for 29 out of 76 samples, concentrations far exceeded federal health and safety standards, in some cases by several orders of magnitude. Moreover, in some instances highly elevated levels of formaldehyde were found up to half a mile from a wellhead. Indeed, in Arkansas, seven air samples contained formaldehyde at levels up to 60 times the level known to raise the risk for cancer.[144] According to the study's lead author 'this is a significant public health risk ... Cancer has a long latency, so you're not seeing an elevation in cancer in these communities. But five, 10, 15 years from now, elevation in cancer is almost certain to happen.'[145]

When considering the fundamental right to clean air (minimally, air that is free from harmful levels of pollution), as a necessary aspect of the 'minimally good life', it is necessary to first note that access to air – like water – 'was an entitlement so natural and fundamental that it was probably inconceivable that the continued availability of this access had to be guaranteed as a human right'.[146] Accordingly, an explicit right to air is not found in any UN human rights instruments or special procedure. Despite this apparent international inattention to the right to clean air, numerous national and regional bodies have recognised the positive obligation of governments to ensure clean air for their populace, either as a component of other internationally recognised rights or as an aspect of the right to a healthy environment.

At the national level, the obligation of the state to protect its people from detrimental pollution has been affirmed in countries across the world. Some of the most explicit references to air pollution have come from Asia, as the Supreme Court of India, in *Subhash Kumar* v. *State of Bihar* (1991), stated that the right to life includes the right to pollution-free water and air.[147] Additionally, the Human Rights Commission of Malaysia, a national human rights institution established by the Malaysian Parliament in 1999, has asserted that the right to liberty within the Malaysian Constitution obliges the government to provide clean air, based on their analysis of Malaysian national and case law.[148] More generally, environmental rights, as such, are recognised in 92 state constitutions, spanning every continent, from Portugal to Mexico to Indonesia, Brazil to Madagascar to Russia.[149] Even with such limited examples of a state-recognised right to clean air specifically, this conglomeration of national acknowledgement of the right to a clean environment demonstrates that the human right to air is broadly recognised, despite the absence of a UN mechanism.

Examining regional human rights law further reveals the general acceptance of a right to clean air, in so far as it is consistent with a general right to a healthy environment. Article 24 of the ACHPR expressly states the right of '[a]ll peoples ... to a general satisfactory environment favourable to their development'.[150] In the Americas, the Additional Protocol to the American Convention on Human Rights in the Area of Economic, Social and Cultural Rights affirms in Article 11 that '[e]veryone shall have the right to live in a healthy environment', and that it is the state's obligation to 'promote the protection, preservation, and improvement of the environment'.[151] Within Europe, the European Court of Human Rights (ECtHR) ruled that air pollution specifically could be a violation of the right to respect for home and private and family life in *Lopez Ostra* v. *Spain* (1994).[152] The court has also found that denying access to *fresh* air contributes to degrading and inhumane treatment.[153] In the case of *Öneryildiz* v. *Turkey* (2004), the ECtHR ruled that the government has a duty to protect private property from environmental risks, as an element of the right to the peaceful enjoyment of possessions.[154] Thus, evidence within each of the three most prominent regional human rights legal systems suggests that there exists a general right to a healthy environment – which must arguably include the right to clean air.

Finally, while the UN system has not recognised the right to clean air as it has the right to water, connections between human rights and a healthy environment have recently been enhanced at the global level. The introduction of an independent expert on human rights and the environment in 2012 demonstrates the growing acceptance that '[a] safe, clean, healthy and sustainable environment is integral to the full enjoyment of a wide range of human rights, including the rights to life, health, food, water and sanitation'.[155] More recently, the HRC has recognised that 'environmental damage has negative implications

… for the effective enjoyment of human rights, in particular of the right to life, the right to the enjoyment of the highest attainable standard of physical and mental health, [and] the right to an adequate standard of living and its components … '[156] On air quality specifically, the NGO Subcommittee on Poverty Eradication submitted, in a report to the UN Human Rights Council, that there exists an inherent right to clean air that should be universally enjoyed as a component of the right to 'life-sustaining natural resources'.[157] As of 2012, 177 UN member states recognise the right to a healthy environment either 'through their constitution, environmental legislation, court decisions, or ratification of an international agreement … '[158] Whether or not the right to clean air is explicitly stated, it is vital to a healthy environment, the rights to life and health (discussed below) and many others, in short it is vital to the minimally good life. Thus, the current and potential effects of fracking upon air quality represent not just an environmental threat, but also a threat to the enjoyment of human rights.

Land

Fracking production has a considerable visual and physical impact on local landscapes. Indeed, fracking involves cluster well-pads, compressor stations, new site access roads, waste water containers/ponds and high-volume site traffic. Industry and government denials aside, the empirical reality of fracking developments is a considerable industrialisation of rural areas.[159] Land can also be impacted through water, air or soil pollution as we have seen above, along with damage to livestock, vegetation and wildlife[160] and damage associated with fracking-induced seismic activity.[161] While earthquakes may not be very serious for local properties, although some have certainly been damaged, they can damage the cement well casing, increasing the likelihood of what the industry calls 'zonal isolation failure' – in other words well casing failure – as happened already at the exploration stage in the UK at Cuadrilla's Presse Hall test site in Lancashire[162] – and which could result in methane leaks and groundwater contamination.

Colorado has seen significant direct and indirect effects on wildlife, including population declines and direct mortality, in gas development areas and recent discoveries of new oil reserves and changing industry technology have dramatically altered the course of development as well as the landscape of the state.[163] In the mountainous regions of the Marcellus shale region fracking drilling leads to soil ground erosion, and loosened sediments quickly enter surface streams, contaminating cold-water fish habitats and drinking water sources.[164] Even so, beyond these issues, perhaps the impact that will draw the most attention from local residents is the likely impact on local property values. As US researcher Richard Heinberg writes 'the various forms of land damage from fracking often result in decreased property values, making resale and farming difficult, and also making it harder to acquire mortgages and insurance. Properties adjoining drilling sites are often simply unsellable, as no one wants to live with the noise, the bad air, and the possibility of water pollution.'[165]

These impacts will of course multiply with each new development instigated in response to the short production cycle of the average fracking cluster. Indeed, fracking requires 'heroic rates'[166] of drilling to maintain production levels, and therefore enormous numbers of drilling sites. Fracking also impacts land far from drilling sites as it requires key material inputs such as sand – which itself needs to be mined and is used as a proppant (to hold hydraulic-induced fractures open).[167] For example, fracking in Pennsylvania, Texas and North Dakota uses sand mined in Wisconsin, Minnesota and Iowa, which itself destroys farmland, impacts wildlife and degrades waterways, while tiny silica particles dislodged by mining, when taken up by winds, can result in higher rates of silicosis and cancer in local populations.[168]

In this context, the right to land can be viewed as the right to land free from severe ecological destruction and its negative effects upon human health and property values. This right, as a human right threatened by fracking, is comprised of the rights to respect for privacy, the family, and home, and protection of property – both of which have been legally established in numerous national, regional and international legal instruments. The 1966 International Covenant on Civil and Political Rights (ICCPR) includes the right not to be 'subjected to arbitrary or unlawful interference' to one's 'privacy, family, home or correspondence'.[169] This right is also found in the European Convention on Human Rights (ECHR),[170] the American Convention on Human Rights (ACHR),[171] and the Arab Charter on Human Rights.[172] Within the European context especially, this right to privacy, family and home has been used in cases of environmental degradation before the ECtHR. Although in most cases – relevant to the discussion of fracking's impact on the land – the court found no violation of this right, it did assert that violation was possible due to environmental destruction that directly affects human well-being (*Kyrtatos* v. *Greece* (2003)),[173] damage to a home by nearby industry (*Dubetska and Others* v. *Ukraine* (2011)),[174] or excessive levels of noise and dust (*Martinez Martinez and María Pino Manzano* v. *Spain* (2012)).[175] Such findings are largely related to the right to protection of property, found in the Protocol to the ECHR,[176] the ACHR,[177] the ACHPR,[178] the Arab Charter on Human Rights,[179] in addition to numerous national constitutions.[180] The ECtHR case of *Flamenbaum and Others* v. *France* (2012)[181] highlights the connection between these two rights as the court asserted that a drop in the market value of property, due to industry activities that could violate the right to privacy, the family and home, would be a violation of the right to protection of property.[182] Therefore, when the rights to privacy, family, home and protection of property are read to include protection from pollution, environmental harm that affects human well-being, and damage to the home – including protection from arbitrary property devaluation due to nearby industrial activities – it is apparent that the effects of fracking on the land are capable of legally violating human rights.

Health

While scientific studies on the health impacts of fracking are still in their relative infancy, partially due to the time lag between environmental impacts and provable human health consequences, there is an emerging body of literature and growing awareness of recurring health defects found in residents living near fracking sites.[183] The recently publicised Texas lawsuit by Robert and Lisa Parr against Aruba Petroleum, in which a jury awarded the family $3 million, was based on the health effects they experienced following the arrival of fracking to their community. The Parrs complained of nosebleeds, vision problems, nausea, rashes and blood pressure issues[184] – symptoms similar to those which have been reported near drilling sites in Colorado,[185] Pennsylvania[186] and other unconventional natural gas operations.[187]

Recent reports have also noted connections between maternal proximity to unconventional drilling sites and birth defects, including congenital heart defects, neural tube defects and low birth-rates, though these studies again lack the robust and comprehensive nature required to find a causal link between fracking-related pollution and health impairments.[188] Despite this, the quantity of studies showing correlations between fracking and health problems is rising fast, with people living near fracking wells in Pennsylvania more than twice as likely to report upper-respiratory and skin problems.[189] Serious ailments have been reported by families living in close proximity to drilling operations of the Eagle Ford Shale in South Texas,[190] and increases in coughs, chest tightness, rashes, difficulty sleeping, joint pains, muscle pains and spasms, nausea and vomiting, spontaneous nose bleeds and skin irritations have been observed among residents living near CBM wells in Tara, Queensland.[191]

These reports are also deeply concerning for people living in countries at the exploration stage, especially where the authorities mean to protect public health in the development process but fail to take on board the latest peer-reviewed health studies. Indeed, for those UK residents living near proposed fracking sites, such as Preston New Road and Roseacre in Lancashire, Public Health England's (PHE) 25 June 2014 report was so inadequate in its coverage that there is some suggestion that it amounted to 'gross scientific misconduct'.[192] A robust interdisciplinary human rights-based investigation seeking health indicator data would go well beyond PHE's meagre review of just 25 publications,[193] up until their arbitrary cut-off date of December 2012, as there have been over 90 relevant reports published since. Many of these reports were considered in the New York State Department of Health's far more comprehensive report, which was instrumental in New York State recently issuing a moratorium on all fracking development on the basis that the public health risks were too great.[194]

The various aspects of fracking's ecological footprint holistically demonstrate the potential for environmental rights violations to reach a severity capable of abusing the human rights to health and life. These rights, enshrined in numerous national and international instruments, including the International Bill of Rights, have been defined broadly by the UN and other bodies to include rights related to ecological preservation.[195] The right to health is 'an inclusive right', comprising not only the right of access to health care but also the right to reasonable protection from detriments to health, such as 'access to safe and potable water and adequate sanitation' (see above) and to a healthy natural environment.[196] The right to life is, of course, intrinsically linked to the right to health, as human life may be endangered by environmental degradation severe enough to damage human health.[197] The European Court of Human Rights has, for instance, ruled that a state may violate right to life by not informing residents of nearby potential environmental safety risks or by failing to enact practical measures to avoid those safety risks.[198]

In the following section we discuss the currently under-researched civil and political dimensions of proposed fracking development in a key emerging context: the UK's 'second dash for gas'.[199] The research sought to explore official responses to anti-fracking protests in the UK, with specific reference to the police response to anti-fracking protests. The discussion refers to civil and political rights that are all recognised in the UK's 1998 Human Rights Act (HRA), the ECHR and the ICCPR. These encompass the right to freedom of peaceful assembly, the right to freedom of expression, the right to liberty and security of the person, the right to a fair trial, and the right to respect for a private and family life. All of the rights discussed stem from the context of protest as a response to the proposed introduction of fracking in the UK, and are supported by primary research gathered through an online survey and interviews.

Freedom of peaceful assembly

Our UK-based primary research focussed on two exploratory (potential fracking) sites and their targeted protests: Balcombe in West Sussex[200] and Barton Moss in Salford.[201] Conflict arose at both of these locations due to the responses of Sussex Police and Greater

Manchester Police (GMP), respectively, to these peaceful protests, conducted most commonly by protesters attempting to delay the delivery of equipment or chemicals by walking in front of the lorries delivering these items to the drilling site. The results of these actions by the police have been threats to, and arguable violations of, civil and political rights recognised in the HRA, ECHR and ICCPR. The right to peaceful assembly is articulated in Article 11 of both the HRA[202] and the ECHR,[203] and Article 21 of the ICCPR.[204] All of these articles place restrictions upon how the right to freedom of peaceful assembly can be expressed, which are of immediate relevance to this discussion, seeking as they do to balance the right of the individual citizen with the legal powers of the state. In the context of this discussion, as a protest is an assembly, any action which prevents individuals from peacefully protesting is a violation of the right to peaceful assembly.

Article 11(2) of both the HRA and the ECHR detail how the only restrictions placed upon the freedom of peaceful assembly should be those 'prescribed by law', and are required 'in the interests of national security or public safety' or 'for the prevention of disorder or crime'. In addition, Article 11(2) in both the HRA and ECHR also states that '[t]his Article shall not prevent the imposition of lawful restrictions on the exercise of these rights by members of the armed forces, of the police or of the administration of the State'. Article 21 of the ICCPR gives less detail as to how the right to peaceful assembly should be controlled by the state, as it does not reference armed forces, police or state administration. The right to freedom of peaceful assembly in the ICCPR is therefore less restrictive than the expression of the same right in the HRA of the UK, drafted over three decades later.

The online survey gave valuable insight into the general experience of anti-fracking protestors, at least as far as can be gauged from a selective form of research. Of the 168 respondents, 98 had personal experience of direct action against fracking in the UK. Of that 98, 79 had either interacted with the police or witnessed interactions between the police and other protesters during that experience. Of those interactions, 56 (over 76%) experienced or witnessed excessive use of force by members of the police, 64 (over 87%) experienced or witnessed unnecessary use of force by members of the police, and 61 (over 83%) experienced or witnessed unnecessary arrests. These figures provide, minimally, a generalisation of how the police responded to anti-fracking protests in the UK.

The overwhelming majority of both survey and interview respondents believed their right to freedom of peaceful assembly was prevented from being realised by the actions of police officers. The majority of comments below therefore illustrate the ways in which police failed to facilitate the right to freedom of peaceful assembly, as expressed in peaceful protest. This failure mostly involved the use of violence to inhibit individuals' ability to peacefully protest, but also extended to the removal of individuals from the protest site (without arrests being made) and unlawful arrests. Most interview respondents made reference to the fact that police were not facilitating any form of peaceful protest. With reference to Barton Moss, one respondent described how 'in terms of actual policing […] It was very difficult to run a campaign', due to GMP's control over the protestors' actions.[205] Another respondent described how they were removed from the Barton Moss protest by two police officers who 'were interfering with my right to protest' as 'they did stop me from actually demonstrating',[206] illuminating the extent to which police were capable of forcibly preventing peaceful protest without making arrests. With regard to lorries, around which most protest activity revolved, one respondent described how police tactics changed between Balcombe, where one lorry was escorted at a time by the police, and Barton Moss: 'When we went to Barton Moss they decided to use the convoy system, bringing in anywhere between ten and fifteen trucks at a time […] that way they undermined our ability to slow the process down.'[207]

The change between Balcombe and Barton Moss was suggested as police altering their response to anti-fracking protest 'in light of what they learnt at Balcombe'.[208] Aside from the changes to the escorting of lorries, a consistently referenced constant between the two protests was the use of violence by members of the police to prevent the realisation of the right to freedom of peaceful assembly through protest. In interactions with the police at both Balcombe and Barton Moss, interview respondents described how they were 'kicked and pushed and punched',[209] 'pushed and shoved in the back',[210] 'pushed off the road by the police',[211] and 'shoved in the back repeatedly'.[212] Police interactions were described as 'rough',[213] 'ultra aggressive',[214] and 'very, very aggressive',[215] resulting in interactions in which 'bones got broken'.[216] The interactions of police with other protestors was described as 'shoving people, pushing people, trying to knock people over, trying to get people on the ground',[217] 'kicking their ankles',[218] and 'deliberately kicking up the backs of legs'.[219] These data, gathered from interviews and alluded to in the experiences of survey respondents, indicate the primary method by which GMP and Sussex Police prevented the realisation of peaceful protest, supplemented by unlawful arrests, and is a far cry from police claims of acting 'professionally and fairly'.[220]

Further to police interference, indications of county council involvement in the controlling and dismantling of protests have appeared. The West Sussex County Council obtained a possession order for land where Balcombe protesters were camped, forcing them to relocate. Though the council provided a new area for the protest, it forbade camping on the site due to the safety risk posed by a nearby unlit road.[221] The Salford City Council, covering the Barton Moss site, has been shown to meet regularly with the GMP and IGas during anti-fracking protests, sharing information and intelligence and discussing levels of acceptable police force. This is in contrast to the council's level of cooperation with protesters, as reportedly none of the councillors visited the protest site.[222] To be sure, there have been significant issues with suppression of anti-fracking protests outside the UK. The fracking industry and governments in the US, Canada and Australia appear to often consider resistance by local people to be an 'insurgency', and anti-fracking groups, particularly in poorer or maginalised communities (HRIAs would need to disaggregate data in this regard), are routinely labelled as terrorists,[223] subjected to psychological warfare operations,[224] intimidation[225] and police violence.[226]

Freedom of expression

The right to freedom of expression is detailed in Article 10 of both the HRA[227] and ECHR[228] and Article 19 of the ICCPR.[229] This freedom is understood in Article 10(1) of the HRA and the ECHR as the 'freedom to hold opinions and to receive and impart information and ideas without interference by public authority', and in Article 19(2) of the ICCPR as the 'freedom to seek, receive and impart information and ideas of all kinds [...] either, orally, in writing or in print'. With relevance to the preceding discussion on the right to peaceful assembly, this freedom can be expressed in the form of protest.[230] Although every instance in which police responses have restricted the right to peaceful assembly could also be discussed here, it will suffice to say that any unlawful restriction of protest through 'interference by public authority' can be considered a violation of the right to freedom of expression.

In addition, as indicated by the human rights legislation, the right to freedom of expression is concerned more generally with the imparting of information or ideas. One interview respondent made reference to banners outside the homes of residents on Barton Moss Lane, who lived in proximity to both the Barton Moss protestors' camp and IGas' exploratory drilling site. The interview respondent explained how the occupants of the buildings had made banners saying 'No shale' and 'No methane gas mining here'.[231] These banners, although located on the private property of the residents, had prompted GMP to visit and request that the banners be removed – seemingly in contravention of the right to freedom of expression. As with police response to protest, the interference by public authority is explicit here: GMP's actions interfered with the ability of the residents to 'hold opinions' and 'impart information and ideas' through the medium of anti-fracking banners. If this request did not violate the right of the residents to freedom of expression then reference must be found within the domestic and international legislation for legitimate interference by public authority.

The HRA, ECHR and ICCPR all contain details as to how and why the right to freedom of expression may be curtailed by the representatives of the state. Article 10(2) of both the HRA and the ECHR state that this right 'may be subject to such formalities, conditions, restrictions or penalties as are prescribed by law', which are clarified as 'the interests of national security' and 'the prevention of disorder or crime'. Similarly, Article 19(3) of the ICCPR states that the right to freedom of expression 'may […] be subject to certain restrictions, but these shall only be such as are provided by law', which are, in Article 19(3), described as being 'For the protection of national security or of public order'. For the request by GMP not to have violated the residents' right to freedom of expression, the presence of the banners must be considered a threat to national security or public order, or their removal must be considered necessary to prevent crime. These three scenarios appear to be legally unfounded, unless the anti-fracking movement itself is considered a threat to 'national security'. The banners may have encouraged activity at the Barton Moss protest camp, but that would only prompt legal justification for their removal if said activity was considered to be a threat to public order, or to constitute a crime. As the majority of protest activity fell within the remit of the right to peaceful assembly, such claims would appear to be legally unfounded, rendering GMP's request unlawful.

Liberty and security of person

The right to liberty and security of person is articulated in Article 5 of both the HRA[232] and ECHR,[233] and Article 9 of the ICCPR.[234] This right is of relevance to the context of UK anti-fracking protests due to the arrests made by GMP and Sussex Police, which are required by domestic and international legislation to be lawful in order to not violate this particular right. Indeed, Article 5(1)(c) of both the HRA and the ECHR require 'lawful arrest […] on reasonable suspicion of having committed an offence', and Article 9(1) of the ICCPR states that 'No one shall be subjected to arbitrary arrest or detention.' In addition, Article 5(2) of both the HRA and the ECHR states that 'Everyone who is arrested shall be informed promptly […] of the reasons for his arrest and of any charge against him', and Article 9(2) of the ICCPR states that '[a]nyone who is arrested shall be informed, at the time of arrest, of the reasons for his arrest and shall be promptly informed of any charges against him'. Any arrest made which could be deemed unlawful under the above descriptions would therefore violate the right of the individual arrested to liberty and security of person.

First, references were made in several interviews to the concept of arrest quotas, whereby police would carry out specific numbers of arrests over consecutive days. At Barton Moss, throughout the autumn and winter of 2013, one interview respondent recalled how 'there were five arrests every day', and that 'officers were heard to say "We need one more arrest."'[235] There was a belief that the use of arrest quotas was 'almost certainly planned in advance', and designed as 'a long term plan' which would ensure that 'eventually everyone would be arrested'.[236] More explicitly, patterns of arrest seemed to follow this trajectory: 'you're arrested, you get bailed, next time you get arrested in breach of bail'.[237] Over a period of time, such a cycle would decrease the effectiveness of the protest camp's actions and increase the likelihood of its disbandment.

In addition to arrest quotas,[238] interview respondents referenced the use of arbitrary arrests in both Balcombe and Barton Moss, whereby individuals felt arrests had no legal basis and were used as a way of 'undermining people's morale' because 'it puts people off protesting'.[239] Arrests were described variously as 'clearly random',[240] 'quite random'[241] and 'completely random',[242] with one respondent expressing the most telling sentiment, that: 'there was a risk that at any time you could be arrested'.[243] Such arrests, made without legal basis, would be in direct contravention of the right to liberty and security of person. The prevalence of violations is best indicated by the discrepancy between the numbers of arrests of anti-fracking protestors in Balcombe, 126 in total, with those who have been found guilty and sentenced in court, a mere 14.[244] In addition to quotas and arbitrary arrests, allegations were made during an interview of arrests being knowingly made on unlawful charges by GMP. At Barton Moss, the lorries travelled down Barton Moss Lane to reach the IGas drilling site, a designated private road with footpath access for the public, which is, according to an interview respondent who resides in the area, 'clearly signposted at the top'.[245] The same respondent described how police made arrests on Barton Moss Lane for 'the crime of obstructing a public highway', which is an entirely unlawful charge given that the road is private with public footpath access, and therefore does not constitute a public highway.[246] Furthermore, the respondent described how, at a court hearing of individuals charged with this crime in November 2013, 'a solicitor informed the court that Barton Moss Lane was a private road which has public footpath access'.[247] However, the respondent states that GMP 'continued to make arrests under that crime until […] February', meaning that, 'for nearly three months they continued to arrest for a crime that wasn't a crime'.[248]

Thus in this example, both the initial and later arrests are therefore unlawful, causing violations of the right to liberty and security of person through failing to comply with basic requirements of lawful detention. As an additional requirement of making lawful arrests, police officers must, as indicated above, inform individuals of the charges under which they are being arrested. One interview respondent described how, at Barton Moss '[…] when people were arrested, if they were told anything, it was when they were separated from the walk […] once they were actually in the police van they might be told what they were being arrested for'.[249] Another respondent stated, also with reference to Barton Moss and the GMP, 'the police have been acting illegally at various times and they've been impeding the legal right to protest', with specific reference here to unlawful arrests.[250] Such testimony suggests that the GMP's actions were designed to disrupt the anti-fracking protestors' right to freedom of peaceful assembly, apparently through unlawful activity.

Fair trial

The right to a fair trial is articulated in Article 6 of the HRA[251] and ECHR[252] and Article 14 of the ICCPR.[253] Article 6(3) of the HRA and ECHR detail the 'minimum rights' which an individual charged with a criminal offence is entitled to, and Article (14)(3) of the ICCPR is similarly concerned with such 'minimum guarantees'. Under these provisions an individual must 'be informed promptly […] and in detail, of the nature and cause of the accusation against him'. Consequently, any instance in which an anti-fracking protestor is arrested and not informed 'promptly' of the charges or suspicion under which he or she is being charged, would contravene the right to a fair trial in the HRA, ECHR and ICCPR. As we outlined earlier, such circumstances have been experienced at Barton Moss protests.

The arrest of protestors on Barton Moss Lane for the crime of obstructing a public highway also concerns the right to a fair trial through connections with the provision of legal aid. As discussed above, protestors were unlawfully arrested in 2013 and early 2014 for obstructing a public highway whilst walking in front of lorries on Barton Moss Lane. An interview respondent involved with the Barton Moss protests described how individuals 'can't claim legal aid for an offence of obstruction of a public highway under the current rules',[254] and expressed concern that GMP's continued arrest of protestors under this crime was a deliberate ploy to ensure protestors 'wouldn't be able to defend themselves' financially.[255] In legislative terms, Article 6(3)(c) of the HRA and ECHR detail the minimum right that any individual charged with an offence and without financial provision for legal representation 'be given it free when the interests of justice so require', and Article 14(3)(d) of the ICCPR similarly states that any such individual must 'have legal assistance assigned to him, in any case where the interests of justice so require'. By charging protesters with a crime which legal aid was not provided for, GMP and, perhaps more so – the Crown Prosecution Service, were knowingly prompting judicial proceedings in which many protesters would be unable to meet the financial costs of a court case. If protesters had instead been arrested for crimes which did receive legal aid, and indeed were actual crimes in this context, such a tactic would have no basis. Fortunately, pro bono legal support was provided, or protesters would have been prevented from being able to obtain legal representation against the charges they faced. In that scenario, given the unlawful nature of the initial arrest, the 'interests of justice' would have been seriously compromised.

Respect for a private and family life

The right to a private and family life is articulated in Article 8 of both the HRA[256] and the ECHR,[257] as 'Everyone has the right to respect for his private and family life, his home and his correspondence', while Article 17(1) of the ICCPR states that 'No one shall be subjected to arbitrary or unlawful interference with his privacy, family, home or correspondence.' It is the precise wording of these articles which allows for interpretations to be made as to how this right has been threatened or violated in the context of anti-fracking protests, through monitoring of communications and covert surveillance of protestors.

Several interview respondents raised concerns of police surveillance of email accounts, telephones and social media. Although, as one interview respondent indicated, such activities are 'difficult to prove',[258] other interview respondents were insistent in their belief of surveillance activity, stating that 'We knew that they were monitoring our Facebook pages, our emails and our phones' at both Balcombe and Barton Moss,[259] and 'I have no doubt that they were bugging certain people's phones' and 'keeping a close eye on people's Facebook pages' in Balcombe.[260] Concerns for some anti-fracking protestors over the security of information were such that one respondent described how, when important details about protest action in Balcombe required discussion, the individuals involved would 'get together and speak about it rather than using [social] media'.[261] Seemingly to confirm fears of surveillance, another respondent described how a list of press contacts on an email account were 'scrambled',[262] preventing messages from reaching the majority of the list.

In addition to covert surveillance through technology, members of the anti-fracking movement have become increasingly concerned over police infiltration via social media accounts or undercover individuals joining specific campaigns or protest camps. Indeed, a request made as part of this primary research for online survey respondents was met with the suggestion that the collation of such information was likely to be a database for police use. Furthermore, one respondent believed that the police were providing drilling companies with information gathered about protestors, stating that 'We'd have to strongly suspect [...] that covert intelligence was shared between Greater Manchester Police and iGas.'[263] Such mistrust indicates significant concerns surrounding the police, the internet and confidentiality. It also demonstrates why concerned individuals, as mentioned above, prefer face-to-face conversations over online or telephone interactions.

In order for any surveillance of communications to be lawful, Article 8(1) of both the HRA and ECHR require that any restrictions placed upon the right to respect for a private and family life are '[...] in accordance with the law and [are] necessary in a democratic society in the interests of national security, public safety or the economic well-being of the country, for the prevention of disorder or crime'. The use of covert surveillance by either GMP or Sussex Police would indicate a belief that anti-fracking protesters threatened 'national security' or 'public safety', or increased the possibility of 'disorder or crime'. As mentioned previously with reference to the right to freedom of expression, given that the majority of protest activity fell within the remit of the right to peaceful assembly, such claims would appear to be without legal foundation.

In the UK, potential future rights concerns may well go beyond circumstances surrounding specific protest sites if the behaviour of Kent police towards an open academic debate is indicative of a national policing approach towards this issue. In November 2014 they asked a university to provide a list of members of the public who were due to attend a public debate on fracking.[264] From subsequent 'freedom of information' requests it was revealed that if such a list were forthcoming Kent police would have conducted 'some R&D'[265] – presumably meaning the individuals would be researched somehow. Such police behaviour should not be analysed as if it occurs in a vacuum. It is vital to consider the broader political context and in particular the 'political spectacle'[266] that has been constructed around fracking in the UK. On the surface it may seem that the extraction of shale gas is considered necessary for 'the economic well-being of the UK' and hence 'in the national interest', and is simply being prioritised over individuals' fundamental civil and political rights; but if we were to investigate a little deeper, a more politically concerning picture may emerge, especially considering recent evidence likening the precarious nature of the US 'fracking boom'[267] to that of a government supported 'Ponzi scheme'.[268]

As Noam Chomsky warns, 'the terms, United States, Australia, Britain, and so on, are now conventionally used to refer to the structures of power within such countries: the "national interest" is the interest of these groups, which correlates only weakly with the interests of the general population'.[269] A critical awareness of such observations is vital to conducting nuanced interdisciplinary HRIAs in our view. Such assessments should, as far as possible, investigate and analyse the 'close relationship between governments and powerful multinational corporations', which de Rijke[270] warned of with unconventional gas production in the Australia, and its impact on policy and the subsequent policing of dissenting voices. For example, in the UK much of the public fracking debate has been conducted in a context which involves a government wanting to 'go all out for shale' while at the same time having a 'lead non-executive director' at the Cabinet Office, Lord Browne, who is also the Chairman of shale gas company Cuadrilla Resources. There have been illuminating 'freedom of information' requests in the UK that have demonstrated collusion between key politicians and industry figures on such matters as how best to 'manage' public perceptions and manufacture consent in order to 'fast track' fracking development.[271] Environmental consultant and extreme energy expert Paul Mobbs has highlighted numerous political-industry connections that are deserving of public attention and which raise fears of 'malfeasance' in public office.[272] Mobbs argues, 'politicians might call for a "balanced debate on shale", but arguably it is they who are peddling a manufactured rhetoric.[273] This is because the political process has been hijacked by lobbyists paid by the industry, whose manipulative tendrils reach right inside the Government.'[274]

By drawing upon the experience of individuals in the UK, this discussion has sought to expose the extent to which the civil and political rights of anti-fracking protestors and individuals living in proximity to exploratory drilling sites have been threatened or violated as a result of the proposed introduction of fracking. The police response to anti-fracking protests, seemingly prompted by the need to protect governmental policy, has violated the right to freedom of peaceful assembly itself, in addition to threatening and violating other rights in the context of anti-fracking protests. Arguably then, the proposal of introducing fracking in the UK has already violated internationally and domestically recognised rights, with actual implementation of this particular method of energy extraction expected to only further impact human rights, of an economic, social and cultural nature as well as civil and political.

Anthropogenic climate change

While issues such as industrialisation of the landscape, water, air, noise pollution and citizens' ability to participate and protest are all important issues to consider in human rights impact assessments, perhaps the most important issue to consider is fracking's impact on greenhouse gas emissions and anthropogenic climate change. The latest climate science suggests that we can only burn approximately one-third[275] of known conventional fossil fuel reserves if we are to avoid catastrophic, runaway climate change.[276] Thus, scientists such as James Hansen and Kevin Anderson argue that unconventional sources such as shale gas need to be left in the ground. Indeed, taking recent climate science seriously calls into question the whole idea of 'unconventional' extraction. If we are to avoid runaway climate change and a potential extinction event for mankind, then, as leading climate scientist James Hansen puts it, 'we must rapidly phase out coal emissions, leave unconventional fossil fuels in the ground, and not go after the last drops of oil and gas. In other words, we must move as quickly as possible to the post-fossil fuel era of clean energies.'[277] Tyndall Centre climate scientist Kevin Anderson concurs, 'the only responsible action with regard to shale gas, or any 'new' unconventional fossil fuel, is to keep it in the ground – at least until there is a meaningful global emissions cap forcing substitution. In the absence of such an emissions cap, and in our energy hungry world, shale gas will only be combusted in addition to coal – not as a substitution, as many analysts have naively suggested.'[278] Despite this, there is considerable industry and government propaganda concerning the use of unconventional gas as a so-called 'bridge fuel', a proposition which is highly dubious and likely false. Robert Howarth's recent paper 'A Bridge to Nowhere: Methane Emissions and the Greenhouse Gas Footprint of Natural Gas' shows that over the crucial 20-year-period (in which we need to drastically reduce emissions to avoid the worst of climate change), both shale gas and conventional natural gas have a larger GHG footprint than do coal or oil, largely due to fugitive methane emissions.

While no explicit legal right to protection from climate change – or similar – exists, the negative effect of climate change on the enjoyment of numerous human rights is well documented. A connection between climate change and human rights was first drawn by the Inuit Circumpolar Council in their 2005 petition to the Inter-American Commission of Human Rights Case against the US.[279] The Inuit Council claimed that excessive greenhouse gas emissions from the US violated their right to culture through advancing climate change. While this case was dismissed by the Inter-American Commission as inadmissible,[280] it brought considerable attention to two important texts: the International Council on Human Rights Policy report which highlighted the 'human rights concerns raised by anthropogenic climate changes'[281] and Human Rights Council Resolution 7/23 which explicitly states '... climate change poses an immediate and far-reaching threat to people and communities around the world and has implications for the full enjoyment of human rights'.[282] An Office of the High Commissioner for Human Rights (OHCHR) study on climate change, called for in Resolution 7/23, was conducted later that same year and not only elaborated on human rights violations due to climate change, but also upon the legal mechanisms in human rights, environmental and other areas of law that oblige states to address climate change and protect their denizens from its consequences.[283] Following the study, in 2009 Human Rights Council Resolution 10/4 stated that climate change is currently directly and indirectly negatively affecting human rights,[284] a view that was affirmed by the Human Rights Council Panel Discussion on the relationship between climate change and human rights later that year.[285] A seminar convened by the OHCHR in 2012 also found the same conclusion.[286] Indeed, from the above discussions of various human rights and their relationship to the environment, as well as the consequences of climate change, the threat of climate change to the minimally good life is immediately apparent, and, therefore, the right to live free from the negative effects of climate change should be considered implicit within the human rights legal framework. Thus, via its contribution to anthropogenic climate change we find another possible avenue through which fracking activities are capable of violating human rights.

Conclusion

The hegemonic neoliberal version of capitalism under which most of us now live has such a significant thirst for fossil fuels that their extraction tends to trump all other concerns. As resources become scarcer and we scrape the bottom of the fossil fuel barrel through the use of more energy intensive, higher risk and environmentally destructive extraction processes, the relationship between resource development and human rights becomes ever more problematic. Indeed, human rights violations due to climate change are but another side effect of humanity's dependence on fossil fuels that is growing in magnitude with each passing decade. These violations are likely to increase and be felt more acutely as resources are depleted, quite possibly until the sharp population decline predicted in *The Limits to Growth* occurs. If there were not considerable evidence emerging, on an almost daily basis, concerning the actual, and potential, impacts and dangers of fracking development in countries with a mature industry such as the US, Canada and Australia,[287] it is highly likely that the UK's anti-fracking movement would not be its fastest growing social movement and the protests in which violations of civil and political rights have occurred may not have taken place. As things stand, however, it seems that citizens' civil and political rights are being violated in defence of their environmental, economic, social and cultural rights.

This article has shown the extent to which the process and infrastructure of fracking developments has the capacity to threaten and violate a wide range of internationally recognised human rights, including rights to water, air, land and health. Additionally, our research suggests the rights to peaceful assembly, freedom of expression, liberty and security of the person, fair trial and a private and family life have also been violated in the state response to protests opposing fracking development. These rights encompass the principles codified in international human rights legislation and the civil liberties recognised in many state constitutions. It is only with more research into the actual impact of these energy technologies on human rights that violations can be identified and hopefully stopped and remedied. Importantly this research must be industry independent, and must do more than appear on annual CSR statements. It should also be independent of government given the close relationships between governments and extractive industries and the tendency of government-sponsored reports to be suspiciously limited[288] or to include dubious 'REDACTED' sections on public release.[289] In sum, there is an urgent need for independent, comprehensive, evidence-based interdisciplinary HRIAs to provide valuable impact data and analysis. Such assessments will be a vital tool for communities in the defence of their rights when faced with immanent extreme energy developments and governments intent on unsustainable fossil fuel extraction.

Disclosure statement

No potential conflict of interest was reported by the authors.

Notes

1. Olivia Ball and Paul Gready, *No-nonsense Guide to Human Rights* (Oxford: New Internationalist, 2006); Upendra Baxi, *The Future of Human Rights* (New Delhi: Oxford University Press, 2002); Rhonda L. Callaway and Julie Harrelson-Stephens, eds, *Exploring International Human*

Rights: Essential Readings (London: Lynne Reiner, 2007); Marie-Bénédicte Dembour and Richard Wilson, eds, *Culture and Rights: An Anthropological Perspective* (Cambridge: Cambridge University Press, 2001), 1–26; Jack Donnelly, *Universal Human Rights in Theory and Practice* (Ithaca, NY: Cornell University Press, 2003); Michael Freeman, *Human Rights: An Interdisciplinary Approach* (Cambridge: Polity, 2002); Michael Goodhart, ed., *Human Rights Politics and Practice* (Oxford: Oxford University Press, 2010); Gerd Oberleitner, *Global Human Rights Institutions* (Cambridge: Polity, 2007); Rhona Smith and Christien van den Anker, *The Essentials of Human Rights* (London: Hodder Arnold, 2005).

2. 'Minimalist' in the sense that Nickel argues, correctly in our view, that human rights are not ideals of the good life for humans, they are rather concerned with ensuring conditions, negative and positive, of a 'minimally good life'.
3. James Nickel, *Making Sense of Human Rights*, 2nd ed. (Oxford: Blackwell, 2007), 138.
4. Ibid.
5. Martin Crook and Damien Short, 'Marx, Lemkin and the Genocide-Ecocide Nexus', *International Journal of Human Rights* 18, no. 3 (2014): 298–319 (Special Issue: Climate Change, Environmental Violence and Genocide, ed. Jurgen Zimmerer).
6. Rhoda Howard-Hassmann, 'The Second Great Transformation: Human Rights Leapfrogging in the Era of Globalization', *Human Rights Quarterly* 27, no. 1 (2005): 1–40; Adamantia Pollis, 'Commentary on the Second Great Transformation', *Human Rights Quarterly* 27, no. 3 (2005): 1120–1; Rhoda Howard-Hassmann, 'Reply to Adamantia Pollis', *Human Rights Quarterly* 28, no. 1 (2006): 277–8.
7. Donella H. Meadows et al., *The Limits to Growth: A Report for the Club of Rome's Project on the Predicament of Mankind* (New York: Universe Books, 1972).
8. Graham Turner, *A Comparison of the Limits to Growth with 30 Years of Reality*, Socio-Economics and the Environment in Discussion CSIRO Working Paper Series 2008–09 (Canberra: CSIRO Sustainable Ecosystems, 2007).
9. As oil and natural gas production peaks and declines, coal becomes increasingly pivotal in maintaining global energy consumption rates; however, this renewed focus on coal, seen in the 'record rate' of coal gasification and coal-to-liquid plant construction of the last decade, will only further exacerbate strained coal resources. Indeed, world coal production continues to increase annually, with an overall increase of over 67% between 1990 and 2013. Even with more conservative estimates of coal production growth and the most opportunistic estimates of global coal reserves – relying on the World Coal Association's production growth rate of 0.4% between 2012 and 2013 remaining constant and the German Federal Institute for Geosciences and Natural Resources' estimate of 1052 billion tonnes of reserves – the world will 'run out' of coal in just over a century. As that figure assumes no 'updates' to reserve figures (despite nearly every state with 'significant coal resources' reporting a 'substantial downward revision' in reserve estimates made since 1986) or increase in production rate (despite the sharp decreases in available oil and natural gas during the upcoming decades), it is reasonable to conclude that the limits to coal-dependent growth will also soon be reached. Richard Heinberg, 'Peak Coal: Sooner Than You Think', *On Line Opinion*, 21 May 2007, http://www.onlineopinion.com.au/view.asp?article=5869; World Coal Association, 'Coal Statistics', http://www.worldcoal.org/resources/coal-statistics.
10. Richard Heinberg, *Snake Oil: How Fracking's False Promises of Plenty Imperils Our Future* (West Sussex: Clairview Books, 2014).
11. James Murray and Jim Hansen, 'Peak Oil and Energy Independence: Myths and Reality', *Eos* 94, no. 28 (2013): 245–52.
12. Natural gas liquids (NGLs) are 'hydrocarbons with longer molecular chains', such as propane and butane, within natural gas that are captured and used for heating and industrial purposes. Heinburg, *Snake Oil*, 25.
13. Paul Mobbs, 'Sheet E1. Peak Energy: The Limits to Oil and Gas Production', Free Range 'Energy Beyond Oil' Project, http://www.fraw.org.uk/publications/e-series/e01/e01-peak_energy.html; Heinberg, *Snake Oil*, 25.
14. Conventional natural gas production follows a similar peak and decline bell-curve and is expected to reach its plateau before the mid-twenty-first century. See: Mobbs, 'Sheet E1'; Gaetano Maggio and Gaetano Cacciola, 'When Will Oil, Natural Gas, and Coal Peak?', *Fuel* 98 (2012): 111–23.

15. We have in mind here both the Gulf War of 1990/1991 and the Iraq War of 2003–2011, though the UN Security Council sanctions against Iraq in the interim also indicate the willingness of Western states to take international action to gain control of oil exports when their native government is considered unreliable.
16. Jon Barnett, 'Environmental Security and U.S. Foreign Policy', in *The Environment, International Relations, and U.S. Foreign Policy*, ed. P. G. Harris (Washington, DC: Georgetown University Press, 2001), 68–91.
17. See: US National Security Strategy, *A National Security Strategy for a New Century* (Washington, DC: The White House, 1998).
18. Exxon's revenue is greater than the gross domestic product of Thailand, for instance. Vincent Trivett, '25 US Mega Corporations: Where They Rank If They Were Countries', *Business Insider*, 27 June 2011, http://www.businessinsider.com/25-corporations-bigger-tan-countries-2011-6?op=1.
19. Jane Mayer, 'Covert Operations: The Billionaire Brothers Who Are Waging a War Against Obama', *The New Yorker*, 30 August 2010, http://www.newyorker.com/magazine/2010/08/30/covert-operations.
20. Fred Bedell, 'Economic Injustice as an Understanding of the Existence of Two Americas – Wealth and Poverty', *Open Journal of Political Science* 4, no. 3 (2014): 101–8.
21. Paul Mobbs, 'Economically and Politically Fracked: "Behind Every Picture Lies a Story" – Statistical Reality versus PR-Hype within the Political Project of Unconventional Gas in Britain', *Mobbsey's Musings*, 25 July 2013, http://www.fraw.org.uk/mei/musings/2013/20130725-behind_every_picture_lies_a_story.html.
22. See the excellent work of investigative journalist Greg Palast on this point – Greg Palast, *The Best Democracy Money Can Buy: An Investigative Reporter Exposes the Truth About Globalization, Corporate Cons and High Finance Fraudsters* (Pluto Press: London, 2002).
23. United States Congress, *Energy Policy Act*, Pub.L. 109–58 (2005).
24. BBC, 'Lords: Fracking Should Be "Urgent Priority" for UK', *BBC News: Business*, 8 May 2014, http://www.bbc.co.uk/news/business-27312796.
25. Damian Carrington, 'UK Defeats European Bid for Fracking Regulations', *The Guardian*, 14 January 2014, http://www.theguardian.com/environment/2014/jan/14/uk-defeats-european-bid-fracking-regulations.
26. Michael J. Lynch, Ronald G. Burns, and Paul B. Stretesky, 'Global Warming and State-Corporate Crime: The Politicalization of Global Warming under the Bush Administration', *Crime, Law and Social Change* 54, nos 3–4 (2010): 213–39.
27. *The Economist*, 'Energy Firms and Climate Change: Unburnable Fuel', *The Economist*, 4 May 2013, http://www.economist.com/news/business/21577097-either-governments-are-not-serious-about-climate-change-or-fossil-fuel-firms-are.
28. For more on corporate-state connections, see: Noam Chomsky, 'Can Civilization Survive Capitalism?', *AlterNet*, 5 March 2013, http://www.alternet.org/noam-chomsky-can-civilization-survive-capitalism; Palast, *The Best Democracy Money Can Buy.*
29. For example, the American Enterprise Institute, which receives funding from ExxonMobil and other companies in the energy sector, 'offered a $10,000 incentive to scientists and economists to write papers challenging the IPCC findings' after the Intergovernmental Panel on Climate Change released its fourth assessment report in 2007. Charles A. Jones and David L. Levy, 'Business Strategies and Climate Change', in *Changing Climates in North American Politics*, ed. H. Selin and S.D. VanDeveer (Cambridge: MIT Press, 2009), 219–240.
30. IPCC, 'Summary for Policymakers', in *Climate Change 2013: The Physical Science Basis. Contribution of Working Group I to the Fifth Assessment Report of the Intergovernmental Panel on Climate Change*, ed. T.F. Stocker et al. (Cambridge: Cambridge University Press, 2013), 3–29.
31. Bärbel Hönisch et al., 'The Geological Record of Ocean Acidification Science', *Science* 335, no. 6072 (2012): 1058–63.
32. IPCC, *Climate Change 2013: The Physical Science Basis. Contribution of Working Group I to the Fifth Assessment Report of the Intergovernmental Panel on Climate Change* (Cambridge: Cambridge University Press, 2013).
33. IPCC, 'Summary for Policymakers'.
34. Office of the Chief Economist, *World Energy Outlook: 2011* (Paris: International Energy Agency, 2011).

35. Joel Bakan, *The Corporation: The Pathological Pursuit of Profit and Power* (London: Constable and Robinson, 2005).
36. Robert C. Hinkley, 'How Corporate Law Inhibits Social Responsibility', *Humanist* 62, no. 2 (2002): 26. Also: Bakan, *The Corporation*. For further reading on the economic model and psychology under which corporations operate, see: Diane Elson, 'Human Rights and Corporate Profits: The UN Global Compact – Part of the Solution or Part of the Problem?', in *Global Tensions: Challenges and Opportunities in the Global Economy*, ed. L. Bernia and S. Bisnath (London: Routledge, 2002); and Nicholas Connolly, 'Corporate Social Responsibility: A Duplicitous Distraction?', *International Journal of Human Rights* 16, no. 8 (2012): 1228–49. Notably, even privately held companies, such as Koch Industries, have a monetary interest in maintaining global fossil fuel use, as long as non-renewable energy sources continue to generate profit.
37. US Energy Information Administration, 'Renewable & Alternative Fuels', http://www.eia.gov/renewable/.
38. For example, in 2009 approximately $43–46 billion was provided to renewable and biofuel technologies, projects and companies by the governments of the world, compared with the $577 billion spent on fossil fuel subsidies in 2008. Bloomberg: New Energy Finance, 'Subsidies for Renewables, Biofuels Dwarfed by Supports for Fossil Fuels', http://about.bnef.com/press-releases/subsidies-for-renewables-biofuels-dwarfed-by-supports-for-fossil-fuels/.
39. This concept is perhaps best illustrated by the insistence from both industry and governments that hydraulic fracturing will allow natural gas to replace the use of coal and thus reduce the emission of greenhouse gases, when in actuality the abundance of hydraulic fracturing in the US has simply lowered the price of US coal and driven up exports. Damian Carrington, 'Fracking Boom Will Not Tackle Global Warming, Analysis Warns', *The Guardian*, 15 October 2014, http://www.theguardian.com/environment/2014/oct/15/gas-boom-from-unrestrained-fracking-linked-to-emissions-rise; Thoman K. Grose, 'As U.S. Cleans Its Energy Mix, It Ships Coal Problems Abroad', *National Geographic: News*, 15 March 2013, http://news.nationalgeographic.com/news/energy/2013/03/130315-us-coal-exports/.
40. Ibid.
41. UNEP, 'Athabasca Oil Sands, Require Massive Investments and Energy and Produce Massive Amounts of Oil and CO2 – Alberta (Canada)', *United Nations Environment Programme* 54, Global Environment Alert Service (2011): 1–5; UNEP, 'Oil Palm Plantations: Threats and Opportunities for Tropical Ecosystems', *United Nations Environment Programme* 73, Global Environment Alert Service (2011): 1–10.
42. Michael Klare, 'The Era of Extreme Energy: Life after the Age of Oil', *The Huffington Post*, 25 May 2011, http://www.huffingtonpost.com/michael-t-klare/the-era-of-xtreme-energy_b_295304.html.
43. Edward Lloyd-Davies, 'Defining Extreme Energy: A Process not a Category', *Extreme Energy Initiative: Working Paper Series*, 25 July 2013, http://extremeenergy.org/2013/07/25/defining-extreme-energy-a-process-not-a-category/.
44. Euran Mearns, 'The Global Energy Crises and its Role in the Pending Collapse of the Global Economy' (Paper presented at the Royal Society of Chemists, Aberdeen, Scotland, 29 October 2008).
45. At the time of writing oil prices were in decline but the finite nature of the resource guarantees that prices will again rise.
46. David J. Murphy, 'EROI, Insidious Feedbacks, and the End of Economic Growth' (Paper presented at the Sixth Annual Conference of the Association for the Study of Peak Oil (ASPO), Washington, DC, 7–9 October 2010).
47. On this point see also Heinberg, *Snake Oil*.
48. Stephen J. Purdey, *Economic Growth, the Environment and International Relations: The Growth Paradigm* (Oxon: Routledge, 2010).
49. International Energy Agency, *Key World Energy Statistics* (Paris: International Energy Agency, 2013).
50. Lloyd-Davies, 'Defining Extreme Energy'.
51. Notwithstanding the current, inevitably temporary, geo-politically induced price reduction, prices will undoubtedly rise over time as supply declines, see Mobbs, P. 'Environmentalists' Oil Price Panic Reflects their Own Existential Crisis', *The Ecologist*, 8 January 2015,

http://www.theecologist.org/blogs_and_comments/commentators/2703420/environmentalists_oil_price_panic_reflects_their_own_existential_crisis.html.
52. Heinberg, *Snake Oil*.
53. Stephanie Malin, 'There's No Real Choice but to Sign: Neoliberalization and Normalization of Hydraulic Fracturing on Pennsylvania Farmland', *Journal of Environmental Studies and Sciences* 2014, no. 4 (2013): 17–27.
54. Lloyd-Davies, 'Defining Extreme Energy'. See also: Jennifer Huseman and Damien Short, 'A Slow Industrial Genocide: Tar Sands and the Indigenous Peoples of Northern Alberta', *The International Journal of Human Rights* 16, no. 1 (2012): 216–37; Stephen Humphreys, *Climate Change and Human Rights: A Rough Guide* (Geneva: International Council on Human Rights Policy, 2008).
55. IPCC, 'Summary for Policymakers', in *Climate Change 2007: The Physical Science Basis. Contribution of Working Group I to the Fourth Assessment Report of the Intergovernmental Panel on Climate Change*, ed. S. Solomon et al. (Cambridge: Cambridge University Press, 2007), 1–18.
56. Jonathan Patz et al., 'Impact of Regional Climate Change on Human Health', *Nature* 438 (2005): 310–17.
57. Laboratory for Aviation and the Environment, 'Air Pollution Causes 200,000 Early Deaths Each Year in the U.S.', Massachusetts Institute of Technology, http://lae.mit.edu/?p=2821.
58. Peter Stott, Dáithí Stone, and Myles Allen, 'Human Contribution to the European Heatwave of 2003', *Nature* 432 (2004): 610–14.
59. Alok Jha, 'Boiled Alive', *The Guardian*, 26 July 2006, http://www.theguardian.com/environment/2006/jul/26/science.g2.
60. Meadows et al., *The Limits to Growth*.
61. IPCC, 'Projections of Future Changes in Climate', in *Climate Change 2007: The Physical Science Basis. Contribution of Working Group I to the Fourth Assessment Report of the Intergovernmental Panel on Climate Change*, ed. S. Solomon et al. (Cambridge: Cambridge University Press, 2007), 12–18.
62. World Health Organisation (WHO) Regional Office for Europe, *Euroheat: Improving Public Health Responses to Extreme Weather Heat-Waves. Summary for Policy-Makers* (Copenhagen: World Health Organization, 2009).
63. IPCC, 'Projections of Future Changes in Climate'.
64. IPCC, *Climate Change 2014: Impacts, Adaptation, and Vulnerability. Part A: Global and Sectoral Aspects. Contribution of Working Group II to the Fifth Assessment Report of the Intergovernmental Panel on Climate Change* (Cambridge: Cambridge University Press, 2014).
65. See: John Barry and Kerri Woods, 'The Environment', in *Human Rights: Politics and Practice*, ed. M. Goodhart (Oxford: Oxford University Press, 2010), 380–395; Nafeez Ahmed, 'Are You Opposed to Fracking? Then You Might Just Be a Terrorist', *The Guardian*, 21 January 2014, http://www.theguardian.com/environment/earth-insight/2014/jan/21/fracking-activism-protest-terrorist-oil-corporate-spies; Human Rights Council, 'Report of the Special Rapporteur on the Human Right to safe Drinking Water and Sanitation: Mission to the United States of America', A/HRC/18/33/Add.4, (2011): 10–11.
66. See Huseman and Short, 'A Slow Industrial Genocide'.
67. S. Perry, 'Development, Land Use, and Collective Trauma: The Marcellus Shale Gas Boom in Rural Pennsylvania', *Culture, Agriculture, Food and Environment* 34, no. 1 (2012): 81–92, 81.
68. See Heinberg, *Snake Oil*.
69. Reports of considerable negative impacts go well beyond the anecdotal realm, see for example environmental and health studies such as V.J. Brown, 'Radionuclides in Fracking Wastewater: Managing a Toxic Blend', *Environmental Health Perspectives* 122, no. 2 (2014): A50–A55; R. McDermott-Levy, N. Kaktins, and B. Sattler, 'Fracking, the Environment, and Health: New Energy Practices May Threaten Public Health', *American Journal of Nursing* 113, no. 6 (2013): 45–51; C.W. Moore, B. Zielinska, G. Petron, and R.B. Jackson, 'Air Impacts of Increased Natural Gas Acquisition, Processing, and Use: A Critical Review', *Environmental Science and Technology* (2014), dx.doi.org/10.1021/es4053472; S. Osborn, A. Vengosh, N.R. Warner, and R.B. Jackson, 'Methane Contamination of Drinking Water Accompanying Gas-well Drilling and Hydraulic Fracturing', *Proceedings of the National Academy of Sciences of the United States of America* 108, no. 20 (2011), http://www.pnas.org/cgi/doi/10.1073/pnas.1100682108; and A. Vengosh, R.B. Jackson, N. Warner, T.H. Darrah, and A. Kondash, 'A Critical Review of the Risks to Water Resources from

Unconventional Shale Gas Development and Hydraulic Fracturing in the United States', *Environmental Science and Technology* (2014), dx.doi.org/10.1021/es405118y; and social scientific enquiries such as Perry, 'Development, Land Use, and Collective Trauma'; B.J. Anderson and G.L. Theodori, 'Local Leaders' Perceptions of Energy Development in the Barnett Shale', *Southern Rural Sociology* 24, no. 1 (2009): 113–29; B.E. Apple, 'Mapping Fracking: An Analysis of Law, Power, and Regional Distribution in the United States', *Harvard Environmental Law Review* 38 (2014): 217–44; D. Beach, 'How the Fracking Boom Impacts Rural Ohio', *EcoWatch: Transforming Green*, 16 September 2013, http://ecowatch.com/2013/09/16/fracking-boom-impacting-rural-ohio/; R. Gramling and W. Freudenburg, 'Opportunity-Threat, Development, and Adaptation: Toward a Comprehensive Framework for Social Impact Assessment', *Rural Sociology* 57, no. 2 (1992): 216–34; D.A. Fleming and T.G. Measham, 'Local Economic Impacts of an Unconventional Energy Boom: The Coal Seam Gas Industry in Australia', *Australian Journal of Agricultural and Resource Economics* (2014), doi:10.1111/1467-8489.12043.

70. Environment and Human Rights Advisory, *A Human Rights Assessment of Hydraulic Fracturing for Natural Gas* (Oregon: EHRA, 2011), http://www.earthworksaction.org/files/publications/EHRA_Human-rights-fracking-FINAL.pdf.
71. See: Damien Short, Karen Hulme, and Steffen Bohm, 'Don't Let Human Rights Fall to Wayside in Fracking Debate', *The Conversation*, 24 March 2014, http://theconversation.com/dont-let-human-rights-fall-to-wayside-in-fracking-debate-24652; Jess Elliot and Damien Short, 'Fracking is Driving UK Civil and Political Rights Violations', *The Ecologist* (2014); Anna Grear 'Fracking – Human Rights Must Not be Ignored!' *The Ecologist*, 30 October 2014; Anna Grear, Tom Kerns, Evadne Grant, Karen Morrow, and Damien Short, 'A Human Rights Assessment of Hydraulic Fracturing and Other Unconventional Gas Development in the United Kingdom', Extreme Energy Initiative Report Commissioned by The Bianca Jagger Human Rights Foundation, http://www.sas.ac.uk/sites/default/files/files/UK%20HRIA%20w%20appdx-hi%20res.pdf.
72. UNEP, 'Gas Fracking: Can We Safely Squeeze the Rocks?', United Nations Environment Programme, Global Environment Alert Service (2012).
73. Ibid., 6–7.
74. Ibid., 7–9, 12.
75. Robert Howarth, Renee Santoro, and Anthony Ingraffea, 'Methane and the Greenhouse-gas Footprint of Natural Gas from Shale Formations', *Climatic Change* 106, no. 4 (2011): 679–90; Robert Howarth et al., *Methane Emissions from Natural Gas Systems: Background Paper for the National Climate Assessment* (2012), http://www.eeb.cornell.edu/howarth/publications/Howarth_et_al_2012_National_Climate_Assessment.pdf; Robert A. Howarth, 'A Bridge to Nowhere: Methane Emissions and the Greenhouse Gas Footprint of Natural Gas', *Energy Science and Engineering* 2, no. 2 (2014): 47–60.
76. Stephen Osborn, Avner Vengosh, Nathaniel R. Warner, Robert B. Jackson, 'Methane Contamination of Drinking Water Accompanying Gas-well Drilling and Hydraulic Fracturing', *Proceedings of the National Academy of Sciences of the United States of America* 108, no. 20 (2011): 8172–6. See also: Isaac Santos and Damien Maher, *Fugitive Emissions from Coal Seam Gas*, Centre for Coastal Biogeochemistry Research Submission to Department of Climate Change and Energy Efficiency (2012), http://www.scu.edu.au/coastal-biogeochemistry/index.php/70/.
77. Walter Brasch, *Fracking Pennsylvania: Flirting with Disaster* (Sacramento, CA: Greeley and Stone, 2012).
78. Environment and Human Rights Advisory, 'A Human Rights Assessment'.
79. For example, *Gasland*, directed by Josh Fox (New York: HBO Productions, 2012); *Drill Baby Drill*, directed by Lech Kowalski (France: Kowalski Productions, 2013).
80. Kim de Rijke, 'Hydraulically Fractured: Unconventional Gas and Anthropology', *Anthropology Today* 29, no. 2 (2013): 13–17; Kim de Rijke, 'Coal Seam Gas and Social Impact Assessment: An Anthropological Contribution to Current Debates and Practices', *Journal of Economic and Social Policy* 15, no. 3 (2013): 3; Kim de Rijke, 'The Agri-Gas Fields of Australia: Black Soil, Food, and Unconventional Gas', *Culture, Agriculture, Food and Environment* 35, no. 1 (2013): 41–53.
81. Anderson and Theodori, 'Local Leaders' Perceptions of Energy Development in the Barnett Shale'; Kai Schafft, Yetkin Borlu, and Leland Glenna, 'The Relationship between Marcellus

Shale Gas Development in Pennsylvania and Local Perceptions of Risk and Opportunity', *Rural Sociology* 78, no. 2 (2013): 143–66; Kai A. Schafft, Leland L. Glenna, Brandn Green, and Yetkin Borlu, 'Local Impacts of Unconventional Gas Development within Pennsylvania's Marcellus Shale Region: Gauging Boomtown Development through the Perspectives of Educational Administrators', *Society & Natural Resources: An International Journal* 27, no. 4 (2014): 389–404.

82. Matthew Cotton, Imogen Rattle, and James Van Alstine, 'Shale Gas Policy in the United Kingdom: An Argumentative Discourse Analysis', *Energy Policy* 73 (2014): 427–38.
83. Malin, 'There's No Real Choice but to Sign'.
84. Paul B. Stretesky, Michael A. Long, and Michael J. Lynch, 'Does Environmental Enforcement Slow the Treadmill of Production? The Relationship between Large Monetary Penalties, Ecological Disorganization and Toxic Releases within Offending Corporations', *Journal of Crime and Justice* 36, no. 2: (2013): 233–47.
85. Tara Shelley and Tara Opsal, 'Energy Crime, Harm, and Problematic State Response in Colorado: A Case of the Fox Guarding the Hen House?', *Critical Criminology* 22, no. 4 (2014): 561–77.
86. de Rijke, 'Hydraulically Fractured'.
87. Ibid., 17.
88. S. Bakker, M. Van Den Berg, D. Düzenli, and M. Radstaake, 'Human Rights Impact Assessment in Practice: The Case of the Health Rights of Women Assessment Instrument (HeRWAI)', *Journal of Human Rights Practice* 1, no. 3 (2009): 436–58; G. De Beco, 'Human Rights Impact Assessments', *Netherlands Quarterly of Human Rights* 27, no. 2 (2009): 139–66. J. Harrison, 'Human Rights Measurement: Reflections on the Current Practice and Future Potential of Human Rights Impact Assessment', *Journal of Human Rights Practice* 3, no. 2 (2011): 162–87; P. Hunt and G. MacNaughton, 'Impact Assessments, Poverty, and Human Rights: A Case Study Using the Right to the Highest Attainable Standard of Health', Submitted to UNESCO (2006), http://www.who.int/hhr/Series_6_Impact%20Assessments_Hunt_MacNaughton1.pdf; G. MacNaughton and P. Hunt, 'A Human Rights-based Approach to Social Impact Assessment', in *New Directions In Social Impact Assessment: Conceptual and Methodological Advances*, ed. F. Vanclay and A.M. Esteves (Cheltenham, UK: Edward Elgar Publishing, 2011), 355–69.
89. John Ruggie, 'Guiding Principles on Business and Human Rights: Implementing the United Nations "Protect, Respect and Remedy Framework"' (2011), http://www.ohchr.org/Documents/Publications/GuidingPrinciplesBusinessHR_EN.pdf.
90. Simon Walker, *The Future of Human Rights Impact Assessments of Trade Agreements* (Brussels: Intersentia, 2009), 43; and Simon Walker, 'The United States–Dominican Republic–Central American Free Trade Agreement and Access to Medicines in Costa Rica: A Human Rights Impact Assessment', *Journal of Human Rights Practice* 3, no. 2 (2011): 188–213.
91. Harrison, 'Human Rights Measurement', 167; G. De Beco, 'Human Rights Impact Assessments', *Netherlands Quarterly of Human Rights* 27, no. 2 (2009): 139–66, 147.
92. MacNaughton and Hunt, 'A Human Rights-based Approach to Social Impact Assessment', 361.
93. Ibid., 355.
94. Anderson and Theodori, 'Local Leaders' Perceptions of Energy Development in the Barnett Shale.
95. Average figures obtained from the US-based www.fracfocus.org website. FracFocus is the national hydraulic fracturing chemical registry. FracFocus is managed by the Ground Water Protection Council and Interstate Oil and Gas Compact Commission, two organisations whose missions both revolve around conservation and environmental protection. FracFocus, 'FracFocus 2.0: Hundreds of Companies. Thousands of Wells', FracFocus, http://www.fracfocus.org.
96. Melissa Stark et al., 'Water and Shale Gas Development: Leveraging the US Experience in New Shale Developments', *Accenture* (December 2012).
97. Queensland Water Commission, *Underground Water Impact Report for the Surat Cumulative Management Area* (Queensland: Queensland Water Commission, 2012), http://www.dnrm.qld.gov.au/__data/assets/pdf_file/0016/31327/underground-water-impact-report.pdf.

98. See for example: Sandra Postel, 'As Oil and Gas Drilling Competes for Water, One New Mexico County Says No', *National Geographic*, 3 May 2013, http://voices.nationalgeographic.com/2013/05/02/as-oil-and-gas-drilling-competes-for-water-one-new-mexico-county-says-no/.
99. Mark Fischetti, 'Groundwater Contamination May End the Gas-Fracking Boom', *Scientific American*, 20 August 2013, http://www.scientificamerican.com/article/groundwater-contamination-may-end-the-gas-fracking-boom/.
100. Anthony Ingraffea et al., 'Assessment and Risk Analysis of Casing and Cement Impairment in Oil and Gas Wells in Pennsylvania, 2000–2012', *Proceedings of the National Academy of the Sciences* 111, no. 30 (2014): 10955–60.
101. Sheila M. Olmstead et al., 'Shale Gas Development Impacts on Surface Water Quality in Pennsylvania', *Proceedings of the National Academy of the Sciences* 110, no. 13 (2013): 4962–7.
102. Paul Mobbs, 'An Abuse of Science – Concealing Fracking's Radioactive Footprint', *The Ecologist*, 8 July 2014, http://www.theecologist.org/News/news_analysis/2469495/an_abuse_of_science_concealing_frackings_radioactive_footprint.html.
103. Nathaniel R. Warner et al., 'Impacts of Shale Gas Wastewater Disposal on Water Quality in Western Pennsylvania', *Environmental Science & Technology* 47 no. 20 (2013): 11849–57.
104. Ibid.
105. Sean Nicholls, 'Santos Coal Seam Gas Project Contaminates Aquifer', *Sydney Morning Herald*, 8 March 2014, http://www.smh.com.au/environment/santos-coal-seam-gas-project-contaminates-aquifer-20140307-34csb.html.
106. Read some examples of such in Matthew Currell, 'Coal Seam Gas Water Leaks Could be a Problem for Decades', *The Conversation*, 24 March 2014,http://theconversation.com/coal-seam-gas-water-leaks-could-be-a-problem-for-decades-24718; and see farmer Brian Monk's experiences here: https://frackinginkent.wordpress.com/2014/02/01/the-ugly-truth-in-queensland-australia/.
107. Avner Vengosh et al., 'A Critical Review of the Risks to Water Resources from Unconventional Shale Gas Development and Hydraulic Fracturing in the United States', *Environmental Science and Technology* 48, no. 15 (2014): 8334–48.
108. United Nations Sub-Commission on the Promotion and Protection of Human Rights, *Realization of the Right to Drinking Water and Sanitation, Report of the Special Rapporteur, El Hadji Guissé*, E/CN.4/Sub.2/2005/25 (2005).
109. United Nations Human Rights Council, *Human Rights and Access to Water*, A/HRC/2/104 (2006).
110. United Nations Human Rights Council, *Annual Report of the United Nations High Commissioner for Human Rights on the Scope and Content of the Relevant Human Rights Obligations Related to Equitable Access to Safe Drinking Water and Sanitation under International Human Rights Instruments*, A/HRC/6/3 (2007).
111. United Nations Human Rights Council, *Human Rights and Access to Safe Drinking Water and Sanitation Resolution 7/22*, A/HR/RES/722 (2008).
112. United Nations Human Rights Council, *The Human Right to Safe Drinking Water and Sanitation*, A/HRC/RES/16/2 (2011).
113. United Nations Human Rights Council, *Human Rights and Access to Safe Drinking Water and Sanitation*, A/HRC/RES/15/9 (2010).
114. United Nations, *Convention on the Elimination of All Forms of Discrimination against Women*, (1979) Article 14(2).
115. International Labour Organization, *Occupational Health Services Convention C161*, (1985) Article 5.
116. United Nations, *The Convention on the Rights of the Child*, (1989) Article 24.
117. African Commission on Human and Peoples' Rights, *African Charter on the Rights and Welfare of the Child*, (1990) Article 14; African Commission on Human and Peoples' Rights, *Additional Protocol to the African Charter on Human and Peoples' Rights on the Rights of Women in Africa*, (2003) Article 15.
118. United Nations, *Convention on the Rights of Persons with Disabilities*, (2006) Article 28.
119. United Nations Human Rights Council, *Report of the Special Rapporteur on the Human Right to Safe Drinking Water and Sanitation, Catarina de Albuquerque: Mission to the United States of America*, A/HRC/18/33/Add.4 (2011).

120. See: US Environmental Protection Agency, *Plan to Study the Potential Impacts of Hydraulic Fracturing on Drinking Water Resources*, (Washington, DC: US Environmental Protection Agency, 2011), http://www2.epa.gov/hfstudy; and their study plan, http://water.epa.gov/type/groundwater/uic/class2/hydraulicfracturing/upload/hf_study_plan_110211_final_508.pdf.
121. Ingraffea et al., 'Assessment and Risk Analysis'.
122. Vengosh et al., 'A Critical Review'.
123. Shelley and Opsal, 'Energy Crime, Harm, and Problematic State Response'.
124. *Wall Street Journal*, 'Online List IDs Water Wells Harmed by Drilling', *Wall Street Journal*, 28 August 2014, http://online.wsj.com/article/AP16a162b66b5946d0837c7395cab7a5f4.html (accessed 5 September 2014).
125. Larysa Dyrszka, Kathleen Nolan, and Sandra Steingraber, 'Statement on Preliminary Findings from the Southwest Pennsylvania Environmental Health Project Study', *Concerned Health Professionals of New York*, 27 August 2013, http://concernedhealthny.org/statement-on-preliminary-findings-from-the-southwest-pennsylvania-environmental-health-project-study/.
126. Dustin Bleizeffer, 'Pristine to Polluted: More Drilling Proposed near Pinedale Despite Ozone Spikes', *WyoFile*, 17 May 2011, http://wyofile.com/dustin/pristine-to-polluted/.
127. A dangerously toxic substance, see National Institute for Occupational Safety and Health (NIOSH), 'Emergency Preparedness and Response: Facts about Benzene', *Centers for Disease Control and Prevention*, 14 February 2013, http://www.bt.cdc.gov/agent/benzene/basics/facts.asp.
128. Mariann Lloyd-Smith, 'License to Drill? Is Australia's Present Britain's Future?' (Presentation, School of Advanced Study, London, 20 May 2013), http://www.sas.ac.uk/sites/default/files/files/events/london%20uni%20talk%20Impacts%20of%20UG.pdf.
129. Dave Fehling, 'State Impact, Like Working in a Refinery: Fracking's New Chemical Hazards for Workers', *State Impact*, 24 July 2012, http://stateimpact.npr.org/texas/2012/07/24/like-working-in-a-refinery-frackings-new-chemical-hazards-for-workers/.
130. Physicians for Social Responsibility, *Hydraulic Fracturing and Your Health: Air Contamination* (Washington, DC: PSR, 2014), http://www.psr.org/assets/pdfs/fracking-and-air-pollution.pdf.
131. Theo Colborn et al., 'Natural Gas Operations from a Public Health Perspective', *International Journal of Human and Ecological Risk Assessment* 17, no. 5 (2011): 1039–56. For an analysis of chemicals found in wastewater pits, see: The Endocrine Disruption Exchange, *Potential Health Effects of Residues in 6 New Mexico Oil and Gas Drilling Reserve Pits Based on Compounds Detected in at Least One Sample: Revised November 15, 2007* (Paonia, Colorado: TEDX, 2007), http://endocrinedisruption.org/assets/media/documents/summary_of_pit_chemicals_revised_2-1-08.pdf.
132. Jessica B. Gilman et al., 'Source Signature of Volatile Organic Compounds from Oil and Natural Gas Operations in Northeastern Colorado', *Environmental Science & Technology* 47, no. 3 (2013): 1297–305.
133. Wendy Koch, 'Wyoming's Smog Exceeds Los Angeles' due to Gas Drilling', *USA Today*, 9 March 2011, http://content.usatoday.com/communities/greenhouse/post/2011/03/wyomings-smog-exceeds-los-angeles-due-to-gas-drilling/1; Detlev Helmig, 'Highly Elevated Atmospheric Levels of Volatile Organic Compounds in the Uintah Basin, Utah', *Environmental Science & Technology* 48, (2014): 4707–15.
134. Helmig, 'Highly Elevated Atmospheric Levels'. See also: American Lung Association, 'State of the Air 2014', American Lung Association, http://www.stateoftheair.org/.
135. National Institute for Occupational Safety and Health (NIOSH), 'Emergency Preparedness and Response: Facts about Benzene', *Centers for Disease Control and Prevention*, 14 February 2013, http://www.bt.cdc.gov/agent/benzene/basics/facts.asp.
136. Lisa M. McKenzie et al., 'Human Health Risk Assessment of Air Emissions from Development of Unconventional natural Gas Resources', *Science of the Total Environment* 424 (2012): 79–87.
137. Wolf Eagle Environmental, *Town of DISH, Texas, Ambient Air Monitoring Analysis* (Flower Mound, TX: Wolf Eagle Environmental, 2009), http://townofdish.com/objects/DISH_-_final_report_revised.pdf.
138. Ibid., 5.
139. Ibid., 6.

140. Theo Colborn et al., 'An Exploratory Study of Air Quality Near Natural Gas Operations', *Human and Ecological Risk Assessment* 20, no. 1 (2014): 86–105.
141. David Brown et al., 'Understanding Exposure from Natural Gas Drilling Puts Current Air Standards to the Test', *Reviews Environmental Health* (March 2014), http://www.degruyter.com/view/j/reveh.2014.29.issue-1-2/issue-files/reveh.2014.29.issue-1-2.xml.
142. Physicians for Social Responsibility, *Hydraulic Fracturing*.
143. G.P. Macey, R. Breech, M. Chernaik, C. Cox, D. Larson, D. Thomas, and D.O. Carpenter, 'Air Concentrations of Volatile Compounds Near Oil and Gas Production: A Community-based Exploratory Study', *Environmental Health* 13, no. 82 (2014), doi:10.1186/1476-069X-13-82
144. Ibid.
145. Quoted in Alan Neuhauser, 'Toxic Chemicals, Carcinogens Skyrocket Near Fracking Sites', 30 October 2014, http://www.usnews.com/news/articles/2014/10/30/toxic-chemicals-and-carcinogens-skyrocket-near-fracking-sites-study-says.
146. Surya Deva, 'Submission to the Office of the High Commissioner for Human Rights in Relation to Equitable Access to Safe Drinking Water and Sanitation', 15 April 2007, http://www2.ohchr.org/english/issues/water/contributions/universities/CityUniversityHongKong.pdf, 2.
147. *Subhash Kumar* v. *State of Bihar and Ors*, Supreme Court of India, 1991 AIR 420.
148. Asia Pacific Forum of National Human Rights Institutions, 'Human Rights and the Environment: Final Report and Recommendations' (Final report, Asia Pacific Forum of National Human Rights Institutions, Sydney, 24–27 September, 2007), 39, http://www.ohchr.org/Documents/Issues/ClimateChange/Submissions/Asia_Pacific_Forum_of_NHRIs_1_HR_and_Environment_ACJ_Report_Recommendations.pdf. Though as this statement comes from an organisation established by the state government – and not the government itself – implementation and acceptance of such an obligation is not as assured as in the Indian context. However, as this assertion is based on numerous examples of Malaysian national and case law upholding the right of its population to a clean environment, it is relevant to include it in a discussion of the national government recognition of the right to clean air.
149. David R. Boyd, 'The Constitutional Right to a Healthy Environment', *Environment: Science and Policy for Sustainable Development* 54, no. 4 (2012): 3–15.
150. Organization of Africa Unity, *African Charter on Human and Peoples' Rights* (1981).
151. Organization of American States, *Additional Protocol to the American Convention on Human Rights in the Area of Economic, Social, and Cultural Rights 'Protocol of San Salvador'* (1988).
152. *Lopez Ostra* v. *Spain*, European Court of Human Rights, 16798 ECtHR 90 (1994). The court made a similar ruling in: *Giacomelli* v. *Italy*, European Court of Human Rights, 59909 ECtHR 00 (2006).
153. See: *Novoselov* v. *Russia*, European Court of Human Rights, 66460 ECtHR 01 (2005); *Khudoyorov* v. *Russia*, European Court of Human Rights, 6847 ECtHR 02 (2005); *Ananyev and others* v. *Russia*, European Court of Human Rights, 42525 ECtHR 07 (2012); and *Arutyunyan* v. *Russia*, European Court of Human Rights, 48977 ECtHR 09 (2012).
154. *Öneryildiz* v. *Turkey*, European Court of Human Rights, 48939 ECtHR 99 (2004).
155. Office of the High Commissioner for Human Right, 'Independent Expert on Human Rights and the Environment', United Nations, http://www.ohchr.org/EN/Issues/Environment/IEEnvironment/Pages/IEenvironmentIndex.aspx.
156. Human Rights Council, *Human Rights and the Environment*, A/HRC/25/L.31 (2014).
157. Sub-Committee on Poverty Eradication, *NGO Consultation on the Draft Guiding Principles on Extreme Poverty and Human Rights* (New York: Sub-Committee on Poverty Eradication, 2011), http://www.ohchr.org/Documents/Issues/Poverty/ConsultationDGP/NGO/SubcommitteeonPovertyEradication31May2011.pdf.
158. David R. Boyd, 'The Constitutional Right to a Healthy Environment', *Environment: Science and Policy for Sustainable Development* 54, no. 4 (2012): 3–15.
159. See George Jucha, 'Google Earth Tour of Oil & Gas Wells, Pads and Impoundments' (2013), https://www.youtube.com/watch?v=7jN6TSSPZwU; and Food and Water Watch, 'Fracking Infrastructure is Carving Up Pennsylvania', *Food and Water Watch: Fact Sheet* (December 2013), http://documents.foodandwaterwatch.org/doc/fracking_infrastructure_pennsylvania.pdf.
160. See: Michelle Bamberger and Robert E. Oswald, 'Impacts of Gas Drilling on Human and Animal Health', *New Solutions* 22, no. 1 (2012): 51–77; Judith Kohler, 'Report Says Drilling

Threatens Colorado Wildlife', *Aspen Times*, 20 January 2010, http://www.aspentimes.com/news/1426301-113/regional-leadstories-regionalivg-leadstoriesivg.

161. Paresh Dave, 'Ohio Finds Link between Fracking and Sudden Burst of Earthquakes', *Los Angeles Times*, 12 April 2014, http://www.latimes.com/nation/nationnow/la-na-nn-ohio-finds-link-fracking-earthquakes-20140411,0,570007.story#ixzz30C04ddBj.
162. Fiona Harvey, Damian Carrington, and Terry McCallilster, 'Fracking Company Cuadrilla Halts Operations at Lancashire Drilling Site', *The Guardian*, 13 March 2013, http://www.theguardian.com/environment/2013/mar/13/fracking-cuadrilla-halts-operations-lancashire.
163. Shelley and Opsal, 'Energy Crime, Harm, and Problematic State Response'.
164. Heinberg, *Snake Oil*, 88.
165. Ibid., 89.
166. Ibid., 88.
167. Ibid.
168. Ibid.
169. United Nations, *International Covenant on Civil and Political Rights*, (1966) Article 17.
170. Council of Europe, *European Convention on Human Rights*, (1950) Article 8.
171. Organization of American States, *American Convention on Human Rights*, (1969) Article 11.
172. League of Arab States, *Arab Charter on Human Rights*, (2004) Article 21.
173. *Kyrtatos* v. *Greece*, European Court of Human Rights, 41666 ECtHR 98 (2003).
174. *Dubetska and Others* v. *Ukraine*, European Court of Human Rights, 30499 ECtHR 03 (2011). In this case the court did rule in favour of the complainants that a mine and factory near their homes had caused damage to their houses and therefore violated their right to respect for their private and family life and home.
175. *Martinez Martinez and María Pino Manzano* v. *Spain*, European Court of Human Rights, 61654 ECtHR 08 (2012).
176. Council of Europe, *Protocol to the Convention for the Protection of Human Rights and Fundamental Freedoms*, (1950) Article 1.
177. Organization of American States, *American Convention on Human Rights*, (1969) Article 21.
178. Organization of Africa Unity, *African Charter on Human and Peoples' Rights*, (1981) Article 14.
179. League of Arab States, *Arab Charter on Human Rights*, (2004) Article 31.
180. See the US and South African constitutions, as examples.
181. *Flamenbaum and Others* v. *France*, European Court of Human Rights, 23264 ECtHR 04 (2012).
182. The court also references property value in relation to environmental degradation in: *Dubetska and Others* v. *Ukraine*, European Court of Human Rights, 30499 ECtHR 03 (2011).
183. Sheila Bushkin-Bedient, Larysa Dyrszka, Yuri Gorby, and Mary Menapace, 'Compendium of Scientific, Medical, and Media Findings Demonstrating Risks and Harms of Fracking (Unconventional Gas and Oil Extraction)', *Concerned Health Professionals of New York*, 2nd ed. (December 2014), http://concernedhealthny.org/wp-content/uploads/2014/07/CHPNY-Fracking-Compendium.pdf. For a report on the uncertain effects of fracking on health in Australia, see: Alicia Coram, Jeremy Moss, and Grant Blashki, 'Harms Unknown: Health Uncertainties Cast Doubt on the Role of Unconventional Gas in Australia's Energy Future', *The Medical Journal of Australia* 200, no. 4 (2014): 210–13.
184. Jason Morris, 'Texas Family Plagued with Ailments Gets $3M in 1st-of-its-kind Fracking Judgment', *CNN*, 26 April 2014, http://edition.cnn.com/2014/04/25/justice/texas-family-wins-fracking-lawsuit/.
185. Shelley and Opsal, 'Energy Crime, Harm, and Problematic State Response'.
186. Nadia Steinzor, Wilma Subra, and Lisa Sumi, 'Investigating Links between Shale Gas Development and Health Impacts through a Community Survey Project in Pennsylvania', *New Solutions* 23, no. 1 (2013): 55–83.
187. For a general discussion of the chemicals released by fracking and their associated potential health effects, see: John L. Adgate, Bernard D. Goldstein, and Lisa M. McKenzie, 'Potential Public Health Hazards, Exposures and Health Effects from Unconventional Natural Gas Development', *Environmental Science & Technology* 48, no. 15 (2014): 8307–20.
188. Ibid.
189. Steinzor, Subra, and Sumi, 'Investigating Links'.

190. Sharon Wilson et al., *Reckless Endangerment While Fracking the Eagle Ford* (Washington, DC: Earthworks, 2013), http://www.earthworksaction.org/files/publications/FULL-Reckless Endangerment-sm.pdf.
191. Geralyn McCarron, *Symptomatology of a Gas Field: An Independent Health Survey in the Tara Rural Residential Estates and Environs* (2013), http://www.gabpg.org.au/wp-content/uploads/2013/11/2013-04-symptomatology_of_a_gas_field_Geralyn_McCarron.pdf.
192. Paul Mobbs, 'Shale Gas and Public Health – The Whitewash Exposed', *The Ecologist*, 6 May 2014. And for a detailed critique of Public Health England's methods and conclusions see Paul Mobbs, 'A Critical Review of Public Health England's Report – "Review of the Potential Public Health Impacts of Exposures to Chemical and Radioactive Pollutants as a Result of Shale Gas Extraction – Draft for Comment"', http://www.fraw.org.uk/mei/archive/phe_shale_gas_and_health_report-critical_analysis.pdf.
193. Adam Law, 'Public Health England's Draft Report on Shale Gas Extraction: Mistaking Best Practices for Actual Practices' (2014); Adam Law et al., *British Medical Journal* 348, 17 April 2014, http://www.bmj.com/content/348/bmj.g2728; and Mobbs, 'Shale Gas and Public Health'.
194. New York State Department of Health, 'A Public Health Review of High Volume Hydraulic Fracturing for Shale Gas Development', https://www.health.ny.gov/press/reports/docs/high_volume_hydraulic_fracturing.pdf.
195. See: UN Committee on Economic, Social and Cultural Rights, *General Comment No. 14: The Right to the Highest Attainable Standard of Health*, E/C.12/2000/4 (2000). Also important to note is that a right to health is not found in the European Convention on Human Rights, and thus the European Court often finds violations of the right to privacy in cases involving health defects from environmental degradation. See, for example: *Tatar* v. *Romania*, European Court of Human Rights, 67021 ECtHR 01 (2009).
196. Office of the High Commissioner for Human Rights, 'Special Rapporteur on the Right of Everyone to the Enjoyment of the Highest Attainable Standard of Physical and Mental Health', United Nations, http://www.ohchr.org/EN/Issues/Health/Pages/SRRightHealthIndex.aspx.
197. Anna Grear et al., *A Human Rights Assessment of Hydraulic Fracturing and Other Unconventional Gas Development in the United Kingdom* (London: The Bianca Jagger Human Rights Foundation, 2014), http://extremeenergy.org/category/eeiresearch/.
198. See: *Öneryildiz* v. *Turkey*, ECtHR.
199. Paul Ekins, 'The UK's New Dash for Gas is a Dangerous Gamble', *The New Scientist*, 6 December 2012, http://www.newscientist.com/article/dn22594-the-uks-new-dash-for-gas-is-a-dangerous-gamble.html#.VMjJI8Yl2dM.
200. It is often suggested that Balcombe had little to do with fracking as it did not happen there, but in 2010 the company Cuadrilla were granted temporary planning permission by West Sussex County Council to do exactly that. 'WSCC notes that under planning permission WSCC/027/10/BA Cuadrilla can use hydraulic fracturing at this site.' In effect, Cuadrilla were a permit away from fracking. Furthermore, in 2011 Cuadrilla sent a letter to DECC, discovered through the court process, stating 'In order for Bolney to be successful in its Weald Basin Kimmeridge Oil Shale Project (KOSP), Bolney will need to rely, to a significant degree, on being able to undertake hydraulic fracture stimulation(s) of this unconventional reservoir.' Bolney Resources Ltd became Cuadrilla Balcombe Ltd in April 2013. (Copies of the above are held on file by the authors.)
201. For basic site information see Richard Wheatstone, 'Environmental Groups Voice Fracking Fears After "Encouraging Results" From Barton Moss Drilling', *Manchester Evening News*, 4 November 2014, http://www.manchestereveningnews.co.uk/news/greater-manchester-news/environmental-groups-voice-fears-over-8049913; and for the view of the company involved see http://www.igas-engage.co.uk/our-work-in-barton-moss/
202. HMSO, *Human Rights Act*, (1998) Article 11.
203. Council of Europe, *European Convention on Human Rights*, Article 11.
204. United Nations, *International Covenant on Civil and Political Rights*, Article 21.
205. Interview with protestor, 18 July 2014. This and the following interviews were conducted confidentially, and as such the interviewees' names have been withheld by mutual agreement.
206. Interview, 21 July 2014.
207. Interview, 18 July 2014.

208. Ibid.
209. Ibid.
210. Interview, 21 July 2014.
211. Interview, 19 July 2014.
212. Interview, 21 July 2014.
213. Ibid.
214. Interview, 19 July 2014.
215. Interview, 21 July 2014.
216. Ibid.
217. Ibid.
218. Interview, 19 July 2014.
219. Interview, 18 July 2014.
220. Chief Superintendent Paul Morrison of Sussex police quoted in: Sandra Laville, 'Sussex Police Under Fire for "Criminalising" Fracking Protests', *The Guardian*, 15 May 2014, http://www.theguardian.com/environment/2014/may/15/sussex-police-criminalising-fracking-protest-acquittals-balcombe.
221. BBC, 'Balcombe Anti-fracking Camp Moves to Council HQ', *BBC News: Sussex*, 17 November 2013, http://www.bbc.co.uk/news/uk-england-sussex-24978363. A legal challenge, brought by the Frack Free Balcombe Residents Association against the decision of the West Sussex council to permit tests for oil after polling showed 60% of responding residents were against it, further highlights possible collusion between the council and the fracking firm Cuadrilla. Emily Gosden, 'Legal Challenge Over Plans for Fracking Firm Cuadrilla to Return to Balcombe', *The Telegraph*, 1 August 2014, http://www.telegraph.co.uk/earth/energy/11006938/Legal-challenge-over-plans-for-fracking-firm-Cuadrilla-to-return-to-Balcombe.html.
222. *Salford Star*, 'Salford Council Daily Barton Moss Intelligence Meetings with IGas, GMP and Peel Holdings', *Salford Star*, 6 August 2014, http://www.salfordstar.com/article.asp?id=2358.
223. Paul Slomp, 'Hey CSIS, Farmers Are Not Terrorists', *The Star*, 5 March 2013, http://www.thestar.com/opinion/commentary/2013/03/05/hey_csis_farmers_are_not_terrorists.html.
224. Robert Johnson, 'Fracking Insiders Admit To Employing Military "Psychological Operations" On American Citizens', *Business Insider*, 9 November 2011, http://www.businessinsider.com/the-fracking-industry-admits-to-employing-military-psychologial-operations-on-american-citizens-2011-11.
225. *Sunshine Coast Daily*, 'Gas Protestors Stand Their Ground Despite Shots Being Fired', *Sunshine Coast Daily*, 24 May 2013, http://www.sunshinecoastdaily.com.au/news/shots-fired-coal-seam-gas-protest-tara/1880952/.
226. Sarah Lazare, 'Protests Sweep Canada Following Paramilitary Assault on Indigenous Fracking Blockade', *Common Dreams*, 18 October 2013, http://www.commondreams.org/news/2013/10/18/protests-sweep-canada-following-paramilitary-assault-indigenous-fracking-blockade.
227. HMSO, *Human Rights Act*, Article 10.
228. Council of Europe, *European Convention on Human Rights*, Article 10.
229. United Nations, *International Covenant on Civil and Political Rights*, Article 19.
230. Conor Gearty, *Civil Liberties* (Oxford: Oxford University Press, 2007), 31.
231. Interview, 21 July 2014.
232. HMSO, *Human Rights Act*, Article 5.
233. Council of Europe, *European Convention on Human Rights*, Article 5.
234. United Nations, *International Covenant on Civil and Political Rights*, Article 9.
235. Interview, 18 July 2014.
236. Ibid.
237. Ibid.
238. A total of 120 people were arrested by the GMP during protests in Barton Moss (with most cleared of wrongdoing as of June 2014), while 126 were arrested by Sussex police in Balcombe (with only 29 convictions resulting). Dan Thompson, 'Most Barton Moss Protesters Cleared after Arrests', *Manchester Evening News*, 28 June 2014, http://www.manchestereveningnews.co.uk/news/greater-manchester-news/most-barton-moss-protesters-cleared-7339995; Laville, 'Sussex Police under Fire'.
239. Interview with protestor, 21 July 2014.
240. Ibid.
241. Interview, 18 July 2014.

242. Ibid.
243. Interview, 21 July 2014.
244. As of April 2014 – see *Drill or Drop?*, 'Update on Balcombe Anti-fracking Court Cases', *Drill or Drop?*, 8 April 2014, http://drillordrop.com/2014/04/08/update-on-balcombe-anti-fracking-court-cases/#more-1879.
245. Interview, 18 July 2014.
246. Ibid.
247. Ibid.
248. Ibid.
249. Ibid.
250. Interview, 21 July 2014.
251. HMSO, *Human Rights Act*, Article 6.
252. Council of Europe, *European Convention on Human Rights*, Article 6.
253. United Nations, *International Covenant on Civil and Political Rights*, Article 14.
254. Interviews, 21 July 2014.
255. Ibid.
256. HMSO, *Human Rights Act*, Article 8.
257. Council of Europe, *European Convention on Human Rights*, Article 8.
258. Interview, 18 July 2014.
259. Ibid.
260. Interview, 21 July 2014.
261. Interview, 19 July 2014.
262. Ibid.
263. Interview, 18 July 2014.
264. Rob Evans, 'Police Asked University for List of Attendees at Fracking Debate', *The Guardian*, 15 December 2014, http://www.theguardian.com/uk-news/2014/dec/15/police-university-list-fracking-debate.
265. Rob Evans, 'Police Under Scrutiny After Seeking to Obtain Names of People Who Wanted to Attend University Debate', *The Guardian*, 5 February 2015, http://www.theguardian.com/uk-news/undercover-with-paul-lewis-and-rob-evans/2015/feb/05/police-under-scrutiny-after-seeking-to-obtain-names-of-people-who-wanted-to-attend-a-debate-organised-by-academics.
266. Murray Edelman, *Constructing the Political Spectacle* (Chicago, IL: University of Chicago Press, 1998).
267. See James Perkins, 'Biggest Weekly Oil Rig Decline since 1987', *The Shale Energy Insider*, 2 February 2015, http://www.shaleenergyinsider.com/2015/02/02/biggest-weekly-oil-rig-decline-since-1987/; and for a UK perspective Anthony Hilton, 'Fracking Just Doesn't Pay So Why Bother?' *The Evening Standard*, 3 February 2015, http://www.standard.co.uk/business/markets/anthony-hilton-fracking-just-doesnt-pay-so-why-bother-10020898.html.
268. Paul Mobbs, 'With Sub-$60 Oil, Fracking and Tar Sands Losses Threaten the Whole Financial System'. *The Ecologist*, 17 December 2014, http://www.theecologist.org/News/news_analysis/2679765/with_sub60_oil_fracking_and_tar_sands_losses_threaten_the_whole_financial_system.html.
269. Noam Chomsky, *Profit over People: Neoliberalism and the Global Order* (New York: Seven Stories Press, 1999), 96.
270. de Rijke, 'Hydraulically Fractured', 15.
271. Damian Carrington, 'Owen Paterson Held Urgent Meeting for Fracking Boss, Documents Show', *The Guardian*, 21 March 2014, http://www.theguardian.com/environment/2014/mar/21/owen-paterson-urgent-meeting-fracking-cuadrilla-lord-browne; and 'Emails Reveal UK Helped Shale Gas Industry Manage Fracking Opposition', *The Guardian*, 17 January 2014, http://www.theguardian.com/environment/2014/jan/17/emails-uk-shale-gas-fracking-opposition; and 'George Osborne Urges Ministers to Fast-track Fracking Measures in Leaked Letter', *The Guardian*, 26 January 2015, http://www.theguardian.com/environment/2015/jan/26/george-osborne-ministers-fast-track-fracking.
272. Paul Mobbs, 'Economically & Politically Fracked: "Behind Every Picture Lies a Story" – Statistical Reality Versus PR-hype Within the Political Project of Unconventional Gas in Britain', *Extreme Energy Initiative*, Working Papers Series (2013), http://extremeenergy.org/2013/07/25/economically-and-politically-fracked-behind-every-picture-lies-a-story-statistical-reality-versus-pr-hype-within-the-political-project-of-unconventional-gas-in-britain/.

273. David Cameron, 'We Cannot Afford to Miss Out on Shale Gas', *The Telegraph*, 11 August 2013, http://www.telegraph.co.uk/news/politics/10236664/We-cannot-afford-to-miss-out-on-shale-gas.html.
274. Paul Mobbs, 'Fracking Policy and the Pollution of British Democracy', *The Ecologist*, 20 January 2015, http://www.theecologist.org/News/news_analysis/2721027/frackingnbsppolicy_and_the_pollution_of_british_democracy.html.
275. International Energy Agency, *Word Energy Outlook 2012* (2012), Executive Summary, 3, http://www.iea.org/publications/freepublications/publication/English.pdf.
276. Christophe McGlade and Paul Ekins 'The Geographical Distribution of Fossil Fuels Unused When Limiting Global Warming to 2 °C', *Nature* 517 (2015): 187–90.
277. James Hansen, *Storms of my Grandchildren: The Truth about the Coming Climate Catastrophe and Our Last Chance to Save Humanity* (London: Bloomsbury, 2009), 289.
278. *Yale Environment 360*, 'Forum: Just How Safe Is "Fracking" of Natural Gas?', *Yale Environment 360*, http://e360.yale.edu/feature/forum_just_how_safe__is_fracking_of_natural_gas/2417/. See also http://kevinanderson.info/blog/uk-international-commitments-on-climate-change-are-incompatible-with-the-development-of-a-national-shale-gas-industry/.
279. Shelia Watt-Cloutier, *Petition to the Inter American Commission on Human Rights Seeking Relief from Violations Resulting from Global Warming Caused by Acts and Omissions of the United States* (Nunavut, Canada: Inuit Circumpolar Conference, 2005), http://earthjustice.org/sites/default/files/library/legal_docs/petition-to-the-inter-american-commission-on-human-rights-on-behalf-of-the-inuit-circumpolar-conference.pdf.
280. Ariel E. Dulitaky to Paul Crowley, *Inadmissibility of Watt-Cloutier Petition*, Washington, DC, 16 November 2006, http://graphics8.nytimes.com/packages/pdf/science/16commissionletter.pdf.
281. Humphreys, *Climate Change and Human Rights*.
282. United Nations Human Rights Council, *Resolution 7/23* (2008).
283. Office of the High Commissioner for Human Rights, *Report of the Office of the United Nations High Commissioner for Human Rights on the Relationship between Climate Change and Human Rights*, A/HRC/10/61 (2009).
284. United Nations Human Rights Council, *Resolution 10/4* (2009).
285. Office of the High Commissioner for Human Rights, *Human Rights Council Panel Discussion on the Relationship between Climate Change and Human Rights* (Geneva: Office of the High Commissioner for Human Rights, 2009).
286. Office of the High Commissioner for Human Rights, 'Human Rights and Climate Change: Overview', United Nations, http://www.ohchr.org/EN/Issues/HRAndClimateChange/Pages/HRClimateChangeIndex.aspx.
287. The recent vote in Denton, Texas to ban fracking highlights the sentiments of residents who are no stranger to the fossil fuel industry. Suzanne Goldenberg, 'Texas Oil Town Makes History as Residents Say No to Fracking', *The Guardian*, 5 November 2014, http://www.theguardian.com/environment/2014/nov/05/birthplace-frackingboom-votes-ban-denton-texas.
288. Mobbs, 'Shale Gas and Public Health'.
289. Zachary Boren, 'Energy Files: Social impacts of fracking REDACTED', *Greenpeace Energy Desk*, 11 August 2014, http://energydesk.greenpeace.org/2014/08/11/energy-files-social-impacts-fracking-redacted/.

'From naming and shaming to knowing and showing': human rights and the power of corporate practice

Christian Scheper

Institute for Development and Peace, Faculty of the Social Sciences, University of Duisburg-Essen, Germany

A recent phenomenon in corporate governance discourses is a strong recourse to human rights. Human rights awareness and corporate policies have become part of the credo of 'good' business. This is also taken up in international institutions, such as the United Nations Guiding Principles on Business and Human Rights, which assign a distinct human rights responsibility to transnational enterprises. The article interprets this transformation through the lens of the 'sociology of critique'. It argues that the concept of corporate responsibility for human rights represents a capacity of capitalism to absorb fundamental criticism and incorporate the very values that formed the ground for critique. The article proceeds in three steps: First, I present the corporate responsibility to respect human rights as a reaction to fundamental critique against global corporate giants that emerged as part of a broad 'anti-globalisation' movement in the 1990s. Second, I argue that today multinationals 'know and show' responsibility and make human rights a subject of management strategies and tools. Human rights are being incorporated and translated into corporate policy programmes. This allows companies to disarm most fundamental strands of criticism. Third, I draw conclusions from this perspective on the productive power of business practice and implications for critique.

Introduction

One of the recent trends in the human rights story is an increasing incorporation of the human rights concept into corporate social responsibility (CSR) discourses. While there had long been a clear divide between human rights debates and the modern, business-driven movement of CSR,[1] we often find an explicit adherence to human rights by transnational enterprises today. A great deal of literature and many controversial debates are devoted to CSR, but the trend towards a human rights responsibility of business marks a noteworthy shift.[2] While the actual role of private transnational corporations is still somewhat difficult to define under contemporary human rights law,[3] the recent trend is significant because it is backed by a remarkably consensual international institutional framework. The concept of the corporate responsibility to respect human rights is currently in the process of being institutionalised on international, supranational and increasingly national policy levels.[4] Thus, it might not be exaggerated when Scott Jerbi notes: '[T]he movement towards greater corporate responsibility is one of the most deep-rooted developments in the human rights story of the first decade of the twenty-first century'.[5]

The question remains, however, *how* exactly this development affects the human rights story. Some authors optimistically argue that it indicates the emergence of human rights norms for private corporations.[6] The human rights idea would further diffuse to the realm of private actors, as corporations are increasingly under pressure to justify their transnational activities and show their adherence to universal norms of 'good' business. Others, quite to the contrary, doubt that this trend has any significant effects on corporate practice. Critics emphasise that – like the whole 'movement' of CSR – the idea of a corporate responsibility for human rights evolves mostly from the business sector[7] and marks another victory of a 'public-relations exercise'[8] by multinational firms, rather than a victory of human rights norms over transnational corporate misconduct.

In this article I offer an interpretation of the concept of the corporate responsibility to respect human rights through the lens of Luc Boltanski's 'sociology of critique'. This French strand of pragmatist sociology is not well-known in international human rights debates, so a few words of clarification seem in order. Boltanski primarily intends to offer an alternative to Bourdieu's critical sociology by giving more weight to the norm judgements and critical capacities of actors. In his collaborative works, especially with Laurant Thevenaut[9] and Eve Chiapello,[10] Boltanski conducts a comprehensive analysis of the ideological characteristics of capitalist society by referring to the normative fundaments of both capitalist practice and its criticisms. While Boltanski and Chiapello analyse management literature in order to illustrate dominant normative regimes, my use of their theoretical lens is somewhat unorthodox: I link the sociological perspective to elements of political discourse theory, specifically to a Foucauldian conception of *productive power*. Assuming that the concept of human rights is (re-)produced in transnational corporate regimes of practices,[11] I analyse corporate references to human rights in order to understand their increasing entanglement with management discourse. By doing this I emphasise an important effect, which has rather been neglected in the literature on business and human rights, including critical voices from within the human rights canon: the effect of successfully disarming public critique through referring to universalistic norms, without necessarily making fundamental changes to the practices that caused this critique.[12]

I take the discourse on corporate responsibility and human rights as a case in point for how public critique and capitalist transformation develop in close interdependence. While the actual impacts of the trend towards a corporate responsibility for human rights are at least vague and subject to controversies, the trend is indeed remarkable if we look at the ways in which it has led transnational enterprises to incorporate a concept that was a major source of criticism against them just a few years ago. The corporate recourse to human rights represents a capacity of capitalism to absorb fundamental criticism and to incorporate the very 'values in whose name it was criticized'.[13] As Eve Chiapello states with regard to ecological criticism, capitalism is now 'embarking on a new cycle of recuperation',[14] especially through engagement in CSR efforts. We can note that this is the case not only with regard to ecological criticism, which is reflected in the evolution of a 'green economy' business movement in recent years, but also in respect to human rights. Both topics together constitute the most important pillars in many of today's CSR departments, and they influence the debate on corporate conduct more generally. Noting that such CSR trends unfold a reformist character and might lead to significant changes in business strategies, my central argument here is that they also represent a remarkable ability to disarm parts of a fundamental critique against economic globalisation that had been quite manifest by the end of the 1990s, most visible as part of the so-called anti-globalisation movement.

We can therefore understand the trend towards business responsibilities for human rights as a case for the *productive* power of business practice: The trend *enables* transnational enterprises to take over a leading role in the human rights discourse.[15]

While the identification of this enabling aspect is the focus of this article, it is important to note from the outset that this trend is, of course, no one-way street. It might already open new doors for public contestation and critique. The modern concept of human rights includes the role of actors' critical capacities and right to 'struggle', and the very openness and universalistic normative background of the human rights discourse has the potential to produce new forms of 'ungovernability'.[16] Transnational business and international rights discourse constitute a field of contradictions that lie at the heart of advanced capitalist societies, and many parts of public critique against neoliberal globalisation are also very alive. Thus, my argument is not to be misunderstood as a normative dismissal of the human rights story in the business context. Instead, I am interested in the ways in which the socio-moral indignation due to inhumane conditions under globalised production is directly responded to by companies themselves, by actively adhering to the concept of human rights. This represents an astonishing ability of capitalism to adapt to critique and turn it into a tool for 'quick recovery'.

The article will proceed in three steps: First, I briefly present the current trend in the field of human rights and transnational enterprises and qualify the kinds of criticisms which preceded it in the 1990s. At the time, fundamental critique towards globalisation developed in a way that brought together a wide variety of civil society fractions. I present two sample narratives that illustrate this, which I refer to through the images of 'evil oil' and 'the sweatshop'. Second, I argue that within the last decade human rights have become an object of management knowledge and corporate governance techniques. While this is far from reaching the level of a general standard and is more or less limited to the largest corporations,[17] we can already assume a twofold character of this development: On the one hand, the discourse on the human rights responsibility of business has certain reformist potentials; on the other hand, there is a process of *translation* of human rights to the logics of management and business practice, allowing it to keep more fundamental transformations of global production systems at bay. In a third step I draw conclusions on the politics of corporate human rights responsibility and claim that it enables corporations to account for human rights-based critique and thus produce new justificatory ground for transnational business practice.

The new discourse on business and human rights

Although the relationship between transnational business and human rights has a much longer history,[18] there has been a growing interest among human rights scholars and business managers in recent years.[19] This new interest corresponds to an increasing acknowledgement of corporate responsibilities for human rights in international institutions and related policy efforts. The main institutional landmark in this context is provided by the UN Guiding Principles on Business and Human Rights, which were unanimously endorsed by the Human Rights Council in 2011.[20] The guiding principles were the outcome of two mandates of the UN Special Representative on Business and Human Rights, a position held by John Ruggie from 2005 to 2011. Besides the traditional concept of state duties to protect human rights from harm by third parties, and an emphasis of the need for effective remedy for victims of corporate misconduct, the guiding principles suggest a distinct *corporate responsibility to respect human rights*.[21] Since Ruggie published his first main report in 2008,[22] this concept has also been taken up by other international standards and guidelines for transnational corporate conduct, such as the OECD Guidelines for Multinational

Enterprises.[23] Today, the idea of the 'responsibility to respect' can be regarded as the current normative gold standard in the international debate on business and human rights. Transnational enterprises themselves have been actively involved in the process towards the UN guiding principles and have started to develop corporate human rights policies.[24]

The bulk of the academic debate that has accompanied these global governance efforts and private CSR strategies has focused on the *normative* conception of the role of private enterprises in the human rights regime, which is mostly discussed in terms of corporate legal obligations (or lack thereof),[25] and business ethics in respect to human rights.[26] Others have compared normative considerations on human rights responsibilities to actual business approaches, especially practices, limits and myths of CSR and corporate governance strategies.[27] While some authors are more optimistic than others as to what the impact of businesses taking over responsibility for human rights might be (or whether there is a noteworthy impact at all), there has been no broader debate on the effects that this development might more generally have on the concept of human rights, understood *via* business practice.[28] More specifically, we can say that there has not yet been much consideration of the *reflexive* dimension of the relationship between corporate everyday practices, their routines and ways of implementing policies on the one hand, and international human rights discourse on the other. In the following I will incorporate this reflexive aspect: I am less interested in the ways in which the notion of responsibility might change business practice, but how it involves the process of human rights becoming an object of management knowledge and practice. I call this the *corporatisation of human rights*. I will add a new perspective to the debate on business and human rights by claiming that the concept of a corporate human rights responsibility can be understood as a powerful reaction to a crisis, which effectively disarms fundamental forms of critique against global capitalist practice. The crisis has emerged as an increasing public critique against multinational firms under neoliberal globalisation. The incorporation of human rights into business practice then involves the construction of new justificatory ground. A key assumption I am following here is this: Where the modern human rights concept is transposed from its historical context of the capitalist, liberal-democratic nation state, to transnational business relations, our understanding of its normative and justificatory meaning and scope needs to include an investigation of corporate governance as a process of translation. In this process human rights offer a universalistic, abstract normative foil, which is translated into the logics of corporations and practices of business management. The ontology of practice lays the ground for a conceptualisation of human rights not merely as international norms, but as a discursive whole, that is, the language and actions[29] of human rights policies. It offers us a perspective on the productive power of business relations: The 'responsibilisation'[30] of business in the field of human rights provides moral agency to management in the construction of rights-based rules of conduct and enables the corporation to transpose the concept of international rights into the grammar of markets, corporate hierarchies and networks. I understand power here in Foucauldian terms of productivity: 'it produces reality; it produces domains of objects and rituals of truth'.[31] Through this productive process we can assume that the human rights concept *qua* corporate practice is subject to transformations. Understood in this sense, the movement towards corporate responsibility indeed is a very deep-rooted development in the human rights story.

Facets of criticism against transnational corporations in the 1990s

The above-mentioned crisis of global corporate practices has occurred mostly in the early to mid-1990s in many OECD countries, in times of accelerated economic globalisation after the end of the Cold War, when various downsides of global capitalism found an increasing resonance in public protests and campaigns against corporations. While such protests existed before, public criticism towards the social and ecological downsides of globalisation became much more visible at the time.[32] Human rights provided one of the concepts that captured a broad range of criticisms we could subsume under the label of the 'anti-globalisation movement'.[33] Peter Utting describes the latter as an 'umbrella movement – sometimes called the movement of movements – encompassing a disparate array of organisations, networks, and movements concerned with social, environmental, and human rights issues, which have emerged or come under the spotlight in the current era of globalisation'.[34] It bundled formerly latent concerns and diffuse strands of critique, some of them fundamental in character, and targeted not only international institutions but also some of the largest multinational brand firms. The underlying 'sources of indignation'[35] that aroused criticism against capitalist developments were manifold. They inspired what Boltanski and Chiapello in *The New Spirit of Capitalism* refer to as *social* and *artistic* forms of critique, and also what Chiapello in a later contribution[36] calls the *conservative* and the *ecological* criticisms. In the following I will give a brief account of these four forms of public criticism in order to then refer these to human rights-based critique against transnational corporations and the succeeding corporatisation of human rights discourse.

Boltanski and Chiapello define artistic critique as targeting the loss of authenticity and the 'disenchantment'[37] of capitalism, and its various forms of oppression. Part of this critique is also the rejection of the capitalist tendency towards a hypocritical invocation of morality.

> This critique foregrounds the loss of meaning and, in particular, the loss of the sense of what is beautiful and valuable, which derives from standardization and generalized commodification, affecting not only everyday objects but also artworks (the cultural mercantilism of the bourgeoisie) and human beings.[38]

Social critique is rather focused on sources of indignation linked to poverty and inequality and the opportunism and egoism that is produced and encouraged by capitalism.[39] 'The social criticism is concerned with what capitalism imposes on the people whose labour is used: they are reduced to production components in the economic machinery, and lose all value if they cannot find employment.'[40] It is thus a very different form of critique than the artistic strand – and partly its harsh rejection, especially where it draws on Christian morality, as it dismisses the allegedly immoral, individualist, and egoistic character of the artistic critique.[41] Chiapello adds to these forms of criticism the notion of conservative criticism, which is closely related to social criticism, but is much more focused on the moral value that is ascribed to labour. 'For conservatives, labour is precious because it contributes to moral education and provides a path to a virtuous life, not because, as in social criticism, it is through labour that man expresses his humanity. (…) Wealth creates bad morals.'[42] Whereas the 'idle lifestyle of the rich'[43] is the main target of the conservative criticism, the positive ideal of the 'honourable merchant', which is often understood as being rooted in Christian social ethics, can be successfully incorporated in this justificatory scheme. I interpret the honourable merchant as a central figure in the justificatory narrative of capitalism vis-à-vis the conservative criticism. It impersonates the construct of *morally responsible self-interest*. Finally, Chiapello adds the notion of ecological criticism, which 'challenges the ability of the capitalist system to guarantee the future of mankind, beginning with its reproducibility'.[44]

As it will become more obvious below, we can understand the recourse to human rights by businesses as a normative conception that speaks to all four strands of criticism, whereas in the following I deem the first three forms most important. While some forms of criticism, especially in the Marxist tradition, are sceptical of the bourgeois idea of individual rights, it is especially the conservative criticism that is obviously akin to the liberal human rights movement as it evolved in the second half of the twentieth century. It resembles the kind of strong recourse to liberal rights that became more dominant than questions of equality and justice at the beginning of the 1990s.[45] Conservative criticism offers an attractive alley for capital to react, as it leaves fundamental questions of equality and distribution of wealth untouched. However, we can argue that the modern human rights concept – with its emphasis on the interdependence and indivisibility of civil, political as well as social, economic and cultural rights – is also able to align the social and at least parts of artistic criticism. In the following I will present two popular narratives of critique against transnational corporate conduct in order to make this claim more plausible and to characterise key forms of criticisms that later found a normative anchor in the upcoming debate on human rights and multinational enterprises. I interpret these examples as representations of powerful narratives that assembled under the umbrella of 'globalisation critique' and that trigger current transformations of the business and human rights discourse.

The image of 'evil oil': global resource extraction as a source of public indignation

The first example draws on the extensive struggles that various indigenous groups alongside environmental and human rights activists around the world have led against giant extractive companies. Emblematic in this respect is the long battle that the Ogoni people have fought against Royal Dutch Shell in Nigeria since the 1980s. In 1995 it led to the execution of nine members of the Ogoni people by the Nigerian government and became a tragic symbol of the anti-globalisation movement. Shell was accused of the deep involvement with the Nigerian government and the executions of the Ogoni leaders. The killing of Ken Saro-Wiwa, the president of the Movement for the Survival of the Ogoni People and well-known environmental activist, has since become one of the main symbols of struggles against corporate misconduct in the extractive industries and their deep entanglement with corrupt and authoritative governments, as well as their devastating ecological impacts. The case became a representative icon that stood for the massive problems that oil giants like Shell could bring to local communities in the areas of resource extraction and the close ties between the global use of natural resources and corrupt and authoritarian governments in distant areas of the globe. We can interpret this case as representing a form of criticism that very much resembles the focus of the international human rights regime at the time: The attention was on civil and political rights of the Ogoni people, which were violated by an untransparent and irresponsible consortium of a government and a multinational corporation.

Public outrage at extractive companies and the situation of indigenous peoples represents what Chiapello describes as the ecological critique combined with the conservative critique: It is linked to the sentiments of the insatiable global hunger for oil which leads to 'immoral' multinationals working in concert with corrupt governments. It is also linked to the perceived tendency of global enterprises, due to their mere size and their geographical distances to local effects, to lose their moral ground. In this scandal Shell stands for the exact opposite of the honourable merchant: The firm is emblematic of capitalism's tendency to construct 'gigantic enterprises which through the effect of numbers and geographical distance prevent the upkeep of personal connections between rich and poor'.[46] Although the conservative criticism has much in common with social criticism, it is focused rather on the question of 'dignity in difference' than on equality and a fair distribution of wealth. Neither is it interested in social classes. 'The classes are interdependent, parts of a whole that are naturally differentiated; they experience unequal conditions, but all have equal dignity.'[47] Therefore, we can state that this example of human dignity-based critique is very close to the modern, liberal tradition of the human rights regime as it has evolved in the context of capitalist nation states since World War II. It is, as it were, a critique that accepts global enterprises and their business in general, but expects a certain code of conduct and the treatment of the individual human being with dignity. Thus, we can understand this strand of criticism as one that would be relatively easily accepted and taken up by multinational corporations in the succeeding years.

The image of the sweatshop: giant lifestyle brands as source of public indignation

The second powerful narrative is that of the sweatshop. The 'anti-sweatshop' movement experienced its peak popularity more or less contemporaneously in the early to mid-1990s. After an initial study commissioned by the United States Agency for International Development in 1989, which had found that Nike's suppliers in Indonesia were paying the lowest wages in the sector, soon massive international campaigns targeted Nike and other brand companies in the clothing and sports goods industries. They also involved US-American and some European consumer boycotts.[48] They were first launched by US-American activist groups but soon included various European organisations.[49] The anti-sweatshop movement developed as a strong critical narrative based on the claim that workers' dignity was not respected by the company and its suppliers.

The focus here was on social critique. It reached from various safety issues, violence and slave labour to the problem of low wages, and thus formed a new, more fundamental critique of labour conditions and of the level of exploitation under globalisation. It targeted the societal and increasingly political role that transnational giants played in the world order, finding its expression in the degrading treatment of workers, those who lose in the game of global manufacturing, especially in labour-intensive industries such as the footwear, clothing and sports goods industries. The core of social criticism indeed seemed to be awakened with regard to the new global scale of capitalist expansion. Since manufacturing sites had been outsourced and moved to 'cheap labour' countries, criticism in OECD countries started to 'name and shame' the new dimensions of exploitation. In light of the apparent incapability of states (or their unwillingness) to regulate global capital, linked to the partly successful '"progressive release" of firms from their legal and political shackles',[50] criticism moved its target more towards global brand firms.

But the indignation based on the social situation of those 'on the other side' of global systems of production and consumption was not limited to social criticism. Instead, we can also find important elements of artistic criticism which were combined in the anti-sweatshop movement, particularly with regard to the ways in which Western *lifestyles* and consumerist societies forged the exploitative character of global production regimes. In this vein, the success of the anti-sweatshop campaigns was closely linked to its understanding as 'lifestyle politics',[51] an allegedly individualised form of political engagement with the world that focused on personal issues, perhaps also taking up ideas of post-materialism that were directed against new levels of global brand fetishism.

The two sample narratives of cruel extractives and hyper-exploitative sweatshops illustrate a strong reference to ideas of dignity. In sum, we can say that human dignity and fundamental rights can be understood as an important semantic container for the diversity of criticisms directed against neoliberal globalisation and multinational firms. The anti-globalisation movement, combining such different strands of critique, gained much ground in light of corporate scandals and successful civil society campaigns in the 1990s, transgressing national and class boundaries. It found public resonance, for instance, in the 'Battle of Seattle', in which joint transnational protests against various facets of globalisation resulted in violent street fights around the World Trade Organisation ministerial conference. Human rights became an obvious normative reference in this movement, as the concept combines those very different causes of indignation, from civil and political rights to economic, social and cultural rights, and the independence and indivisibility of these different categories, which were increasingly emphasised at the time. As two authors of a working paper for the International Council on Human Rights Policies comment with regard to the anti-globalisation protestors in 2001:

> By now, they have made it quite clear what they are against. Somewhere in the din of media coverage, and of protesters clashing with police, we seem to have missed out on an important message. These protesters are for social and economic rights, as well as the right to livelihood, health, and sanitary and safe environments.[52]

Thus, while addressing central aspects of the social critique, the human rights concept also allowed emphasis of the aspect of individuality, which is so closely linked to the idea of capitalism itself and inherent in the artistic 'life-style criticisms' of the consumer boycotts.

Recapturing ground: 'knowing and showing' as the new business of human rights

Since the mid-1990s, the discourse on business and human rights has gathered momentum.[53] The critical narratives increasingly found their way onto corporate executive floors and into international organisations. They triggered attempts to normatively underpin transnational business activities by transforming the international human rights regime and giving an active role to corporations. In 1998 the UN Sub-Commission on the Promotion and Protection of Human Rights established the Working Group on Transnational Corporations. It developed the Norms on the Responsibilities of Transnational Corporations and Other Business Enterprises with Regard to Human Rights (often referred to as the 'UN Norms'[54]). This document attempted to establish various binding human rights obligations for transnational corporations under international law. While some major human rights groups, such as Amnesty International, welcomed the UN Norms, sharp critics from the business side together with most national governments opposed them and argued that they would effectively grant private corporations the status of legal subjects under international law. They would, so claimed some of the critics, give companies both rights and duties comparable to states. The harsh dismissal by influential states and corporations led to a political stagnation. Eventually the UN Commission on Human Rights decided that the document would not be legally binding in any way. In order to resolve the debate, Kofi Annan appointed a Special Representative on the Issue of Human Rights and Transnational Corporations and Other Business Enterprises, a mandate that was granted to John Ruggie from 2005 to 2008 and then for a second mandate to 'operationalise' his policy framework until 2011. John Ruggie developed a policy framework based on three pillars: the 'state duty to protect', the 'corporate responsibility to respect' and 'access to remedy'.[55] The second mandate resulted in the UN Guiding Principles on Business and Human Rights, which were officially endorsed by the UN Human Rights Council in 2011.[56] From the outset Ruggie worked in close cooperation with transnational corporations, governments and civil society organisations. But already the institutional attempts to establish the UN Norms, combined with a strong involvement of civil society, urged businesses to get involved and actively take up the concept of human rights. As Preuss and Brown note: 'From a business perspective, the danger arises that if business does not get involved in shaping the debate it risks leaving the interpretation of human rights entirely to NGOs and IGOs.'[57]

It is against the background of the massive opposition to the UN Norms and the cooperative work of the Special Representative that the corporate responsibility to respect human rights quickly became a mantra-like concept in the UN context and found a broad consensus among both governments and transnational corporations. Although the framework does not explicitly refer to the business-driven idea of CSR,[58] the corporate responsibility to respect clearly resembles the spirit of the CSR world. The notion of responsibility is contrasted to 'duties' which is assigned to states alone. Businesses are presented as having a licence to operate as long as they do their business with 'due diligence'.[59] At the same time the concept reacts to resentments against the CSR agenda which became increasingly apparent in transnational civil society networks because of the dominance of voluntaristic ideas inherent in the concept. It was necessary to introduce a stronger element of accountability.[60] The fundamental nature of human rights emphasises the non-arbitrariness of business conduct, and the guiding principles add the principle of 'access to remedy' to the idea of corporate responsibility, stressing the need for accountability. They keep the spirit of corporate self-regulation but give these initiatives more substance by formulating more clearly what would be expected from corporations vis-à-vis the state duties to protect human rights and by emphasising the necessity for victims of human rights violations to gain access to remedy. This closes the lines of criticism by non-governmental organisation (NGO) networks and activist groups which disapprove of the voluntarism of the CSR movement. John Ruggie calls this a 'smart mix'[61] of different forms of regulation which overcome the divide between voluntary and mandatory solutions.

The corporate responsibility to respect therefore is a further progression of the UN course that started with other initiatives and debates in the early 2000s, such as the UN Global Compact.[62] The corporate responsibility to respect human rights and the concept of due diligence are the institutionalised concepts that were much needed in order to refer transnational business back to the normative underpinnings of globalisation. They are the names that represent the general apprehension of the idea that it is in the best interest of transnational corporations to consider human rights as part of their business strategy:

> Human rights due diligence can be a game-changer for companies: from 'naming and shaming' to 'knowing and showing'. Naming and shaming is a response by external stakeholders to the failure of companies to respect human rights. Knowing and showing is the internalization of that respect by companies themselves through human rights due diligence.[63]

We should therefore understand corporate responsibility for human rights as a semantic compromise that establishes the possibility of a general confirmation of transnational corporations' licence to develop their own form and format of human rights policies. It is a concept that lays the ground for the development of a *managerial form* of human rights policy.

The productive power of business practice: corporatising human rights

On a normative level the guiding principles aim to establish a 'global standard of practice that is now expected of all States and businesses with regard to business and human rights'.[64] What concerns me here is how the concept of the corporate responsibility to respect, which is increasingly backed by institutions at international and national levels, forms the semantic basis for the process in which human rights are becoming an element of management strategies, tools and knowledge – thus constituting a changing practice of human rights.

Companies now take up ideas of human rights much more comprehensively than only a few years ago. Given the transnational scale of business activities, especially in global production networks, corporate policy commitments often go beyond compliance with national laws and refer to normative concepts that transgress the state level, like environmental sustainability and human rights.[65] Ideas of human rights and CSR have increasingly merged. In light of the discourse on corporate responsibility, brand firms now actively seek to make human rights 'governable' for corporate management.

So far I have presented the criticisms of neoliberal globalisation as an important background for the momentum that the business and human rights debate has recently gathered. But human rights policies of transnational corporations today should not be understood as mere *reactions* to scandals and campaigns. To the contrary, I understand the notion of responsibility less as a mere international-legal work-around that is forced upon companies in order to 'tame' them, but rather as an enabling discourse that allows companies to actively create and define human rights standards in their own terms, implement them and define 'good human rights practice' with their own means. Today some argue that the commitment to human rights constitutes a genuine business interest:

> There is growing evidence that good [human rights] practice enhances reputation, resulting in improved staff morale, leading to higher motivation, productivity, and the ability to attract and retain the best employees; strengthens the licence to operate, giving improved access to new markets, consumers and investors; creates more stable operating environments; and promotes better community relations.[66]

Rights discourse is less seen as a costly social standard which decreases profits, than as an opportunity which can be incorporated into discourses of profit generation. The process of corporatisation makes human rights manageable, that is, predictable and governable, and performance visible.

I will highlight transformations in two fields of management practices related to global business networks in order to underline this claim and then interpret them with regard to the conception of corporate power and the implications this has for human rights-based critique. Traditions of science and technology studies[67] as well as social anthropology[68] offer informative insights with regard to the productive power of standards and indicators in shaping social realities. My examples partly draw on these strands of thought. With the rise of indicators, audits[69] and performance measurement we witness shifting ideas of governance, 'a shift from a command-and-control strategy of governance to collaborative, consensus-building discussions focused on problem solving and improvement'.[70] The first field of corporate practice is created by the emergence of human rights policies as a part of supply chain management strategies, including efforts for transparency and stakeholder engagement, especially active collaboration with 'former critics', mostly transnational NGOs. The second is the increasing quest for standardisation through tools of human rights impact and risk assessments. Both examples represent genuine management approaches to the normative concept of human rights through standardisation, quantification and bench-marking, that is, elements that are necessary in order to 'know and show' human rights.

Developing expertise, winning allies: human rights as supply chain management strategy

If we consider the elements of critique against sweatshop conditions, it is obvious that the management of complex supply chains has become a key area of human rights concerns in multinational brand firms. Global networks of supply and demand are a result of outsourcing strategies based on transaction cost economics, massive differences in labour costs, and improving possibilities of global trade and logistics. With the discourse on business and human rights, these production networks become a new kind of *problem*. With the corporate responsibility to respect human rights, the economic power that firms can exert over suppliers and subsidiaries, which is especially essential for the business of many brand firms, has now become an aspect of ethical problematisation. It becomes a liability where it is assumed that a corporation has 'leverage' to make sure that its suppliers comply with human rights.

> Where a business enterprise has not contributed to an adverse human rights impact, but that impact is nevertheless directly linked to its operations, products or services by its business relationship with another entity the situation is more complex. Among the factors that will enter into the determination of the appropriate action in such situations are the enterprise's leverage over the entity concerned, how crucial the relationship is to the enterprise, the severity of the abuse, and whether terminating the relationship with the entity itself would have adverse human rights consequences.[71]

Accordingly, brand firms and some other major supply chain managing companies have started to actively engage with developing strategies to know and show their activities as responsible corporations. The most obvious way of doing this is the inclusion of human rights in policy statements that define a commitment to human rights. This is often combined with reports in which both achievements and remaining problems in the field will be published. Nike Inc., one of the main targets of sweatshop campaigns in the 1990s, today defines its own targets using its leverage over suppliers in order to meet its responsibilities. This, for instance, is Nike's commitment to 'empower workers':

> Aim: Transform our working relationship with contract factories to incentivize changes that benefit their workers. Instill changes in our code, instigate innovation, educate to build management capacities, address root causes in our own processes, work with the industry, and reward factories' progressive achievement. Target: Source from factories that demonstrate commitment to workers by achieving minimum Bronze on our Sourcing & Manufacturing Sustainability Index by the end of FY20.[72]

Note that the 'Sourcing & Manufacturing Sustainability Index' is Nike's invention. Due to the complexity of their production network, a *tailored* index is needed. Who else would be able to understand the complex needs and contexts of the corporate veil? Looking more closely at the practices of manufacturing and trade, human rights commitments are linked to a new industry of governance through social auditing and monitoring alongside production networks.[73] Companies develop tools to monitor and measure their own corporate performance in fields such as labour rights. Whereas brands have the ability to make their network transparent, set targets and provide complex indices for performance measurement, the 'problem' of human rights becomes one of *verification of data* and *trust*, rather than of political and juridical contestation over rights interpretation and the 'sources of indignation'.

Therefore, monitoring and reporting functions are increasingly being taken over by forms of multi-stakeholder arrangements. The latter are often co-founded by brand firms themselves, such as the Fair Labor Association (FLA), which was founded in 1998. Along with other CEOs, Philip Knight, then CEO of Nike Inc, was a board member. Other popular examples for multi-stakeholder initiatives are Social Accountability International (SAI), the Fair Wear Foundation (FWF), and the Ethical Trading Initiative (ETI). These organisations and initiatives perform essential functions in terms of monitoring, verifying and communicating 'how responsible' each member company is and partly offer consumers the possibility to receive information about working conditions in related factories. Their activities and structures as well as their strategies have developed in remarkable ways throughout the last years. Some of them develop tools to conduct auditings in factories, but others develop more elaborate strategies to train supplier factories and workers in fields such as core labour rights; they advance tools to compare factories and company performance in terms of responsible behaviour; they also work towards higher awareness among workers.

The increasing role of multi-stakeholder initiatives in the field of supply chains and production networks is becoming diverse and complex.[74] This development allows those companies that participate in such initiatives to become much more proactive and develop their own ways to address human rights issues. If we recall the Nike example, this quote represents its newly established confidence in the field of labour rights:

> Nike has been evolving its mindset and its field operations away from a compliance auditing model towards a coaching model for factory partners focusing on continuing improvement in sustainability. We are looking forward to continued partnership with FLA in the development of industry-wide tools to build sustainable supply chains in the footwear and apparel industry.[75]

Another element of the corporate response closely related to this is the increase of transparency. Through initiatives such as the FLA, social auditing results are published in massive data sets on corporate websites and in sustainability reports. Nike was the first company in its industry to publish a full list of all its supplier companies on its website.[76] Today the company is often presented as a world leader in transparency issues in its sector and is listed in so-called sustainability stock indices. Thus, although the company admits that still many of its supplier factories do not meet its own corporate targets on labour standards, the company is seen as a sustainability leader and has received awards, for instance, for transparency and reporting standards.

Nike thus represents a good example that illustrates the potential for a transnational company to introduce reforms with regard to its global supply chain relations and turn the massive critique experienced in the 1990s into a position of leadership in the emerging discourse on human rights in production networks. Indeed, there are noteworthy improvements for workers, but they are gradual.[77] A more crucial transformation has taken place in terms of a recuperation of the sector, from a critique of globalised production, and a transformation of the many negative social externalities of global production into a *positive image of showing performance*. Nike Inc. and other brands have become experts in the human rights discourse.[78] We can understand production networks as complex regimes of practices in which corporations introduce changes, new sets of expertise and 'test formats'.[79] Today the concept of human rights is transformed into a standard that can and *needs to be* operationalised and measured by management tools and through the use of experts. This becomes possible by problematising human rights aspects in terms of supply chain management discourse. If the problem is one of management, the solution has to be one of management, too. The problem of the human rights violation and the various sources of indignation has turned into a problem of defining the right tools of measurement and verifying the numbers. By actively seeking cooperation with civil society groups, the necessary trust and expertise is provided and serves as a resource for the company. Knowing and showing human rights responsibility becomes a commodity: The result is an industry of consultants, multi-stakeholder initiatives, standards, sets of data on factory performances, auditings, trainings, and management actions taken. Human rights policy in global production networks is a complex field in which it is hard to identify drivers and obstacles, and which depends on the definition of business targets.

Assessing risk, measuring performance: human rights as aggregated risk and impact

Another field of practice that can further illustrate the process of translation in the corporate form is the evolution of human rights as a subject of risk and impact assessment. While human rights indicators have been subject to discussions,[80] their development and use by private companies adds a new dimension to this debate. Approaches to human rights impact and risk assessments seek to offer tools for standardising procedures and minimising human rights risks at manageable costs. One of the leading consultancies specialised in this field is the British company Maplecroft, which advertises one of its 'human rights products' as follows: 'The Human Rights Risk Atlas 2013 is an ideal tool to assess, quantify and compare human rights risks and responsibilities in 197 countries around the world with scorecards for each country and maps for each theme.'[81] Human rights risks here have become a specific knowledge resource. It draws on the emerging business case for knowing the possibilities for minimising human rights risks. Companies need to assess human rights risks to optimise their performance. In a similar vein, the Danish Institute for Human Rights, in cooperation with Royal Dutch Shell, has developed a 'Human Rights Compliance Assessment' tool, based on more than 1000 indicators, which allows companies to assess fields of risk, that is, fields in which they might not comply with human rights, through a standardised list of questions.

> The tool is available online to subscribers, and the Web interface allows companies to develop a tailored assessment tool from the database by screening out questions based on country risk and features of the company operation. Companies answer the relevant questions and receive a final report identifying areas of compliance and non-compliance in their operations. Numeric scores allow companies to track their performance from year to year.[82]

Extractive industry companies, such as Shell, have been actively engaged in developing standards for assessing potential risks and impacts of their large-scale operations.[83]

Tools like this allow companies to know their risk of being blamed as irresponsible and lift the question of human rights, which has formally been rather foreign to management practice, to a level on which they can use expert services and are able to 'prove' that they act with responsibility, even if instances of rights violations still happen. Companies show this, for instance, by using the standards of the Global Reporting Initiative (GRI), an international non-profit initiative that develops global reporting standards for social and ecological issues. It has taken up the concept of a human rights responsibility of business and developed indicators that allow companies to report on their human rights 'performance'. It translates rights into reporting standards: For instance, the right to non-discrimination is measured as the 'total number of incidents of discrimination and corrective actions taken'; the rights of indigenous groups become the 'total number of incidents of violations involving rights of indigenous people and actions taken'.[84] Again, in such details we clearly see the moment of translation that allows businesses to produce 'manageability' of a diffuse problem that was the basis for fundamental criticisms. The human rights violation becomes an instance that can be accounted for by showing *positive* engagement, and a quantified image of the company's progress. Numbers of total incidents contain the political 'problem' by inventing relative, aggregated targets. This further contributes to the process of corporatising human rights: it changes the logic of the rights concept – someone is entitled to claim a right – into a tool of control over an organisation's performance.

Implications for critique

My interpretation of the concept of a human rights responsibility of business as *enabling* a process of corporatising human rights in reaction to public criticism can lay the ground for a further assessment of the political implications of this trend. I focus here on my initial starting point of human rights-based critique.

Where human rights become part and parcel of a business-driven discourse on CSR, their critical impetus might lead to actual reforms that – to a certain extent – satisfy the criticisms towards globalisation and improve the situation in transnational networks of production. At the same time the political impetus of human rights as a normative reference for critique against transnational corporations and related global scales of labour exploitation become transposed to the *management discourse itself*, in which corporate experts, consultancies and governance tools provide the foil against which criticism has to be levelled. We can assume that the idea of human rights and their constant, systematic deprivation represent fundamental contradictions under advanced capitalist societies. Thus, it is not surprising that approaches to human rights in transnational business networks entail fundamental flaws and paradoxes, contributing to what Lane and Probert have described as a 'bottom-up private regulatory regime, in the face of continuing intense price- and time-based competition'.[85] Nevertheless, in light of successful commitments by transnational companies, even though they do not lead to fundamental changes in global production regimes, the incorporation of the human rights discourse can be understood as a way to *stabilise* systems of production and their justificatory frameworks. The contradictions are at least partly turned into a collaborative undertaking by transnational corporations and transnational civil society networks. More importantly, the corporate responsibility to respect human rights and related corporate policies use the normative *references* of the original critique, but the form in which they are *tested* is transposed to the regimes of business practices in transnational networks.

As a result, the simple but fundamental criticism based on the idea of dignity and rights – blaming the brand firm for the inhumane conditions of its operations – is confronted with a complex system of new industries and actors (consultancies, suppliers, auditors, civil society groups, stakeholder forums, etc.), each understood as bearing certain levels of responsibilities, according to their fields of leverage and expertise. A web of practices of auditing, monitoring, bench-marking, standardisation and performance measurement creates a novel basis of judgement. Impacts on rights and effects on human dignity then are addressed in terms of *degree* and *gradual change* (for example, '14 percent less violent incidents in factories'). It renders any critique unqualified, which is formulated in principled, *absolute* terms and thus ignores these numbers (and test formats). Instead, it requires either a level of inside knowledge and expertise of a company's own managerial regimes of practice in order to criticise it in these very own terms ('it could have been 38 percent less instead of 14 percent because … ', or '14 percent is wrong, the correct number would be 5 percent because … '); or the necessity to give a qualified account of why the underlying *test formats* cannot be applied and need to be replaced by others.

The first path is usually limited to those multi-stakeholder initiatives that closely cooperate with the company and thus also provide it with an increased licence to operate. The latter path is open to more critical civil society groups which 'name and shame'. But this path is confronted with the managerial 'effects of domination'[86] at work in networks of transnational production relations and the constant changes inherent to the managerial form (for instance, innovations in supply chain management).

> These systems are therefore not primarily geared towards the preservation of established qualifications and test formats, but intervene to alter sometimes the test formats, sometimes *the reality* constructed and validated by the outcome of tests and sometimes the world. It is through this plurality of interventions that critique finds itself disarmed.[87]

This means that while the effects of corporate human rights policies for public critique are quite manifest, it is rather unclear to what extent corporations actually change the regimes of managing global supply chains and/or rather transform the ways in which human rights are translated in corporate practice.

Conclusion

The sociology of critique provides an interesting foil for reading the recent trend towards a corporate responsibility to respect human rights. Linking it to a Foucauldian notion of productive power, I have offered a perspective on the power of business with regard to human rights. It allows a critical re-assessment of the concept of 'rights responsibility' as enabling new practices of governance through self-regulation. The human rights discourse has provided a capacity for businesses to react to various forms of social, artistic, conservative and partly even ecological public criticisms, which were strongly aligned in the anti-globalisation movement. This reaction to a crisis of justification constitutes a change in discourse which includes international institutional transformations. The latter have formed the grounds for a principled, normative confirmation of transnational business as an 'ally' of the human rights idea and an agent in the field of human rights policies.

By way of illustrative examples I have hinted at some of the practices in which companies incorporate human rights. The managerial forms that human rights policies take and their underlying test formats based on the logics of industrial hierarchies, markets and production networks, constitute an incorporation of the human rights discourse into complex regimes of domination, thereby disarming critique based on the normative ideas of dignity and rights. The example of the corporate responsibility for human rights thus shows very well an appropriation process of capitalism. It shows how criticism 'contributes to the construction of the normativity that accompanies capitalism, and consequently justifies it while placing constraints on it, making capitalism incorporate the values that just a short while before served to criticize it'.[88] My focus in this article was on the tendency of corporations not to change in fundamental ways based on international norms, but rather to translate the very norms that have served to criticise them into their very own regimes of practice. This does *not* directly change the normative representation itself, the semantic 'content'; human rights covenants and international-legal interpretations are still relatively independent of the processes described here. It is rather the ways in which we consider and accept a rule to be followed, the *form* in which a practice is perceived as being in line with a rule. In this sense I have called the process of corporate human rights policy a process of translation. The latter makes the rights concept fit the transnational practices of businesses, thereby diffusing and replacing the space for criticism with a realm of expertise and inside knowledge, of dispersed responsibility and complex processes of 'managing constant change'.[89]

Acknowledgements

A first draft of this article was presented at the 8th EISA Pan-European Conference on International Relations in Warsaw, in September 2013. I would like to thank all participants and commentators of the panel 'Resilience: Critique and the New Spirit of Capitalism' for their valuable comments and critique.

Disclosure statement

No potential conflict of interest was reported by the author.

Notes

1. See, for example, Florian Wettstein, 'CSR and the Debate on Business and Human Rights', *Business Ethics Quarterly* 22, no. 4 (2012): 739–70.
2. See Wesley Cragg, Denis G. Arnold, and Peter Muchlinski, 'Human Rights and Business', *Business Ethics Quarterly* 22, no. 1 (2012): 1–7; Stephen J. Kobrin, 'Private Political Authority and Public Responsibility: Transnational Politics, Transnational Firms, and Human Rights', *Business Ethics Quarterly* 19, no. 3 (2009): 349–74; Delphine Rabet, 'Human Rights and Globalization: The Myth of Corporate Social Responsibility?' *Journal of Alternative Perspectives in the Social Sciences* 1, no. 2 (2009): 463–75.
3. See, for example, for a legal discussion on corporate responsibility and international human rights law: Steven R. Ratner, 'Corporations and Human Rights: A Theory of Legal Responsibility', *The Yale Law Journal* 111, no. 3 (2001): 443–545.
4. The European Commission, for instance, recommended the development of national action plans to implement the United Nations (UN) Guiding Principles on Business and Human Rights on the level of member states; see European Commission, 'Communication from the Commission to the European Parliament, the Council, the European Economic and Social Committee and the Committee of the Regions. A Renewed EU Strategy 2011-2014 for Corporate Social Responsibility'. Brussels, 25/10/2011 (2011), 14. By the time of writing, several governments in and outside of the European Union (EU) have followed this recommendation, several others will probably follow in the near future.
5. Scott Jerbi, 'Business and Human Rights at the UN: What Might Happen Next?' *Human Rights Quarterly* 31, no. 2 (2009): 299–320.
6. Mantilla Casas and Giovanni Fabrizio, 'Emerging International Human Rights Norms for Transnational Corporations', *Global Governance* 15, no. 2 (2009): 279–98.
7. See Rabet, 'Human Rights and Globalization'.
8. Tony Evans, *The Politics of Human Rights. A Global Perspective*, 2nd ed. (London: Pluto Press, 2005), 90.
9. Luc Boltanski and Laurent Thévenot, *On justification. Economies of Worth* (Princeton, NJ: Princeton University Press, 2006).
10. Luc Boltanski and Eve Chiapello, *The New Spirit of Capitalism* (London; New York: Verso, 2007).

11. The notion 'regime of practice' draws on Glynos' and Howarth's Political Discourse Theory. A regime is a discursive formation, with its systems of meaning, of material objects and of doing things. It has 'a structural function in the sense that it orders. 'a system of social practices, thus helping us to characterize the latter', Jason Glynos and David R. Howarth, *Logics of Critical Explanation in Social and Political Theory* (London; New York: Routledge, 2007), 106.
12. With this approach I also intend to offer a critical alternative to dominant strands of norm research in international relations, which tend to assume a rather progressive development towards increasing human rights commitments by transnational corporations, moving from 'norm denial' towards 'compliance' and 'norm entrepreneurship'; see for example Nicole Deitelhoff and Klaus D. Wolf, 'Business and Human Rights: How Corporate Norm Violators Become Norm Entrepreneurs', in *The Persistent Power of Human Rights: From Commitment to Compliance*, ed. Thomas Risse; Stephen C. Ropp; Katherine Sikkink (Cambridge: Cambridge University Press, 2013), 222–38.
13. Boltanski and Chiapello, *The New Spirit of Capitalism*, 28.
14. Eve Chiapello, 'Capitalism and Its Criticisms', in *New Spirits of Capitalism? Crises, Justifications, and Dynamics*, ed. Paul Du Gay and Glenn Morgan (Oxford: Oxford University Press, 2013), 60–81, at 61.
15. I use 'discourse' in the Wittgensteinian sense of 'language games'. Wittgenstein refers to the semantic and extra-semantic dimensions of practice. In this vein, discourse is the name of a logic or grammar of a practice, it is not limited to language and speech acts; see Glynos and Howarth, *Logics of Critical Explanation in Social and Political Theory*, 134f.
16. Chiapello, 'Capitalism and its Criticisms', 63.
17. In their content analysis of corporate policy commitments Preuss and Brown found that of the FTSE 100 firms 60% had a particular human rights policy; see Lutz Preuss and Donna Brown, 'Business Policies on Human Rights: An Analysis of Their Content and Prevalence Among FTSE 100 Firms', *Journal of Business Ethics* 109, no. 3 (2012): 289–99.
18. See, for example, Philip Alston, ed., *Non-State Actors and Human Rights* (Oxford; New York: Oxford University Press, 2005); Philip Alston, 'Labour Rights as Human Rights: The Unhappy State of the Art', in *Labour Rights as Human Rights*, ed. Philip Alston (Oxford; New York: Oxford University Press, 2005).
19. See, for example, Cragg et al., 'Human Rights and Business'; Rory Sullivan, ed., *Business and Human Rights. Dilemmas and Solutions* (Sheffield: Greenleaf, 2003).
20. Office of the High Commissioner for Human Rights (OHCHR), 'Guiding Principles on Business and Human Rights – Implementing the United Nations "Protect, Respect and Remedy" Framework' (2011). http://www.ohchr.org/Documents/Publications/GuidingPrinciplesBusinessHR_EN.pdf (accessed 10 June 2013).
21. Ibid., §§11–24. Of course, the Universal Declaration of Human Rights already emphasised the need for all individuals and organs of society to promote respect for human rights. Thus, the guiding principles can be seen as a specification of this idea with regard to transnational corporations.
22. United Nations Human Rights Council (UNHRC), 'Report of the Special Representative of the Secretary General on the Issue of Human Rights and Transnational Corporations and Other Business Enterprises, John Ruggie: Protect, Respect, and Remedy: A Framework for Business and Human Rights', UN Doc. A/HRC/8/5 from 07/04/2008 (2008). http://daccess-ddsny.un.org/doc/UNDOC/GEN/G08/128/61/PDF/G0812861.pdf (accessed 27 March 2014).
23. Organisation for Economic Co-operation and Development (OECD), 'OECD Guidelines for Multinational Enterprises'. Paris: OECD Publishing, 2011. http://dx.doi.org/10.1787/9789264115415-en (10 February 2014).
24. See Preuss and Brown, 'Business Policies on Human Rights'.
25. See Casas and Fabrizio, 'Emerging International Human Rights Norms for Transnational Corporations'; Jordan J. Paust, 'Human Rights Responsibilities of Private Corporations', *Vanderbilt Journal of Transnational Law* 35, no. 3 (2002): 801–25; Rabet, 'Human Rights and Globalization'.
26. Wesley Cragg, 'Business and Human Rights: A Principle and Value-Based Analysis', in *Oxford Handbook of Business Ethics*, ed. George Brenkert and Tom Beauchamp (Oxford: Oxford University Press, 2010), 267–305; Cragg et al., 'Human Rights and Business'; Florian Wettstein, *Multinational Corporations and Global Justice. Human Rights Obligations of a Quasi-Governmental Institution* (Stanford, CA: Stanford Business Books, 2009).

27. See, for example, David J. Karp, 'The Location of International Practices: What is Human Rights Practice?', *Review of International Studies* (2012): 1–24; Kobrin, 'Private Political Authority and Public Responsibility'; Tineke Lambooy, 'Corporate Due Diligence as a Tool to Respect Human Rights', *Netherlands Quarterly of Human Rights* 28, no. 3 (2010): 404–48; Wettstein, 'CSR and the Debate on Business and Human Rights'.
28. Human rights (like other rights) always need to be interpreted in a given context. Not only are they subject to political contestation, they also imply a decision in individual cases. My focus on *rights as practice* draws on this assumption but also goes beyond it: I assume that the perspective on human rights as corporate practice shows us how the concept of rights is partly *decoupled from legal discourse.* While the latter acknowledges the contested character of legal norms, the need of interpretation and judgement based on a specific case, human rights via corporate practice rather mark a minimum standard of governance.
29. Ludwig Wittgenstein, *Philosophical Investigations*, translated by G.E.M. Anscombe, (Oxford: Basil Blackwell, 1986 [c.1958]), 5.
30. Ronen Shamir, 'The Age of Responsibilization: On Market-Embedded Morality', *Economy and Society* 37, no. 1 (2008): 1–19.
31. Michel Foucault, *Discipline and Punish*, translated by A. Sheridan (New York: Pantheon, 1977), 194.
32. See Geoffrey Chandler, (2003): 'The Evolution of the Business and Human Rights Debate', in *Business and Human Rights*, ed. Sullivan, 22–32; Cragg, 'Business and Human Rights'.
33. The notion 'anti-globalisation' obliterates many different positions and should thus be understood as a catchword, rather than a definition of political demands. Of course, many of the critical advocates were not actually positioned against globalisation per se. They rather criticised globalisation in its current form and particular characteristics, especially with regard to global justice. There are many labels that often refer to the same phenomenon, such as 'global justice movement' or 'movement against neoliberal globalisation'.
34. Peter Utting, 'Corporate Responsibility and the Movement of Business', *Development in Practice* 15, nos 3–4 (2005): 275–388, 383.
35. Boltanski and Chiapello, *The New Spirit of Capitalism*, 37.
36. Chiapello, 'Capitalism and its Criticisms'.
37. Ibid.
38. Ibid., 38.
39. Ibid., 37.
40. Ibid., 64f.
41. Boltanski and Chiapello, *The New Spirit of Capitalism*, 38.
42. Chiapello, 'Capitalism and its Criticisms', 70.
43. Ibid.
44. One should note that this definition of ecological criticism is not to be misunderstood as representing the very different facets of ecological movements, which of course incorporate various forms of artistic, social, conservative, and ecological criticisms. Chiapello's definition attempts to distil a specific characteristic here, which is the relative indifference of the ecological criticism towards the political system. 'It is possible, for instance to be anti-democracy and pro-ecology' (Ibid., 74).
45. Boltanski and Chiapello, *The New Spirit of Capitalism*, 517.
46. Ibid., 70.
47. Ibid.
48. See Ann Harrison and Jason Scorse, 'Multinationals and Anti-Sweatshop Activism', *American Economic Review* 100, no. 1 (2010): 247–73.
49. See for the series of events and publications Jeff Ballinger's chronology. http://depts.washington.edu/ccce/polcommcampaigns/NikeChronology.htm (accessed 2 September 2013).
50. Chiapello, 'Capitalism and its Criticisms', 68.
51. Lance W. Bennett, 'The Un-Civic Culture: Communication, Identity, and the Rise of Lifestyle Politics', *Political Science & Politics* 31, no. 4 (1998): 741–61.
52. Kumi Naidoo and Indira Ravindran, 'A Rights-Based Understanding of the Anti-Globalisation Movement' (Working Paper Commissioned by the International Council on Human Rights Policies, 2002). http://www.ichrp.org/files/papers/74/118_-_A_Rights-based_Understanding_of_the_Anti-globalisation_Movement_Naidoo__Kumi___Ravindran__Indira__2002.pdf (accessed 10 February 2014).

53. Some exceptional activities by transnational companies had already occurred earlier. They referred to the more liberal understanding of human rights as civil and political liberties, such as the apparel company Levy Strauss that withdrew its business from Myanmar in the early 1990s, stating that it would not be possible to do business there without actively supporting a military state that massively violated human rights (see Preuss and Braun, 'Business Policies on Human Rights'). But beyond such rather exceptional steps there was no broader development in corporate strategies to actively adhere and refer their actions to human rights norms.
54. David S. Weissbrodt and Muria Kruger, 'Norms on the Responsibilities of Transnational Corporations and Other Business Enterprises with Regard to Human Rights', *American Journal of International Law* 97, no. 4 (2003): 901–22.
55. UNHRC, 'Report of the Special Representative of the Secretary General on the Issue of Human Rights and Transnational Corporations and Other Business Enterprises, John Ruggie: Protect, Respect, and Remedy: A Framework for Business and Human Rights'.
56. OHCHR, 'Guiding Principles on Business and Human Rights – Implementing the United Nations "Protect, Respect and Remedy" Framework'.
57. Preuss and Brown, 'Business Policies on Human Rights', 290.
58. Wettstein, 'CSR and the Debate on Business and Human Rights'.
59. UNHRC, 'Report of the Special Representative of the Secretary General on the Issue of Human Rights and Transnational Corporations and Other Business Enterprises, John Ruggie: Protect, Respect, and Remedy: A Framework for Business and Human Rights'.
60. See Utting, 'Corporate Responsibility and the Movement of Business', 383f.
61. OHCHR, 'Guiding Principles on Business and Human Rights – Implementing the United Nations "Protect, Respect and Remedy" Framework'. § 3, Commentary.
62. The guiding principles are now in the process of being taken up by other international organisations and there are also efforts to transpose them into rules and standards on regional and national levels (for example, in the EU). For instance, the OECD Guidelines on Multinational Enterprises, which were already developed in the wake of the debate on the New Economic Order in the 1970s, have been revised for the fifth time and now include a human rights chapter that resembles the spirit of the guiding principles. Further examples are the OECD standards for export credit guaranties ('Common Approaches for Officially Supported Export Credits and Environmental and Social Due Diligence', usually referred to as the 'Common Approaches'), the Performance Standards of the International Finance Corporation, which inform not only World Bank projects with private companies but are also an important basis of major transnational banking standards for project finance; the European Commission has also taken up the guiding principles in its 'CSR Strategy' (see European Commission, 'Communication from the Commission to the European Parliament, the Council, the European Economic and Social Committee and the Committee of the Regions. A Renewed EU Strategy 2011–2014 for Corporate Social Responsibility').
63. UNHRC, 'Report of the Special Representative of the Secretary General on the Issue of Human Rights and Transnational Corporations and Other Business Enterprises, John Ruggie: Business and Human Rights: Further Steps toward the Operationalization of the "Protect, Respect and Remedy" Framework'.
64. OHCHR, 'The Corporate Responsibility to Respect Human Rights. An Interpretive Guide', HR/PUB/12/02 (New York; Geneva, United Nations, 2012), 1.
65. Casas and Fabrizio, 'Emerging International Human Rights Norms for Transnational Corporations'; Rabet, 'Human Rights and Globalization'; Tom Campbell, 'Corporate Social Responsibility: Beyond the Business Case to Human Rights', in *Business and Human Rights*, ed. Cragg, 47–73.
66. Castan Centre for Human Rights Law; International Business Leaders Forum; Office of the United Nations High Commissioner for Human Rights; United Nations Global Compact Office, 'Human Rights Translated: A Business Reference Guide' (2008). http://human-rights.unglobalcompact.org/doc/human_rights_translated.pdf (accessed 2 January 2014), viii.
67. Michel Callon, Cécile Méadel and Vololona Rabeharisoa, 'The Economy of Qualities', *Economy and Society* 31, no. 2 (2002): 194–217.
68. Sally E. Merry and Susan B. Coutin, 'Technologies of Truth in the Anthropology of Conflict'. AES/APLA Presidential Address, 2013. *American Ethnologist* 41, no. 1 (2014): 1–16.

69. Michael Power, *The Audit Society: Rituals of Verification* (Oxford: Oxford University Press, 1999).
70. Merry and Coutin, 'Technologies of Truth in the Anthropology of Conflict'.
71. OHCHR, 'Guiding Principles on Business and Human Rights – Implementing the United Nations "Protect, Respect and Remedy" Framework', § 19, Commentary.
72. Nike Inc., 'Raising the Bar' (2012). http://www.nikeresponsibility.com/#targets-commitments (accessed 24 April 2014).
73. Dara O'Rourke, 'Multi-Stakeholder Regulation: Privatizing or Socializing Global Labor Standards?' *World Development* 34, no. 5 (2006): 899–918; Gale Raj-Reichert, 'The Electronic Industry Code of Conduct: Private Governance in a Competitive and Contested Global Production Network', *Competition & Change* 15, no. 3 (2011): 221–38.
74. O'Rourke, 'Multi-Stakeholder Regulation'.
75. Fair Labor Association, 'Nike Inc.' (2012). http://www.fairlabor.org/affiliate/nike-inc (accessed 2 February 2014).
76. Nike Inc., 'Sustainable Business at Nike Inc.' (2013). http://nikeinc.com/pages/responsibility (accessed 10 September 2013).
77. For an assessment of the ETI see Stephanie Barrientos and Sally Smith, 'Do Workers Benefit from Ethical Trade? Assessing Codes of Labour Practice in Global Production Systems', *Third World Quarterly* 28, no. 4 (2007): 713–29.
78. We can also interpret this development in terms of the politics of translation, see Noémi Lendvai and Paul Stubbs, 'Policies as Translation: Situating Transnational Social Policies', in *Policy Reconsidered. Meanings, Politics and Practices*, ed. Susan M. Hodgson, Zoë Irving (Bristol, UK: Policy Press, 2007), 173–89.
79. Luc Boltanski, *On Critique. A Sociology of Emancipation* (Cambridge; Malden: Polity, 2011), 129.
80. Todd Landman and Edzia Carvalho, *Measuring Human Rights* (London: Routledge, 2009).
81. Maplecroft, 'Human Rights' (2013). http://maplecroft.com/themes/hr (accessed 9 September 2013).
82. Danish Institute for Human Rights, 'Human Rights Compliance Assessment' (2013). https://hrca2.humanrightsbusiness.org (accessed 9 September 2013).
83. See Royal Dutch Shell, 'Human Rights' (2013). http://reports.shell.com/sustainability-report/2013/our-approach/living-by-our-principles/human-rights.html (accessed 2 February 2014).
84. Global Reporting Initiative (GRI), 'Indicator Protocol Set Human Rights. Version 3.1' (2011). https://www.globalreporting.org/resourcelibrary/G3.1-Human-Rights-Indicator-Protocol.pdf (accessed 9 September 2013).
85. Christel Lane and Jocelyn Probert, *National Capitalisms, Global Production Networks. Fashioning the Value Chain in the UK, US, and Germany* (Oxford: Oxford University Press, 2009), 258.
86. Boltanski, 'On Critique. A Sociology of Emancipation', 129.
87. Ibid.
88. Chiapello, 'Capitalism and its Criticisms', 63.
89. Boltanski, 'On Critique. A Sociology of Emancipation', 130.

Global production, CSR and human rights: the courts of public opinion and the social licence to operate

Sally Wheeler

School of Law, Queens University Belfast, Northern Ireland

This article takes as its starting point the responsibility placed upon corporations by the United Nations' (UN) Protect, Respect and Remedy Framework as elaborated upon by the Guiding Principles on Business and Human Rights to respect human rights. The overt pragmatism and knowledge of the complex business relationships that are embedded in global production led John Ruggie, the author of the framework, to adopt a structure for the relationship between human rights and business that built on the existing practices of corporate social responsibility (CSR). His intention was that these practices should be developed to embrace respect for human rights by exhorting corporations to move from 'the era of declaratory CSR' to showing a demonstrable policy commitment to respect for human rights. The prime motivation for corporations to do this was, according to Ruggie, because the responsibility to respect was one that would be guarded and judged by the 'courts of public opinion' as part of the social expectations imposed upon corporations or to put it another way as a condition of a corporation's social licence to operate. This article sets out the background context to the framework and examines the structures that it puts forward. In its third and final section the article looks at how the framework requires a corporation's social licence to be assembled and how and by whom that social licence will be judged. The success or failure of the framework in persuading corporations to respect human rights is tied to whether 'the courts of public opinion' can use their 'naming and shaming power' effectively.

1. A contextual background to Ruggie's appointment

This article takes as its starting point the responsibility placed upon corporations by the United Nations' (UN) Protect, Respect and Remedy Framework as elaborated upon by the Guiding Principles on Business and Human Rights to respect human rights. The overt pragmatism and knowledge of the complex business relationships that are embedded in global production led John Ruggie, the author of the framework, to adopt a structure for the relationship between human rights and business that built on the existing practices of corporate social responsibility (CSR). His intention was that these practices should be developed to embrace respect for human rights by exhorting corporations to move from 'the era of declaratory CSR'[1] to showing a demonstrable policy commitment to respect for human rights. The prime motivation for corporations to do this was, according to

Ruggie, because the responsibility to respect was one that would be guarded and judged by the 'courts of public opinion' as part of the social expectations imposed upon corporations or to put it another way as a condition of a corporation's social licence to operate.[2]

Accounts of what appear to be at worst flagrant disregard, and at best disinterest, by corporations of the human rights of individuals reach the mainstream Western media on a regular but atomised basis. Many people in the developed world are aware in very general terms that the production activities of corporations involve power imbalances between the various factors of production and the nation states they are located in. What is much less well known is the complexity of business relationships involved in productive activity. Any attempt to deal with human rights infractions by corporations needs to offer a strategy that addresses this complexity. Examples of recent publicised infractions would be the technology corporation Apple[3] and the mineral extractive corporation Rio Tinto,[4] both of which were accused of benefitting from labour practices that abused the human rights of workers in China and Indonesia respectively, with Rio Tinto additionally accused of land grabbing and forced evictions in Madagascar. In both examples neither corporation is in an employer/employee relationship with the workers concerned. In Indonesia Rio Tinto is in an investment role as part of a joint venture at Grasberg mine which is controlled by Freeport (90.6% shareholding), with the remaining shares held by the Indonesian government. In Madagascar the mine in question was part owned by the Madagascan government.

China, Indonesia and Madagascar have very different political and institutional structures from each other and from the United States (US), United Kingdom (UK) and Australia where these corporations are incorporated and listed. Apple and Rio Tinto fit the classic model of large-scale corporations attracting foreign inward investment into lower cost labour or resource rich economies resulting in export-orientated industrialisation in those states.[5] Apple's production facilities in China are enclosed in a contractual web involving locally based manufacturers who both produce components and obtain them from other manufacturers for further work and onward supply. This illustrates the development of the outsourced production paradigm into global value chains as the inward investment vehicle.[6] For many industries production is becoming increasingly fragmented into trade in value-generating intermediate goods and services with activity located in webs of long-term co-production relationships, franchises, affiliated business structures and more traditional arm's length supply contracts, hence the name global value chains.[7] The presence of these chains makes the tracking of responsibility for human rights abuses much more difficult. The collapse of the structurally unsound Bangladeshi clothing factory, Rana Plaza, in April 2013 that killed over 1100 workers revealed the tangled web of supply, subcontracting and labeling relationships that lies behind some consumer products. It is still not clear exactly which fashion chains were sourcing garments or parts of garments from this factory and on what legal basis they were doing so but they were numerous.[8] Some have admitted their involvement while suggesting darkly that others were also involved.[9] This makes locating an appropriate corporation with sufficient funds to satisfy a tort action in the correct jurisdiction very difficult from a victim perspective.

These issues are not simply about business actors based in northern and western states exploiting low-cost regulatory regimes in the global south. Capital in the form of foreign direct investment (FDI) no longer flows inexorably from the global north to the global south.[10] The contours of globalisation have shifted in recent years to cast new or emerging economies as the host country for corporations which then provide inward investment into other such economies across the global south.[11] Nor is it always the case that global value chains are constituted with the largest and so most influential corporation in the chain located in a developed state.[12] Manufacturers in emerging economies are increasingly able to capture more locally driven production and supply more than one customer thus inverting the power base of the chain.[13] Domestic markets in the global south have expanded enormously with India and China both becoming Asian Driver economies.[14] Global business in terms of FDI flows is much more complex and granular than traditional accounts would suggest it is. This creates a geopolitical dimension to corporate activity that is subtler in terms of a pattern of winners and losers in relation to human rights abuses and protection than can be addressed by focusing solely on the regulatory relationship between a corporation and its host state.

The example of Apple in China is illustrative of the complex relationship that exists between states and corporations in the control of global production activity. The classic observation is that the growth of corporations in number and economic significance signals a decline in the influence of the nation state and its regulatory power. This is usually supported by the observation that the turnover of the world's largest corporation is greater than the gross domestic product (GDP) of a large number of states.[15] While technically true this is a rather static description that does not capture the full picture of the interplay between production on a global scale, a global finance system and the desire to industrialise rapidly on the part of many individual states. In fact, the Apple and Rio Tinto examples illustrate the fluidity and complex nature of economic globalisation.[16] Industrialisation through FDI has changed some parts of some states significantly very quickly and this brings new problems for host nations. The effects of global production produce for some states problems that are not of their making, for example the environmental degradation that results from natural resource extraction. However this activity also allows an economic growth model for that state to be predicated on adding value to natural resources.[17] The proliferation of bilateral investment treaties[18] might restrict the space for host countries to develop their domestic policy in relation to the regulation of corporations, but as these are interstate arrangements in theory they do not directly lead to a leeching of power between the state and the inward investing corporation.[19]

Corporations sometimes act in support of strong governments and sometimes against them. Corporations might, in a weak state, offer a form of stability that the state cannot. On occasions this is done from an altruistic standpoint such as corporate participation in the Global Fund initiative, an international public-private partnership, to fight Aids, tuberculosis and malaria in Somalia.[20] In other instances it is done from a more self-interested perspective; for example, by providing Aids-related health services in parts of South Africa Mercedes Benz is able to secure the supply of a healthier workforce.[21] States in the neoliberal era opened up new service markets for corporations by privatising state monopolies under the blueprint offered by proponents of the new public management school.[22] Since the financial crisis of 2008 there has been a further wave of stripping back state functions in favour of private sector provision to serve the interests of austerity. The relationship between the state and corporations is one that is constantly evolving, with individual citizens more likely to be in direct contact with corporate activity as the role of the state changes in response to a variety of political and economic imperatives that are more nuanced than the naked growth of Western-based corporations.

Into this world of complex networked global production came John Ruggie, a Harvard-based academic who for some years had worked on globalisation and markets and had been Kofi Annan's Assistant Secretary-General for Strategic Planning from 1997 to 2001. He was appointed the UN Special Representative for Business and Human Rights in 2005.[23] This was not the first attempt by the UN[24] to force an acceptance or even an acknowledgment of responsibility for the effects of business practices onto the corporate sector.[25] In

2000, the Global Compact[26] (of which Ruggie was one of the leading architects) was introduced and encouraged businesses to declare themselves in support of ten core principles based around environmental standards, employment practices, human rights and corrupt practices, and to observe them in their activities.[27] Prior to the compact's promulgation there was the UN Draft Code of Conduct for Transnational Corporations which set up in 1980. The UN was not the only supra-national organisation suggesting that there should be interventions into the relationship between the corporate sector and the advancement of human rights. The Organisation for Economic Co-operation and Development (OECD) and the International Labour Organization (ILO) both developed positions expressed through codes in 1976 and 1977 respectively.[28]

What this demonstrates is that the latter years of the twentieth century saw the supporters of an influential international human rights discourse[29] increasingly interrogating free market actors about the human rights impacts of their activities.[30] The public/private divide in the context of corporations has broken down and for many this is not a desirable state of affairs. In a neoliberal worldview, corporations are purely private accumulators of capital and should be required to take little interest in the provision of public benefits.[31] From a civil society perspective any corporate intervention in the social world is fundamentally anti-democratic; corporations are, in terms of structure, largely unaccountable in the provision of societal goods, unlike a government which has an electoral mandate[32] based on the articulation of particular ideological principles. Furthermore, corporate executives are likely to be inexperienced in the design and delivery of social interventions.[33]

However corporations are both political and public actors, not least because of the way in which state governments have systematically ceded their functions to the corporate sector.[34] Ruggie's appointment can be seen as the UN's response to the need to manage the convergence of global production regimes and the supporting neoliberal discourse of both states[35] and corporations with the discourse of human rights recognition and protection.[36] The emergence of CSR as a central feature of corporate behaviour at the level of the individual firm and at industry sector level is the response offered by capital to ameliorate demands from wider society for greater accountability, transparency and ultimately regulation[37] of the activities that generate corporate profit.[38] The framework eventually produced by Ruggie, echoing views he had expressed prior to his appointment,[39] invites links to be drawn between the discourse of human rights and the discourse and practice of CSR, as the next section of the article explains. Concern for human rights has not to date played a significant role in CSR debates or in corporate policies.[40] Preuss and Brown report that in their study of human rights policies in FTSE 100 listed companies, 42.8% of corporations did not address human rights at all despite having at least one CSR tool in place.[41] The desire to behave in a socially responsible manner did not include the observance of human rights, it seems. The commonality between the two discourses that is being advocated, in effect, by the Ruggie framework forces us to recognise not only that both discourses require proactive action on the part of corporations but also that these discourses have fundamentally different trajectories, as the text below explains. The third and final section of this article asks whether the norms of behaviour adopted by the corporate proponents of CSR can be subjected to the level of scrutiny required for them to be accepted also as the norms of behaviour that will deliver respect for human rights.[42]

The Global Compact was followed in 2003 by the announcement by the UN Sub-Commission for the Promotion and Protection of Human Rights of the Draft Norms on the Responsibilities of Transnational Corporations and other Business Enterprises with Regard to Human Rights.[43] The norms pertained to a basket of rights broadly mapped onto the Universal Declaration of Human Rights (UDHR) and subsequent international covenants and customary law, although the inclusion of economic and social rights as well civil and political rights marked a significant shift away from the anchoring effect of the UDHR[44] in terms of expressing human rights obligations. The norms advocated imposing on corporations and other enterprises over which they held influence an obligation to observe human rights rather than a negative demand not to infringe them,[45] while still casting states as bearing the primary responsibility for protecting human rights. Criticisms of the norms ranged from the substantive, with concerns around the interpretation placed on existing treaty arrangements and the breadth of liability ascribed to corporations[46] and the meaning of previously unused phrases such as 'respective spheres of activity and influence' to more, albeit disputed, procedural concerns with perceived lack of consultation of relevant, ultimately opposing, stakeholder groups.[47] These norms were expressly not adopted by the Commission on Human Rights in 2004 even though the Sub-Commission on the Promotion and Protection of Human Rights had endorsed them in August 2003.

This is not the place for a detailed discussion of the norms[48] but they are worthy of a short mention at this point for two reasons: The first part of Ruggie's mandate in 2005 involved clarifying some of the contentious concepts used by the norms and the hostile reception that the norms received from much, but not all, of the corporate sector[49] and some states[50] is unlikely not to have had an influence on how Ruggie undertook his task and what he considered was possible in terms of devising a structure that would achieve broad acceptability.[51] In 2006 Ruggie explained that his operating credo was one of 'principled pragmatism'; a commitment to 'strengthening the promotion and protection of human rights … coupled with a pragmatic attachment to what works best in creating change'.[52] This view when taken with his ex post facto comments about the desire to avoid his mandate being side-tracked into lengthy discussions about the status of legal texts and his position being instead that he wanted to get the 'parameters and the perimeters of business and human rights locked down in … policy terms … which could be acted upon immediately and on which future progress could be built' would seem to suggest that the norms and their failure was on his mind throughout his mandate.[53] Ruggie ameliorated two of the most contentious parts[54] of the norms early in his tenure; he set up multi-stakeholder consultations that canvassed opinion across five continents,[55] a practice that he continued throughout his mandate,[56] and he abandoned attempts to base corporate liability on direct obligation, focusing instead on obligations flowing through states for violations of international criminal and humanitarian law.[57] In relation to corporations he sets out responsibilities which while not binding are intended to be a basis for the monitoring and, if necessary, remediation of corporate conduct.

2. The Ruggie framework and guiding principles

By April 2008 Ruggie had produced a report, supported by extensive consultation, that created a framework resting on the three pillars of 'protect', 'respect' and 'remedy'.[58] In the three years that followed, until 2011, he worked on producing implementation guidance for corporations and states and some of this guidance is discussed below. Protection of human rights is the role of the state expressed as a duty; respect for human rights is the second pillar and is the role given to corporations. The difference in liability for states and corporations expressed as 'duty' and 'respect' reflects the established view that no legal liability attaches to non-state actors in international law.[59] Remedying the infringement of human rights is something that corporations should do or they should cooperate in legitimate processes that are advanced by the state to effect a remedy. One part of the norms that Ruggie did retain was contained in this third pillar: corporations should have in place mechanisms for those whose rights have been adversely affected to bring grievances to the corporation's attention and for their swift resolution. The rights which Ruggie wishes corporations to respect are 'all internationally recognised rights',[60] which are defined in the Guiding Principles of 2011[61] as, at a minimum, the International Bill of Human Rights and the principles concerning fundamental rights set out in the ILO's Declaration on Fundamental Principles and Rights at Work.[62] Whether this covers all international human rights or not is a matter of debate.[63] Ruggie's position would appear to be that it does.[64] The principles that Ruggie set out have been endorsed by the UN Human Rights Council, adopted by the OECD,[65] encouraged by the EU,[66] they have influenced the current design of ISO (International Organization for Standardization) 26000[67] and are included in the 2012 International Finance Corporation (IFC) Environmental and Social Performance Standards.[68] They are the most recent and most authoritative statement on the relationship between corporations and human rights.

Both Ruggie's pragmatism and his recognition of the complexity of global production are evidenced in the way that he deals with the issue of a wider responsibility upon corporations beyond clear identifiable acts of theirs that affect particular individuals or groups; this wider responsibility could be expressed as the responsibility to exercise leverage or influence over business associates, states or other actors in respect of adverse impacts on human rights they commit. Relationships such as business networks, brand-based supply chains in areas like apparel production and direct sourcing relationships such as those found in agricultural production would be obvious examples where the idea of a wider responsibility beyond direct impact would have considerable utility. Given his role in constructing the Global Compact which advocated corporations applying its principles 'within their sphere of influence',[69] Ruggie's attachment to leverage is unsurprising. However 'sphere of influence'[70] was a much contested concept when it was included in the UN norms and it is unlikely that inclusion of leverage expressed in those terms would have endeared the Framework of Guiding Principles to the business community.[71] If we track the idea of 'influence' through the various stages of the evolution of the idea of 'responsibility to protect' what we find is a rather malleable, almost slippery approach to the ambit of corporate responsibility.[72] Responsibility for influence fades in and out of the documentary structure.

At various stages of promulgation of the framework and Guiding Principles there appear to be clear statements to the effect that the responsibility of respect is confined to impact-based liability only. Corporations presumably drew comfort from the bold assertion early on in the journey to the Guiding Principles that 'companies cannot be held responsible for the human rights impacts of every entity over which they may have some influence'.[73] This sentiment is buttressed by the commentary to Guiding Principle 17 which refers to the corporation's 'human rights risks' as its 'potential adverse rights impacts'. Complex value chains might make it 'unreasonably difficult' to conduct due diligence in all areas so a concentration on general areas where significant risk is likely to occur is suggested with the added bonus that acting in this way might assist in ameliorating any potential subsequent reputational damage. Again, in Guiding Principle 18 impact-based liability is stressed in terms of the need for the corporation 'to understand the specific impacts on specific people, given a specific context of operations'. The responsibility to protect then occurs in relation to adverse micro-level impacts on defined individuals or groups of individuals.[74]

Guiding Principle 19 seems, however, to entrench the idea of a wider influenced-based responsibility to the extent that after a corporate actor has ended its own conduct that gave rise to the adverse impact, its responsibility is to use its leverage to end the conduct of others. If it cannot do this due to insufficient influence then it should improve the situation by providing capacity building interventions or even ending the business relationship. HSBC, a bank listed in London and Hong Kong, with global interests, has recently found itself accused of providing loan finance and other banking services to at least seven logging companies operating in Sarawak, Malaysia.[75] These companies are said to be infringing the rights of indigenous groups through harassment and forced evictions, engaging in the bribery of public officials[76] and breaking environmental regulations on deforestation. Irrespective of whether these companies are breaking HSBC's own CSR policies and the external validations that it has signed up to, Guiding Principle 19 suggests HSBC should take put pressure on[77] these logging companies to change their practices even if Guiding Principles 17 and 18 would appear to point in the opposite direction. The confusion in the Guiding Principles around whether respect extends to influence-based responsibility or is confined to impact-based activities only perhaps indicates the complexity of global production and how difficult it is to draft to deal with activities that do not centre on a single nodal point but rather exist across a swathe of networks and chains of relationships.

The focus of this article is on the second pillar of the framework accepting that the pillars stand together; the state's duty to protect and the need for both actors to find victims of adverse human rights impacts access to remedies may place increased legal obligations upon corporations as a matter of national law. The responsibility of respect placed upon corporations is housed within a methodology of due diligence. Corporations should have in place a mechanism of due diligence that will allow them to become aware of the impact of their activities on human rights and then act to prevent and/or address adverse impacts.[78] Due diligence within the framework has four elements.[79] Corporations first need to put in place a human rights policy.[80] The remaining three elements coalesce around the ideas of transparency, external participation and independent verification. The second stage is to learn the effect that business activity has upon human rights by conducting assessments of the impact of corporate activities on human rights.[81] Ruggie's concern was that if respect for human rights was not integrated into business practice but instead grafted on as an additional but separate activity it would be cosmetic at best in approach and coverage.[82] Consequently he advocated the idea that a corporation's human right policy should be 'owned' by the whole firm and integrated throughout its activities. Corporate leaders should ensure that respect for human rights is allowed to trickle down through business structure. Employees should be trained, if necessary, to avoid infringing human rights while carrying out their job.[83] The use of monitoring and auditing processes to track corporate progress is advocated.[84]

Due diligence is performing two functions within the framework. It develops what Ruggie terms 'a connectivity' between respect for human rights and the corporate sector on two levels: linguistic and practical.[85] At the linguistic level Ruggie is presumably trying to create a common language of understanding between the two discourses. Due diligence has a particular meaning within the human rights obligations of states; for example, the UN Declaration on the Elimination of Violence Against Women requires states to use *due diligence* to prevent, investigate and punish, in accordance with their own national legal systems, acts of violence against women perpetrated by the state or third parties. This includes creating, if necessary, the appropriate structures of sanction. By using this concept Ruggie is conveying to corporations the idea that despite the non-obligatory nature of 'respect' under the framework the level of attention in terms of resource intensive fact-finding, policy-making and training that is expected of them is akin to what states are legally obliged to do under the human rights obligations they have accepted. The difference between duty and respect at the level of obligation is what makes this a linguistic communality only. Due diligence also has traction within the corporate sector as a practical concept. It is used in corporate management and corporate governance to identify and measure risk in relation to a wide range of business transactions from merger and acquisition to supply chain management. This is tantamount to suggesting that respect for human rights is a business risk rather than a good in its own right.

Opinions differ about the merits of this approach in philosophical terms. While these debates are interesting,[86] of more significance for this article is the link that the idea of human rights as a business risk makes to CSR as a practice. In 2005, before his tenure at the UN began, Ruggie set out the idea that CSR was a risk management strategy for business and offered some suggestions on how CSR might be used in this way. The elements of due diligence bear considerable resemblance to these suggestions[87] which include stakeholder consultation, a system for identifying risks and dealing with them and reporting protocols. When this is added to the grounding of the responsibility in a socio-ethical structure,[88] namely unexplained[89] 'social expectations'[90] and 'prevailing social norms'[91] which are said to underpin the corporate 'social licence to operate', what appears to have happened is that the responsibility to respect has been fused into the rationale for CSR – a management tool for the avoidance of damage to business reputation.

The adoption of particular CSR policies is a choice made by corporate management to present a corporation to the external world in a particular way. CSR policies are not designed by corporations to be assessed by third parties as a reflection of corporate operations even in part, let alone in their entirety. There is insufficient information available in the public domain for accurate independent evaluation to take place. Corporations may encourage, through the giving out of information and financial support, validation of their policies by external bodies they have selected or, more likely, they take part in.[92] There are a variety of different institutional environments for this type of CSR: certification from NGOs and corporate co-governance of organisations (for example the Forest Stewardship Council) to NGOs themselves and to industry coalitions (for example Responsible Care)[93] and literally hundreds of different kinds of certification for products and whole industries.[94] The rationale for corporations participating in these validation exercises is that they trigger a reaction in public opinion and the financial markets that is at least equivocal and at most positive about the societal impacts that particular policies have achieved.[95] CSR discourse identifies its goal as business-orientated social investment with vulnerable groups (defined as those outside the supplier-employee paradigm), seen as stakeholders in the business not as independent bearers of human rights.[96]

Respect for human rights by the corporate sector is about observing at least minimum standards for human existence through recognising liberty rights, political rights, and economic and social rights. This is a very different requirement and policy focus from voluntarily adopting CSR policies for strategic reasons.[97] Corporate managers use CSR as a form of chiaroscuro[98]; certain activities are pushed forward for scrutiny, awards even, while others remain firmly in the shade.[99] This might be seen within the corporate sector as efficient and effective management of risk. Zadek has identified a three-stage development model for CSR which he maps against the changing landscape of societal expectations of corporations. His linear three generations move from CSR as corporate philanthropy that is unconnected with business operations, to CSR that is integrated into a longer-term business strategy, recognising that promotion of ideas like cause-related marketing and socially responsible investment will lead to 'win-win' scenarios, and finally to a form of CSR that tries to interrogate the largest global challenges around environmental degradation, poverty and social and economic exclusion.[100] Other commentators employ similar developmental models for CSR[101] and at heart all of these models are describing how corporations make strategic business decisions to achieve particular market reputations in the context of changing social pressures.[102] Ruggie is pushing the CSR model much further than this by suggesting that what will hold the balance between respect for human rights and corporate indifference is a social licence granted or revoked by the courts of public opinion in line with social expectations and norms. The final section of the article looks at the concept of a social licence, at how they might operate in more detail, at what these courts of public opinion might be and at how they will be able to obtain the evidence for their judgments on the maintenance or not of a social licence.

3. The social licence

Defining the social licence

Social licence, as the term suggests, is about business practice and regulation outside the realm of the legal. It draws on CSR principles[103] and is central to Zadek's third stage of CSR development. Its appearance in the framework is no surprise because it is what is left in the absence of a structure of legal enforcement. It enjoys no particular recognised definition but the most influential analysis of it by Gunningham and his colleagues[104] describes it as 'the demands on and expectations for a business enterprise that emerge from neighbourhoods, environmental groups, community members and other elements of the surrounding civil society'.[105] The focus of Gunnigham's work was on environmental standards in the pulp and paper manufacturing industry and this explains the prominence of environmental interests in the description given. As he acknowledges, within the corporate sector generally there is no agreement about the demands made by those to whom the social licence is presented or how and when their demands should be responded to. This acknowledgment comes against the background of environmental regulation which, while it has its own problems of rigour and enforcement, is more tightly legally defined than the protection required for human rights by the corporate sector. In Gunnigham's work the idea of a social licence was evidenced in a corporate actor choosing to embark upon a course of behavior that went beyond what was required for legal compliance. In Ruggie's framework the social licence stands on its own without a close supporting network of legal regulation addressing the immediate problem. The level at which the licence kicks in is the level of protection supplied by existing but diffuse national and international regulation. This puts the importance of the debate referred to in the preceding section about which rights are included in the framework and which are not in context.

The research carried out by Gunningham et al. identified four related reasons for positive corporate responses to social licence pressure: damage to corporate reputation, fear of increased regulatory enforcement, fear of the imposition of new regulations and fear of the damage of market-based boycotts. At worst this relegates social licence to the realms of 'a calculation of what is required to minimize business risk [and] win … community support to avoid … disruption to … operations'.[106] At best a positive response that supports human rights might result from some of these triggers through pressure from the 'courts of public opinion'. The potential for this is examined below. However it is important before looking at that potential to consider some of the inherent, rather than context specific, limits to social licence enforcement and how the concept of social licence sits internally within the corporation. Not all corporate actors will react in the same way to pressure on their social licence. Reaction depends on how much pressure and by whom the pressure is exerted against any one of the factors identified by Gunningham's research. It is also the case that the internal dynamics of a corporation play a part. Issues such as managerial incentives, the operating culture of a particular corporation, the internal perception of organisational identity and image and the personal attitudes of executives and managers to different issues are all important factors in how the social licence is viewed within the corporation.[107] Corporate reputation is a good example of this. Reputation has a different value to different corporations. What decides its value is not the presence of external pressure factors necessarily but how the corporation's internal operational culture values reputation.[108]

In Schön's idea of 'problem setting', individuals operating in a particular context select the boundaries of a situation and impose upon it a sense of order and coherence by determining what needs attention and in what direction events or policies need to be driven.[109] This is what corporate managers and executives do when they make policy and operational decisions. The idea of mainstreaming human rights respect into corporate conscience through the operation of the due diligence structure that Ruggie advocates plays into the paradigm of problem setting. If the due diligence structure is adopted by corporations it sets the problem of how respect for human rights is upheld within corporate activities and pushes respect for human rights into the consciousness of decision-makers within the corporation. These decision-makers should then ask questions of themselves about how they need to change their operations and possibly their business relationships with other corporations to give effect to respect. The internal factors specified above would determine exactly what action is taken. However the problem is also circular in nature because in the absence of any external pressure it is unlikely that an issue will be translated into a problem that is addressed internally by corporate executives. To return to the example of corporate reputation in the previous paragraph something has to alert corporate executives to the idea that corporate reputation is under attack before a corporation can take a decision to respond in a particular way.

Adoption of the social licence as a description of practice has achieved most popularity in the extractive sector. There it is used by the International Council on Mining Minerals,[110] other industry representative groups such as the Australian Coal Association,[111] the Minerals Council of Australia[112] and many of their corporate members[113] in their publicly available policy statements on sustainability and operational standards.[114] It has come to be used to indicate that a particular extraction project has the consent of the local community in which it is situated.[115] Thus it signifies a negotiation process, often through intermediaries, in which local communities receive and accept assurances that the social, economic and environmental benefits of what is proposed outweigh the potential impact.[116] As an equation this reveals some of the inherent limitations in the idea of a social licence for corporate operations.[117] It assumes that information is a neutral factor between the parties. In a situation where there is likely to be a significant power imbalance between a corporate actor and community it means that the local community have received accurate information not tainted by deceit, corruption or lack of corporate technical knowledge about the long-term effects of a project in a form and timescale which allows them to give free, prior and informed consent.[118] There may be issues here about who is entitled to speak for different groups[119] and whether those who might oppose a social licence have the organisational capacity to prevent consent being simply assumed by a more powerful actor.[120] Extractive projects have an immediate geographical impact and the position of wider society and the local community on the desirability of extraction development may not be the same. This is particularly true in instances where host states do not recognise indigenous land rights or land claims and prefer the possibilities for development offered by inward investment.[121] The traction that the concept of social licence has in the extraction industry is perhaps unfortunate for the future prospects of human rights respect given that this industry was the one that Ruggie described in 2006 as 'dominat[ing] this sample of reported abuses' and as 'account[ing] for most allegations of the worst abuses'.[122]

Constructing the social licence within the Ruggie framework

The social licence that pertains to the Ruggie framework will presumably be shaped through the adoption of the due diligence mechanism, outlined in section 2 above. The Guiding Principles[123] set out a screening process to be undertaken to identify the areas where human rights are at greatest risk, evidence is to be gathered, possibly with the assistance of actors external to the corporation, the evidence is to be examined against the applicable human rights standards and actions to deal with infringements or potential infringements of rights are to be taken. Following this the effectiveness of these actions is to be evaluated and then reported to interested external parties. This process will form the internal part of the licence. This internal stage suggests, although the framework does not describe it in this way, an approach to respect for human rights that looks like a human rights impact assessment (HRIA) more frequently seen in the policy design activities of governments and public sector bodies. It is an evidenced approach to building human rights awareness into business operations. Of course, as noted above, when a HRIA is carried out by these public bodies it is, in most cases, being used to look at the effect of proposed actions on their rights-based legal obligations. In the context of corporations, these assessments, as a social licence, will have eventual traction only through public opinion. Corporations are used to considering the impact upon their business of extraneous risk factors. Most corporate actors are unused to calculating the impact of their entire business operation on categories of rights holders outside perhaps investors, consumers and directly salaried employees.[124] For other corporations whose activities required them to engage in social impact assessments the methodology of assessing the impact on human rights is very different.[125] Social impact assessments encourage selected stakeholders to take part in a process that nominates key issues for attention.[126] The assessment of human rights, using the lens of human rights, unsurprisingly starts from the point of all recognised rights (hence the importance of knowing exactly which rights are included within the framework) and then moves to a position of dialogue participation.[127]

The framework suggests, but does not require, that what it describes as 'meaningful' consultation take place with those likely to be affected by business operations.[128] In that this consultation should also be prior to the business operations in question taking place, the model resembles the free, prior and informed consent model that the extractive industries use, referred to above. It is also likely to be beset by the same difficulties in that there is no right of consultation; whether it occurs and how it occurs is a matter for an individual corporation. There is also an issue of cultural norms and expectations in the context of rights. In the absence of a stronger steer from the framework there is every incentive for a corporation to shelter behind a consultation with the local community, the result of which is further entrenchment of the norm of gender discrimination, which is embedded in the community. On the one hand, a corporation that takes the results of consultation seriously might feel obliged to accept this, not least on the grounds that it should not be imposing different cultural values on a community. On the other hand, a rights impact assessment creates an opportunity to examine the rights of the entire effected community, and consistent with respect is the requirement not to worsen the position of any one group.

A corporation is not really in a position to assert that societal re-engineering of this sort belongs solely to the province of the state when it is charged with respecting the same rights that states are legally obliged to uphold. Failure to respect all rights equally, irrespective of consultation results, leads to those rights and their repeated infringement being hidden until such time as those particular human rights values become part of the community's consciousness.[129]

The due diligence framework is advocating that corporations do what many of them already do: release information about their corporate operations to an external audience. This occurs in the context of complying with the requirements of the plethora of certification mechanisms that already exist within CSR. The different institutional settings for these mechanisms, referred to above, see them fall into six distinct groups, ranging from internationally promulgated and independent codes to codes created by individual corporations. There are model business codes of general application supported by inter-governmental bodies such as the UN-backed Global Compact that corporations can sign up to; there are general codes of business operation agreed between governments such as the OECD Guidelines for Multinational Enterprise; multi-stakeholder codes drafted as a result of agreements between corporations, NGOs and governments such as the Ethical Trading Initiative; industry-wide codes such as the Sustainable Development Framework of the International Council on Mining and Metals; individual company codes which contain operating principles in relation to everything from bribery to environmental management to supply chain assurance,[130] and independent reporting standards such as the ISO 14001 standard for environmental management.[131] These reporting initiatives all have the same outcome: they facilitate corporations benchmarking their performance against common standards and against each other. The choice of policy area and business segment that is certified belongs to the corporation. That choice might be made for a variety of strategic reasons: to focus audience awareness on positive actions in a particular arena or to distract attention from a particular event for example.[132] The potentially misleading nature of selective certification by corporations is something that has consistently undermined the credibility of CSR.[133]

What is very different in the context of the Ruggie framework is the absence of a reporting structure or template and hence the absence of any lower (or upper) limit to policy ambition. There is no minimum floor requirement that must be passed. For CSR certification the emphasis for a corporation is on achieving a limit to policy while still attracting certification; in the context of human rights the goal should be limitless and for some corporations, given the nature of their business, recognised as unachievable.[134] Choice for the corporation is not part of the due diligence framework. Both the corporation's human rights policy and its calculation of the impact of its business upon human rights should be all-encompassing of its business operations. However, as Harrison points out, the danger of corporations conducting their own assessments of their own risks, albeit with some external consultation and participation, is that what occurs is a validation of their assessment and policy response rather than an enhancement of respect for human rights.[135] A corporation's credibility may be lost in the eyes of an expert[136] if it proceeds in this way, but, as the text that follows explains, judgment on the adequacy of the impact assessment is unlikely to be solely in the hands of an expert audience.

Notwithstanding Ruggie's stated preference[137] for corporations to publicise the methodology they have used to undertake due diligence, the absence of any template or indicative methodology in the framework for constructing the social licence makes cross-corporation comparison very difficult for an outsider.[138] However such comparison is an essential tool, surely, if the courts of public opinion are to decide whether a corporation's social licence is acceptable and will be maintained. Any opportunity for corporations to learn and share best practice with each other is lost in the absence of a published methodology. The element of competition between corporations is then also lost. While the idea of corporations competing around respect for human rights might be unpalatable it is more likely to drive up the quality of assessment processes and outcomes than the probable absence of inter-firm competition.[139]

Assessing the social licence

The assessment of a corporation's social licence depends upon the view taken of it by the 'courts of public opinion' which will exercise 'naming and shaming' prowess over any licence that does not conform to social expectations. The framework is silent on whose social expectations will be used as the measure but it does indicate particular sites of judgment – investors, employees, communities, consumers, civil society.[140] Whether these actors come to the issue of assessment with the same goals in mind is a moot point. Institutional investors, for example, break into two groups in broad terms: investors who pursue socially responsible investing, sometimes as part of business coalitions to mitigate risk to their business model[141] and ethical investors,[142] and then the much larger group of conventional investors. Nevertheless whatever the rationale for assessment is, assessors will have access to the same information.

Assessment by any of these groups, even before the issue of how they might conduct assessment, requires transparency of reporting and this takes us back to the point made by Harrison[143]; the nature and extent of the internal process that creates the social licence feeds into the evaluation that can be made of it. Possible impacts and actual infringements that are not reported upon cannot be judged. Rio Tinto once again provides a useful illustrative example. Rio Tinto tells the world that it spends US$331 m on socio-economic projects spread across the 40 countries in which it operates.[144] It provides information on 12 case studies that illustrate its commitment to human rights. However these case studies nearly all feature corporate business activities that commenced before 2007. There is no indication of whether any assessment was done of the possible impact on human rights when commercial activity began or since, and if an assessment was carried out what it revealed. What is presented is a story of Rio Tinto's social engagement activities, not a story of what might have needed to be done or should have been done to protect human rights.[145]

For Ruggie's suggested group of assessors to be able to evaluate a corporation's social licence they need to access it and understand what it means. This means taking not only corporate reports that directly reference impacts upon human rights but looking at the entire social licence that a corporation constructs for itself using the third-party certification mechanisms and its own internal codes that are referred to above. There is a problem of asymmetrical information for assessors. Their judgment can be made in one of two ways. One is by relying on certification and corporate reports and the other is by relying on the translation services of an NGO, which, while enjoying the status of assessor itself, breaks down information into a comprehensible format and offers a commentary, additional information and comparisons where possible in the format of report cards, alternative certification and narrative accounts.[146] The reality might be a combination of reliance on both.

Both these assessment avenues raise questions of credibility, product and industrial practice coverage and market place traction. In terms of third-party certification, not only are there the doubts about the absolute reliability of these mechanisms that are set out above but it is also the case that we know very little about the extent to which they are trusted by, or have traction with, consumers. It might be that those that are associated with an NGO are considered more reliable, or alternatively, these NGOs might be viewed as captured by corporations, so giving their shared certificate less value.[147] Product labels might be more influential on consumers than text. In this case, interest in human rights is reduced to the aesthetics of presentation. Starobin and Weinthal, using the example of kosher food certification, produce a model for assessing consumer traction of third-party certification that centres on the display by certifiers of demonstrable and transparent expertise that taps into a group of consumers with strong social capital bonds.[148] This will be a difficult model to replicate in relation to more complex products and practices and in situations where consumers do not share a particular organising identity.

NGOs can engage other assessors of corporate social licences and encourage them to pass negative judgment by targeting the practices of particular corporations or particular products or both. NGOs are not neutral actors, they have values and agendas. They can be in competition with each other to attract and retain significant donors and skilled staff, to affect high profile results and thus to garner respect and influence in the field.[149] This has an impact on their choice of social licence to challenge. Some NGOs are seen as more credible by wider society and thus their campaigns against social licences will be more successful irrespective of the relative merits of the claims made. High credibility is achieved by NGOs that can demonstrate that their claims are supported by a high degree of costly and observable effort that is externally verifiable and that they will suffer significant reputational damage from making false claims.[150]

Even for NGOs with high credibility, target choice and campaign methodology is key to gaining traction for social licence opposition. Awareness of human rights non-observance is dependent on NGOs achieving populist support. Campaign methods might range from raising funds for litigation or share purchase, organising consumer boycotts to direct lobbying for regulatory change or regulatory enforcement. There are a variety of factors that make some firms and some products more attractive as targets than others. Significant factors are the nature of the product. Anti-social products such as weapons and cigarettes are typical targets, as are brands that have a high awareness value within the consumer market place; niche clothing and food brands are two obvious examples. Products or practices with clear externalities like oil drilling or chemical production have high traction. Firms that are representative of particular cultures or lifestyles like McDonalds, or firms which are perceived as securing large amounts of surplus value from the supply chain like Apple would be considered to have traction.[151] Global production is a complex activity spanning many business relationships and jurisdictions. A particular type of consumer is required to respond to many of these campaigns. Expanding consumer markets in new and developing economies may produce consumers with different cultural expectations and preferences. Only those activities that can be simply explained or identified with are suitable for a licence removal campaign. How iPads are soldered together has more traction than how the ruthenium component of their chips is produced.

Conclusion

Through the adoption of pragmatism and the pursuit of compromise John Ruggie has produced a framework that recognises the complex reality of global business production. It acknowledges the importance but also the difficulty of achieving influence-based corporate responsibility and of persuading corporations to use their leverage over others as a way of bringing about change. However, in suggesting that the framework will force corporations to move from declaratory CSR to demonstrable CSR a yawning gap is opened up. Drawing on CSR concepts might offer comfort to corporations but it will also ensure that CSR methods are used to respond to the framework. These methods are likely to be of limited utility – limited in relation to effective protection of human rights. Ruggie is placing a reliance on a broad swathe of different and largely unconnected groups to act as a chain of interrogators and judges. This requires a large degree of happenstance to be even moderately successful. In the absence of a methodology for the production of accurate, relevant and verifiable information and with no clear idea of how it will get to the social and political marketplace much is left to a combination of chance, the offices of NGOs and the sentiments of consumers. Human rights observance by business it seems is being returned to the marketplace of consumption for adjudication by a range of actors with very different agendas.

Disclosure statement

No potential conflict of interest was reported by the author.

Notes

1. See the comments made by Ruggie to the UN General Assembly on 26 October 2010, http://www.ohchr.org/documents/issues/business/2010GA65remarks.pdf (accessed 7 February 2014).
2. Promotion and protection of all human rights, civil, political, economic, social and cultural rights, including the right to development – protect, respect and remedy: A framework for business and human rights report of the special representative of the secretary-general on the issue of human rights and transnational corporations and other business enterprises. UN Doc. A/HRC/8/5 at para. 54.
3. United States (US)-based non-governmental organisation (NGO) China Labor Watch produced two consecutive reports in 2013 and 2014 on Apple's subcontracted production facilities in China which show human rights abuses and environmental standards to be compromised and unimproved in the intervening 12 months: http://www.chinalaborwatch.org/upfile/Jabil_Green_Point.final.pdf; http://www.chinalaborwatch.org/upfile/2014_09_25/2014.09.25%20i Exploitation%20at%20Jabil%20Wuxi%20EN.pdf
4. R. Neate, 'Rio Tinto Blamed by Protesters Over 41 Mine Worker Deaths', *The Guardian*, 5 April 2014. See also http://londonminingnetwork.org/2010/04/rio-tinto-a-shameful-history-of-human-and-labour-rights-abuses-and-environmental-degradation-around-the-globe/. It should be noted that Rio Tinto has compiled a publicly available and very extensive guide to how it integrates human rights into its operations, see http://www.riotinto.com/documents/ReportsPublications/Rio_Tinto_human_rights_guide_-_English_version.pdf (accessed 28 March 2014).
5. M. Hart-Landsberg, *Capitalist Globalization* (New York: The Monthly Review Press, 2013), 13–55, provides an account of the growth of large corporations. See also for some additional statistical depth UNCTAD, *World Investment Report 2011: Non-Equity Modes of International Production and Development* (New York: UN, 2012).
6. G. Gereffi, 'The Organization of Buyer-Driven Global Commodity Chains: How US Retailers Shape Overseas Production networks', in *Commodity Chains and Global Capitalism*, ed. G. Gereffi and M. Korzeniewicz (Westport, CT: Praeger, 1994), 95.
7. The *World Investment Report 2013* (122–40) suggests that more than 60% of global trade by value takes place within global value chains, http://unctad.org/en/PublicationsLibrary/wir2013_en.pdf (accessed 1 February 2014).

8. Some accounts assert that the number of clothing brands sourcing products from Rana Plaza was as high as 27. For a discussion of this and other factory disasters see https://www.cleanclothes.org/news/2013/05/24/background-rana-plaza-tazreen; and D. Robinson, 'Primark Increases Compensation to Rana Plaza Factory Victims in Bangladesh', *Financial Times*, 24 October 2013.
9. Press Association, 'Primark Offers Long-Term Compensation to Rana Plaza Factory Collapse Victims', *The Guardian*, 24 October 2013.
10. A. Rugman, 'How Global are TNCs from Emerging Markets', in *The Rise of Transnational Corporations from Emerging Markets*, ed. K. Sauvant (Cheltenham: Edward Elgar, 2008), 86.
11. R. Applebaum, 'Giant Transnational Contractors in East Asia: Emergent Trends in Global Supply Chains', *Competition and Change* 12 (2008): 69.
12. D. Hoang and B. Jones, 'Why do Corporate Codes of Conduct Fail? Women Workers and Clothing Supply Chains in Vietnam', *Global Social Policy* 12 (2012): 67.
13. G. Gereffi, 'Global Value Chains in a Post-Washington Consensus World', *Review of International Political Economy* 21 (2014): 9.
14. R. Kaplinsky and M. Farooki, 'Global Value Chains, the Crisis, and the Shift of Markets from North to South', in *Global Value Chains in a Postcrisis World*, ed. O. Cattaneo, G. Gereffi and C. Staritz (Washington, DC: The World Bank, 2010), 125.
15. For a discussion of alternative methodologies that are comprehensible to non-economists see D. Kinley, *Civilising Globalisation* (Cambridge: Cambridge University Press, 2009), 163–5.
16. A. Scherer and G. Palazzo, 'The New Political Role of Business in a Globalized World: A Review of a New Perspective on CSR and its Implications for the Firm, Governance, and Democracy', *Journal of Management Studies* 48 (2011): 899.
17. The extent to which this growth model becomes a reality depends on a number of variables, including the terms of investment treaties, the strength of governance in the host country and the quality of infrastructure available to distribute the benefits, see S. Lauwo and O. Otusanya 'Corporate Accountability and Human Rights Disclosures: A Study of Barrick Gold Mine in Tanzania', *Accounting Forum* 38 (2014): 91–108.
18. See UN Doc. A/HRC/8/5 at para 12.
19. M. Sheffer, 'Bilateral Investment Treaties: A Friend or Foe to Human Rights', *Denver Journal of International Law and Policy* 39 (2011): 483.
20. M Schäferhoff, 'External Actors and the Provision of Public Health Services in Somalia: Public Health Services in Somalia', *Governance* 27 (2014): 675.
21. J. Hönke and C. Thauer, 'Multinational Corporations and Service Provision in Sub-Saharan Africa: Legitimacy and Institutionalization Matter: Multinational Corporations in Sub-Saharan Africa', *Governance* 27 (2014): 697.
22. A. Crane, D. Matten and J. Moon, *Corporations and Citizenship* (Cambridge: Cambridge University Press, 2008), at 64f.
23. United Nations Commission on Human Rights, Human Rights Resolution 2005/69.
24. See T. Sagafi-Nejad, *The UN and Transnational Corporations* (Bloomington: Indiana University Press, 2008).
25. Seppala, while concentrating on the continuance of state centrality to the human rights and business activity debate, presents some very interesting commentary about the cumulative processes around these interventions, see N. Seppala, 'Business and the International Human Rights Regime: A Comparison of UN Initiatives', *Journal of Business Ethics* 87 (2009): 401–17.
26. http://www.unglobalcompact.org/
27. http://www.unglobalcompact.org/AboutTheGC/TheTenPrinciples/index.html
28. See S. Asante, 'The Concept of the Good Corporate Citizen in International Business', *Foreign Investment Law Journal* 4 (1989): 1.
29. For an account of how this has become one of the central discourses of our times but has also lost its way in a sea of anti-democratic political activity see S. Hopgood, *The Endtimes of Human Rights* (Ithaca, NY: Cornell University Press, 2013), in particular 119–41.
30. Baxi framed the juncture between these two discourses in terms of a question, 'which are the right language and rhetoric to be used – those furnished by the grammar of human rights or the wider languages of "social responsibility"?': U. Baxi, 'Market Fundamentalisms: Business Ethics at the Altar of Human Rights', *Human Rights Law Review* 5 (2005): 1 at 24.
31. B. Husted and J. Salazer, 'Taking Friedman Seriously: Maximizing Profits and Social Performance', *Journal of Management Studies* 43 (2006): 75.

32. For a framing of this debate see J. Dillard and A. Murray, 'Deciphering the Domain of Corporate Social Responsibility', in *Corporate Social Responsibility*, ed. K. Haynes, A. Murray and J. Dillard (Abingdon: Routledge, 2013), 10, and from a more critical perspective, S. Banerjee, 'Corporate Social Responsibility: The Good, the Bad and the Ugly', *Critical Sociology* 34 (2008): 51.
33. Wilks has a concise but powerful articulation of the critique of corporations taking on the role of governments in the delivery of social programmes, see S. Wilks, *The Political Power of the Business Corporation* (Cheltenham, UK: Edward Elgar, 2013): at 207.
34. A. Scherer, G. Palazzo and D. Matten, 'The Business Firm as a Political Actor: A New Theory of the Firm for a Globalized World', *Business and Society* 53 (2014): 143.
35. S. Aaronson, 'Seeping in Slowly: How Human Rights Concerns are Penetrating the WTO', *World Trade Review* 6 (2007): 1.
36. D. Rabet, 'Human Rights and Globalization: The Myth of Corporate Social Responsibility?' *Journal of Alternative Perspectives in the Social Sciences* 1 (2009): 463.
37. P. Newell, 'CSR and the Limits of Capital', *Development and Change* 39 (2008): 1063.
38. T. Porter, 'The Private Production of Public Goods: Private and Public Norms in Global Governance', in *Complex Sovereignty: Reconstituting Political Authority in the Twenty-First Century*, ed. E. Grande and L. Pauly (Toronto: University of Toronto Press, 2005), 217.
39. J. Ruggie, 'Taking Embedded Liberalism Global: The Corporate Connection', in *Taming Globalization*, ed. D. Held and M. Koenig-Archibugi (Cambridge: Polity, 2003), 93 at 108 and 116–17.
40. T. Campbell, 'A Human Rights Approach to Developing Voluntary Codes of Conduct for Multinational Corporations', *Business Ethics Quarterly* 16 (2006): 255. For a discussion of the surprisingly small overlap that has occurred in CSR and human rights debates see F. Wettstein, 'CSR and the Debate on Business and Human Rights: Bridging the Great Divide', *Business Ethics Quarterly* 22 (2012): 739 at 746–8.
41. L. Preuss and D. Brown, 'Business Policies on Human Rights: An Analysis of Their Content', *Journal of Business Ethics* 109 (2012): 289. Their findings were based on corporate policies from the reporting year 2009.
42. Human rights and CSR have both emerged as norms of behaviour for different groups in the recent past, following the norm life-cycle explained in M. Finnemore and K. Sikkink, 'International Norm Dynamics and Political Change', *International Organization* 52 (1998): 887. For an illustration of this structure of norm emergence in the context of corporate activity and affected communities and stakeholders see H. Dashwood, 'Sustainable Development Norms and CSR in the Global Mining Sector', in *Governance Ecosystems*, ed. J. Sagebien and N. Lindsay (Basingstoke: Palgrave Macmillan, 2011), 31.
43. Norms on the Responsibilities of Transnational Corporations and Other Business Enterprises with Regard to Human Rights, 26 August 2003, E/CN.4/Sub.2/2003/12/Rev.2.
44. K. de Feyter, *Human Rights* (London: Zed Books, 2005).
45. Delimiting corporate responsibility in this way was seen as extending it considerably from previous iterations of the relationship between corporate behaviour and human rights recognition and protection, see W. Meyer, *Human Rights and International Political Economy in Third World Nations: Multinational Corporations, Foreign Aid and Repression* (Westport, CT: Praeger, 1998); and A Voiculescu, 'Human Rights and the Normative Ordering of Global Capitalism', in *The Business of Human Rights*, ed. A. Voiculescu and H. Yanacopulos (London: Zed Books, 2011), 10 at 12–16.
46. Compare the positions taken by D. Weissbrodt and M. Kruger, 'Norms on the Responsibilities of Transnational Corporations and Other Business Enterprises with Regard to Human Rights', *American Journal of International Law* 97 (2003): 901; and J. Knox, 'The Ruggie Rules: Applying Human Rights Law to Corporations', in *The UN Guiding Principles on Business and Human Rights*, ed. R. Mares (Leiden, the Netherlands: Martinus Nijhoff, 2012), 51.
47. D. Kinley, J. Nolan and N. Zerial, '"The Norms are Dead! Long Live the Norms!" The Politics behind the UN Human Rights Norms for Corporations', in *The New Corporate Accountability*, ed. D. McBarnet, A. Voiculescu and T. Campbell (Cambridge: Cambridge University Press, 2007), 459.
48. For detailed accounts of the norms see D. Kinley and R. Chambers, 'The UN Human Rights Norms for Corporations: The Private Implications of Public International Law', *Human Rights*

Law Review 6 (2006): 447; and D. Arnold, 'Transnational Corporations and the Duty to Respect Basic Human Rights', *Business Ethics Quarterly* 20 (2010): 371–99.

49. Some corporations' members volunteered to trial the monitoring of activities suggested by the norms, see http://www.realizingrights.org/pdf/BLIHR3Report.pdf
50. States such as Pakistan and Malaysia, with economic models predicated on supply chain participation, took the view that the norms might make them uncompetitive locations for inward corporate business and/or stifle their own domestic economic development, see S. Jerbi, 'Business and Human Rights at the UN: What Might Happen Next?', *Human Rights Quarterly* 31 (2009): 299. For similar concerns around the Global Reporting Initiative (GRI) and ISO 14000, see K. Dingwerth, 'Private Transnational Governance and the Developing World: A Comparative Perspective', *International Studies Quarterly* 52 (2008): 607 at 617.
51. Ruggie's own analysis of the issues that had to be addressed in a post-norms era can be found at J. Ruggie, 'Business and Human Rights: The Evolving International Agenda', *American Journal of International Law* 101 (2007): 819.
52. Report of the Special Representative of the Secretary-General on the Issue of Human Rights and Transnational Corporations and Other Business Enterprises, UN E/CN.4/2006/97.
53. J. Ruggie *Just Business* (New York: Norton & Co., 2013), at pxlv.
54. Ruggie described the norms as a 'train wreck' full of exaggerated legal claims and conceptual and procedural ambiguities, see *Promotion and Protection of Human Rights*, Interim Report of the Special Representative of the Secretary-General on the Issue of Human Rights and Transnational Corporations and Other Business Enterprises, UN ESCOR, Commission on Human Rights, 62d Sess, Provisional Agenda Item 17, UN Doc. /CN.4/2006/97 (2006).
55. See UN Doc. A/HRC/8/5 at para. 4; and J. Ruggie, *Prepared Remarks at Clifford Chance* (London: Clifford Chance, 19 February 2007), http://www.reportsand-materials.org/Ruggie-remarks-Clifford-Chance-19-Feb-2007.pdf
56. S. Aaronsen and I. Higham, '"Re-Righting Business": John Ruggie and the Struggle to Develop International Human Rights Standards for Transnational Firms', *Human Rights Quarterly* 35 (2013): 333.
57. See n. 46; and S. Ratner, 'Corporations and Human Rights: A Theory of Legal Responsibility', *Yale Law Journal* 111 (2001): 443.
58. See note 2.
59. A. Clapham, ed., *Human Rights and Non-State Actors* (Cheltenham, UK: Edward Elgar, 2013).
60. See UN Doc. A/HRC/8/5 at para. 52.
61. 'Guiding Principles on Business and Human Rights: Implementing the United Nations "Protect, Respect and Remedy" Framework', (GP), http://www.ohchr.org/Documents/Issues/Business/A-HRC-17-31_AEV.pdf (accessed 6 February 2014).
62. See GP 12.
63. Muchlinski asserts that several important human rights instruments in the context of business operations, for example, Convention for the Elimination of all forms of Discrimination Against Women (CEDAW) are not caught by the framework, P. Muchlinski, 'Implementing the New UN Corporate Human Rights Framework: Implications for Corporate Law, Governance and Regulation', *Business Ethics Quarterly* 22 (2012): 145 at 148.
64. See Ruggie *Just Business*, 20–3, 96.
65. http://www.oecd.org/newsroom/newoecdguidelinestoprotecthumanrightsandsocialdevelopment.htm
66. http://ec.europa.eu/enterprise/policies/sustainable-business/corporate-social-responsibility/human-rights/
67. S. Atler, 'The Impact of the United Nations Secretary-General's Special Representative and the UN Framework on the Development of the Human Rights Components of ISO 26000', *Corporate Social Responsibility Initiative Working Paper No. 64* (Cambridge, MA: John F. Kennedy School of Government, Harvard University, 2011).
68. See IFC Performance Standards on Environmental and Social Sustainability, January 2012, http://www.ifc.org/wps/wcm/connect/115482804a0255db96fbffd1a5d13d27/PS_English_2012_Full-Document.pdf?MOD=AJPERES (accessed 30 September 2014).
69. A. Rasche, '"A Necessary Supplement": What the United Nations Global Compact Is and Is Not', *Business and Society* 48 (2009): 511.

70. Macdonald recasts sphere of influence into 'sphere of responsibility' built around an idea of agent-centred responsibility for harm mediated through others. This has the potential to encourage the changing of harmful business practices and the adoption of improved business practices as distinct actions in their own right where the corporation was not the primary actor, see K. Macdonald, 'Re-thinking "Spheres of Responsibility": Business Responsibility for Indirect Harm', *Journal of Business Ethics* 99 (2011): 549.
71. D. Kinley, J. Nolan and N. Zerial, 'The Politics of Corporate Social Responsibility: Reflections on the United Nations Human Rights Norms for Corporations', *Company and Securities Law Journal* (2007): 30 at 37.
72. The possibilities for a leveraged-based responsibility is offered in S. Wood, 'The Case for Leverage-Based Corporate Human Rights Responsibility', *Business Ethics Quarterly* 22 (2012): 63. An equally rigorous case for a narrower view of the ambit of responsibility can be found in J. Douglas-Bishop, 'The Limits of Corporate Human Rights Obligations and the Rights of For-Profit Corporations', in *Business and Human Rights*, ed. W. Cragg (Cheltenham, UK: Edward Elgar, 2012), 74.
73. See UN Doc. A/HRC/8/5 at paras 68–9.
74. A real commitment to leverage would see the Ruggie architecture suggest that the largest or most financially powerful corporate actors should have a wider purview of human rights responsibility that causes them to think in a global sense about what the effect of particular business activities might be, see M. Dowell-Jones and D. Kinley, 'Minding the Gap: Global Finance and Human Rights', *Ethics and International Affairs* 25 (2011): 183.
75. See http://www.globalwitness.org/hsbc
76. See http://www.globalwitness.org/library/open-letter-sarawak-chief-minister-taib-mahmud-accepting-offer-debate-land-and-forest-use
77. The challenge of engaging the finance industry in what respect for human rights means is set out by Dowell-Jones in 'Financial Institutions and Human Rights', *Human Rights Law Review* 13 (2013): 423.
78. See UN Doc. A/HRC/8/5 at para. 56.
79. Report of the Special Representative of the UN Secretary-General on the Issue of Human Rights, and Transnational Corporations and Other Business Enterprises. Business and Human Rights: Further Steps Towards the Operationalization of the 'Protect, Respect and Remedy' Framework, 9 April 2010. UN Doc. A/HRC/14/27 at para. 80.
80. See UN Doc. A/HRC/8/5 at para. 60.
81. Ibid., at para. 61.
82. J. Ruggie, 'The Construction of the UN "Protect, Respect and Remedy" Framework for Business and Human Rights: The True Confessions of a Principled Pragmatist', *European Human Rights Law Review* (2011): at 131.
83. See UN Doc. A/HRC/8/5 at para. 62.
84. See ibid., at para. 63.
85. J. Ames, 'Taking Responsibility', *European Lawyer* (2011): 15.
86. For a review of possible positions on this point see D. Arnold, 'Transnational Corporations and the Duty to Respect Basic Human Rights', *Business Ethics Quarterly* 20 (2010): 371; and W. Cragg, 'Ethics, Enlightened Self-Interest, and the Corporate Responsibility to Respect Human Rights: A Critical Look at the Justificatory Foundations of the UN Framework', *Business Ethics Quarterly* 22 (2012): 9.
87. B. Kytle and J. Ruggie, 'Corporate Social Responsibility as Risk Management: A Model for Multinationals', *Corporate Social Responsibility Initiative Working Paper No. 10* (Cambridge, MA: John F Kennedy School of Government, Harvard University, 2005).
88. B. Horrigan, *Corporate Social Responsibility in the 21st Century* (Cheltenham, UK: Edward Elgar, 2010), at 323–5.
89. For a discussion of this point see C. Lopez, 'The "Ruggie Process": From Legal Obligations to Corporate Social Responsibility?', in *Human Rights Obligations of Business*, ed. S. Deva and D. Bilchitz (Cambridge: Cambridge University Press, 2013), 58.
90. See UN Doc. A/HRC/8/5 at paras 54–61.
91. Business and Human Rights: Towards Operationalising the 'Protect, Respect and Remedy' Framework. UN Doc A/HRC/11/13 at paras 46–9.

92. T. Büthe and W. Mattli, 'International Standards and Standard-Setting Bodies', in *The Oxford Handbook of Business and Government*, ed. D. Coen, W. Grant and G. Wilson (Oxford: Oxford University Press, 2010), 440 at 455f.
93. S. Bernstein and B. Cashore, 'Can Non-State Global Governance be Legitimate? An Analytical Framework', *Regulation and Governance* 1 (2007): 347.
94. D. Vogel, 'Taming Globalization', in *The Oxford Handbook of Business and Government*, ed. D. Coen, W. Grant and G. Wilson (Oxford: Oxford University Press, 2010), 472.
95. There is an extensive debate as to whether a positive CSR profile improves corporate financial performance. There are numerous studies on this with some looking at particular CSR activities such as corporate charitable giving and others looking at a corporation's total CSR portfolio. It seems that CSR does not have a negative impact on financial performance and in some cases can be shown to have a positive one, see P. van Buerden and T. Gössling, 'The Worth of Values – A Literature Review on the Relation between Corporate Social and Financial Performance', *Journal of Business Ethics* 82 (2008): 407; and A. Carroll and K. Shabana, 'The Business Case for Corporate Social Responsibility: A Review of Concepts, Research and Practice', *International Journal of Management Reviews* 12 (2010): 85. More worrying is the finding contained in S. Scalet and T. Kelly, 'CSR Rating Agencies: What is their Global Impact', *JBE* 94 (2010): 69, that being omitted from a particular rating index or certificate programme because of poor performance does not lead to an improved corporate performance in the future but to a greater emphasis on other more positive CSR stories.
96. R. Mayes, B. Pini and P. McDonald, 'Corporate Social Responsibility and the Parameters of Dialogue with Vulnerable Others', *Organization* 20 (2013): 840.
97. R. McCorquodale, 'Corporate Social Responsibility and International Human Rights Law', *Journal of Business Ethics* 87 (2009): 391.
98. N. Jackson and P. Carter, 'Organizational Chiaroscuro: Throwing Light on the Concept of Corporate Governance', *Human Relations* 48 (1995): 875.
99. J. Conley and C. Williams, 'Engage, Embed and Embellish: Theory versus Practice in the Corporate Social Responsibility Movement', *Journal of Corporate Law* 31 (2005–2006): 1.
100. S. Zadek, *The Civil Corporation* (London: Earthscan, 2001); and S. Zadek, 'The Path to Corporate Responsibility', *Harvard Business Review* (December 2004).
101. Stage models of CSR development pre-date Zadek, see P. Sethi, 'Dimensions of Corporate Social Performance: An Analytical Framework', *California Management Review* 75 (1975): 58. For a more modern example see A. Warhurst, 'Past, Present and Future Corporate Responsibility: Achievements and Aspirations', in *The Responsible Corporation in Global Economy*, ed. C. Crouch and C. Maclean (Oxford: Oxford University Press, 2011): 55–83.
102. B. Holzer, *Moralizing the Corporation* (Cheltenham, UK: Edward Elgar, 2010), 94–6.
103. J. Owen and D. Kemp, 'Social Licence and Mining: A Critical Perspective', *Resources Policy* 38 (2013): 29 at 33.
104. N. Gunningham, R. Kagan and D. Thornton, 'Social License and Environmental Protection: Why Businesses Go Beyond Compliance', *Law and Social Inquiry* 29 (2004): 307.
105. Ibid., 308.
106. J. Owen and D. Kemp, 'Social Licence and Mining: A Critical Perspective', *Resources Policy* 38 (2013): 31.
107. J. Howard-Grenville, J. Nash and C. Coglianese, 'Constructing the License to Operate: Internal Factors and Their Influence on Corporate Environmental Decisions', *Law and Policy* 30 (2008): 73, provide a fantastic account of intrafirm factors that influence the fate of the social licence. Their account deserves much more attention than it is possible to give it here. A summary of the factors that they identify with the supporting evidence for them can be found at p. 80.
108. Of course there may be other external factors at play in valuing reputation, such as the position taken on it by debt and equity finance, but importance of this position has to be calculated by corporate executives based upon their own internal view of things. What shapes their view is the culture they operate in, see J. Howard-Grenville, 'Inside the "Black Box": How Organizational Culture and Subcultures Inform Interpretations and Actions on Environmental Issues', *Organization & Environment* 19 (2006): 46.
109. D. Schön, *The Reflexive Practitioner* (New York: Basic Books, 1983), at 40.
110. http://www.icmm.com/document/3716 (accessed 2 February 2014).
111. http://www.australiancoal.com.au/social-licence-to-operate.html (accessed 2 February 2014).

112. http://www.minerals.org.au/file_upload/files/resources/enduring_value/EV_GuidanceForImplementation_July2005.pdf (accessed 2 February 2014).
113. For example, Anglo American PLC, http://www.angloamerican.com/~/media/Files/A/Anglo-American-Plc/reports/annual-report-2013/AA-SDR-2803.pdf (accessed 31 January 2014); and Lonmin PLC, http://sd-report.lonmin.com/2013/home (accessed 31 January 2014).
114. S. Bice, 'What Gives You a Social Licence? An Exploration of the Social Licence to Operate in the Australian Mining Industry', *Resources* (2014): 62.
115. E. Salim, *Striking a Better Balance: Extractive Industries Review: The World Bank Group and Extractive Industries (Volume 1)* (Washington, DC: World Bank, 2003).
116. J. Prno and D. Slocombe, 'Exploring the Origins of "Social Licence to Operate" in the Mining Sector: Perspectives from Governance and Sustainability Theories', *Resources Policy* 37 (2012): 346.
117. Gunningham, Kagan and Thornton, 'Social License and Environmental Protection', 332–6.
118. O. Ololade and H. Annegarn, 'Contrasting Community and Corporate Perceptions of Sustainability: A Case Study within the Platinum Mining Region of South Africa', *Resources Policy* 38 (2013): 568.
119. R. Howitt and R. Lawrence, 'Indigenous Peoples, Corporate Social Responsibility and the Fragility of the Interpersonal Domain', in *Earth Matters*, ed. C. O'Faircheallaigh and S. Ali (Sheffield: Greenleaf Publishing, 2008), 83.
120. R. Hamann, 'Is Corporate Citizenship Making a Difference?', *Journal of Corporate Citizenship* 4 (2007): 15.
121. The UN Declaration on the Rights of Indigenous Peoples, article 32 of which enshrines free, prior and informed consent as the standard to be applied to protect the land rights of indigenous communities, is endorsed by 148 states, but without host state recognition of actual land rights and claims competing claims to preservation and wider development are likely to conflict, see B. Haalboom, 'The Intersection of Corporate Social Responsibility Guidelines and Indigenous Rights: Examining Neoliberal Governance of a Proposed Mining Project in Suriname', *Geoforum* 43 (2012): 969.
122. In 2006, early in his mandate, Ruggie presented an interim report which focused on 65 cases of corporate abuses of human rights drawn from 27 countries, see *Promotion and Protection of Human Rights*, Interim Report of the Special Representative of the Secretary-General on the Issue of Human Rights and Transnational Corporations and Other Business Enterprises, 22 February 2006, E/CN.4/2006/97.
123. See 'Guiding Principles on Business and Human Rights: Implementing the United Nations "Protect, Respect and Remedy" Framework', GPs 17–21.
124. For an account of some HRIAs that have been conducted by corporate actors in relation to very specific activities see J. Harrison, 'Measuring Human Rights: Reflections on the Practice of Human Rights Impact Assessment and Lessons for the Future', *Warwick School of Law Research Paper No. 2010/26*, November 2010, http://ssrn.com/abstract=1706742
125. T. Maassarani, M. Tatgenhorst Drakos and J. Pajkowska, 'Extracting Corporate Responsibility: Towards a Human Rights Impact Assessment', *Cornell International Law Journal* 40 (2007): 135 at 144–50.
126. A.M. Esteves, D. Franks and F. Vanclay, 'Social Impact Assessment: The State of the Art', *Impact Assessment and Project Appraisal* 30 (2012): 34.
127. D. Kemp and F. Vanclay, 'Human Rights and Impact Assessment: Clarifying the Connections in Practice', *Impact Assessment and Project Appraisal* 31 (2013): 86.
128. See 'Guiding Principles on Business and Human Rights: Implementing the United Nations "Protect, Respect and Remedy" Framework', the supporting commentary to GP 18.
129. Cragg, 'Ethics, Enlightened Self-Interest, and the Corporate Responsibility to Respect Human Rights', 14.
130. S. Barrientos and S. Smith, 'Do Workers Benefit from Ethical Trade? Assessing Codes of Labour Practice in Global Production Systems', *Third World Quarterly* 28 (2007): 713.
131. O. Borial, 'Corporate Greening Through ISO 14001: A Rational Myth?', *Organization Science* 18 (2007): 127.
132. N. Andrew, M. Wickham, W. O'Donohue and F. Danzinger, 'Presenting a Core-Periphery Model of Voluntary CSR Disclosure in Australian Annual Report', *Corporate Ownership and Control* 9 (2012): 438.

133. See M. Delmas and V. Burbano, 'The Drivers of Greenwashing', *California Management Review* 54 (2011): 64; and I. Alves, 'Green Spin Everywhere: How Greenwashing Reveals the Limits of the CSR Paradigm', *Journal of Global Change and Governance* 2 (2009): 1.
134. K. Salcito, J. Utzinger, M. Weiss et al., 'Assessing Human Rights Impacts in Corporate Development Projects', *Environmental Impact Assessment Review* 42 (2013): 39.
135. J. Harrison, 'Human Rights Measurement: Reflections on the Current Practice and Future Potential of Human Rights Impact Assessment', *Journal of Human Rights Practice* 3 (2011): 162 at 172.
136. For concerns about the accuracy and quality of what is released in existing governance environments see A. Fonesca, 'How Credible are Mining Corporations' Sustainability Reports? A Critical Analysis of External Assurance under the Requirements of the International Council on Mining and Metals', *Corporate Social Responsibility and Environmental Management* 17 (2010): 355.
137. Ruggie, *Just Business*, 68–77.
138. J. Harrison, 'Establishing a Meaningful Human Rights Due Diligence Process for Corporations: Learning from Experience of Human Rights Impact Assessment', *Impact Assessment and Project Appraisal* 31 (2013): 107 at 114.
139. L. Fransen, 'Why do Private Governance Organizations not Converge? A Political-Institutional Analysis of Transnational Labor Standards Regulation', *Governance* 24 (2011): 359.
140. UN Doc. A/HRC/8/5.
141. See for example http://www.unpri.org, http://www.ceres.org, http://www.incr.com, http://www.iigcc.org. While this is not a point to be taken here, there is a distinction drawn in investment practice between responsible ownership and socially responsible investment, now rather better known as ethical investing.
142. S. Viviers, 'Is Responsible Investing Ethical?', *South Africa Journal of Business Management* 39 (2008): 15. Co-operative Financial Service figures for 2009 (constructed using information from the Investment Management Association and the British Bankers Association) place the amount of money held in ethical financial instruments at £19.2 billion up from £5.2 billion in 1999. Although showing strong growth, this figure represents only 1.8% of the amounts held in UK-based financial instruments.
143. Harrison, 'Establishing a Meaningful Human Rights Due Diligence Process for Corporations', 113.
144. http://www.riotinto.com/annualreport2013/_pdfs/rio-tinto-2013-strategic-report.pdf (accessed 28 March 2014).
145. See n. 4.
146. T. Melish and E. Meidinger, 'Protect, Respect, Remedy *and Participate*: "New Governance" Lessons for the Ruggie Framework', in *The UN Guiding Principles on Business and Human Rights: Foundations and Implementation*, ed. R. Mares (The Netherlands: Brill, 2011), 303.
147. I. Nooruddin and S. Wilson Sokhey, 'Credible Certification of Child Labor Free Production', in *The Credibility of Transnational NGOs*, ed. P. Gourevitch, D. Lake and J. Gross Stein (Cambridge: Cambridge University Press, 2012), 62.
148. S. Starobin and E. Weinthal, 'The Search for Credible Information in Social and Environmental Global Governance', *Business and Politics* 12 (2010): 1.
149. J. Hendry, 'Taking Aim at Business: What Factors Lead Environmental Non-Governmental Organizations to Target Particular Firms?', *Business and Society* 45 (2006): 45.
150. P. Gourevitch and D. Lake, 'Beyond Virtue: Evaluating and Enhancing the Credibility of Non-governmental Organizations', in *The Credibility of Transnational NGOs*, ed. Gourevitch, Lake and Gross Stein, at 3f.
151. M. Yaziji and J. Doh, *NGOs and Corporations* (Cambridge: Cambridge University Press, 2009), at 57–73.

These are financial times: a human rights perspective on the UK financial services sector

Manette Kaisershot and Samuel Prout

Human Rights Consortium, School of Advanced Study, University of London, UK

This article explores the relationship between finance, financial institutions and human rights in an increasingly financialised world. Though developments have been made in human rights with respect to business, particularly with the United Nations' endorsement of UN Special Representative John Ruggie's *Guiding Principles in Business and Human Rights*, there remains a dearth of research into the ways that, specifically, the financial industry maligns human rights worldwide. This article bolsters discussion of the financial sector, human rights and the government and explores how these organisations, specifically in the United Kingdom and United States context, exploit the defuse nature of their operations and the lax government regulations on the financial industry to ensure the continuing prosperity of the financial and business world to the detriment of human rights.

1. Introduction

The United Kingdom (UK) has a large and active financial services industry. Over the decade prior to the financial collapse of 2008, financial services[1] grew twice as much as the rest of the UK economy.[2] The House of Commons Library's report on the financial services sector's contribution to the UK economy suggests that 9.4% of nationwide gross value added is attributable to the financial sector.[3] The financial services sector is the largest contributor to the UK economy, the second largest being other business services.[4] Financial services are the largest UK export, bringing valuable international investment into the UK's economy.

In addition to having a large financial sector on which they are economically reliant, the UK has also signed and ratified six major United Nations (UN) conventions on human rights.[5] These agreements are legally binding in theory, although suffer greatly from a lack of enforceability. Acceding to these international agreements clearly states the UK's commitment to pursue a human rights agenda. Due to the relative strength of the UK's financial sector, and its disproportionate reliance on financial services for national income, the UK serves as an excellent example for a discussion on the financial services industry, financial services regulation, and the implications these have for human rights.

Due to this developed reliance on professional services, and financial services in particular, the financial crisis of 2008 hit the UK economy hard and highlighted the country's budget deficit and relaxed approach to financial regulation. Despite government intervention to alleviate the impact of the economic turmoil and return to positive growth, the aftermath of the crisis can still be felt even though, as the UK approaches a general election, much is being made in the media of a positive recovery (in house prices and gross domestic product (GDP) growth).[6] That recovery has been cautioned as too reliant on house prices[7] and predictions abound that the economic stagnation being experienced in the 'developed' economies could continue for, potentially, another decade or beyond.[8] The UK remains heavily reliant on financial services.

The blame for the prolonged period of economic stagnation has been placed partially on badly prescribed policies,[9] however the actions of governments towards financial services before, during and after the financial crisis would suggest that the policies were not simply short-sighted, but were, in fact, intended to promote the financial sector and foster an attractive environment for its development (for, as Joseph Stiglitz says, the economic crisis was something that was allowed to happen).[10] This article seeks to demonstrate that despite the UK being a signatory to all the aforementioned conventions (and many others; perhaps too numerous to name) the actions of policymakers in fact suggest that business interests are better protected by policy and law[11] than any of the purported human rights enshrined in those treaties and covenants.

2. Overlooking of economic, social and cultural rights

Of perhaps obvious relevance to a discussion of financial services' impact on human rights is the emerging raft of research on economic, social and cultural rights (ESC). These rights, whilst perhaps providing some obvious foundations for a rights-impact assessment of macroeconomic or financial activities, have not always been afforded the recognition that other, more 'traditional' rights have enjoyed in higher-level academic, legal and political discourse.

Jeremy Sarkin and Mark Koenig, in their research on the right to work, discuss overlooked and underdeveloped economic rights.

> Developmental narratives of specific human rights have, in most cases, been carefully explored for most fundamental civil and political rights. These so-called first generation rights are still deemed by many the apex of a hierarchy, and thus more worthy of protection relative to other rights.[12]

In the West there is a historic argument that ESC rights conflict with the capitalist model on which Western states have built their empires.[13] This conflict of interest is perhaps why ESC rights have historically been given less attention than civil and political (CP) rights and the definitions of ESC rights remain less specific than those of CP rights.[14] The International Covenant on Economic, Social, and Cultural Rights (ICESCR) and the Committee on Economic, Social, and Cultural Rights (CESCR) left the discretion of defining and enacting these rights to the state. Diane Elson explains that this discretion is to recognise that ESC matters vary widely from state to state and, thus, need to be decided at the state level, which is by no means an excuse to ignore the obligations of the state to realise ESC rights.[15] The prioritising of CP rights is a common theme in human rights discourse,[16] but the distinction between the two sets of rights seems artificial and, as it is often noted, is largely motivated by political and economic considerations.

Studies of the interdependence and indivisibility of ESC rights and CP rights reveal that both sets of rights need equal recognition for basic rights realisation to occur.[17] When considering the achievement of so-called 'basic rights', the means to achieving CP rights are tied up in ESC rights in such a way that both 'sets' of rights need to happen concurrently for lasting advancements in either 'set' of rights to be made. As Lanse Minkler and Shawna Sweeney observe: '[o]ne cannot enjoy subsistence rights if one is not also free from murder, just as one cannot enjoy security rights if one has starved to death'.[18] Not only are ESC rights underdeveloped, but the nature of rights means that ESC and CP rights are interrelated, so that the retardation of development in one area will have a substantive effect on the development and enjoyment of rights in other areas.

Some have suggested that the West has struggled to make progress in this area and go so far as to state that any perceived realisation of ESC rights is a 'Western myth'.[19] With the emergence of corporate social responsibility (CSR) as a means of advancing (or seeming to advance) human rights globally there is a feeling, amongst some scholars and activists, that progress to secure rights is being made[20] but some recent literature argues that in fact global inequality is increasing at an alarming rate.[21] While disadvantaged communities in some countries may look superficially better off (perhaps because they own a television, a smart phone, or a pair of Nike trainers[22]) when their wealth is compared to the global wealth distribution they are, in fact, in a worse place now than they would have been 10 or 20 (or more) years ago.[23]

ESC rights can seem less compelling and unethical practices in the financial services industry, for example, may seem trivial if we consider that people in many countries still face starvation, torture, disenfranchisement, murder and rape as a daily reality. As explained above, however, the two forms of rights are interconnected and ESC rights, for all the benefits they add to this discussion, are not the extent to which high finance, regulation and economic policy engage with a consideration of human rights. The impact of aggressive financial services activity impacts upon the more 'traditional', basic human rights and fundamental equalities. Not only do business practices in these areas directly or indirectly disadvantage groups of people for the profit of others (a consequence of zero-sum financial markets) but government intervention to protect and promote financial services also benefits classes of people by transferring its cost onto a far-greater majority. The financial crisis has directed renewed attention to the gulf between those who enjoy a great deal of wealth and those who do not. This is thrown into particular relief in the UK given the prominence and privilege enjoyed by the financial services sector.

The difficulty in this area is that causal links tying the activities of businesses to human rights abuses are often not particularly obvious.[24] While conclusions can be drawn establishing that decisions that the financial services sector makes, and the policies and laws that governments put in place to protect those decisions, can do a great deal to malign the rights, both ESC and CP, of people worldwide, proving and regulating these practices is much more difficult. Contributing to the lack of direct causal links between the financial industry and human rights abuses it is often the case that the abuses occur across national borders, which eliminates almost all available agency in redressing rights abuses.[25] The curtailing of human rights as a result of financial services practices, however, is not reserved for people working at the bottom of the supply chain.

3. Inequality

Inequality is said to have been increasing over the last quarter of a century, and its effects can be felt in a myriad of ways. Ed Howker and Shiv Malik, for example, use educational funding as the main argument in their analysis of inequality increasing in the UK. In their book on student debt in Britain, Howker and Malik state that 'when unemployment becomes focused on the generation that should be driving the economy, they cannot fuel growth'[26]; it should be blindingly obvious that inequality serves no one well.

Students are taking on more and more student debt, but the potential for earning is decreasing. The current levels of high-unemployment amongst young people in the West mean that even those students with university qualifications are struggling to find work. The burden of debt is enormous on the UK's 'jilted generation' (which Howker and Malik define as those born in the late 1970s or after)[27] and yet this is the generation that will be responsible for supporting an economy with an unprecedented number of pensioners.[28] As Stiglitz observes, student debt is a great perpetuator of inequality.[29] In addition to persistent unemployment and mounting student debt, the 'jilted generation' will not make the same salaries as their parents' generation, nor will they be able to retire as soon,[30] or live as long. In this way, mounting student debt, unemployment and stagnant wages might well have repercussions for the economy as a whole and will impact future generations.

Inequality is the prevailing theme of Thomas Piketty's *Capital in the Twenty-First Century*, which was published in early 2014 to much popular acclaim.[31] Piketty, through historical and empirical economic analysis, shows how inequality, which was decreasing after the turn of the twentieth century, is again on the rise. Piketty also links the increase in economic inequality to its current outrageous level in the US to political agendas in the 1980s and the prevalence of neo-conservative economic policies.[32] Piketty makes further strong observations regarding inherited wealth, which he finds returning to the level experienced in the times of Balzac and Austen. He identifies an elite group of wealthy heirs[33] whose capital will accumulate more wealth, purely by virtue of its existence.[34] As Stiglitz points out, many of the wealthiest people alive now owe their wealth to inheritance, which is a quite significant indicator of levels of inequality.[35] Stiglitz also points to inequality and, importantly, dysfunctional financial systems, as two factors that are contributing to a prolonged economic slowdown post the 2008 crisis[36] in both the US and the Eurozone. This ever-increasing disparity of wealth, if not corrected, will have enormous future impacts on the social, economic and political wellbeing of various people.[37]

4. The effect of inequality on human rights

Inequality has an obvious effect on human rights, which manifests in a multitude of different ways. Piya Mahtaney focuses on the effects that inequality – and the policies that uphold inequality – have on driving growth and sustainable development.[38] Of concern is that many policies have not focused on supporting the poor and marginalised, particularly those subsistence farmers who rely on agriculture for their very means of survival but whose livelihoods are not protected or enhanced by the many so-called assistance programmes in place the world over.

> The large-scale capital-intensive model of agriculture production is clearly unsuited to the conditions and requirements of the agrarian economy in poorer nations. The few beneficiaries of the gains that arise from this are outweighed considerably by the employment that it hardly creates, the poverty that it does not mitigate and even worsens, and the corrupt rent-seeking political class that it fosters.[39]

As an example, between 2008 and 2011 rising prices of food drove the increasing costs of food imports, pushing 126 million people below the poverty line (in this case the poverty line is defined as living on less than $2 a day). When the price of food rises, the demand for certain goods (such as staples like corn or fat) remains the same, but the portion of income allocated to obtaining those essentials increases – as does revenue from selling these goods. For the poor these rises in price hugely affect their income distribution and allow them less money to spend on other goods, while the wealthy and their income distribution remain mostly unaffected by the price changes to staple goods. Mahtaney reports that when prices dropped after the period (2008–2011) the food prices in low-income, food-deficit countries did not experience a corresponding drop. What can be surmised here is that the drop in prices must have benefited those who could easily afford to purchase life's essentials (particularly the world's most affluent class of people), while the poorest and most vulnerable continued to struggle. That prices have failed to fall to their pre-2008 trends has thereby wiped out any advancements that may have been made in this area prior to 2008.

Mahtaney, like Piketty, points out the return to a system by which those with a great deal of wealth can amass even more by doing little other than holding onto their wealth. The rich-get-richer social-economic construct, with a very wealthy asset-holding upper class and a rent-beholden lower class, echoes conditions in medieval Europe by which land and resources were owned by a few select individuals and institutions. The foundations for such uneven distribution of wealth were laid, as stated previously, in the 1980s return to conservative politics in America and the UK, and the results came into sharp focus in the economic crisis of 2008. The crisis, and subsequent austerity policies in the West, have severely enhanced and will severely prolong the wealth disparity that has been deepening since the 1980s. There is a great deal of consensus amongst scholars, economists and commentators of other kinds of bad policy; policy that does not properly address the root causes of inequality, or policy that does not seek to serve the most vulnerable amongst the population is a key factor in the current state of the world. If social and economic policies are not amended then it is highly likely that the post-crisis conditions experienced at present, and the wealth divide driving global inequality, will persist for years or decades to come.[40]

Inequality has also been fostered by state policies which do not adequately consider the human rights effect of policy changes. As Elson demonstrates[41] in her breakdown of the UK budget deficit policy, the austerity measures the UK took to compensate for the huge deficit the government faced after the financial crisis of 2008 failed to meet the UK's obligations under the CESCR. According to Elson, the austerity measures meant that hundreds of thousands of children would be living in poverty in the UK[42]; the austerity measures disproportionally affected women, especially single mothers.[43] Austerity in the UK had a limiting effect not just on social provisions for housing, food, health and mental health care but also on legal aid, educational funding for higher education (not to mention higher tuition fees), infrastructure repair, and research and development funding. Away from services provided by the public sector, the impact of the financial crisis has meant reduced access to credit for many people (many of whom rely on borrowed money to provide their basic needs such as housing, food and power), rising inflation and stagnant wages, increases in taxes (such as VAT; which cut off resources and cause financial strain on the general public), and many of the people who have borne the brunt of these changes were not active participants in the market that caused the financial crisis.

As Elson aptly points out, part of a state's duty to acknowledge and realise ESC rights is to not engage in any policy that would be considered retrogressive.[44]

> An example of a potentially retrogressive measure would be cuts to expenditures on public services that are critical for realization of economic and social rights; or cuts to taxes that are critical for funding such services.[45]

The measures outlined above can be seen to be retrogressive in the achievement of rights and no reasonable justification was given by the state to its people – a violation of the terms and obligations as stated in the CESCR. Not to mention that the financial crisis and subsequent credit crunch and fiscal deficit were the reasons why austerity measures were put in place. In addition to limiting people's access to their human rights, the burden of these austerity measures falls mostly on those who are paid average salaries and rely on public sector services. For those who can afford to be educated privately, access private health care, and employ creative professional services to help offset their tax burdens, the cost of austerity has been somewhat cushioned. The burden of these measures is therefore felt most by those who can least afford it, and the wealth gap is consequently expanded.

Mahtaney points to the lack of education and the lack of research and development funding as two key issues on the path to creating a sustainable system of economic development.[46] The UK's austerity programmes have seen a reduction in government funding in both of these areas. Stiglitz[47] points out that spending on industrial infrastructure projects is a viable way of crawling out of the current economic slump (a point Mahtaney also makes[48]); with much of the old regime of industry (namely manufacturing) being performed largely outside of Western economies, the West should concentrate on services, like health care and education, to revitalise the economy. Austerity in the UK has seen a reduction, as aforementioned, in education (at all levels) and also in spending in the health care sector.

At the root of all the issues of inequality, of all the myriad of contributing factors to the growing increases in poverty and the loss of rights, is wealth (or the lack of wealth). It is clear from the way policy and global market movements affect the distribution of wealth and all that wealth brings that access to it has a huge bearing on rights. Dowell-Jones and Kinley state:

> [h]uman rights do, of course, have distinctive qualities: they are essential minimum standards, and are backed by purportedly enforceable legal obligations. At their core, however, they are fundamentally matters of welfare. As such, human rights are intimately tied up with the economic health of the state […].[49]

Dowell-Jones and Kinley mention minimum standards, which do need to be delineated and enforced, as well as temporarily revised, because human rights are fundamentally a matter of welfare. Welfare is a physical state – as well as a psychological one – which is why the inequality discussion is so relevant because it is also concerns where people perceive the minimum to be. Dowell-Jones and Kinley also state the need for human rights to engage with finance; prior to the crisis there had been a lack of this type of discourse. Finance and the structures and mechanisms used by the financial services sector have had a huge and costly effect on human rights, as demonstrated by the crisis of 2008. The connection between business, finance and human rights has not gone unnoticed by the wider public, and popular nonfiction, newspaper editorials, and even senior human rights lawyers have commented on the impacts the economic crisis has had on human rights.[50]

It is not sufficient to wait for the development of ESC rights to catch up with political rights protection before financial services and economic policy are subjected to a critical analysis from a human rights perspective. In fact, disagreement over which rights should be preferred is, in the view of this article, neither helpful nor productive. Rather than competing for which rights should be considered first, efforts should be directed towards ensuring that rights are a first consideration, whether those rights could be sub-classified as political, individual, economic or cultural.

That is somewhat easier said than done, and, as in many areas of business and human rights, identifying where the human rights impact of financial services activity actually occurs requires a far more nuanced analysis. There are some examples which show where the decisions of financial services firms – or the actions of government in promoting their financial services sectors – have directly curtailed individuals' access to rights. While some of these examples are stark, they are frequently anecdotal and distinctively narrative. This area of research would benefit greatly from quantitative, directly verifiable examples of rights infringement, if only to bring this area of study to the attention of finance and economics academics.

5. Financial decisions and human rights in context

One of the more popularly referenced examples of financial services firms playing a direct role in individuals' enjoyment of their human rights involves speculative activity in food pricing.[51] In speculative commodity trading, professional services firms buy, sell and exchange real commodities (for example, grains, fuels and meats) or the promise of these real commodities amongst themselves. These commodity trading companies are amongst the biggest in the world (see, for example, Glencore[52]) and large financial services firms employ teams who advise, broker and even directly engage in these speculative activities themselves (see, for example, Barclays,[53] Goldman Sachs[54] and Macquarie[55]).

The past decade has seen a dramatic increase in the volume and purpose of commercial speculation in agricultural commodities,[56] with institutional investors buying and selling positions in agricultural futures for profit, rather than (as traditionally was the case) to hedge against changes in physical market values. Media[57] and non-governmental organisations[58] have linked the recent global increase in food prices to excessive speculation by financial institutions, although it should be stated that empirical evidence to prove this connection establishes correlation rather than causation.

Unlike many financial derivatives, agricultural commodity prices actually have the potential to be life-threatening: inflating physical food prices and restricting supplies to those who cannot compete with institutional investors when it comes to winning bids on contracts for basic foodstuffs. Unconvinced, however, the European Commission reports that there appears to be no link between speculation and price rises or increasing volatility in food prices,[59] despite the correlation between massive growth in agricultural commodity prices and increasing investor interest in agricultural commodities since the early 2000s. It does seem that this is an area in need of more detailed research, particularly research mindful of the human rights implication of rising food prices.

The European Commission response optimistically suggests that rising agricultural commodity prices are perhaps not entirely a bad thing, and explain that the price rise in food may be due to a short-lived competition with using crops for biofuels, which are also staple foodstuffs.[60] This does raise the interesting argument about how agricultural land is purposed (according to financial incentives, for example government subsidies, rather than according to real world demand) and provides a helpful emerging link between the empirical study of finance and economics and the qualitative analysis of social science and human rights. The companies involved in these activities, although global in reach, have headquartered themselves in well-financialised Western economies (predominantly the UK, Switzerland and the US), and the toll of higher food prices broadly fell on those, as described above, who had to allocate a far greater share of their daily income to buying food as a result (and who mostly lived outside the financialised West).

Companies being held accountable for their actions wherever the actions take place seems recently to have been rolled back, not rolled out. The conventions on human rights have become a smokescreen for *less* corporate accountability (the repeal of Glass-Steagal,[61] the end of Alien Tort[62]). Corporations aggressively seek profit and are encouraged to do so by financial policy and government budgets. Governments increasingly prioritise growth and subsidise, incentivise or promote high-growth industries (for example, in the UK recently, technology, financial services and luxury goods). In promoting these industries governments implicitly mandate an 'at all costs' business model, incentivising corporations to pursue aggressive or negligent tactics in order to continue to enjoy tax breaks, low-regulation and access to government decision makers.[63]

There are numerous illustrative examples of how financial and economic decisions affect human rights. The links, however, are not direct, which has the effect of somewhat obscuring responsibility.[64] Take, for instance, the Foxconn factory in China.[65] Foxxconn is a Taiwanese-owned company whose factories in China manufacture technological parts for tech companies, Apple being the most high profile of these. In 2010 there were numerous cases of workers at these factories committing suicide – the working conditions found in the factories were blamed for the rash of deaths. The conditions at Foxxconn included forced labour, unhealthy and dangerous factory conditions, no allowances for personal time, and no adequate remuneration (that is, workers were not paid a living wage). Additionally, Foxxconn employed armed guards at its factories to ensure that workers complied and did not attempt to escape. Clearly these conditions are in violation of even the most basic of human rights. After several suicides and subsequent media coverage, Foxxconn fixed nets to windows and stairwells so as to prevent further suicide attempts.[66]

Foxxconn makes Apple products. Apple is a registered company in the US, the US is a signatory to many of the same UN conventions as the UK which oblige a state to fulfil certain duties in protecting and developing human rights and, as such, should take responsibility for the situation even if China (who, incidentally, is also signatory to the ICESCR[67]) refuses to. UN treaties are supposed to be legally binding, despite the mechanisms for enforcing them being less than apparent. By a strict reading of the ICESCR, of course, the aforementioned conditions at the Foxxconn factories should be unlawful. It is sadly obvious from the continued abuse and neglect of these principles – not only those contained in the ICESCR but also in other UN treaties – that these supposed legally binding treaties and covenants have yet to become effective in enforcing the rights delineated within.

After actions had been taken by Apple to monitor the situation at the Foxxconn factories, more press coverage reported that there were subsequent deaths happening at Foxxconn.[68] After some investigation into the matter Apple announced that a 15-year-old boy, who had been working long hours of overtime, had died from other causes and not as a result of his working conditions. The official reports suggested the boy died in hospital from pneumonia but, using the same sort of logic applied to the working conditions of the poor in Victorian industrial England, Apple decided that the young man's death (from pneumonia, having worked in a factory with the aforementioned unhealthy and dangerous living conditions, owned by a company known to habitually force workers to work untold amounts of overtime) had in fact nothing to do with said working and living conditions.[69] The reaction from Apple was to assess the conditions at Foxxconn and to pressure them into making changes; however, they also continued to pressure Foxxconn to produce more goods, at a faster pace, to meet rising consumer demand.

A short-time later, Apple published press statements confirming that it was submitting to voluntary audits of the working conditions in factories to which it outsourced work.[70] Although a positive step, it was regrettable that such audits were not conducted at the start of its working relationship with Foxconn. Perhaps it would benefit major companies to include human rights assessments in their due diligence before they agree project financing, or submit for tendering or contracting processes – if only to avoid the embarrassment of having to answer questions on the subject of factory conditions later on.

The results of Apple's decision to submit to voluntary audits were a series of follow-up inspections of the Foxconn factories to confirm that conditions had improved[71]; 98% of the 'action items' highlighted in the initial audit had apparently been completed by July 2013.[72] The burden for remedying these 'action items' fell, of course, on the local factories overseen by Foxconn itself and allowed Apple to publish conscientious press statements to assure the public (not to mention investors) that it had taken decisive actions to rectify the situation. While Foxxconn should certainly be held responsible for its part in the violations, the pressures it is under come from far further afield (from Apple, and Apple's consumers, and international trade agreements providing for attractive industrial centres like China and India). The uncomfortable truth is that the demand for Apple's affordable, desirable and high-quality electronics is driven by consumers in the West,[73] many of whom are only too aware of the disparate levels of poverty worldwide.

Of course, providing firms comply with local employment laws, it is next-to impossible to link the activities of financial services corporations (headquartered, for example, in London, New York or Zurich) with overt human rights abuses. While it is more easy (as in the Apple example above) to link the activities of manufacturers, mineral extractors and heavy industry with neglectful or degrading practices, it is far more difficult to attribute responsibility for these actions to the financial services firms who encourage, oversee or influence these activities in their capacity as shareholders, advisors or outright managers.

6. Financialisation

Many rights violations are, in some way, extrapolated to be the result of a global trend towards financialisation.[74] Financialisation is a broad term, which generally attributes trends in corporate behaviour to an increasing pursuit of finance (here meaning the accumulation and exchange of money and investment) for its own sake; rather than (as was historically the case) positioning finance more broadly as a support service for production and trade.

According to Thomas I. Palley,

> [f]inancialization transforms the functioning of the economic system at both the macro and micro levels. Its principal impacts are to (1) elevate the significance of the financial sector relative to the real sector, (2) transfer income from the real sector to the financial sector, and (3) contribute to increased income inequality and wage stagnation.[75]

Given the predominance of financial institutions and financial goals in other industries, corporations have adopted common, aggressive strategies to deliver fuller balance sheets and attract greater investment. Joel Bakan[76] points out that the ever-present goal of profit maximisation in corporate decision-making turns human casualties into economic formulas.[77] Casualties in this sense may not always be deaths or serious injuries (as in industrial human rights abuse cases), but may be economic losses, such as mortgage repossessions and refusal of credit. In this way human concerns are placed second to financial concerns.

Incidentally, inequality has also been pinpointed as a common side effect of financialisation.[78] We saw above how speculation in food prices by investment banks and commodities traders (who seek profits from trading resources, but who have no use for the actual asset) has mirrored the global rise in food prices.

By its very nature, speculation in purely financial assets is a gamble – the outcome is uncertain and the sums of money involved can be immense. It is therefore extremely risky behaviour; it was the cause of the Wall Street Crash and subsequent Depression of 1929 in the US. But the very history of capitalism has its basis in financial innovation, which means that capitalist societies, and indeed any society that engages in heavy commerce and industry, give undue power to financiers,[79] which results in complicated and diverse financial products, inventions and transactions that are not always subjected to detailed impact assessments and are not always traded responsibly.

7. The 2008 financial crisis

In the late 2000s the banking system faced its biggest crisis since the Great Depression of the 1930s. The crisis was not only long-lasting but it exposed the interdependencies and fragilities shared across national economies around the world. Because of the amount of widely shared risk in the global marketplace and the speed at which financial markets now move, the crisis spread quickly and resulted in significant losses in a very short time. These losses were not as quickly repaired as they had been caused, and had consequences far beyond company balance sheets and pension statements.

In the aftermath of the crisis there were attempts made by many to investigate, understand and explain why this crisis happened and how to change the financial system in order to prevent another such crisis from happening. The cause of the crisis, it is generally agreed, started in the sub-prime mortgage lending market in the US. Although falling beyond the scope of this article, the proliferation of sub-prime lending in the US involved cynical and – in cases – malicious exploitation of low- or no-income consumers. The rights implications of those corporate actions deserve treatment of their own.

When the housing bubble in the US collapsed it revealed the way in which the financial sectors of developed nations are now intricately balanced and connected. In this way, a shock to one residential property market (in the US) brought down some of the world's biggest and most powerful economies, and caused banking crises as far away as mainland Europe. The defaults on these poorly managed and inappropriately assessed mortgages spread quickly to financial institutions with no direct interest in housing debt – a result of the rapid globalisation of financial securitisation since the mid-1980s.[80]

Securitisation involves repackaging underlying debts or obligations into some kind of financial product (this might take the form of an agreement between the parties to swap their debts or to negotiate repayment of one another's debts on some agreed date in the future) that can be bought and sold between market participants. By selling debts on, securities allow an individual or company to take on a debt, and then arrange for another individual or company to shoulder the burden of repayment. Securitisation is frequently used as a more liquid form of insurance (liquid as it can be bought and sold almost infinitely; the debt takes on a value of its own and selling it to someone else can even become profitable).

Newly devised securities can be exchanged, bought or sold by interested parties or individuals in the same way as many other structured financial products (like stocks, shares or bonds). Securitisation is not necessarily a bad thing – it can help to diversify risk and create a form of insurance.[81] Considerable problems arise, however, when the perceived sophistication of the 'insurance' on offer appears to engineer away the risks inherent in that debt.

In this way, and this happened particularly in the lead up to the financial crisis, the issuers of debts come to believe that the securitisation provides adequate protection if the original borrower can no longer repay their debt.[82]

This was a particularly prevalent belief in Western property markets, where a steady upwards trend in house prices ensured that even in the case of default, repossession and sale of mortgaged property could turn the mortgage lender a profit (as the property was sold for more than its mortgaged value). This, along with readily available credit derivatives, provided a disincentive for lenders to adequately background check borrowers. Sub-prime mortgages, which were poorly assessed and securitised, were instrumental to the housing bubble's link to the global financial crisis. In a sense, the careless lending contributed to the housing market's demise: the more readily available mortgages became, the more demand for property rose.

Diversifying the risk of mortgage lending by selling securitised debt packages to other financial institutions shared the responsibility of default between many financial institutions. One of the key factors behind the crisis was that mortgage-backed securities were not only exchanged between mortgage lenders, but were packaged (sometimes with other forms of debt) and sold onto institutional or private investors – many of whom contest that they were ignorant to the underlying risks.[83] This information asymmetry was not helped by an over-reliance on the accuracy of external credit assessments, which were often more influenced by the perceived risk of the issuer than that of the component debt. In this way even positive assurances of national banks' credit health, such as those issued in Iceland by the International Monetary Fund[84] months before the Icelandic collapse, were often proved to be unreliable.

This was particularly possible under regulatory regimes and governments who were more sympathetic to banks than predecessors had been (see for example the repeal in the US of the Glass-Steagal Act in 1999). Valdez and Molyneux identify securities trading as the cause of the rise of US financial institutions from occupying one entry in the global top 20 banks (ranked by assets) in 1990, to occupying four places in the top 20 in 2008.[85] Even the investment bank listed as globally earning the most money from merger and acquisition advice in 2008[86] actually earned considerably more of its total revenue that year from trading activities (40% compared to 23%).[87] Trading and securitisation, as outlined above, provided ways for banks to reduce their balance sheet risk and offer attractive returns to investors.[88] This competition continues to push rival institutions to trade beyond their means.[89]

Not only did securitisation coincide with favourable treatment of financial markets by governments, it also allowed financial institutions to circumvent the regulatory controls that were in place. The Basel I[90] agreement (in place from 1988) required banks to hold a minimum amount of capital in reserve (8% after 1993) in order to cover liabilities. This 8% did not apply to the total value of the bank's liabilities however, it was based on a value that assigned varying weight distributions to different securities according to their perceived risk.[91] Although the requirements applied directly to banks, special purpose vehicles (the legal entities which banks used to provide credit derivatives) could circumvent these capital requirements, and much concern has recently been expressed over these and other 'shadow banking' entities.[92] Many regulatory overseers (both pre- and post-crisis) permitted value at risk (VAR) assessment as a way for banks to calculate their future liquidity needs based on forecasts drawn from past events.[93] While complex math allows banks to quantify history and analyse past market movements, its reliability for accurately explaining what will happen tomorrow has been overemphasised by managers.[94]

The failure of academics, governments and economists to accurately model increasing risk and signal concerns to the wider market has been criticised.[95] Even before the crisis it appears the Bank for International Settlements (BIS) was aware of the potential risks inherent in credit derivatives and securitisation.[96] That more was not done to address these issues is further evidence of the insufficiency of banking regulation leading up to the crisis (poor regulation was also a cause of crisis in the 1930s in America).[97] The banks that suffered the worst of the financial crisis, of course, were subsequently bailed out by the UK government, increasing the government's budget deficits and imposing the cost of this prior poor regulation onto the general public (through the austerity measures described above). Regulatory regimes which focus on limiting the speculative activities of banks are often described as dissuading lending and contributing to the development of credit crunch situations (such as the European Sovereign debt crisis) and they are, in any event, unpopular with the UK government.[98]

The UK, which historically enjoys a close economic relationship with the US, was particularly hard hit by this collapse. Financial regulation was the preserve of the Financial Services Authority (FSA), a quasi-government organisation tasked with monitoring, licensing and regulating the actions of financial services firms trading in the UK. It was the philosophy of the FSA that markets were self-correcting, that responsibility for risk assessment should lie with firms rather than regulators, and that customer protection should lie with market transparency – not with 'product regulation or direct intervention'.[99] These principles of course were not exclusive to the FSA, or even to the UK – assumptions about the efficiency of markets hold much influence over global economic and financial decision-making and give little regard to the impact of economic decisions on society.

7.1 *The crisis and its impact on people*

After the recession hit and the banks were bailed out, what remained was a huge deficit in governments' current accounts. In the UK, the taxpayer money that the government used to prop up the banks left the state budget in a serious deficit and in order to address this deficit the UK entered a state of austerity, even though analysis has suggested austerity is ineffectual at allowing an economy to recover from recession.[100] After America's Great Depression of the 1930s, President Franklin Delano Roosevelt used the New Deal programme – a programme that used spending, not austerity – to get the American people working again and helped the economy to recover from a crippling crash that was, as in the present instance, caused by poorly regulated financial institutions taking huge speculative risks.[101]

The mainstream media has a way of obscuring the concept of austerity[102]; for example, in a *Financial Times* article from 24 June 2013, which says 'on Wednesday George Osborne will announce in his spending review that he has clawed back a further £11.5bn of spending cuts from departmental budgets for the financial year that straddles the next election'[103] austerity is simply a figure – and one so large that it is hard to relate to what that figure means in real terms. The presentation of facts and figures in terms of politics or economics manages to leave out that the reality of a cut to government spending (even if, as in the case of the aforementioned, the cuts are not yet finalised), that is, the impact these cuts will have on people dependent on government programmes, working in government jobs, or receiving government aid. Austerity measures mean cuts to housing budgets, which could mean children commuting huge distances to attend schools,[104] which will undoubtedly have an effect on attendance, and perhaps has implications for a child's success at school. Additionally, there are environmental implications of austerity measures, with carbon emissions rising a considerable amount as a result of the extra distance added to children's commutes to school.[105] Austerity is portrayed as a number that politicians throw about, but the reality of austerity is that people, often the most marginalised or vulnerable in society, are affected by the cuts to the social system of a state that they rely on.

7.2 *The crisis, UK financial regulation and consumer protection*

The actions of banks and lending institutions leading up to the financial crisis attest to the publicly held opinion that these entities considered themselves too big and too clever to run into trouble even though they knew that they were playing with risks larger than they could support. Unregulated, the largest financial services firms attracted the popular maxim 'too big to fail', to describe a firm whose value, size and wide-ranging operations made it critically important to the functioning of economies in the Western hemisphere.

That banks were allowed to grow this large, and that national economies were allowed to become so reliant on the operations of financial services firms, was no mistake. A period of large-scale deregulation, accompanied by corresponding amounts of lobbying by financial services firms, had created a loose regulatory environment in which positive, unsubstantiated growth figures were given greater weight by governments than a consideration of how these banks could be supported if they did fail. Despite being popularly recognised as too big to fail, little thought was given to what could be done if these firms actually did fail.

Shortly after the crisis these same institutions ran into severe liquidity problems: the most severe cases include the multinational insurance company AIG (American Insurance Group – one of the largest investment firms in the world), Lehman Brothers, and the government-sponsored mortgage lending institutions Freddie Mac and Fannie Mae. Other huge financial service providers like Morgan Stanley and Goldman Sachs were left haemorrhaging money as a result of the crisis and had to accept government intervention (mostly in the form of costly bailouts). This scenario was not unique to the US; governments in most developed nations have bailed out banks and financial institutions to try and prevent the recession from snowballing into a full-blown depression.

The financial regulation industry often employs individuals who have formerly worked for the very same companies that the regulators are attempting to oversee. As the regulation bodies are made up of industry insiders it is easy to understand why, due to conflicts of interests, regulators are largely impotent. Though it might not be entirely accurate to say that the FSA was broken up as a result of the financial crisis, soon after the financial crisis the FSA was disbanded and broken into two new financial regulatory bodies: the Financial Conduct Authority (FCA) and the Prudential Regulation Authority (PRA).

The FCA,[106] which is now providing the UK financial industry's consumer protection, is a private body entirely funded by 'contributions' from the financial industry. The PRA,[107] which is supposed to monitor banks and banking activity, is now housed in the Bank of England. The PRA does not deal directly with consumers and the FCA deals only with people directly invested in financial markets or products; they do not recognise at an institutional level the effects of the financial institutions on those individuals not directly invested in financial markets or products.

There is little redress in the UK for those individuals who take the view that the financial industry is responsible for indirect abuse. The Financial Ombudsman[108] and the Citizens Advise Bureau (CAB),[109] while undoubtedly worthy organisations, can provide support in the form of recommendations, mediation or advice. The CAB states that it influences, or that it intends to influence, policy, but in light of earlier information in respect to the allocation of power in governments (that is, to the financiers who drive the engine of capitalism) and the failure of government to enact those international agreements in such a way as to provide a human rights-appropriate and protective policy with respect to economic and financial institutions. Against institutions that are systemically so critical to the functioning of Western economies that they cannot be allowed to go bankrupt for their own mistakes, it is hard to imagine that the CAB is large or influential enough to provide the systemic changes needed. With both the Ombudsman and the CAB, an individual seeking redress would have to be able to prove direct causal harm; there is no agency for those who do not have direct *consumer* complaints.

The European Court of Human Rights (ECtHR) is the final court of appeal in the UK. It is a forum for citizens of member states (that is, states which have acceded to the European Convention on Human Rights) to challenge their governments where government action (or inaction) has in some way restricted an individual's access to their rights. It should be stated that the European Convention on Human Rights does not enshrine ESC rights in law. That should not, however, preclude ESC rights being exercised by way of the explicit protection of CP rights.[110]

The ECtHR typically does not involve itself in matters of commerce; its ambit is limited to individuals' grievances against state shortcomings, but of recent interest is the shareholder rights case of *Grainger* v. *UK*, in which a pool of investors challenged the UK government's decision to nationalise the Northern Rock bank in order to protect the ailing firm from a catastrophic run on its deposits and prevent sales of its shares. Following the government's actions, the bank became effectively worthless to its shareholders, and the appellant investors in *Grainger* suffered significant losses as a result. The ECtHR dismissed the appeal, and supported the government's actions, and in so doing made a number of telling statements about the nature of the convention regarding the application of human rights to financial matters.

Of particular note is the way the ECtHR restates the amount of leeway national governments are allowed when it comes to ensuring economic policy respects human rights. The court states in its judgment:

> As noted above, the Court accepts that the Government's objective throughout its dealings with Northern Rock during this period was to protect the United Kingdom's financial sector […] the Court has stressed on many occasions that [a state's obligation to respect human rights] cannot be interpreted as imposing any general obligation on the Contracting States to cover the debts of private entities.[111]

The court agrees with the decisions of the domestic courts that governments taking decisions in the context of macroeconomic policy should be allowed a wide margin of appreciation when it comes to respecting and guaranteeing rights under the European Convention on Human Rights. With such power left in the hands of individual states it remains to be seen how great a loss, or how blatantly culpable a government would have to be in order for citizens to rely – if at all – on their convention human rights against economic policy.

Consumer protection, however, covers only some of the impact that finance and economics has on members of the public. Certainly in their capacity as account holders, depositors and borrowers, members of the public are exposed to banks, building societies, insurers and pension funds. The majority of people however are neither directly involved in, nor for the most part even aware of, the systemically risky worlds of securitisation or derivative trading, for example. Securitisation (as a means of supposedly 'diversifying' risk), derivative trading (as a means of sharing this risk amongst market participants for profit) and proprietary trading (as a means for financial firms to keep the profit for themselves) have been highly profitable and hugely valuable areas of operation for industry-leading financial firms and have attracted much attention for their role in causing the financial crisis.[112]

Notwithstanding the recent interest in limiting, criticising and regulating financial firms to constrain their activities in these areas, the actions of northern hemisphere governments in the immediate aftermath of the financial crisis demonstrated that when these risky practices incur potentially fatal losses for financial firms, tax-payer money can be deployed to support the banks (providing they are considered to be 'systemically important' enough). In the aftermath of the bailouts the UK government chose to plug its spending deficits by reducing public expenditure[113] and requiring public services to become self-financing (for example, social housing).[114] The areas that have suffered in the UK from reductions in government spending include education, justice, welfare, health care and social housing.

The development of rights realisation since World War II has placed the burden for ensuring individuals have access to their human rights squarely at the door of central government. To access these rights, individuals must be able to rely on government to provide adequate and appropriate services and protection on a national and local level. Of particular concern is the response of the UK government to its spending deficit by requiring public services to become self-financing; certain public services (health care, mental health support and education, for example) can never be profitable if their services are provided free of charge at the point of use. These services have, for decades in the UK, been provided free at the point of use and, in many respects, the UK led the social-democratic trend towards an integrated welfare state after World War II. For the government to limit and impose such strict financial constraints on those public services not only fails to appreciate the 'public' nature of them, but also appears as a drastic reduction in the rights realisation that at the beginning of the century was developing so well.

The argument is not that one generation should always have more than the next, so that a retraction becomes a violation by virtue of being socially retrogressive; however, there is a point to be made about services being free, but then not being free anymore. Social services, like health care in the UK, are a sign that at some time in the past the state was recognising ESC rights and the repeal of them is, therefore, a slide backwards. Social services were hard won benefits that took decades, and the risky actions of an elite few are seeing cuts to social welfare systems that were hard won. The state cannot jeopardise the social systems in place and not provide an explanation. In its guide for National Human Rights Institutions (NHRIs) the UN Office of the High Commissioner for Human Rights says that, where ESC rights are concerned, that:

> [a]ny deliberately regressive measures, such as rescinding legislation affecting the enjoyment of economic, social and cultural rights, can only be justified by reference to the totality of the rights provided for in the Covenant and in the context of the full utilization of a State's maximum available resources. Similarly, the Committee on Economic, Social and Cultural Rights has emphasized that 'policies and legislation should […] not be designed to benefit already advantaged social groups at the expense of others'.[115]

The austerity measures seem to be woefully misguided in light of the empirically provable causes of the financial crisis. Those who are being punished are not those who were responsible for the crisis, nor those who directly benefitted from the bailouts (as private individuals' deposits were already guaranteed by the government up to a certain amount). It is worth noting that as government spending (on education and health, for example) has been capped or decreased (in real terms) in response to the financial crisis, corporation tax has remained unchanged.[116]

8. Conclusion

The financial services sector enjoys a particularly unchallenged relationship with government regulation, as actions taken, ostensibly, in the macroeconomic interests of the country (for example, cutting public spending or underwriting the losses of banks and insurance firms) fall outside of the government's obligation to protect and promote human rights. This is not an attitude limited to the UK and the US, but appears to be endorsed on a European-wide basis too (see above in the case of *Grainger*). As the fortunes of the UK economy are so intrinsically linked to the health of the financial services sector policies which promote a more lenient economic climate frequently have a beneficial impact on financial services firms (as demonstrated in the deregulation of financial services after 1986).[117]

The financial crisis has, amongst other things, thrown these repeat endorsements of the importance of financial services firms into greater relief. In political rhetoric the public are assured of the systemic importance of the financial sector, of the value it contributes to national economies and how much worse things could have been.[118]

There have at least been efforts to provide consumers with a degree of protection, or recourse, as the financial crisis has highlighted aspects of bad practice and market manipulation. For example, the miss-selling of payment protection insurance in the UK has seen retail banks face significant fines and compensation payments as a result of their bad business practices. In these instances there have typically been direct links between an individual's losses (for example, over-paying for needless options related to one's mortgage) and the actions of financial services firms. Far less well recognised, and almost untreated even in human rights literature, is the extent to which individuals have incurred losses (or face the prospect of sustained or future losses) as a result of macroeconomic policy, government attitudes towards regulation, and the actions of financial services firms operating.

Financial services firms are operating under an implied licence of low regulation, minimal oversight and collateral security (in the form of assured government bailouts) so long as they remain so influential and so systemically important to the national economy that they are considered too big to (be allowed to) fail. All the time the sector is contributing heavily to GDP its business practices are a somewhat lesser concern (see also the actions of tech-sector companies in the US, for example, Apple; also the oil and gas industry is of strategic importance too). Corporate interests trump those of individuals and, in many cases, corporations enjoy protection of the law that are sometimes not extended to individuals.[119]

Take, for example, Credit Suisse, which has come under considerable scrutiny - and attracted criminal charges - for engaging in illegal activities, including apparently helping clients to evade tax.[120] Credit Suisse escapes criminal charges and is let off with very light fines, leading journalists to comment that (in reference to the adage that banks are 'too big to fail') in many instances banks are 'too big to jail'.[121] Because of the wealth, power and importance of banks like Credit Suisse, many other governments – even supposedly world leaders such as the UK and the US – lack either the power or the ambition to penalise banks for aiding and abetting criminal activities like tax evasion and money laundering.

Though the UK government has signed and ratified many treaties that express its desire and intent to protect human rights, it is clear from the actions of the government that there is no recourse to address human rights issues in relation to financial actors except in cases where an individual is directly invested in financial markets. In these cases the recourse is compensation rather than ex ante protection.

There is an increasing raft of academic and popular discussion on the extent to which corporations, their activities and agendas, curtail human rights. As some of the largest and most amorphous corporations, financial services firms are ripe for criticism of their human rights records, despite expensive and well-publicised CSR campaigns. The financial crisis has highlighted, however, that even when the activities of financial services firms are instrumental in changing people's fortunes and creating a climate in which rights realisation has a minimum price, the firms are largely supported and (in some cases) encouraged by governments, through loose regulation and growth-at-all-costs economic policy.

Governments should be human rights gatekeepers; they should ensure that actors headquartered in their jurisdictions comply with the international standards that the state has signed up to. It seems to be the case, however, that in matters of business far more of a free reign is given, allowing greater leeway in business activities before they will be challenged on their human rights records. Where corporations are challenged on their human rights records, it is likely that this challenge comes from the press, rather than from presiding governments. Even where firms headquartered in convention signatory states comply with local legislation, there appears to be a degree of outsourcing, shifting the worst human rights abuses to countries where local legislation is more lax (and the cost of settlement for non-compliance is lower). Despite the increasing raft of literature on business interaction with individual rights, few efforts have been made to engage the human rights discussion with complimentary analysis in other disciplines (for example, business, finance and economics). As the international business environment has become increasingly reliant on financial services as an industry in itself, little has been done to critically examine financial practices for the impact they have on human lives. This article has identified a distressing series of examples which show that there are many areas of crossover between the activities of financial services firms and human rights. More work is needed.

Disclosure statement

No potential conflict of interest was reported by the author.

Notes

1. Joshua Zumbrun, 'World's Most Economically Powerful Cities', *Forbes*, 15 July 2008, http://www.forbes.com/2008/07/15/economic-growth-gdp-biz-cx_jz_0715powercities.html (accessed 4 August 2013).

2. Stephen Burgess, Conjunctural Assessment and Projections Division, Bank of England, 'Measuring Financial Sector Output and its Contribution to UK GDP', *Quarterly Bulletin* (2011), Q3.
3. United Kingdom House of Commons, *Financial Services: Contribution to the UK Economy*, Standard Note by Lucinda Maer and Nida Broughton (SN/EP/06193), 21 August 2012.
4. Department for Business Innovation and Skills, *Industrial Strategy: UK Sector Analysis*, BIS Economic Paper No.18, September 2012, http://www.bis.gov.uk/assets/BISCore/economics-and-statistics/docs/I/12-1140-industrial-strategy-uk-sector-analysis.pdf (accessed 4 August 2014).
5. Those being the International Covenant on Economic Social and Cultural Rights (ICESCR), the International Covenant on Civil and Political Rights (ICCPR), the Convention Against Torture (CAT), the Convention on the Elimination of Racial Discrimination (CERD), the Convention on the Elimination of Discrimination Against Women (CEDAW), and the Convention on the Rights of the Child (CRC). Found at http://www.publications.parliament.uk/pa/jt200405/jtselect/jtrights/112/11209.htm (accessed 4 August 2013).
6. William Schomberg and Ana Nicolaci Da Costa, 'UK Economy Basks in Manufacturing Growth, IMF Upgrade', *Reuters*, 8 April 2014, http://uk.reuters.com/article/2014/04/08/uk-britain-economy-manufacturing-idUKBREA370H120140408 (accessed 4 August 2014).
7. 'IMF Warns UK Government over Housing Bubble Risk', *BBC*, 6 June 2014, http://www.bbc.co.uk/news/business-27731567 (accessed 4 August 2014).
8. Joseph Stiglitz, 'The North Atlantic Malaise: Failures in Economic Policy' (public lecture, Oxford Martin School, Oxford, 22 May 2014), https://www.youtube.com/watch?v=asV5_O6glbA&list=UUmXB98lpzelFrlryV2llXUQ (accessed 26 May 2014).
9. Ibid.
10. Ibid.
11. Joel Bakan, *The Corporation: The Pathological Pursuit of Profit and Power* (New York: Free Press, 2004).
12. Jeremy Sarkin and Mark A. Koenig, 'Developing the Right to Work: Intersecting and Dialoguing Human Rights and Economic Policy', *Human Rights Quarterly* 33, no. 1 (2011): 2.
13. Alex Kirkup and Tony Evans, 'The Myth of Western Opposition to Economic, Social, and Cultural Rights: A Reply to Whelan and Donnelly', *Human Rights Quarterly* 3, no. 1 (2009): 354.
14. Ibid.
15. Diane Elson, 'The Reduction of the UK Budget Deficit: A Human Rights Perspective', *International Review of Applied Economics* 26, no. 2 (2012): 180.
16. See for example: Lanse Minkler and Shawna Sweeney, 'On the Interdependence and Indivisibility of Basic Rights in Developing Countries', *Human Rights Quarterly* 33, no. 2 (2011): 351–96; Kirkup and Evans, 'The Myth of Western Opposition to Economic, Social, and Cultural Rights', 354; Elson, 'The Reduction of the UK Budget Deficit', 177–90.
17. Minkler and Sweeney, 'On the Interdependence and Indivisibility of Basic Rights in Developing Countries', 351–95.
18. Ibid., 354.
19. Daniel J. Whelan and Jack Donnelly, 'The West, Economic and Social Rights: Setting the Record Straight', *Human Rights Quarterly* 29, no. 4 (2007): 908–49.
20. Sethi S. Prakash, David B. Lowry, Emre A. Veral, H. Jack Shapiro, and Olga Emelianova, 'Freeport-McMoRan Copper & Gold, Inc.: An Innovative Voluntary Code of Conduct to Protect Human Rights, Create Employment Opportunities, and Economic Development of the Indigenous Peoples', *Journal of Business Ethics* 103, no. 1 (2011): 1–30.
21. Thomas Piketty and Arthur Goldhammer, *Capital in the Twenty-first Century* (Cambridge, MA: Belknap of Harvard University Press, 2014); Joseph E. Stiglitz, *The Price of Inequality* (New York: W.W. Norton, 2012); Ed Howker and Shiv Malik, *Jilted Generation: How Britain Has Bankrupted Its Youth* (London: Icon, 2010); Piya Mahtaney, *Globalization and Sustainable Economic Development: Issues, Insights, and Inference* (London, Palgrave Macmillan, 2013); Darnell Hunt and Ana-Christina Ramon, *Black Los Angeles: American Dreams and Racial Realities* (New York: New York University Press, 2010).
22. A phenomenon which is explained by Abhijit Banerjee and Esther Duflo in *Poor Economics* (London: Penguin, 2011).
23. Ibid.

24. Mary Dowell-Jones and David Kinley, 'Minding the Gap: Global Finance and Human Rights', *Ethics & International Affairs* 25, no. 2 (2011): 183–210.
25. Penelope Simons, 'International Law's Invisible Hand and the Future of Corporate Accountability for Violations of Human Rights', *Journal of Human Rights and the Environment* 3, no. 1 (2012): 5–43.
26. Howker and Malik, *Jilted Generation*, 2.
27. For more discussion of student debt and its effects see: Manette Kaisershot, 'The Next Crisis: Student Debt', Human Rights Consortium Blog, 7 March 2014, http://humanrights.blogs.sas.ac.uk/2014/03/07/the-next-crisis-student-debt/ (accessed 26 May 2014).
28. Stephen Valdez and Philip Molyneux, *An Introduction to Global Financial Markets* (Basingstoke and New York: Palgrave Macmillan, 2012), 201–4.
29. Stiglitz, 'The North Atlantic Malaise'.
30. Ibid.
31. Robert Shrimsley, 'The Nine Stages of The Piketty Bubble', *The Financial Times*, 30 April 2014, http://www.ft.com/cms/s/0/2d492786-cf90-11e3-bec6-00144feabdc0.html (accessed 26 May 2014).
32. Piketty and Goldhammer, *Capital in the Twenty-first Century*, 294.
33. Ibid.
34. Ibid., 377–429.
35. Stiglitz, 'The North Atlantic Malaise'.
36. Ibid.
37. Stiglitz, *The Price of Inequality*.
38. Mahtaney, *Globalization and Sustainable Economic Development*.
39. Ibid., 190.
40. Piketty and Goldhammer, *Capital in the Twenty-first Century*; Mahtaney, *Globalization and Sustainable Economic Development*; Stiglitz, *The Price of Inequality*; Elson, 'The Reduction of the UK Budget Deficit'; Howker and Malik, *Jilted Generation*.
41. Elson, 'The Reduction of the UK Budget Deficit'.
42. Ibid., 182.
43. Ibid., 183.
44. Ibid., 180.
45. Ibid., 181.
46. Mahtaney, *Globalization and Sustainable Economic Development*.
47. Stiglitz, 'The North Atlantic Malaise'.
48. Mahtaney, *Globalization and Sustainable Economic Development*.
49. Dowell-Jones and Kinley, 'Minding the Gap', 183–210.
50. Judge Julia Laffranque, 'Opening of the Seminar on Implementing the European Convention on Human Rights in Times of Economic Crisis' (European Court of Human Rights, Strasbourg, 25 January 2013), http://www.echr.coe.int/Documents/Speech_20130125_Laffranque_ENG.pdf (accessed 4 August 2014).
51. Mahtaney, *Globalization and Sustainable Economic Development*.
52. Eric Onstad, Laura MacInnis, and Quentin Webb, 'Special Report: The Biggest Company You Never Heard Of', *Reuters*, 25 February 2011, http://uk.reuters.com/article/2011/02/25/us-glencore-idUSTRE71O1DC20110225 (accessed 4 August 2014).
53. Barclays Investment Bank, 'Commodities', http://realizations.barclays.com/global-markets/commodities#.U5MtmvldX4U.
54. Goldman Sachs, 'Securities Commodities', http://www.goldmansachs.com/what-we-do/securities/products-and-business-groups/products/commodities.html.
55. MacQuarie, 'Commodities', http://www.macquarie.com/mgl/com/globalcapabilities/trading/commodities.
56. Ben Lilliston and Andrew Ranallo, 'Excessive Speculation in Agriculture Commodities: Selected Writings from 2008–2011' (Institute for Agriculture and Trade Policy, 2011), http://www.iatp.org/documents/excessive-speculation-in-agriculture-commodities (accessed 4 August 2014).
57. Johann Hari, 'How Goldman Gambled on Starvation', *The Independent*, 2 July 2010, http://www.independent.co.uk/opinion/commentators/johann-hari/johann-hari-how-goldman-gambled-on-starvation-2016088.html (accessed 4 August 2014); F. Kaufman 'The Speculative Scrum Driving Up Food Prices' *The Guardian*, 20 December 2011.

58. Murray Worthy, *Broken Markets: How Financial Market Regulation Can Help Prevent Another Global Food Crisis* (London: World Development Movement, 2011), http://www.wdm.org.uk/sites/default/files/files/resources/broken-markets.pdf.pdf (accessed 18 December 2014).
59. European Commission, 'Commission's Response to the High Oil and Food Prices EC MEMO/08/421' (Press release, 10 June 2008), http://europa.eu/rapid/pressReleasesAction.do?reference=MEMO/08/421.
60. Ibid.
61. Glass-Steagal, The Banking Act 1933 (US) enacted June 1933; effectively repealed - in this context - by the Financial Services Modernization Act (US) 1999.
62. Odette Murray, David Kinley, and Chip Pitts, 'Exaggerated Rumours of the Death of an Alien Tort: Corporations, Human Rights and the Peculiar Case of Kiobel', *Melbourne Journal of International Law* 12, no. 1, (2011): 57–94.
63. See for example: Bakan, *The Corporation*; Noam Chomsky, *Profit over People: Neoliberalism and Global Order* (New York: Seven Stories, 1999); Greg Palast, *Vultures' Picnic: In Pursuit of Petroleum Pigs, Power Pirates, and High-finance Carnivores* (New York: Plume, 2012).
64. Dowell-Jones and Kinley, 'Minding the Gap'.
65. 'Foxconn Admits Labour Violation at China Factory', *BBC News*, 11 October 2013, http://www.bbc.co.uk/news/business-24486684 (accessed 21 May 2014); 'Five Ex-Employees of Taiwan's Foxxconn Indicted for Bribery', *Yahoo! Finance*, 21 May 2014, https://uk.finance.yahoo.com/news/five-ex-employees-taiwans-foxconn-085549226.html (accessed 21 May 2014).
66. Tom Randall, 'Inside Apple's Foxconn Factories', *Bloomberg*, 30 March 2012, http://www.bloomberg.com/slideshow/2012-03-30/inside-apple-s-foxconn-factory.html#slide9 (accessed 4 December 2014).
67. See UN, 'Status of Ratification Interactive Dashboard' (at http://indicators.ohchr.org/) for the most up-to-date information on the status of all UN covenants by country.
68. David Barboza, 'Worker Deaths Raise Questions at an Apple Contactor in China', *New York Times*, 12 December 2013, http://www.nytimes.com/2013/12/12/business/international/worker-deaths-raise-questions-at-an-apple-contractor-in-china.html?_r=1& (accessed 9 June 2014).
69. Connie Gugliemo, 'Apple's Supplier Labor Practices In China Scrutinized After Foxconn, Pegatron Reviews', *Forbes*, 12 December 2013, http://www.forbes.com/sites/connieguglielmo/2013/12/12/apples-labor-practices-in-china-scrutinized-after-foxconn-pegatron-reviewed/ (accessed 21 May 2014).
70. Apple, 'Fair Labor Association Begins Inspections of Foxconn', 13 February 2012, http://www.apple.com/uk/pr/library/2012/02/13Fair-Labor-Association-Begins-Inspections-of-Foxconn.html (accessed 21 May 2014).
71. Fair Labor Association, *Final Foxconn Verification Status Report*, December 2013, http://www.fairlabor.org/sites/default/files/documents/reports/final_foxconn_verification_report_0.pdf.
72. Ibid.
73. Charles Duhigg and David Barboza, 'In China, Human Costs Are Built Into an iPad', *The New York Times*, 25 January 2012, Business Day, http://www.nytimes.com/2012/01/26/business/ieconomy-apples-ipad-and-the-human-costs-for-workers-in-china.html?pagewanted=all&_r=0 (accessed 21 May 2014).
74. Thomas I. Palley, 'Financialization: What It Is and Why It Matters', Working Paper No. 525 (Washington, DC: The Levy Economics Institute, 2007), http://www.levyinstitute.org/pubs/wp_525.pdf (accessed 4 August 2013); Bakan, *The Corporation*; Stiglitz, *The Price of Inequality*.
75. Palley, 'Financialization'.
76. Bakan, *The Corporation*.
77. Ibid., 63. In the case of *Anderson* v. *General Motors*, a car accident resulting in a fire from a badly designed car that left the plaintiff, her three children, and a friend horribly disfigured was the result of a known fault in a general motors car that was not recalled based on a financial computation that worked out it would cost the company more to pay out damages than to recall the faulty vehicle.
78. Elson, 'The Reduction of the UK Budget Deficit', 177–90.

79. David Harvey, *The Crisis of Capitalism* (London: *RSA* Animate, 2010), http://davidharvey.org/2010/05/video-the-crises-of-capitalism-at-the-rsa/ (accessed 1 December 2014).
80. Valdez and Molyneux, *An Introduction to Global Financial Markets*, 273–4.
81. Ugo Albertazzi, Ginette Eramo, Leonardo Gambacorta, and Carmelo Salleo, 'Securitization Is Not That Evil After All', Bank of International Settlements Working Papers No. 341 (Basel: Monetary and Economic Department, March 2011).
82. Benjamin J. Keys, Tanmoy Mukherjee, Amit Seru, and Vikrant Vig, 'Did Securitization Lead to Lax Screening? Evidence from Subprime Loans', *The Quarterly Journal of Economics* 25, no. 1 (2010): 307–62.
83. Financial Conduct Authority, 'FCA Fines RBS and NatWest For Failures in Mortgage Advice Process' (Press release, 27 August 2014), https://fca.org.uk/news/fca-fines-rbs-and-natwest-for-failures-in-mortgage-advice-process (accessed 4 December 2014); Kate Palmer, 'RBS-NatWest Fine: Were You Also Mis-sold a Mortgage?', *The Telegraph*, 27 August 2014, http://www.telegraph.co.uk/finance/personalfinance/borrowing/mortgages/11058040/RBS-NatWest-mortgage-mis-selling-were-you-also-mis-sold-a-mortgage.html (accessed 4 December 2014).
84. International Monetary Fund, 'Iceland: Financial System Stability Assessment –Update', *IMF Country Report*, No.08/368 (Washington, DC: IMF, December 2008), 5.
85. Valdez and Molyneux, *An Introduction to Global Financial Markets*, 43–4.
86. Ibid., 116.
87. Goldman Sachs, *Goldman Sachs Annual Report*, 2008, http://www.goldmansachs.com/investor-relations/financials/archived/annual-reports/2008-entire-annual-report.pdf (accessed 4 December 2014).
88. For a brief discussion of this subject see Eichengreen, B. (2008) Origins and Responses to the Crisis, University of California, Berkeley, http://emlab.berkeley.edu/users/webfac/eichengreen/e183_sp07/origins_responses.pdf (accessed 29.08.2014).
89. See, for example, the collapse of MF Global in 2011.
90. Basle Committee on Banking Supervision, *International Convergence of Capital Measurement and Capital Standards* (Basel: BIS, 1988).
91. Valdez and Molyneux, *An Introduction to Global Financial Markets*, 37–8.
92. European Commission Green Paper, *Shadow Banking* (Brussels: European Commission, 19 March 2012), http://ec.europa.eu/internal_market/bank/docs/shadow/green-paper_en.pdf; Financial Services Authority, *The Turner Review: A Regulatory Response to the Global Banking Crisis* (London: FSA, March 2009), http://www.fsa.gov.uk/pubs/other/turner_review.pdf; Financial Stability Board, *Shadow Banking: Strengthening Oversight and Regulation*, Recommendations of the Financial Stability Board, 27 October 2011; George Osborne and Jun Azumi, 'Beware the Risks of the Rush to Regulate', *The Financial Times*, Opinion, 22 February 2012.
93. Financial Services Authority, *The Turner Review*, 22–4.
94. Ibid., 22.
95. David Colander, Hands Follmer, Armin Haas, Michael Goldberg, Katarina Juselius, Alan Kirman, Thomas Lux, and Brigitte Sloth, 'The Financial Crisis and Systemic Failure of Academic Economics', Working Paper No. 1489 (Kiel, Germany: Kiel Institute for the World Economy, February 2009), https://www.ifw-members.ifw-kiel.de/publications/the-financial-crisis-and-the-systemic-failure-of-academic-economics/KWP_1489_ColanderetalFinancial%20Crisis.pdf (accessed 4 December 2014).
96. Basel Committee on Banking Supervision, *The Joint Forum: Credit Risk Transfer* (Basel: BIS, March 2005), http://www.bis.org/publ/joint13.pdf (accessed 4 December 2014).
97. James Crotty, 'The Great Austerity War: What Caused the US Deficit Crisis and Who Should Pay to Fix It?', *Cambridge Journal of Economics* 36, no. 1 (2011): 79–104.
98. Basel Committee on Banking Supervision, *Core Principles for Effective Banking Supervision* (Basel: BIS, September 2012), http://www.bis.org/publ/bcbs230.pdf (accessed 4 December 2012); House of Commons Library, *Voting Behaviour in the EU Council*, Standard Note SN/IA/6646, 23 May 2013, 17.
99. Financial Services Authority, *The Turner Review*, 89.
100. Crotty, 'The Great Austerity War'.
101. Ibid.
102. 'Osborne and the Politics of Austerity', *The Financial Times*, 24 June 2013, http://www.ft.com/cms/s/0/aa1b570e-dcc3-11e2-9700-00144feab7de.html#axzz2b6jsfUg1 (accessed 5 August

2013); Jeffrey Dorman, 'Austerity in Europe: It Will Work If It's Ever Tried', *Forbes*, 1 August 2013, http://www.forbes.com/sites/jeffreydorfman/2013/08/01/austerity-in-europe-it-will-work-if-its-ever-tried/ (accessed 5 August 2013).

103. Ibid.
104. Ed Ferrari, 'Excess Commuting to School', Blog, 27 July 2011, http://ed-ferrari.staff.shef.ac.uk/blog/blog/2011/07/27/excess-commuting-to-school/ (5 August 2013); Jill Sherman, 'Children Join Big Commute as Benefit Cap Forces Out Families', *The Sunday Times*, 23 May 2014, http://www.thetimes.co.uk/tto/news/politics/article3773349.ece (accessed 5 August 2014).
105. Ibid.
106. Financial Conduct Authority, 'How We Are Funded', http://www.fca.org.uk/about/how-we-are-funded# (accessed 28 July 2013).
107. Bank of England, 'Prudential Regulation Authority', http://www.bankofengland.co.uk/PRA/Pages/default.aspx (accessed 28 July 2013).
108. Financial Ombudsmen, 'About', http://www.financial-ombudsman.org.uk/about/index.html (accessed 28 July 2013).
109. Citizens Advice Bureau, http://www.citizensadvice.org.uk/ (accessed 28 July 2013).
110. Laffranque, 'Opening of the Seminar on Implementing the European Convention on Human Rights in Times of Economic Crisis'.
111. *Grainger and Others* v. *The United Kingdom*, 34940/10, 10 July 2012, Paragraph 42.
112. House of Lords and House of Commons Parliamentary Commission on Banking Standards, *Proprietary Trading: Third Report of Session 2012–2013*, Vol. I & II, 15 March 2013, http://www.publications.parliament.uk/pa/jt201213/jtselect/jtpcbs/138/138.pdf, http://www.publications.parliament.uk/pa/jt201213/jtselect/jtpcbs/138/138vw.pdf (accessed 4 December 2014).
113. Cabinet Office, The Rt Hon Francis Maude MP and Civil Service Reform, 'Future of Government Services: 5 Public Service Reform Principles' (Speech, 10 February 2014), https://www.gov.uk/government/speeches/future-of-government-services-5-public-service-reform-principles (accessed 4 December 2014).
114. Department for Communities and Local Government, *Implementing Self-financing for Council Housing*, February 2011, https://www.gov.uk/government/uploads/system/uploads/attachment_data/file/6005/1831498.pdf (accessed 4 December 2014).
115. United Nations Office of the High Commissioner for Human Rights, *Economic, Cultural and Social Rights: A Handbook for National Human Rights Institutions* (Geneva: UN, 2005), 12.
116. HM Treasury and Office of National Statistics, *Country and Regional Analysis*, November 2013, https://www.gov.uk/government/uploads/system/uploads/attachment_data/file/264286/Country_and_Regional_Analysis_2013.pdf (accessed December 2014); HM Revenue & Customs, *Rates and Allowances: Corporation Tax*, 14 April 2013, https://www.gov.uk/government/publications/rates-and-allowances-corporation-tax (accessed 4 December 2014).
117. Valdez and Molyneux, *An Introduction to Global Financial Markets*.
118. National Audit Office, 'Taxpayer Support for UK Banks: FAQS', National Audit Office webpages, http://www.nao.org.uk/highlights/taxpayer-support-for-uk-banks-faqs/, (accessed 4 December 2014); 'Taxpayers Bail-Out of Banks is "Justified", says NAO', *BBC News*, 4 December 2009, http://news.bbc.co.uk/1/hi/8394393.stm (accessed 4 December 2014); HM Treasury and The Rt Hon George Osborne MP, 'Chancellor Says Today's Figures Show that Britain is Coming Back', UK Government, 29 April 2014, https://www.gov.uk/government/news/chancellor-says-todays-figures-show-that-britain-is-coming-back (accessed 4 December 2014).
119. Bakan, *The Corporation*.
120. Frances Coppola, 'Credit Suisse is Too Big To Jail', *Forbes*, 24 May 2014, http://www.forbes.com/sites/francescoppola/2014/05/24/credit-suisse-is-too-big-to-jail/ (accessed 4 December 2014).
121. Ibid.

Company-created remedy mechanisms for serious human rights abuses: a promising new frontier for the right to remedy?

Sarah Knuckey and Eleanor Jenkin

Columbia Law School, Columbia University, USA; New York University School of Law, New York University, USA

This article identifies and analyses a new type of process by which corporations are seeking to directly remedy serious violations of human rights associated with their operations. We call this process a 'company-created human rights abuse remedy mechanism' (CHRM). We argue that while this new type of process is often discussed as an operational-level grievance mechanism (OGM), it differs in key respects from OGMs as they have been generally conceived. Typically, OGMs are viewed as early-warning, prevention-oriented, and dialogue-based complaint and resolution processes for a wide range of (often low-level) adverse impacts. In contrast, the new process we describe here is designed to provide a largely fixed remedy for a known class of past serious human rights violations, is more adjudicative than dialogue-based, and seeks to impose final settlement on claims. Drawing on a case study of a CHRM created by a Canadian company at a goldmine in Papua New Guinea to provide remedies to victims of sexual assault committed by company guards, we argue that while CHRMs may promise more accessible and convenient remedies, they may also entail unique and serious risks to rights-holders and the right to remedy. Such mechanisms should be subjected to heightened scrutiny because of the risks to victims' rights inherent in a mechanism designed by a company to remedy adverse impacts associated with its own operations, and should be used only sparingly and in accordance with stringent safeguards. Future project-level direct remediation efforts would benefit from a shift towards mechanisms created and administered as a partnership between a company and affected communities.

Introduction

Securing redress for individuals and communities adversely impacted by the activities of multinational corporations in the Global South is notoriously difficult. Remedy gaps abound: host states often lack the capacity or will to hold companies to account, and judicial recourse in a corporation's home state or a third state is sometimes impossible, always legally and logistically difficult, and infrequently successful.[1] In addition, many non-judicial grievance mechanisms – such as Organisation for Economic Co-operation and Development (OECD) national contact points, industry-wide complaints processes, and international financial institution ombudsmen – often lack adequate investigation, determination, or enforcement powers, or are inaccessible or simply unknown to rights-holders.[2]

In this remedy-deficient landscape, company-created 'operational-level grievance mechanisms' (OGMs), a type of non-judicial non-state grievance mechanism, have emerged as a prominent form of complaint and remediation process. They have also been the subject of increasing study, debate, civil society scrutiny, and policy guidance. Endorsed as a path to remedy in the United Nations (UN) Guiding Principles on Business and Human Rights, OGMs are mechanisms through which companies receive complaints and may directly provide remedies at the operational or project level to those harmed by the company's operations. They may be implemented without the intervention of governmental, judicial, or international institutions, or multi-stakeholder processes. Generally, OGMs are understood to be ongoing procedures through which low-level complaints about a diverse array of issues such as employee complaints, property damage, and relocation issues, can be addressed through dialogue and flexible alternative dispute resolution processes before they escalate. They are primarily viewed as advancing two important goals: the early identification of adverse corporate impacts; and the early resolution of grievances with a view to mitigating the escalation of abuse or conflict. Analysis has not focused on how they might be used to remedy grave or widespread human rights impacts and abuses.[3]

Recently, a new type of corporate-created process has emerged which challenges existing assumptions about and analyses of OGMs, and which entails unique opportunities and risks for rights-holders and their right to remedy. This article seeks to shed light on this new form of transnational, privatised remedy mechanism. It does so through a close examination of a controversial mechanism at a remote Papua New Guinea (PNG) mine created by one of the world's largest gold mining companies to remedy over 100 cases of sexual violence, including numerous gang rapes, committed by the company's security guards and other employees.[4] Canadian miner Barrick Gold Corporation created the *Olgeta Meri Igat Raits* (All Women Have Rights) Framework of Remediation Initiatives in 2012,[5] a remedy mechanism through which women allegedly sexually assaulted by Barrick employees may submit a complaint. If found eligible and legitimate, and in return for signing a waiver of her legal rights to sue Barrick, the complainant may receive a remedy package of a business grant and services valued at on average (as of December 2014) 23,630 kina (US$8,920) plus (as of June 2015) an additional amount of 30,000 kina (US $10,905).[6] As of June 2015, the claims of 137 women had been deemed eligible, and 119 claims had been settled through the remedy mechanism.[7]

This mechanism exhibits several features which distinguish it from OGMs as commonly discussed. Its primary function is not to serve early warning or escalation mitigation functions, but to provide a remedy to a defined class of victims of widely known and serious human rights abuses committed over many years. It is single issue, time-bound, retrospective, provides a largely fixed remedy, seeks final settlement, and employs a corporation-created decision-making process which is closer to adjudication than to dialogue-based 'decide together' approaches. Together, these features represent a significant shift in the nature, purpose, and scope of OGMs as otherwise generally conceived.[8] To distinguish this type of process from the archetypal general complaints resolution OGM model, we refer to it as a 'company-created human rights abuse remedy mechanism' (CHRM).

This kind of mechanism opens up a potentially promising new frontier for addressing adverse human rights impacts or violations associated with business activities. In particular, it creates the possibility of comparatively swift and potentially effective remedies for rights-holders who may otherwise have limited access to national or foreign judicial systems, or who have little prospect of success due to jurisdictional and procedural barriers, or for cases where other non-judicial paths have limited remedy prospects. However, our case study also reveals that serious concerns may arise – in both principle and practice – when companies seek to remedy serious human rights impacts through company-created non-judicial mechanisms. This is especially so where the ability of rights-holders to assert their rights is constrained by the lack of other feasible remedy options, where there is a significant power differential between rights-holders and the company, and where rights-holders face economic disadvantage and a lack of access to education or legal assistance. In this article, we highlight some of the key design and implementation issues which may impact the rights-compatibility, and perceived legitimacy and effectiveness of a company-created mechanism designed to remedy serious human rights impacts. These issues include: the nature of consultation and dialogue with victims and stakeholders; mechanism accessibility and the scope of harms addressed; the amount and nature of remedies; interaction with judicial processes and conditioning remedy on the claimant's release of the company from legal liability; and transparency, external review, and continuous improvement.

Company-created remedy mechanisms which address serious human rights issues, (ostensibly) impose final settlement on claims, and which deal with especially vulnerable claimants and communities, should be subjected to heightened scrutiny. The new type of remedy mechanism identified here would benefit from additional research and tailored design and implementation guidance. Such mechanisms may justifiably seek to fill a governance or accountability gap in relation to human rights abuses, and they have the potential to advance rights-holders' interests. But they are at particular risk of undermining the right to remedy where, as is often the case, there is a power asymmetry between companies and affected communities. In the long-term, there is also a risk that focus on company-created mechanisms may displace efforts to improve state-based or independent remediation processes. In light of these risks, company-created remedy mechanisms should be implemented only in narrow circumstances and where stringent safeguards are met. Future project-level direct remediation efforts would benefit from a shift towards mechanisms created and administered as a partnership between a company and affected communities.

Locating operational-level grievance mechanisms

The third pillar of the UN 'Protect, Respect, and Remedy' framework recognises the 'need for greater access by victims to effective remedy'.[9] In operationalising the framework, the UN Guiding Principles on Business and Human Rights[10] describe the duty of states to ensure access to an effective remedy as a 'foundational principle', and use the term 'grievance mechanism' to 'indicate any routinized, State-based or non-State-based, judicial or non-judicial process through which grievances concerning business-related human rights abuse can be raised and remedy sought'.[11] The Guiding Principles state that business enterprises 'should provide for or cooperate in' remedy processes where they bear responsibility for 'adverse impacts'.[12] Among the array of grievance mechanisms constituting the remedy system,[13] the Guiding Principles specifically highlight operational-level grievance mechanisms as one 'effective' process, which can allow grievances 'to be addressed early and remediated directly'.[14]

In recognition of the potential for poorly designed or implemented mechanisms to undermine rights and to have other negative impacts, the Guiding Principles also set out eight effectiveness criteria which OGMs should satisfy.[15] These criteria, which aim to provide a benchmark for designing, revising, or assessing non-judicial grievance mechanisms, require that OGMs be legitimate, accessible, predictable, equitable, transparent, rights-compatible, a source of continuous learning, and based on engagement and dialogue.[16]

The Commentary to the Guiding Principles identifies two key functions of OGMs. First, they provide a way for a company to learn about its specific negative human rights or other impacts, understand system-level concerns, and alter practices to avoid future harm. Second, they provide a process through which harmful impacts (explicitly not only human rights abuses, but of any kind of adverse impact) can be remedied 'early and directly … thereby preventing harms from compounding and grievances from escalating'.[17] Thus, in significant part, OGMs are conceived as entailing core *warning* and *preventative* functions.[18] In this sense, OGMs as conceptualised in the Guiding Principles are rooted in concepts of corporate self-regulation, and fit within the canon of complaints resolution processes and stakeholder engagement which have long been the subject of discussion in corporate social responsibility and organisational management discourse.[19]

This corporate social responsibility orientation is also reflected in the research which preceded (and informed the drafting of) the Guiding Principles, and which has proliferated since their adoption. Corporations and non-governmental and international organisations have all sought to understand what role project-level non-judicial grievance mechanisms can and should play in the new business and human rights landscape,[20] and numerous workshops and projects designed to map, understand, share lessons and best practices, and improve OGMs have taken place.[21] Several organisations have issued general guidance to companies on designing and implementing operational-level mechanisms.[22]

Much of this research has focused on identifying best practices for the operationalisation of the eight effectiveness criteria – determining what these criteria mean, or ought to mean, in practice. Most of this guidance has also been distilled through the analysis of case studies of existing OGMs,[23] and many of the guides for grievance mechanisms assume OGMs with the kinds of core warning and preventative purposes and qualities evident in the Guiding Principles.[24] This existing work on OGMs generally assumes or describes a mechanism with the following features: it is *ongoing* (without a specific end-date), has *broad eligibility* (in order to address a wide array of complaints of varying seriousness), privileges *dialogue* and incorporates *flexible alternative dispute resolution (ADR) processes* (including informal discussion, arbitration, and mediation),[25] and aims to *intervene early* in complaints, thereby preventing serious harms and contributing to improved overall company–community relations. We refer to this as the 'complaints resolution' model of OGM. This grievance model – the typical OGM – is increasingly acknowledged by a variety of actors as an essential mechanism for any project or operation, a position we support.

The type of mechanism analysed in this article is a significantly different species of OGM. While categorised and discussed as an OGM by the UN, NGOs, and grievance mechanism experts,[26] it departs in notable respects in both purpose and process from the complaints resolution model of OGMs. The mechanism analysed in our case study is *single issue* (only cases of sexual assault are eligible); *time-bound* (complaints are only received for a limited time period); *retrospective* (designed to deal with known past abuses rather than designed to address issues before they escalate); *fixed-remedy* (providing a largely non-negotiable remedy); seeks *final settlement* (receipt of remedy is contingent on relinquishing the right to sue); uses a *decision-making process* which is closer to adjudication than to dialogue-based 'decide together' approaches; and, importantly, seeks to remedy large numbers of *serious human rights abuses*.

A close examination of this new type of mechanism is therefore warranted, both on its own merits and to provide analysis of and guidance on the potential benefits and risks of such mechanisms for the right to remedy. In doing so, we seek to foreground the experiences and perspectives of those directly impacted by the company's actions, including alleged sexual assault victims who are the users of the mechanism as well as those unable or unwilling to access it, and other affected stakeholders within the local community.

Human rights issues and concerns in the design and implementation of company-created human rights abuse remedy mechanisms

In October 2012, Barrick launched the *Olgeta Meri Igat Raits* (All Women Have Rights) Framework of Remediation Initiatives, which included an individual reparations programme to provide remedies to victims of sexual assault by company guards and other personnel at the Porgera Joint Venture (PJV) mine site in PNG. The launch followed years of investigations, allegations, and advocacy by victims, the local community, and international and foreign groups about extreme violence by security guards at the mine.[27] Company documents setting out the remedy programme explicitly describe it as intended to align with the Guiding Principles and international human rights.[28] Through a case study of this novel mechanism, we outline here some of the key human rights issues and concerns that may arise in the design and implementation of CHRMs generally. We specifically address five interconnected issues which we have identified in the course of our research as being particularly important, complex, or concerning. These include: the nature of consultation and dialogue; accessibility and the scope of harms addressed; amount and nature of remedy; legal waivers, and interaction with judicial processes; and transparency, external review, and continuous improvement. Close analysis of these dimensions highlights the distinctiveness of CHRMs as a remediation process, and their divergence from OGMs as they are generally conceptualised. It also reveals unresolved questions about CHRMs, and heightened risks to effective remediation posed by the use of CHRMs – risks which we argue necessitate careful scrutiny of existing and future mechanisms created by companies to remedy serious human rights impacts. These risks are best mitigated by, at a minimum, limiting the use of CHRMs to very narrow circumstances, and, more substantially, by shifting the creation and design of remedy mechanisms from companies to affected communities and companies jointly.

Consultation and dialogue

Thorough and meaningful consultation and dialogue are crucial to the legitimacy and success of a remedy mechanism. The Guiding Principles emphasise that OGMs should be 'based on engagement and dialogue', meaning that companies should consult with stakeholders on a mechanism's design and performance, and focus on dialogue as the means to address and resolve grievances. In contrast, the CHRM in Porgera was more adjudicative than dialogue-based in its resolution of individual complaints. There was limited direct dialogue between the company and rights-holders, and the mechanism offered largely fixed, non-negotiable remedies to rights-holders. Grievance mechanisms which share more in common with adjudication or arbitration than mediation have been used in the past, and community involvement in the design of a mechanism has fostered trust in decision-making processes (and sometimes direct participation, for example through community representation on adjudication panels).[29] In certain respects, the Barrick CHRM stands as a positive precedent for consultation and dialogue, demonstrating how it can improve a mechanism. In other respects, however, consultation and dialogue were inadequate because of the exclusion or shallow level of engagement with key stakeholders (most importantly, assault victims),[30] and the absence of flexibility and meaningful dialogue during the resolution of individual grievances. Where a grievance process is designed and implemented by the company itself (or its agents), attention to consultation and dialogue processes in the design and implementation of the mechanism is particularly important.

Barrick states that it conducted an 18-month consultation process with national and international NGOs, human rights and gender violence experts, as well as the former UN Special Representative for Business and Human Rights, John Ruggie.[31] Such consultation with subject-matter experts was an important step in tailoring the mechanism to the specific context and promoting rights-compliance, and should be repeated for any future similar mechanisms.[32] However, during the design phase of the mechanism, the most important stakeholders – the assault victims who were directly impacted by the company's security guards' violence and for whom the mechanism was intended – were not consulted. Many victims we interviewed in Porgera were eager and willing to enter into good faith discussions prior to the mechanism being launched, but were not given the opportunity.[33] Importantly, the failure to engage rights-holders in the design phase limited the designers' access to local expertise about what would make the mechanism effective, and led to scepticism about and a lack of confidence in the mechanism among numerous potential claimants.[34]

In addition, the local voices in Porgera who had been vocally condemning the security guard violence and who were most engaged on the issue of remedy, were not brought substantively into the consultation process.[35] Notably excluded was a local civil society group, led by men, which focuses specifically on the human rights impacts of the Porgera mine, and an association that represents traditional landowners, also led by men.[36] In defending the decision to exclude these groups, Barrick has referred to advice that including 'patriarchal groups' would potentially discourage women from coming forward, and to concerns regarding the 'good faith and integrity' of the groups.[37] Whatever legitimate concerns exist about aspects of the groups' operations – concerns which should not be ignored and which should inform *how* they might be engaged – excluding them came at a high cost. Many of their members have been *the* most important local stakeholders advocating an end to and redress for security guard violence. It is indisputable that these groups have been the primary actors engaged on issues of human rights at the Porgera mine, are trusted by many victims, and deserve significant credit for the fact that international groups and Barrick itself even became aware of the abuse allegations. In addition, while it is essential that proactive steps be taken to counteract existing gendered power asymmetries and to ensure that women are not spoken *for*, when 'gatekeeper' groups and leaders are engaged constructively, they have the potential to enable rather than block rights-holders' engagement.[38] In this case, members of these groups occupy positions of authority and trust within the community, as landowners, leaders, and especially through their work over many years reporting on and advocating to end human rights violations at the mine. Consequently, many victims reported their cases to the groups in the first instance, and when the mechanism opened, a number of women expressed hesitation in filing a complaint unless the groups 'vouched for' the process.[39] This meant that male leaders were called on by potential claimants to provide information and advice on the mechanism, but were hamstrung by the reluctance of Barrick to engage with them. Despite this, men in the groups have been extremely active in encouraging and assisting women to access the mechanism.

Excluding stakeholders who have directly suffered, or those with leadership positions, extensive networks, and a long-term stake in the local area, is counter-productive to the long-term effective resolution of grievances, and, in this case, unnecessarily impacted the effectiveness and perceived legitimacy of the mechanism, particularly in its early phases. Early and meaningful engagement with rights-holders and other key local stakeholders might have fostered improved company–community/victim trust from the start, and may also have produced a mechanism which better met the expectations, needs, and wishes of rights-holders and the community (or, equally, might have provided an early opportunity to manage some of these expectations and wishes).

The Guiding Principles also emphasise the need to focus on dialogue as the means to address and resolve grievances, noting that if adjudication is needed, an independent and legitimate third party is necessary.[40] In this case, decisions relating to individual cases, including those on eligibility and legitimacy were made by Barrick's third-party implementing agency, and an "Independent Expert" appointed by Barrick. However, Barrick determined eligibility and legitimacy criteria (the third-party implementer applied criteria which had already been determined). Moreover, consultations with victims to ascertain their views on the specific nature of reparation are critical to ensuring adequate and appropriate reparations.[41] However, interviews with claimants and their representatives indicate that dialogue about remedies with the third party implementer was generally limited. Indeed, numerous claimants expressed to us that the mechanism did not provide them a meaningful opportunity to participate in determining the remedy,[42] and those who did attempt to negotiate the quantum of compensation through the mechanism were rebuffed.[43]

This highlights clearly the relationship between the participatory design of CHRMs, and the actual and perceived legitimacy of their implementation and outcomes. The failure to meaningfully engage rights-holders and affected communities during the design phase meant that, although Barrick engaged a third-party during the implementation phase, many key aspects of the mechanism had been unilaterally determined. The constraints imposed also meant that rights-holders often did not perceive the process as being independent of the company. It is essential therefore that crucial phases of CHRMs – including design and monitoring – are based, at minimum, on meaningful dialogue with relevant stakeholders, in particular rights-holders and affected communities, if they are to embody the actual and perceived legitimacy expounded in the Guiding Principles. Failure to do so risks placing the power to determine core CHRM questions effectively in the hands of companies, and in doing so, creating mechanisms which risk better meeting the imperatives of corporations, rather than the needs of rights-holders.

Accessibility and scope of harms addressed

OGMs generally are understood as mechanisms set up to receive a wide array of complaints on an ongoing basis. This broad scope is crucial to their early warning and prevention functions, and a necessary step towards the resolution of all grievances. A defining feature of the Barrick mechanism is its narrow scope – in terms of both time (the mechanism's period of operation is limited, and only incidents occurring before a particular date may be eligible) and subject matter (only incidents of sexual assault are potentially eligible, abuses of a non-sexual nature are excluded). Given the distinct remedy purposes and retrospective focus of CHRMs, and in contrast to OGMs, there are potentially sound reasons for limiting a CHRM to, for example, a class of specific human rights violations. The limitation may improve mechanism effectiveness by tailoring processes and remedies to a particularly vulnerable group, or to the context of a particular event or series of connected abuses. A specialised mechanism may itself fulfil an expressive function, signalling the seriousness with which a company intends to respond to a set of abuses. However, in this case study, the Barrick mechanism's design limitations presented practical difficulties to ensuring that all eligible claimants could access the mechanism, and meant that a wide range of alleged abuses, even those closely connected in cause and form to the types of claims accepted in the mechanism, remain unaddressed and un-remedied. Our research suggests that in their implementation, the limitations adversely impacted the full effectiveness and perceived legitimacy of the mechanism.

The scope of issues eligible for consideration through the Barrick mechanism is limited to sexual violence, despite longstanding, extensive, and serious allegations of non-sexual abuses committed by company personnel against male and female community members.[44] These include allegations of: security personnel beating individuals with wooden sticks and butts of guns; kicking, punching, slapping, and hosing individuals; unjustified use of firearms; and in some cases, unlawful killings.[45] These alleged abuses occurred in similar and often overlapping contexts as the sexual assaults, and share causes and dynamics. Like the sexual assaults, they also resulted in local residents reporting great fear and insecurity, as well as a strong desire for investigation and redress (indeed, originally, alleged non-sexual assaults were one of the driving forces behind local advocacy efforts seeking compensation for security guard abuse).[46] The exclusion of such abuses from the mechanism has led to confusion and consternation among some local stakeholders, who question why the remedy mechanism's scope does not reflect the nature or extent of harms allegedly experienced by the local community. Many community members have welcomed remedies for sexual assault victims, but some nevertheless report feeling that other serious harms now remain arbitrarily or unfairly un-remedied, a perception that has aggravated long-standing grievances about security guard violence.

While there may be compelling reasons for limiting a CHRM to a specific class of victims or human rights violations, it is imperative that this does not lead to other classes of victims or violations being sidelined or silenced. Even where an issue-specific CHRM has been established, victims of non-eligible violations must be able to access effective and adequate remedy through other means, such as ongoing complaint-resolution OGMs or other CHRMs. Moreover, it is important to acknowledge that CHRMs (like other reparation processes) are part of, and shape, the narrative of human rights violations and community-company relations. As such, it is critical that they reflect the concerns, experiences, and needs of the community at large, as well as the priorities of the company in question.

In addition to the scope of issues eligible for consideration by the Barrick mechanism, the timeframe of operation was also limited. Unlike most OGMs, the mechanism was not a permanent and ongoing complaints system; the period of time for lodging a claim in the mechanism was limited to approximately 18 months, during which time mechanism staff periodically visited Porgera to receive complaints.[47] Potential claimants' capacity to access the mechanism during staff visits was impacted by a lack of effective outreach. The mechanism employed a limited outreach strategy which relied on certain actors, including a Barrick-created and funded local women's group, the Porgera District Women's Association (PDWA)[48] and some women in the community to distribute information about the mechanism to their networks, and, informally, on voluntary targeted outreach undertaken by intermediaries (including the authors) to previously identified victims. The decision to rely on 'word of mouth' rather than a public and media-based awareness campaign may have been well-intentioned and motivated by concern for women's security.[49] However, as implemented, and paired with the mechanism's limited focus on sexual assault, it ultimately proved insufficient. Our interviews indicate that information spread very unevenly across villages, clans, and networks, was sometimes quite inaccurate (seemingly a product of a 'telephone' effect), and did not reach numerous potential claimants, in particular those who had moved away from Porgera. The result is that it appears likely that some eligible women may have missed the opportunity to lodge claims during the life of the mechanism.[50] These dynamics highlight a right to remedy challenge for mechanisms tailored to one class of violations – accessing them may 'out' individuals as victims in ways that may threaten their privacy and security interests. (A mechanism designed for all kinds of security guard concerns, for example, would have mitigated fears that merely being seen at the mechanism's office would be to declare oneself a rape victim.) Where vulnerable groups may be at risk, and softer roll-out strategies are adopted, CHRMs may need to adopt extra steps to ensure accessibility, such as extending operating timeframes, multiple points of entry (including the ability to make complaints from 'neutral' locations, such as hospitals, as well as individually tailored meeting locations), and particularly pro-active and repeated outreach to target populations.

Amount and nature of reparations

The Guiding Principles require that remedies 'accord with internationally recognized human rights', but say little about how to specifically assess remedies.[51] International human rights law guarantees victims the right to remedy, with the overarching requirement that reparations are 'proportional to the gravity of the violations and harm suffered', [52] and are awarded on an equitable basis.[53] A major issue of contention in the Barrick CHRM is whether the compensation offered on a 'take it or leave it' basis was at an appropriate level to remedy the serious abuses victims experienced. The debate around the remedy highlights the need for further international guidance about CHRM remedies and about the kinds of safeguards that might be required to mitigate the risk that the inequality between companies and rights-holders will result in unfair 'remedies'. Such risks are particularly acute in contexts where potential claimants have few other options for pursuing remedies, and have little choice but to take what they are offered.

It has been difficult at times over the past few years for those outside the mechanism or Barrick to obtain a precise understanding of the compensation packages offered. In our initial interviews with claimants, women stated that mechanism staff offered services (such as medical care) and provided lists of items, such as crates of chickens or bales of second-hand clothes to resell, from which women could choose for their 'compensation' package.[54] Many women were offended and deeply unsatisfied with the offers as they understood them, and expressed a strong desire for other forms of compensation.[55] They welcomed medical or other services or goods, but not to the exclusion of compensation in cash or pigs, in keeping with local custom and traditional justice, and their sense of what would fairly remedy extreme violence.[56] These concerns and perspectives were communicated to Barrick by some groups during the first implementation periods of the mechanism.

Subsequently, it appeared that the packages as finalised, and signed by claimants, included, together with some medical services, school fees, counselling, and business training, a 'business grant' of around 15,000 kina (approximately US$5,662.51) together with in some cases (for example, where the claimant did not have children and thus had no need of school fees) a supplement of 5,000 kina (approximately US$1,887.50).[57] In public documents (December 2014), Barrick stated that the average value of settled packages was 23,630 kina (US$8,920.00). As this article was being finalized for publication, Barrick informed the authors that each woman would soon receive an additional 30,000 kina amount (approximately US$10,905.00).[58] According to claimants and Barrick, the money is going directly into the rights-holder's bank account, which she can access and use at her discretion. In July 2015, claimants told us that the supplements were given after the women discovered that eleven women represented by the US-based NGO ERI received what they understood to be remedies ten times greater than those awarded through the remedy mechanism. The women said that they organized themselves, and demanded that Barrick offer them similar amounts, seeing no justification for the difference, except that the eleven had their own lawyers.

These packages appear to be an attempt to balance victims' desire for monetary compensation with the potential risks entailed in cash payments to women in the Porgera context.[59] In our interviews, women spoke positively of their business training experience, and some found the counselling to be important (although others said they had never received counselling and did not know what it was). Yet numerous claimants expressed the view that the compensation package did not reflect the severity of the abuses, which included, in some cases, gang rapes and severe beatings, including enduring physical harm (scars, hearing damage, miscarriage) as well as shame, stigma, and the breakdown of their marriages and families.[60] Because of the near-uniformity of the packages, it is not clear whether or how the specific nature of each claimant's harm was a factor in the determination of their compensation. Those who were dissatisfied and had accepted the package indicated that they did so because they felt there were no feasible alternatives – either outside the mechanism (for example, pursuing a civil claim) or within it (such as negotiating a different compensation package). One woman explained, 'I don't think it's enough. But I have to get it. Some people died, waiting.'[61]

Concerns have also been expressed about whether the final packages (as at December 2014), meet international legal standards on remedies. According to Barrick's public documents, "the range of damages awards made by PNG courts for proven instances of rape … will be considered as a point of reference for the total value of the remediation packages."[62] In a new communication to the authors, Barrick now states that these national compensation amounts were intended as a "lower limit" only, and that Barrick did not set an upper limit for the third-party implementer.[63] There is some precedent for the principle that awards made in comparable domestic cases are a relevant, though not decisive consideration, in determining just satisfaction.[64] However, proportionality to the abuse is the foundational requirement,[65] and reparations for human rights abuses therefore should not necessarily be constrained by available domestic remedies.[66] Any presumption that awards available through civil litigation in PNG are necessarily fair or equitable requires, at the very least, close scrutiny. Sexual and other forms of violence against women are disturbingly prevalent in PNG, and the justice system has historically responded poorly to these issues.[67] Clearly, the amounts offered through the mechanism and to which claimants agreed, were considerably smaller than those which would typically be awarded to victims of grave sexual assault in Barrick's home state of Canada, or in United Kingdom, Australian, or US courts.[68] Considering that the waivers required of claimants preclude civil action in all foreign jurisdictions, it is reasonable to question whether the compensation offered is in fact equitable, or whether sums offered by multinational corporations should also take into account typical awards in potentially available foreign jurisdictions.

Moreover, it is unclear whether Barrick's research addressed only the upper level of compensation in cases against individual perpetrators for sexual assault, or whether the research also addressed aggravating factors and the many additional kinds of harms women suffered, including what in some cases may amount to torture. It is also unclear what scope of potential individual or corporate liabilities the research addressed. Did it only address the liability that one person might owe for one case of rape, or did it also consider appropriate liabilities for repeated assaults, or any appropriate liabilities for a corporation in a case where employees apparently committed many assaults on indigenous women over a number of years? Given that rights-holders are required to waive all future civil claims against the company, serious consideration at the international level needs to be given to whether the kinds of remedies offered in this case are appropriate.

Legal waivers, and interaction with judicial processes

One of the greatest risks posed to the right to effective remedy by the CHRM examined here emanates from the requirement that successful claimants waive their legal rights to sue in order to receive compensation. At issue is whether imposing a condition of release of liabilities on rights-holders is consistent with the Guiding Principles and human rights, and whether it is appropriate in the circumstances. This has been the subject of vigorous debate in the context of the Barrick mechanism, which requires that successful claimants waive their right to pursue compensation through civil proceedings, in PNG or any other jurisdiction, as a condition of receiving compensation.[69] The issues examined in relation to the Barrick mechanism raise difficult and important questions, with relevance also to any future CHRMs imposing final settlement.

The Commentary to Principle 29 of the Guiding Principles states that OGMs should not be used to preclude access to other judicial and non-judicial grievance mechanisms.[70] A number of NGOs have argued that requiring claimants to release Barrick from any future liability falls foul of this requirement.[71] Barrick has rejected this claim, citing the need for final settlement and certainty. It has also emphasised that claimants are free to pursue concurrent civil claims, only relinquishing any legal claims upon accepting a final offer of compensation from Barrick, and that criminal processes are not part of the waiver.[72]

In July 2013, the Office of the High Commissioner for Human Rights (OHCHR) took the unusual step of offering an opinion on some of the procedural and substantive issues concerning the Barrick mechanism, with a view to providing principled interpretive guidance based on the Guiding Principles.[73] On the question of waivers, the OHCHR offered the following guidance:

> the presumption should be that as far as possible, no waiver should be imposed on any claims settled through a non-judicial grievance mechanism. Nonetheless, and as there is no prohibition per se on legal waivers in current international standards and practice, situations may arise where business enterprises wish to ensure that, for reasons of predictability and finality, a legal waiver be required from claimants at the end of a remediation process.[74]

In reaching this conclusion, the OHCHR applied the legal standards attaching to post-conflict state-based remediation programmes, noting that 'for state-based remediation frameworks there is no consistent practice or jurisprudence on the issue from regional and national courts'.[75] The opinion goes on to note that contextual factors may play a significant role in deciding on the desirability of making reparations programmes final, such as the functioning or not of legal systems; preventing anyone from receiving compensation twice for the same violation; and that the presumption should be to leave the possibility of accessing courts as un-curtailed as possible.

The OHCHR opinion raises a number of issues which require further clarification. These include whether there is a legal basis for transplanting legal standards from post-conflict state-based reparations schemes directly to CHRMs. In addition, the OHCHR opinion does not consider whether the factors posited in favour of finality in post-conflict state-based reparations schemes also apply to CHRMs. Limited and over-stretched national budgets, unwieldy numbers of potential claims which might overwhelm national courts, and the need for broad social reconciliation are often important considerations in designing a state-based reparations scheme, but do not clearly map onto mechanisms created by corporations to provide remedies for human rights violations. In other words, it is unclear exactly how the fact that the presumption against a waiver is displaceable in the case of post-conflict state-based reparations programmes is instructive in determining whether and when the presumption against waivers ought to be displaceable in the case of corporate grievance mechanisms.

Accepting the premise that the presumption against waivers might be displaceable in some cases, the OHCHR opinion provides limited guidance on the factors to be considered when assessing displaceability in specific cases. The OHCHR opinion mentions only one – the desire of the company (which is also the likely defendant in any civil suit) for finality and predictability.[76] The opinion then seems to suggest that this desire may alone be sufficient to displace the presumption against waivers.

However, this fails to take into account potential power dynamics between companies and claimants, and the possibility that settlement through alternative dispute resolution might, in practice, be a coercive or unequal process because of the uneven distribution of resources between the parties.[77] These dynamics are particularly significant where large Western transnational corporations operate in remote regions of countries in the Global South and where business activities impact communities marginalised in the prevailing international economic order. In these circumstances (as in the case of victims in Porgera), there is a real risk that rights-holders will have few other options, and a limited understanding of their rights and options,[78] a disadvantage exacerbated by generally low levels of education and literacy. In comparison to the Northern beneficiaries of transnational corporate activity, rights-holders in the Global South adversely impacted by business activities may be grossly economically disadvantaged, and have been waiting years for compensation for the harms inflicted on them by company employees. Many of these factors are present in the Porgera case, where the need for some compensation to be provided in the near-term was cited by a number of women as an inducement for accepting compensation they felt was otherwise inadequate. Few saw that they had an alternative to the offer made through the mechanism, and many see their domestic judicial system as inefficient and subject to delays, which sexual assault claimants generally lack the resources to access in any event. These factors raise the prospect that, without strict controls, rights-holders' less favourable position may be exploited in future CHRMs to secure legal indemnity for companies, including from action in foreign jurisdictions.

Making the strict compliance of a CHRM with the effectiveness criteria outlined in the Guiding Principles a minimum requirement for the displacement of the presumption against waiver would begin to address this asymmetry of power when assessing the legitimacy and appropriateness of a waiver. This would refocus emphasis on the rights-compatibility of the process and on affected communities. Doing so would require, however, a serious commitment and investment by companies to demonstrating compliance in practice, rather than mere alignment between the effectiveness criteria and a written framework. This will invariably necessitate intensive on-the-ground investigation, and genuine engagement with potential claimants (both those who access the CHRM, and those who opt not to), the broader community, and other stakeholders. It will also require cooperation with independent third parties which are able and willing to monitor implementation. In addition, to the extent that transnational companies seek to indemnify themselves against suits in a range of foreign jurisdictions through CHRM waivers, rights-holders should be ensured access to independent legal advice about their possible international and foreign claims. This is an important measure towards putting companies and communities on a more equal footing. In cases where effective monitoring and third-party oversight is either impossible or not supported by the company, and where legal advice is limited, predicating reparations from CHRMs on the waiver of legal rights should generally be considered illegitimate.

Lastly, it is important to consider the potential implications of CHRMs not only on specific rights-holders, but also on the justice systems of the states in which they are established. Of particular concern is whether CHRMs may in *practice* act as substitutes for rights-holder engagement with the formal (civil) legal system, other existing tribal justice mechanisms, or indeed, criminal processes. This 'parallel justice system', even if beneficial in the short term, might pose a long-term risk to already fragile legal institutions in the Global South, by undermining confidence in, and efforts to improve, state-based judicial processes, in turn entrenching governance gaps. It is too early to say whether such risks will eventuate. However, it is critical that the interaction between CHRMs and the formal legal system is monitored, and any adverse impacts on formal legal processes be considered in assessments of CHRMs.

Transparency, external review, and continuous improvement

The Guiding Principles require that OGMs are transparent,[79] and a 'source of continuous learning', meaning that they draw on relevant measures to identify lessons for improving the mechanism and preventing future grievances and harms.[80] The importance of effective monitoring of and transparency in OGMs is also emphasised in much of the leading commentary on company-created grievance processes, which highlight the importance of releasing information on the registration, management, and outcomes of complaints,[81] in order to demonstrate the mechanism's legitimacy and retain broad trust.[82] The Barrick experience is instructive, suggesting not only that there is a close relationship between these criteria and issues of consultation and engagement, but also that external third parties have a pivotal role to play in providing oversight and advocating for continuous improvement of such mechanisms.

The written documents setting out the mechanism did not address the question of transparency, or set out a procedure for the public release of information, which led to initial concern about whether or how information might be shared. In practice, the company publicly released some updates on the mechanism, including a summary of its progress towards the end of the life of the mechanism which included information about the total number of settled, discontinued, or withdrawn complaints, and the highest, lowest, and average remedy package values.[83] However, outside reviewers and local stakeholders found it difficult at various points in the life of the mechanism to obtain clear details on the progress of its implementation, or on the status of changes.[84] Important information not yet made public includes details about the basis for declined cases, the kinds of harms forming the basis for complaints, and the nature of the perpetrators, as well as the findings of a mid-programme review.[85]

A formal process to enable claimants and others to provide feedback was not created in the original written mechanism documents. During implementation, some valuable informal processes for feedback developed, although their at times ad hoc nature undermined the creation of effective channels of communication with those with valuable views and information. Importantly, and as an example of continuous learning, Barrick made a number of positive changes to the mechanism during implementation, following (frequently unsolicited) feedback and concerns raised by local and international groups (including ourselves) which have had sustained engagement with victims, community members, and other stakeholders.[86]

There are several lessons to be learned from this for future mechanisms. The first is the importance of formalising at the design stage, and ensuring the proper implementation of, channels for feedback from rights-holders and affected communities. Consultation and dialogue should be fostered throughout the lifecycle of a mechanism. This includes two-way communication between the company (providing information regularly on the progress and outcomes of the process), and rights-holders and the broader community (providing feedback on their experiences of the process, needs, and expectations). Effective communication and monitoring by local communities can enhance alignment between the mechanism as it is implemented, and the expectations of rights-holders, and in doing so can contribute to improved relations between the company and community.

The second lesson is that release of information enhances effective external review and mechanism legitimacy, and that limited public release of information hampers the capacity of external monitors to contribute to the continuous improvement of a mechanism. External monitoring by independent third parties can play a positive role in the life of a CHRM, by supporting its effectiveness and legitimacy, and should be facilitated and actively engaged by corporations. While this should be applied to any company-led grievance process, it is particularly important in the case of CHRMs, where the legal rights of victims of serious human rights violations are at stake. As noted in the preceding section, such external oversight is a relevant factor in assessing the legitimacy of a waiver, and is essential in ensuring that a CHRM is a channel rather than an obstacle to the realisation of victims' right to effective remedy.

Conclusions

The right to remedy is a fundamental right, yet there are significant legal and logistical barriers to its realisation for communities adversely impacted by the operations of companies. The Guiding Principles envisage a prominent role for non-state non-judicial company-created operational-level grievance mechanisms in facilitating victims' right to remedy. This article examined in detail one such mechanism, Barrick Gold's PNG *Olgeta Meri Igat Raits* (All Women Have Rights) Framework of Remediation Initiatives, a novel form of company-created remedy mechanism designed to provide remedies to victims of widespread sexual assaults. Based on this analysis, we offer here several concluding thoughts.

A new kind of remedy: company-created human rights remedy mechanisms: We identify the emergence of a new species of operational level non-judicial grievance mechanism, which we refer to as 'company-created human rights remedy mechanisms' (CHRMs). CHRMs represent a significant departure from traditional complaints resolution OGMs, which are generally conceived as early-warning and resolution systems for low-level complaints before they escalate. In contrast, the central feature of CHRMs is their focus on providing remedy for past known human rights impacts. The case study we examine here is also distinct from typical OGMs in that it is narrow in scope, time-bound, retrospective, offers largely fixed remedies, seeks final settlement, uses a decision-making process in which the company sets up a process closer to adjudication than to dialogue-based 'decide together' approaches, and which seeks to remedy large numbers of serious human rights abuses. While few grievance mechanisms of this form exist, the Barrick mechanism has been widely debated in international fora, and is seen as either a potential precedent or warning for new ways of addressing corporate responsibility for human rights abuses. Discussions in international fora indicate that the Barrick mechanism is potentially the start of a new wave of corporate responses to human rights allegations.

Company-created human rights remedy mechanisms offer benefits: The current corporate accountability landscape provides all too few feasible options for rights-holders to obtain remedies and some semblance of justice. CHRMs may justifiably seek to fill existing governance and accountability gaps. They may be useful complementary or supplementary remedy mechanisms, or perhaps even just pragmatic or 'better than nothing' paths to remedies for rights-holders where other options do not exist or have limited viability. Where implemented well, they may enable the participatory development of innovative and tailored remedies, align remediation processes and outcomes with the expectations and needs of victims, provide a swifter, less bureaucratic path to remedy, empower rights-holders, restore dignity by offering acknowledgement and satisfaction, and improve company–community relations. In the case study examined here, the corporation took numerous positive steps and instituted various processes which other companies should look to as instructive precedent. In the design phase, these included consideration of the security and confidentiality of claimants, and consultation with subject-matter experts. During implementation, the reported provision of a suite of services to women (including medical and psychosocial care, as well as livelihoods assistance and cash compensation), should be considered favourably by future CHRMs as an option for ensuring some of the harms experienced by victims are addressed and mitigating some of the risks of large cash payments. Importantly, there was some willingness to alter aspects of the mechanism in response to feedback. While a more structured path for feedback would be desirable, the changes which the company made during the course of implementation improved the mechanism. In this case, the mechanism has encouraged and given some women the confidence to report assaults, provided women with opportunities to improve their economic independence, and provided some with the sense that – finally – they have been heard. Importantly, women who suffered greatly and otherwise would likely have received nothing, have received some compensation for harms suffered at the hands of company employees. The reality described by Rombouts et al. in discussing state-based reparations applies equally to direct remediation by corporations:

> The choice for a very large majority of victims is in any case not between obtaining maximum reparation through court and a lesser form of reparation offered by the government outside court, but rather between the latter and no reparation at all.[87]

Operational-level remedy mechanisms entail risks: Without stringent safeguards, company-run mechanisms may pose risks to the right to remedy. While CHRMs may be a way for companies to meet their responsibilities to ensure victims' right to remedy, companies may be also animated by a number of other interests. A corporation's interest in avoiding embarrassing and reputation-harming litigation or in minimising the risk of potentially more expensive and unpredictable court orders, settlements, or negotiated/arbitrated remedies may influence a company's decision to establish a CHRM as well as the mechanism's design. These corporate interests may sit uneasily or directly conflict with rights-holders' interests and rights. Ultimately, the risk looms large that CHRM processes and outcomes may reflect the power differentials between companies and impacted communities, or that companies may be able to exploit power differentials to undermine victims' rights to an effective remedy. 'One of the most common inadequacies of grievance mechanisms is that they are structured to leave the company in a position of power and the complainant in a position of dependency',[88] and where grave violations of human rights are at stake, the potential for this power differential to lead to unjust outcomes weighs more heavily. These risks are amplified where communities are especially marginalised or vulnerable, and where regular physical access by third-party monitors is hampered due to geographic isolation or insecurity. In addition, CHRMs risk *in practice* acting as substitutes for rights-holder engagement with the formal (civil) legal system, other existing tribal justice mechanisms, or indeed, criminal processes. There is a long-term risk that if corporations regularly create parallel private remedial mechanisms in the Global South, confidence in and efforts to improve state-based judicial processes may be undermined and governance gaps further entrenched.

Thus, the use of company-created remedy mechanisms should be sparing and subject to strict safeguards: Despite the potential benefits of CHRMs, because of the risks they pose to the right to remedy, we urge great caution in their use. They should be subjected to strict safeguards tailored to the *severity* of the claims, the *vulnerability* of the community, and *the finality of the settlement*. Safeguards are required in particular to ensure meaningful consultation and engagement with stakeholders, a mechanism scope which reflects the full range of serious violations of human rights experienced by the local community, adequate and appropriate compensation, transparency, as well as to prevent a mechanism being used to secure finalisation of claims at the expense of rights-holders' interests. Final settlement may be appropriate where the harms involved are less severe and where the mechanism has complied with the highest standards of the effectiveness criteria. However, even in such cases, relying on a company to assess and report on its own compliance with the effectiveness criteria is a risky proposition. This is a result of both the company's potentially conflicting motivations (on the one hand, to administer an effective and fair mechanism, on the other to limit its own exposure to liability), and its capacities (due to the existing power dynamic and relationship between the company and communities, it may be poorly placed to effectively elicit feedback and monitor implementation). This suggests that company mechanisms should only be used to achieve final settlement of claims where there is transparent and effective oversight by an independent third party.[89] Where grave violations of human rights are involved, there should be a very strong presumption against final settlement of claims through waiver, as the risk that a remedy mechanism may be used to limit a company's liability, without sufficient safeguards to ensure substantive and procedural justice for rights-holders, may often be too great to be managed effectively. In cases of serious human rights abuse, a waiver should be used only in rare cases and with, at minimum, clear demonstration of equality of arms, fully informed claimant consent and provision of comprehensive legal advice, and strict compliance with human rights principles and the effectiveness criteria.

Need for further academic and policy research: The potential for the Barrick mechanism to serve as a precedent or model for future mechanisms, and the attendant potential impacts on rights to remedy, call for further research into mechanisms with similar features. To date, complaints-focused OGMs have been the subject of virtually all of the academic, civil society, and policy-level scrutiny of project-level remedy mechanisms. This article has sought to begin the process of understanding CHRMs, and the standards which ought to apply to them. Much more academic and policy research and analysis is needed. Fruitful and important subjects for future research could include: building typologies of the various project-level mechanisms and their key features; considering the impact of these typologies on interpretations of the effectiveness criteria (are the criteria adequate for all types? How should factors such as the severity of the human rights violation in question impact the interpretation of the criteria?); analysing the legality and suitability of the use of waivers; considering the meaning of 'dialogue and engagement', and the relationship between this criterion and legitimacy; suitable models for third-party oversight of mechanisms; and considering how the effectiveness and success of CHRMs can be measured or evaluated.

When considering these questions, it will be important to look beyond the Guiding Principles and existing case studies of OGMs for guidance. CHRMs may well have more in common with some transitional justice or state-based reparations processes, or structured settlements, than they do with complaints-resolution OGMs. It will be valuable to locate these mechanisms within the broader literature not only on corporate social responsibility and management theory, but also international and domestic laws relating to remedy and reparation, global governance, and transitional justice. It will also be valuable to consider how principles of law and practice emerging from these processes may assist in the interpretation of the Guiding Principles, and provide guidance where the Guiding Principles are silent.

A better approach?: company–community remedy mechanisms: In our view, one option for a potentially more effective and legitimate model of project-level direct remediation would be a mechanism created and administered as a *partnership* between a company and primary stakeholders,[90] including rights-holders, their representatives, local civil society, traditional leaders (where relevant), and engaging secondary stakeholders and independent experts. In this model, primary stakeholders would have the power to influence decisions, power would shared, and agendas would be jointly set. In other words, an improved model would involve the corporation and impacted individuals agreeing together to mediation or arbitration, or to a jointly created remedy mechanism. This approach has the benefit of empowering rights-holders and allowing them to share ownership in the remediation process and outcomes, and opening ongoing channels of communication and building trust. Such a mechanism should also, in cognisance of the risks associated with the direct remediation of human rights violations and the power asymmetry between the company and community, incorporate external oversight and the highest possible levels of transparency,[91] and should generally forego the finalisation of claims through legal waiver in cases concerning serious human rights abuses.

Securing redress for violations of human rights by corporate actors is a longstanding global challenge, and so it is unsurprising that operational-level non-judicial mechanisms, allowing direct and potentially swifter and more convenient resolution of disputes, have been embraced as a promising and important path to remedy. However, these mechanisms entail risks, which are amplified where they are used to remedy past serious violations of human rights, rather than as prevention-oriented complaints processes. Significant safeguards and additional research and analysis are required if private remedy processes are to consistently uphold rather than undermine the right to remedy.

Acknowledgements

This article was written in the course of a multi-year investigation of the Porgera Joint Venture Gold Mine, an investigation jointly undertaken by the Global Justice Clinic at New York University School of Law, the International Human Rights Clinic at Harvard Law School, and the Human Rights Clinic at Columbia Law School. The results of those investigations will be published in 2015 by the clinics. Parts of this article were researched and written while the authors worked at New York University School of Law.

We wish to acknowledge the many residents of Porgera, Papua New Guinea, who, at great risk to themselves, have been advocating for human rights and seeking justice for abuses they and their communities have experienced. We particularly thank those who shared with us their experiences of violence and their views about just remedies. We also thank law students in the human rights clinics at Harvard Law School, New York University School of Law, and Columbia Law School for their research and commitment over the years, as well as Philip Alston and Joanne Bauer for their comments on drafts of this article, and Tyler Giannini and Amelia Evans for their invaluable contributions to the research project that informed this article.

Disclosure statement

No potential conflict of interest was reported by the authors.

Notes

1. See for example, Gwynne Skinner, Robert McCorquodale, Olivier De Schutter, and Andie Lambe, *The Third Pillar: Access to Judicial Remedies for Human Rights Violations by Transnational Business*, International Corporate Accountability Roundtable, CORE, the European Coalition for Corporate Justice (December 2013) (analysing ten key obstacles); Nadia Bernaz, 'Enhancing Corporate Accountability for Human Rights Violations: Is Extraterritoriality the Magic Potion?', *Journal of Business Ethics* 117 (2013): 493–511; Richard Meeran, 'Access to Remedy: The United Kingdom Experience of MNC Tort Litigation for Human Rights Violations', in *Human Rights Obligations of Business: Beyond the Corporate Responsibility to Respect?*, ed. Surya Deva and David Bilchitz (Cambridge: Cambridge University Press, 2013), 378 (describing corporate legal accountability as 'generally regarded an almost impenetrable challenge', but providing analysis of some successful efforts in English courts); Tineke Lambooy, Aikaterini Argyrou, and Mary Varner, 'An Analysis and Practical Application of the Guiding Principles on Providing Remedies with Special Reference to Case Studies Related to Oil Companies', in *Human Rights Obligations of Business: Beyond the Corporate Responsibility to Respect?* ed. Surya Deva and David Bilchitz (Cambridge: Cambridge University Press, 2013), 329–78; Gonzalo Aguilar Cavallo, 'Pascua Lama, Human Rights, and Indigenous Peoples: A Chilean Case Through the Lens of International Law', *Goettingen Journal of International Law* 5, no. 1 (2013): 215–49; Justine Nolan and Luke Taylor, 'Corporate Responsibility for Economic, Social and Cultural Rights: Rights in Search of a Remedy?', *Journal of Business Ethics* 87 (2009): 433–51; Chilenye Nwapi, 'Jurisdiction by Necessity and the Regulation of the Transnational Corporate Actor', *Utrecht Journal of International and European Law* 30, no. 78 (2014): 25–31 (describing legal and political obstacles to accountability); Beth Stephens, 'The Amorality of Profit: Transnational Corporations and Human Rights', *Berkeley Journal of International Law* 20 (2002): 45–91; Jérémie Gilbert, 'Corporate Accountability and Indigenous Peoples: Prospects and Limitations of the US Alien Tort Claims Act', *International Journal on Minority and Group Rights* 19, no. 1 (2012): 25–52 (describing the accountability gap faced by indigenous populations when their lands are impacted by large scale extractives projects); Wolfgang Kaleck and Miriam Saage-Maaβ, 'Corporate Accountability for Human Rights Violations Amounting to International Crimes', *Journal of International Criminal Justice* 8 (2010): 699–724 (analysis of enforcement mechanism inadequacy). Numerous guides which provide practical advice for navigating these difficulties also exist. See for example, Accountability Counsel, *Accountability Resource Guide*, Version 7.1 (San Francisco: Accountability Counsel, 2012); The International Federation for Human Rights, *Corporate Accountability for Human Rights Abuses: A Guide for Victims and NGOs on Recourse Mechanisms* (updated March 2012).
2. Other common non-judicial grievance mechanisms include national government-created mechanisms such as national human rights institutions, and multi-stakeholder initiative complaint mechanisms. See, Office of the High Commissioner for Human Rights, 'Taking Stock: 1 ½ Years After the Endorsement of the GP's Pillar III: Access to Non-Judicial Remedy' (Background Note on the Parallel Session, Forum on Business and Human Rights, 4–5 December 2012). For critiques of multi-stakeholder non-judicial remedy mechanisms in practice, see, Luc W. Fransen and Ans Kolk, 'Standards Global Rule-Setting for Business: A Critical Analysis of Multi-Stakeholder Standards', *Organization* 14 (2007): 667; John Morrison and Luke Wilde, *The Effectiveness of Multi-Stakeholder Initiatives in the Oil and Gas Sector: Summary Report* (TwentyFifty Ltd, March 2007); Marina Ottaway, 'Corporatism Goes Global: International Organizations, Nongovernmental Organization Networks, and Transnational Business', *Global Governance* 7 (2001): 265–92. On the effectiveness of the OECD

Guidelines for Multinational Enterprises, see OECD Watch, *Calling for Corporate Accountability: A Guide to the 2011 OECD Guidelines for Multinational Enterprises* (June 2013); Jernej Letnar Černič, 'Corporate Responsibility for Human Rights: A Critical Analysis of the OECD Guidelines for Multinational Enterprises', *Hanse Law Review* 3, no. 1 (2008): 71–100.

3. Many OGMs include violations of human rights within their eligibility criteria, and so it is possible that isolated incidents of grave abuses have been dealt with through OGMs in the past. We are, however, aware of only two OGMs designed specifically to deal with large numbers of grave violations of human rights abuses in this fashion, and following the UN Guiding Principles. These include the mechanism discussed in this article, and a mechanism which has been instituted at African Barrick Gold's (a subsidiary of Barrick Gold Corporation) North Mara mine in Tanzania. See African Barrick Gold, *Update on the North Mara Sexual Assault Allegations* (20 December 2013), http://www.africanbarrickgold.com/~/media/Files/A/African-Barrick-Gold/Attachments/press-releases/2013/abg-update-north-mara-sexual-assault-allegations_20122013.pdf; African Barrick Gold, Letter to Ms Coumans and Ms Feeney Regarding African Barrick Gold's Non-Judicial Remedy Programs at North Mara, Tanzana (11 March 2014), http://www.africanbarrickgold.com/~/media/Files/A/African-Barrick-Gold/Attachments/pdf/abg-response-to-MWC-RAID-march-2014.pdf. We have not studied the North Mara mechanism, but concerns overlapping with those raised in this article have been raised by non-governmental organisations (NGOs). See, CORE, 'Corporate Abuse Victims Sign Away Rights Under UK Company Complaint Process' (Press Release, 20 January 2014), http://corporate-responsibility.org/wp-content/uploads/2014/01/ABG-greivance-mech-PR_140127_final.pdf.
4. This article draws on information obtained by researchers from the Global Justice Clinic and Center for Human Rights and Global Justice (New York University School of Law), the International Human Rights Clinic (Harvard Law School), and the Human Rights Clinic (Columbia Law School) (including the authors) during numerous visits to Porgera between 2006 and 2015, as well as continual external monitoring of the situation in Porgera and regular communication with Porgerans and other stakeholders from 2006 to the present. The research team has conducted hundreds of interviews with local women and other stakeholders. In addition to information gleaned through interviews and field visits, this case study draws on publicly available documents relating to the mechanism, correspondence, communications with Barrick, participation in international grievance mechanism workshops, and secondary literature relating to grievance mechanisms, international law, and victim participation and community engagement. The investigations and methods are described in detail in a report of the clinics to be published in 2015.
5. Barrick Gold Corp., *Olgeta Meri Igat Raits: A Framework of Remediation Initiatives in Response to Violence Against Women in the Porgera Valley* (uploaded 16 May 2013), http://www.barrick.com/files/porgera/Framework-of-remediation-initiatives.pdf.
6. Barrick Gold Corp., *The Porgera Joint Venture Remedy Framework* (1 December 2014), 13, http://www.barrick.com/files/porgera/Porgera-Joint-Venture-Remedy-Framework-Dec1-2014.pdf. The value of individual components of the package is not clear from Barrick's public materials. EarthRights International (ERI), which represents some of the alleged victims, has published some of the agreements (although Barrick has stated that these agreements were drafts and not finalized). Those indicate that within the package, women receive a 'business grant' of 15,000 kina (at that time, approximately US$5,620), with the rest of the package split between medical costs, counselling, business training, school fees, and a financial supplement. ERI assessed the value of the final package at 21,320 kina (or around US$8,176). See, ERI, 'Survivors of Rape by Barrick Gold Security Guards Offered "Business Grants" and "training" in Exchange for Waiving Legal Rights' (Press Release, 21 November 2014), http://www.earthrights.org/media/survivors-rape-barrick-gold-security-guards-offered-business-grants-and-training-exchange. We have also reviewed numerous signed agreements, which are near-identical to the agreements made public by ERI. In June 2015, as this article was being prepared for publication, Barrick informed the authors that each claimant would receive an additional sum of 30,000 kina. (Email from Peter Sinclair, Senior Vice President, Corporate Affairs, Barrick Gold Corporation, to Sarah Knuckey (24 June 2015)).
7. Barrick Gold Corp., *The Porgera Joint Venture Remedy Framework*, 12.
8. Indeed, Barrick itself seems to distinguish its mechanism from the plethora of complaints-based OGMs when, in describing its creation of the mechanism, it states, 'Barrick is among the first

companies to put into practice the Guiding Principle of the "right to remedy" since the ratification of the Principles by the UN Human Rights Council in 2011' (Barrick Gold Corp., 'Barrick Corrects False Claims Concerning Remediation Program at Porgera' (1 February 2013), http://www.barrick.com/files/porgera/Barrick-corrects-false-claims-concerning-Remediation-Program-at-Porgera.pdf).

9. A/HRC/17/31, ¶ 6.
10. Special Representative of the Secretary-General on the Issue of Human Rights and Transnational and other Business Enterprises, *Guiding Principles on Business and Human Rights: Implementing the United Nations 'Protect, Respect and Remedy' Framework*, Human Rights Council, UN Doc. A/HRC/17/31 (21 March 2011). See discussion in Robert McCorquodale, 'Corporate Social Responsibility and International Human Rights Law', *Journal of Business Ethics* 87 (2009): 385–400.
11. Guiding Principles, Principle 25. See also, *Addressing Grievances from Project-Affected Communities* (International Finance Corporation, Good Practice Note No. 7, 2009), 4 (describing operational-level grievance mechanism as, 'a process for receiving, evaluating, and addressing project-level grievances from affected communities at the level of the company, or project'); Oxfam Australia, *Community-Company Grievance Resolution: A Guide for the Australian Mining Industry* (2010), 7 (describing company-level grievance mechanism as, 'a company-supported, locally based and formalised method, pathway or process to prevent and resolve community concerns with, or grievances about, the performance or behavior of a company, its contractors or employees'); International Council on Mining and Metals, *Handling and Resolving Local Level Concerns and Grievances* (2009), 4 (defining 'complaints mechanism' as a 'set of processes a company may have in place to deal with local level concerns and grievances').
12. Guiding Principles, Principle 22.
13. See, Shift, *Remediation, Grievance Mechanisms and the Corporate Responsibility to Respect Human Rights*, Workshop Report No. 5 (May 2014) (conceiving of OGMs within internal ecosystems and external landscapes of remedy processes).
14. Guiding Principles, Commentary, Principle 22; Guiding Principles, Principle 29.
15. Guiding Principles, Principle 31.
16. Ibid. The full criteria are: Legitimate (enabling trust from the stakeholder groups for whose use they are intended, and being accountable for the fair conduct of grievance processes); Accessible (being known to all stakeholder groups for whose use they are intended, and providing adequate assistance for those who may face particular barriers to access); Predictable (providing a clear and known procedure with an indicative time frame for each stage, and clarity on the types of process and outcome available and means of monitoring implementation); Equitable (seeking to ensure that aggrieved parties have reasonable access to sources of information, advice and expertise necessary to engage in a grievance process on fair, informed and respectful terms); Transparent (keeping parties to a grievance informed about its progress, and providing sufficient information about the mechanism's performance to build confidence in its effectiveness and meet any public interest at stake); Rights-compatible (ensuring that outcomes and remedies accord with internationally recognised human rights); A source of continuous learning (drawing on relevant measure to identify lessons for improving the mechanism and preventing future grievances and harms); and Based on engagement and dialogue (consulting the stakeholder groups for whose use they are intended on their design and performance, and focusing on dialogue as the means to address and resolve grievances).
17. Guiding Principles, Commentary, Principle 29.
18. See for examples, United Nations Office of the High Commissioner for Human Rights, *The Corporate Responsibility to Respect Human Rights: An Interpretive Guide* (2012), 58 ('In sum, their primary purpose is to provide an early point of recourse to identify and address the concerns of directly affected stakeholders before they escalate or lead to otherwise preventable harm.'); Cristina Cedillo, *Better Access to Remedy in Company-Community Conflicts in the field of CSR: A Model for Company-Based Grievance Mechanisms* (The Hague Institute for Environmental Security, 2011), 4 ('the objective of a company-based grievance mechanism is providing an early-stage recourse and possible resolution'); International Petroleum Industry Environmental Conservation Association (IPIECA), *Operational Level Grievance Mechanisms: IPIECA Good Practice Survey* (2012), 6 (highlighting 'early identification

and resolution' and 'reduces the potential for complaints to escalate' as key effects of a good OGM).

19. See for example, Brian Husted, 'Organizational Justice and the Management of Stakeholder Relations', *Journal of Business Ethics* 17, no. 6 (1998): 643–51; Brian Bemmels and Janice R. Foley, 'Grievance Procedure Research: A Review and Theoretical Recommendations', *Journal of Management* 22, no. 3 (1996): 359–84.
20. See for example, CSR Europe, *Assessing the Effectiveness of Company Level Grievance Mechanisms* (2013), 4 (explaining that 87% of CSR's members already have an operational-level grievance mechanism in place, and 40% have begun addressing community grievances in a systematic way); Damiano de Felice, 'Measuring the Effectiveness of Grievance Mechanisms: Between Key Performance Indicators and Engagement with Affected Stakeholders', *Measuring B&HR (blog)* (London School of Economics, 11 April 2014), http://blogs.lse.ac.uk/businesshumanrights/2014/04/11/damiano-de-felice-measuring-the-effectiveness-of-grievance-mechanisms-between-key-performance-indicators-and-engagement-with-affected-stakeholders / (discussing challenges in measuring the effectiveness of OGMs).
21. See for example, SOMO, 'Human Rights and Grievance Mechanisms: Summary of Four-Year SOMO Programme Funded by the Dutch Ministry of Foreign Affairs, Human Rights Fund 2012–2015' (November 2012); Corporate Accountability Research, 'Non-Judicial Redress Mechanisms Project', http://corporateaccountabilityresearch.net/project-1/; Shift, *Remediation, Grievance Mechanisms and the Corporate Responsibility to Respect Human Rights*; ACCESS Facility hosted an Expert Meeting on 3–4 April 2014 on the topic 'Sharing experiences and finding practical solutions regarding the implementation of the UNGP's effectiveness criteria in grievance mechanisms.' Sarah Knuckey attended the meeting. For more information, see http://accessfacility.org/3-4-april-expert-meeting-sharing-experiences-and-finding-practical-solutions-regarding.
22. See also, International Finance Corporation, *Addressing Grievances from Project-Affected Communities: Guidance for Projects and Companies on Designing Grievance Mechanisms* (2009); Caroline Rees, *Rights-Compatible Grievance Mechanisms – A Guidance Tool for Companies and their Stakeholders* (Corporate Social Responsibility Initiative, Harvard Kennedy School, 2008); Deanna Kemp and Nora Gotzmann, *Community Grievance Mechanisms and Australian Mining Companies Offshore: An Industry Discussion Paper* (Centre for Social Responsibility in Mining, the University of Queensland, 2008); Office of the Compliance/Advisor Ombudsman for the International Finance Corporation and Multilateral Investment Guarantee Agency, *A Guide to Designing and Implementing Grievance Mechanisms for Development Projects* (2008); Caroline Rees, *Grievance Mechanisms for Business and Human Rights: Strengths, Weaknesses and Gaps*, Working Paper No. 40 (Corporate Social Responsibility Initiative, Harvard Kennedy School, 2008); Deanna Kemp and Carol Bond, *Mining Industry Perspectives on Handling Community Grievances – Summary and Analysis of Industry Interviews* (Centre for Social Responsibility in Mining, the University of Queensland and Corporate Social Responsibility Initiative, Centre for Social Responsibility in Mining, the University of Queensland, and Corporate Social Responsibility Initiative, Harvard Kennedy School, 2009).
23. Many of these studies have employed a similar methodology, relying on the cooperation of the company deploying the mechanism and with limited engagement with local stakeholders and end-users. In fact, a recent publication by the Institute for International Development (IIED) identified a lack of material on the community perspectives on company-led grievance mechanisms as a gap in existing literature (see, Emma Wilson and Emma Blackmore, eds, *Dispute or Dialogue?: Community Perspectives on Company-Led Grievance Mechanisms* (London: International Institute for Environment and Development, 2013), 11.
24. See for example, Caroline Rees, *Piloting Principles for Effective Company-Stakeholder Grievance Mechanisms: A Report of Lessons Learned*; Barbara Linder et al., *The Right to Remedy: Extrajudicial Complaints Mechanisms for Resolving Conflict of Interest between Business Actors and those Affected by their Operations* (Vienna: Ludwig Boltzmann Institute, 2013); Wilson and Blackmore, *Dispute or Dialogue?*; Oxfam Australia, *Community-Company Grievance Resolution*.
25. See for example, Caroline Rees and David Vermijs, *Mapping Grievance Mechanisms in the Business and Human Rights Arena* (describing the case study of Xstrata Copper in Peru and its use of arbitration); Oxfam Australia, *Community-Company Grievance Resolution*

(describing the 'Mesa de Dialogo' or 'Dialogue Table' mediations conducted by Oxfam Australia's Mining Ombudsman at Xstrata's Tintaya copper mine in Peru).

26. See for example, Office of the High Commission for Human Rights, *Re: Allegations Regarding the Porgera Joint Venture Remedy Framework* (2013) ('The Porgera remediation framework is an operational level grievance mechanism that was set up as a direct response to well-founded allegations of sexual violence against women residing in the Porgera Valley, perpetrated by men who were employed at the Porgera mine.'); Access Facility, 'General information on Barrick Gold Corporation's Operational Level Grievance Mechanisms', http://accessfacility.org/general-information-barrick-gold-corporations-operational-level-grievance-mechanisms (referring to the Olgeta Meri Igat Raits Framework as an 'operational level grievance mechanism'); Catherine Coumans, *Brief on Concerns Related to Project-Level Non-Judicial Grievance Mechanisms* (MiningWatch Canada, April 2014), http://www.miningwatch.ca/sites/www.miningwatch.ca/files/brief_on_njgms_access_meeting_april_2014_final.pdf (describing the mechanism as a 'project-level grievance mechanism put in place by Barrick Gold for victims of rape by the mine's security guards').
27. See for example, Akali Tange Association, *The Shooting Fields of Porgera Joint Venture* (2005) (on file with authors); MiningWatch Canada, 'Papua New Guinea Conducts Flawed Investigation of Killings at Barrick Mine' (Press Release, 10 July 2006), http://www.miningwatch.ca/papua-new-guinea-conducts-flawed-investigation-killings-barrick-mine; International Human Rights Clinic, Harvard Law School and Center for Human Rights and Global Justice, New York University School of Law, *Legal Brief before the Standing Committee on the Foreign Affairs and International Development House of Commons Regarding Bill C-300* (2009), http://www.business-humanrights.org/Documents/CanadaParliamentarytestimonyreBarrickPJV; Human Rights Watch, *Gold's Costly Dividend: Human Rights Impacts of Papua New Guinea's Porgera Gold Mine* (New York: Human Rights Watch, 2010).
28. See for example, Barrick Gold Corp., *Olgeta Meri Igat Raits: A Framework of Remediation Initiatives*, 8; Barrick Gold Corp., *The Porgera Joint Venture Remedy Framework*, 9–11.
29. For example, the grievance process established by Xstrata Copper, Peru, in which the final dispute resolution phase involves the appointment of an Arbitration Court, comprising one arbitrator each appointed by the company and the community, and typically an ombudsman. See, Rees and Vermijs, *Mapping Grievance Mechanisms in the Business and Human Rights Arena*, 19–21.
30. Barrick was responsible for the design of the mechanism. Independent agents, namely the PRF Association (an association incorporated to oversee implementation of the mechanism) and Cardno Emerging Markets (Australia) Pty Ltd (a company retained to administer the individual reparation programme on the ground), were engaged to implement the mechanism after it had been finalised.
31. See, Barrick Gold Corp., *Olgeta Meri Igat Raits: A Framework of Remediation Initiatives*, 10–11. See also, Letter from Peter Sinclair, Vice President Corporate Soil Responsibility, Barrick Gold Corp., to Dr Navanethem Pillay, UN High Commissioner for Human Rights (22 March 2013), http://www.barrick.com/files/porgera/Letter-to-UN-High-Commissioner.pdf; Barrick Gold Corp., 'Barrick Corrects Further False Claims Concerning Remediation Program at Porgera' (Press Release, 16 April 2013), http://www.barrick.com/files/porgera/Barrick-corrects-further-false-claims-concerning-Remediation-Program-at-Porgera.pdf.
32. Despite this, the quality and depth of consultation with other stakeholders was also, in some cases, shallow. This was the experience of CHRGJ/HRP. We were invited to provide comments on the draft remedy proposal only very late in the process, and few of our comments and suggestions were taken up.
33. Many now feel resentful at not having been consulted. For example, one woman remarked, 'No one ever spoke to us ... They should have come and talked to us here instead of just starting this framework' (Interview 2-2014).
34. One victim remarked, 'Barrick has never done anything like this before. I don't trust it' (Interview 3-2013).
35. The only local organisations purportedly consulted were the Porgera District Women's Association (PDWA) and Porgera Environmental Advisory Komiti (PEAK). Both organisations receive funding and other support from Barrick; the PDWA has its offices inside Barrick's fences (see, Barrick Gold Corporation, *2011 Responsibility Report* (2012), 44, http://www.barrick.com/files/responsibility-report/2011/Barrick-2011-Responsibility-Report.pdf; PEAK

Association Inc., *Funding Forecast for 2013*, http://www.peakpng.org/resources/Budget_2013.pdf). Neither organisation, to our knowledge, had done any work on the assault issue previously, and it has been our experience that the local community has limited knowledge of the work of the organisations.

36. These groups were the Akali Tange Association (ATA) and the Porgera Landowners Association (PLOA). These groups sometimes work together as the Porgera Alliance. The ATA was founded with the purpose of seeking compensation for victims of human rights violations occurring at the Porgera mine; the PLOA represents traditional landowners. The groups have for a number of years brought allegations to the attention of the company, and the Porgera Alliance is a party to a complaint against Barrick before the OECD National Contact Point in Canada regarding the mine-related abuses (see, Porgera Alliance, 'Background – Issues Related to Barrick Gold's Porgera Joint Venture Mine in Papua New Guinea' (May 2011), http://www.porgeraalliance.net/2011/05/background-issues-related-to-barrick-gold%E2%80%99s-porgera-joint-venture-mine-in-papua-new-guinea-may-2011/). MiningWatch Canada, an NGO which has been actively engaged since 2005 on human rights issues surrounding Porgera and critical of Barrick, also appears to have been excluded from mechanism design consultations.
37. Letter from Peter Sinclair, Vice President Corporate Soil Responsibility, Barrick Gold Corp., to Dr Navanethem Pillay, UN High Commissioner for Human Rights' (22 March 2013), 5–6.
38. Indeed, 'ignoring or refusing to engage least trusted groups' is recognised as a key barrier to responsible grievance handling (Kemp and Bond, *Mining Industry Perspectives on Handling Community Grievances*, 38). See also, Ellie Brodie et al., *Understanding Participation: A Literature Review* (Pathways Through Participation, 2009), 29.
39. Many of the potential claimants we spoke with in 2013 stated that they would not access the mechanism until advised to do so by elders and leaders.
40. Guiding Principles, Principle 29(h).
41. United Nations, *Guidance Note of the Secretary-General: Reparations for Conflict-Related Sexual Violence* (2014), 15.
42. One woman stated, 'They did not ask me what I wanted. They just told me what they were going to do' (Interview 14-2013).
43. According to information provided to us, when claimants requested amounts of compensation greater than 20,000 kina, their claims were rejected by Claims Assessment Team members as being outside the mechanism (Interview 26-2014; Interview 63-2014).
44. A number of female alleged victims of *non*-sexual violence attempted to make claims with the mechanism when it opened, but were turned away. Barrick has issued many public statements about its responses to allegations of sexual assault, but it has remained largely silent on issues of non-sexual violence, and the company's written materials do not explain its decision to exclude claims of non-sexual violence. In its initial response to the allegations of sexual violence made by Human Rights Watch in their report *Gold's Costly Dividend*, Barrick did not acknowledge the allegations of non-sexual violence, including excessive use of force (see, Barrick Gold Corp., 'Addressing Violence Against Women at Porgera' (Press Release, 27 October 2011), http://www.barrick.com/files/porgera/Progress-on-Human-Rights-at-Porgera.pdf), nor are we able to find evidence of Barrick addressing the issue in any subsequent statements or documents posted on its website (see, Barrick Gold Corp., '"Porgera 95%": Human Rights Remedy', http://www.barrick.com/operations/papua-new-guinea/porgera/default.aspx). The mechanism documents also do not acknowledge allegations of non-sexual human rights violations, or specifically explain why it is limited to cases of sexual assault (see, Barrick Gold Corp., *Olgeta Meri Igat Raits: A Framework of Remediation Initiatives*).
45. International Human Rights Clinic, Harvard Law School and Center for Human Rights and Global Justice, New York University School of Law, *Legal Brief before the Standing Committee on the Foreign Affairs and International Development House of Commons Regarding Bill C-300*, 22. In visits to Porgera carried out since the preparation of the legal brief, we have spoken with additional individuals who have alleged excessive force by Barrick security personnel, allegations not previously recorded by our research teams.
46. It would be surprising if security guards – who committed extraordinarily violent gang rapes, rapes that were often coterminous with extensive non-sexual beatings – were otherwise fully compliant with human rights law's restrictions on the use of force in their encounters with community members.

47. The Claims Assessment Team did not have a permanent presence in Porgera, but instead visited in a number of rotations of generally two weeks each. The initial period for lodging claims was in fact extended, at the behest of ERI, for a number of women represented by the NGO.
48. For a discussion of the relationship between the PDWA and Barrick, see note 35.
49. The mechanism implementers had legitimate concerns (which the authors share) about creating a broad, media-driven, and very public awareness campaign for the mechanism. Although the guides for remedy mechanisms emphasise improving accessibility through wide awareness-raising, in Porgera, an important concern was that if the entire Porgeran community (that is, including men) knew about the mechanism and where its complaints office was located, this could have – given the pervasive shaming and harm to sexual assault victims in the area – endangered women or prevented them from making claims due to fear.
50. Our interviews over the last two years indicate that numerous alleged victims did not know about the mechanism, or were not correctly informed about it and therefore did not access it. During a recent visit to the region, in December 2014–January 2015, additional women not previously known to us, came forward to report assaults. We make no assessment as to the legitimacy of their allegations, but like other alleged victims, they should at minimum be able to present their complaints to the mechanism.
51. Guiding Principles, Principle 31(f).
52. *Basic Principles and Guidelines on the Right to a Remedy and Reparation for Victims of Violations of International Human Rights and Humanitarian Law*, G.A. Res. 60/147, UN Doc. A/RES/60/147 (16 December 2005) Annex, Art. 15. Barrick states that the framework was developed using the Basic Principles: see, Barrick Gold Corp., *Olgeta Meri Igat Raits: A Framework of Remediation Initiatives*, 10.
53. *Velásquez-Rodríguez Case, Interpretation of Compensatory Damages* (Art. 67 American Convention on Human Rights), Judgment, Inter-Am. Ct. H.R. (Ser. C) No. 9 ¶ 4 (17 August 1990); Dinah Shelton, *Remedies in International Human Rights Law* (Oxford: Oxford University Press, 2005), 345.
54. Barrick cited concerns for the safety of claimants as the reason for structuring compensation in this fashion, as well as the fear that cash payments would be disbursed to husbands and the clan, noting that 'any award of cash to the Claimant must be carefully considered and discussed with the Claimant to minimise any risk that this would present to the Claimant', in Barrick Gold Corp., *Claims Process Procedures Manual* (undated), 6, http://www.barrick.com/files/porgera/Claims-Process-Procedures-Manual.pdf. Also, Barrick Gold Corp., *Olgeta Meri Igat Raits: A Framework of Remediation Initiatives*, 12.
55. Women interpreted the initial offers as offers of goods. Following numerous visits over two years, we think it is possible that they were initially offered some form of small business grant (for example, for a chicken raising or clothes selling business), but that this was conveyed in a way that led to widespread (mis)understanding that goods were being offered. In any event, it is not clear what the difference between the two offers would be in practice.
56. One woman explained, 'These materials, sewing and things ... are not enough. With what happened to me ... From our customs, we don't pay compensation with these things. We pay with cash and other things' (Interview 14-2013). Village Courts are known to award cash compensation in cases of sexual assault.
57. See ERI, *Factsheet: Abuse by Barrick Gold Corporation* (December 2014), http://www.earthrights.org/legal/factsheet-abuse-barrick-gold-corporation. During interviews in Porgera, some told us women were provided three years of school fees. Direct communications from Barrick to us state three years, however Barrick's public materials state two years: see, Barrick Gold Corp., *The Porgera Joint Venture Remedy Framework*, 14.
58. Barrick stated that these supplements "follow[ed] recent discussions with eligible claimants". (Email from Peter Sinclair, Senior Vice President, Corporate Affairs, Barrick Gold Corporation, to Sarah Knuckey (24 June 2015)).
59. Risks of cash payments include that cash might be appropriated or forcibly taken by family members instead of being used to the benefit of the woman, and women might be coerced into making false claims to the mechanism in order to secure a cash benefit.
60. These views were expressed about the earlier finalized packages. In July 2015, many women interviewed in Porgera were even more disappointed with the remedy mechanism packages. They did not consider the 30,000 kina supplement to be fair or just, in light of their understanding of the much greater amounts awarded to ERI clients.

61. Interview 44-2014. A small number of women who obtained access to legal representation from a United States (US)-based NGO, ERI, opted to reject the packages. As this article was being finalised for publication, Barrick and ERI announced that those cases had been resolved through a negotiated settlement. See, ERI, 'Survivors Who Alleged Rape and Killing at Papua New Guinea Mine Pleased With Barrick Gold Settlement' (Press Release, 3 April, 2015), http://www.earthrights.org/media/survivors-who-alleged-rape-and-killing-papua-new-guinea-mine-pleased-barrick-gold-settlement.
62. Barrick Gold Corp., Olgeta Meri Igat Raits: A Framework of Remediation Initiatives in Response to Violence Against Women in the Porgera Valley, 12. The packages would be "determined based on reference to" (among other factors, such as the type of harm) Barrick's research on the "upper levels of compensation" awarded by PNG courts for sexual assault (as opposed to traditional courts, which may award different remedies, and which many in Porgera have the most familiarity). 'A Summary of Recent Changes to the Porgera Remediation Framework' (Press Release, 7 June 2013), http://www.barrick.com/files/porgera/Summary-of-Recent-Changes-to-the-Porgera-Remediation-Framework.pdf, the document is the 'Summary of Recent Changes' document.
63. Email from Peter Sinclair, Senior Vice President, Corporate Affairs, Barrick Gold Corporation, to Sarah Knuckey (24 June 2015). This is not the impression given by the mechanism's public documents, and it is not clear to the authors whether this was always the case, or is a recent change. The amounts initially awarded by the third-party implementer appear to track the amounts awarded in the PNG justice system.
64. *Z* v. *UK* [2001] 2 FLR 612, ¶ 131, in which the court, in applying the principle that 'the rates applied in domestic cases, though relevant, are not decisive', in fact determined that equity required a departure from the levels of awards in similar cases in domestic courts (applying UK law: *Smith and Grady* v. *the United Kingdom* (just satisfaction), nos 33985/96 and 33986/96, §§ 18-19, ECHR 2000-IX).
65. *Basic Principles and Guidelines on the Right to a Remedy and Reparation for Victims of Violations of International Human Rights and Humanitarian Law*, Annex, Art. 15.
66. *Velasquez Rodriguez Case, Compensatory Damages* (Art. 63(1) American Convention on Human Rights), Judgment of 21 July 1989, Inter-Am. Ct.H.R. (Ser. C) No. 7, ¶ 30 (1990).
67. See for example, Rashida Manjoo, *Report of the Special Rapporteur on Violence against Women, its Causes and Consequences, Rashida Manjoo. Mission to Papua New Guinea*, A/HRC/23/49/Add.2 (18 March 2013); AusAID, *Papua New Guindea Country Report* (2009), at 35 ('the response of the Papua New Guinea justice sector to violence against women has been relatively weak').
68. Awards made in these countries vary greatly, depending on jurisdiction, the facts of the case, and whether punitive or exemplary damages are available. Nonetheless, Elizabeth Grace has identified a trend towards high non-pecuniary awards for sexual assault in Canada. She cites several cases where non-pecuniary awards were CA$250,000 or greater, as well as the case of *Evans* v. *Sproule* [2008] O.J. No. 4518 (ONSC), in which the victim of a sexual assault by a police officer which did not include genital contact received $150,000 in non-pecuniary damages (Elizabeth Grace, 'Trend Develops for Higher Sexual Abuse Non-Pecuniary Awards', *Lawyers Weekly* (February 2010), http://lernerspersonalinjury.ca/lawyers/elizabeth-grace/#selected-publications-presentations). Damages can be even higher. In a groundbreaking 2013 case, a jury in Ontario found a school board directly and vicariously liable for the sexual assault of a student by its employee, awarding the victims damages of CA$3.2 million (*Langstaff* v. *Robert Terry Marson and The Hasting and Prince Edward District School Board*, 2013 CarswellOnt 3819, 2013 ONSC 1448 (S.C.J.)).
69. The waiver clause reads, 'The claimant agrees that, in consideration for the Reparations, on and from the date of signing this Agreement, she will not pursue any claim for compensation, or any civil legal action, that relates in any way to the Conduct [the claimant was the subject of sexual violence attributable to one or more current or former employees of the Porgera Joint Venture], against the Porgera Joint Venture, PRFA or Barrick in Papua New Guinea or in any other jurisdiction. This expressly excludes any criminal action that may be brought by any state, governmental or international entity' (Barrick Gold Corp., *Claims Process Procedures Manual*, Form 9: Individual Reparations Agreement, 45).
70. Guiding Principles, Principle 29.

71. See, Letter from Catherine Coumans, Asia Pacific Program Director, MiningWatch Canada, to Dr Navanethem Pillay, UN High Commissioner for Human Rights (19 March 2013), http://www.miningwatch.ca/sites/www.miningwatch.ca/files/letter_to_unhchr_on_porgera_2013-03-19.pdf; Letter from Catherine Coumans, Asia Pacific Program Director, MiningWatch Canada, to Dr Navanethem Pillay, UN High Commissioner for Human Rights (2 April 2013), http://www.miningwatch.ca/sites/www.miningwatch.ca/files/letter_to_un_high_commissioner_april_2_2013.pdf; Letter from various concerned organisations, to Dr Navanethem Pillay, UN High Commissioner for Human Rights (14 May 2013), http://www.miningwatch.ca/sites/www.miningwatch.ca/files/ltr_to_unhchr_may_14_2013_re_porgera_sign-on.pdf.
72. Barrick Gold Corp., *Olgeta Meri Igat Raits: A Framework of Remediation Initiatives*, 28. Barrick's mechanism is distinct from PNG criminal processes. Following internal investigations before the mechanism was created, Barrick stated that it terminated the employment of a number of its employees suspected of abuse, although the numbers of those terminated and for what specific offences has not been made public. Barrick has also stated that it encouraged police to investigate, and provided evidence to police. See, Barrick Gold Corp., *The Porgera Joint Venture Remedy Framework*, 4. To our knowledge, and based on interviews with local police and prosecutors, no Barrick security guards have been convicted of sexual assault, and no criminal investigations have been launched into whether Barrick itself or Barrick managers bear any criminal responsibility for the actions of security guards.
73. Office of the High Commission for Human Rights, *Re: Allegations Regarding the Porgera Joint Venture Remedy Framework.*
74. Ibid., 8–9.
75. Ibid.
76. The OHCHR opinion does allude, in footnote 25, to another concern of Barrick's, which is the potential for double recovery. The OHCHR Rule of Law Tools for Post-Conflict States: Reparations Programmes (2008) suggests this problem is 'easily addressed', and describes the Peruvian Truth and Reconciliation Commission's position, in which victims who received compensation through the commission, then received a civil award through judicial procedures, were required to return to the state the compensation they had received through the reparations programme (35). While other parts of the OHCHR Rule of Law Tools for Post-Conflict States: Reparations Programmes are referred to this approach for preventing double recovery while preserving access to courts is not mentioned in the OHCHR opinion.
77. Owen M. Fiss, 'Against Settlement', *Yale Law Journal* 93, no. 6 (1984): 1073–90.
78. Barrick provided funding for an Independent Legal Advisor (ILA) to meet with each claimant, and to advise the claimant on: (a) the merits of her claim; (b) the process for pursuing a claim through the mechanism; (c) the availability of translators during her participation in the mechanism; (d) the remedies that may be available to the claimant if her claim is found to be eligible and legitimate; (e) the legal consequences of accepting any offer made by Barrick and signing an agreement releasing the company from civil claims; (f) the legal options available to the claimant; and (g) her possible exposure under PNG law should any false claim be made during her participation in the mechanism process (see, Barrick Gold Corp., *Claims Process Procedures Manual*, Form 10: Signed Statement of Independent Legal Advisor, 48). Our interviews on the ground suggest that the ILA was a committed and thoughtful advisor. However, our interviews also indicate that her perceived independence was undermined (numerous women incorrectly believed that the ILA was Barrick's, rather than their, lawyer), and that many women had a poor understanding of their legal options, and were not advised of potential foreign legal claims or alternative direct mediation options.
79. Guiding Principles, Principle 31(e). For a detailed analysis of the role of transparency in the Guiding Principles, and of the broad, critical role of access to information and corporate transparency in the effective operationalisation of the Guiding Principles, see Nicola Jägers, 'Will Transnational Private Regulation Close the Governance Gap?', in *Human Rights Obligations of Business: Beyond the Corporate Responsibility to Respect?* ed. Surya Deva and David Bilchitz (Cambridge: Cambridge University Press, 2013), 295–328.
80. Guiding Principles, Principle 31(g).
81. Rees, *Rights-Compatible Grievance Mechanisms*, 23–24.
82. Guiding Principles, Commentary on Principle 31.
83. See for example, Barrick Gold Corp., 'A Summary of Recent Changes to the Porgera Remediation Framework'; Barrick Gold Corp., *The Porgera Joint Venture Remedy Framework.*

84. Barrick has cited the need to protect the confidentiality of victims as the reason for not releasing information. The need to protect the confidentiality of victims is undoubtedly a vital consideration. However, as recognised in the Guiding Principles, the need for transparency and the need to protect confidentiality must be balanced. No personal information about victims should ever be released, at least absent properly informed consent and assessment of security risks, but a great deal of anonymised and aggregated information regarding issues such as numbers and types of cases, process and time for handling of cases, and the progress and disposition of cases, can be released without exposing claimants to risk.
85. Barrick committed in November 2013 to making the outcome of the review public (see, Barrick Gold Corp., 'Continued Progress of Claims under the Porgera Remediation Framework' (1 November 2013), http://www.barrick.com/files/porgera/Continued-progress-of-claims-under-the-Porgera-Remediation-Framework.pdf). This has not happened, other than the inclusion of a brief excerpt as an appendix in Barrick's December 2014 document, *The Porgera Joint Venture Remedy Framework*. Barrick has also undertaken to conduct a review now that the mechanism is coming to a close.
86. For example, Barrick announced improvements to translation services for victims, extended the timeframe for lodging of claims, amended the scope of advice provided by the ILA, and seemed to have changed the form of compensation packages (see, Letter from Peter Sinclair, Vice President Corporate Soil Responsibility, Barrick Gold Corp., to Dr Navanethem Pillay, UN High Commissioner for Human Rights (22 March 2013)); Barrick Gold Corp., 'A Summary of Recent Changes to the Porgera Remediation Framework'. Another positive change included the provision of feedback from victims to the third-party implementer, although our research could not determine the scope or nature of this feedback, or how many women provided it: Barrick Gold Corp., *The Porgera Joint Venture Remedy Framework*, 3.
87. Heidy Rombouts et al., 'The Right to Reparation for Victims of Gross and Systematic Violations of Human Rights', in *Out of the Ashes: Reparation for Victims of Gross and Systematic Human Rights Violations*, ed. K. De Feyter et al. (Antwerp: Intersentia, 2005), 492.
88. Rees, *Rights Compatible-Grievance Mechanisms*, 30.
89. Independent third parties could include but are not limited to NGOs (such as Oxfam Australia's now defunct Mining Ombudsman). It would be necessary for victims and key stakeholders to endorse any independent third party exercising oversight.
90. See for example, African Development Bank, *Handbook on Stakeholder Consultation and Participation in ADB Operations* (2001), 2 (engagement with primary stakeholders, including those who are the intended beneficiaries of the intervention, demands a higher level of engagement).
91. While at all times protecting the confidentiality of victims and ensuring their safety.

Beyond the 100 Acre Wood: in which international human rights law finds new ways to tame global corporate power

Daniel Augenstein[a] and David Kinley[b]

[a]*Tilburg Law School, The Netherlands;* [b]*Sydney Law School, Australia*

States and corporations are being forced out of their comfort zones. A consensus is building among international human rights courts and committees that states can and will be held accountable for overseas human rights abuses by corporations domiciled in their respective territories. The authors suggest that this development is rooted in a transition from a territory-based to a subject-based approach to human rights obligations that de-centres international human rights law from state territory. In this article, they construct a conceptual framework for understanding how and why this is happening and articulate what are and will be the consequences for the theory and practice of international human rights law.

"You can't stay in your corner of the Forest waiting for others to come to you. You have to go to them sometimes." AA Milne (per Winnie-the-Pooh)

1. International human rights law between universal aspiration and global corporate power

The universality of human rights is often treated as a truism: human rights are universal because they belong to all human beings by virtue of their being human; or put the other way around, unless they are universal rights they cannot be human rights.[1] This despite the fact that propositions of the kind that all human beings are 'born free and equal in dignity and rights' (Article 1 UDHR) have little empirical purchase. Geography plays a decisive role in the global birth lottery and most Northerners happen to live a freer and less unequal life than people in the so-called Global South. What is more, the criteria for membership in the human family are far from settled, with prospective candidates ranging from animals and artificially intelligent machines to corporate beings that claim protection of their 'human' rights to privacy, property and so on against the rest of 'us'.[2] Both of these challenges combine in the well-known difficulty of 'mapping' humanity's universality-by-abstraction onto concrete right-bearing subjects that come with a gender, age, race, class, and so on. While this would appear to rebut any easy inference from being human to having rights, it arguably leaves unscathed the normative thrust of human rights' proclaimed universality, namely that *we ought to be treated as if* we were born free and equal in dignity and rights.

However, such an approach still falls short of constituting universal *legal* rights of all human beings to be treated as free and equal. The universal aspirations of human rights constantly run up against the limitations inherent in the state-centred ('Westphalian') architecture of international law. Far from giving rise to legal entitlements to have one's human rights respected, protected and fulfilled by anyone and anywhere, the international order of states has traditionally confined them to a territorially circumscribed relationship between public authorities and private individuals. Each state has a singular legal obligation and entitlement (to the exclusion of other states) to respect, protect and fulfil the human rights of individuals located on its own territory in relation to acts of its own public authorities. An important presumption behind this legal compartmentalisation of human rights is that, at least as a general rule, victims and perpetrators of human rights violations will reside in the same state territory. An important consequence thereof is that human rights protection outside the state's borders is traditionally considered to require special justification in the light of the sovereign territorial rights of other states.

What is more, the state-centrism of international human rights law entails that corporations are by and large treated analogously to individual rights holders – that is, as putative victims rather than perpetrators of human rights violations. Corporations enter the world as private legal artefacts subject to the state's territorially confined public authority to assist individuals in accumulating wealth without undue risk of personal liability. *Qua* private subjects of the state they are entitled to its legal protection of their 'disembodied' human rights.[3] At the same time, they are conceptually incapable of violating (as opposed to merely 'abusing') the rights of those human beings they have been fashioned to serve. The result is an uneven treatment of human and corporate beings in international human rights law. As the Council of Europe's Parliamentary Assembly notes, 'while a company may bring a case before the Court [ECtHR] claiming a violation by a state authority of its rights protected under the European Convention on Human Rights, an individual alleging a violation of his rights by a private company cannot effectively raise his or her claims before this jurisdiction'.[4]

The legal compartmentalisation of universal human rights in the international order of states is challenged by the globalisation of corporate power. Today, the Westphalian imaginary of global business entities as 'multi-national' corporations subject to the public authority of territorially confined state entities has lost much of its plausibility. The attribution of multiple state-based 'nationalities' to corporations that operate as globally integrated economic entities appears increasingly factitious – as if, say, the Shell Transport and Trading Company incorporated in Nigeria really 'belonged' to the Nigerian state (and its people) rather than to its Anglo-Dutch parent, the Royal Dutch Shell Petroleum Corporation. Moreover, for all but the most stubborn positivists and government officials, it is far from obvious that states still regulate and control corporations (or have the capacity to do so) rather than corporations assuming regulatory and enforcement powers over the state or states.[5] Indeed, we may – as Catá Backer nicely puts it – be witnessing a shift

> [f]rom a discussion of the legitimacy or foundations of the authority of the United States to impose its legislation over chemicals in consumer products on Chinese manufacturers, to one in which the legitimacy and foundations of the authority of the global corporation *Wal-*

> *Mart* to impose its own standards on the same regulatory subject (by determining the content of the products that it will order and sell) on both the United States and China moves to centre-stage.[6]

From a domestic point of view, global corporate power erodes the substance of public authority that states wield over their territory. Global business operations escape the regulatory grasp of territorial states while at the same time limiting states' ability 'to set the social, economic and political agenda within their respective political space', which undermines their capacity 'to secure the livelihoods of their respective citizens by narrowing the parameters of legitimate state action'.[7] Internationally, global corporate power transforms states' external relations with each other. As de Feyter says, 'companies that organise across borders define the primary role of a state in terms of creating a space for the play of market forces. Not only should a state adopt a market-based system within its own territory ... , the same system should apply to economic relationships *among* countries'.[8] Developed states are under pressure to create a global 'level playing field' for their corporate nationals by further dismantling legal barriers to the free flow of capital, production and labour in the developing world. At the same time, developing states will be reluctant to raise national standards of social and environmental protection for fear of losing their competitive advantage in attracting foreign investment in the global market.

In a nutshell, while human rights are traditionally protected against public emanations of the state for the benefit of individuals located on the state's territory, human rights violations committed in the course of global business operations call for their extraterritorial protection in relation to private actors. Yet the globalisation of corporate power has not been accompanied by a corresponding universalisation of legal human rights obligations. On the contrary, the resilience of the state-centred world-view has hampered international legal reform and propelled the marginalisation of international human rights law. Sections two and three below illustrate this predicament by considering two important legal avenues for taming the human rights impacts of global corporate power – namely the direct imposition of human rights obligations on corporations under international law and the indirect control of corporate power through positive state obligations. Section four examines the presently dominant international business and human rights instrument – the UN Guiding Principles on Business and Human Rights (UNGPs) developed by the Special Representative of the Secretary-General on the issue of human rights and transnational corporations and other business entities (SRSG).[9] We contend that the failure of the international order of states to account for the human rights impacts of global corporate power engenders a transition from territorial human rights government to global human rights governance that challenges the state-centred conception of international human rights law. Against this threefold background, section five argues that taming corporate power overseas requires a subject-based approach to international human rights law that disentangles the territorial nexus between states, corporate human rights 'abusers' and victims of human rights violations into a triangular relationship mediated by state power and control. Section six shows how the proposed subject-based approach to international human rights law yields the recognition of state obligations to regulate and control corporate actors operating from their territory with a view to protecting the human rights of third-country victims against corporate violations. By de-centring international human rights law from the public and territorial state, we conclude, in the seventh and final section, that this contributes to recovering human rights' universal aspirations in the face of global corporate power.

2. 'Public' *versus* 'private': the direct imposition of human rights obligations on corporations under international law

Whereas in certain areas of international law, most prominently international criminal and humanitarian law, states have moved towards imposing direct legal obligations on private actors that (also) serve to vindicate values embodied in human rights,[10] *international human rights law* traditionally has little to say about the human rights impacts of non-state actors other than tying them back to its state-centred premises.[11] According to the Westphalian orthodoxy, states are the principal subjects and authors of international human rights law that only becomes directly effective in the relationship between corporate perpetrators and individual victims of human rights violations through its translation via domestic state laws and legislation. Human rights 'abuses' by 'multi-national' corporations are treated as a domestic failure of the state and as a problem of international cooperation between states; inversely, globally operating business entities only register in international human rights law as corporate nationals of the public and territorial state.

To date, the most prominent attempt to address this lacuna of protection in international human rights law was the 2003 UN Draft Norms on the Responsibilities of Transnational Corporations and Other Business Entities with regard to Human Rights (UN Norms) that suggested, obliquely, that human rights obligations might be directly applicable to private actors.[12] Building on key international human rights instruments, the UN Norms envisaged extending existing human rights obligations of states to transnational corporations and other business entities, within their sphere of influence and activity:

> States have the primary responsibility to promote, secure the fulfilment of, respect, ensure respect of and protect human rights recognised in international as well as national law, including ensuring that transnational corporations and other business enterprises respect human rights. Within their respective spheres of activity and influence, transnational corporations and other business enterprises have the obligation to promote, secure the fulfilment of, respect, ensure respect of and protect human rights recognised in international as well as national law, including the rights and interests of indigenous people and other vulnerable groups.[13]

Whatever the shortcomings of the UN Norms (and let it be made clear that they were presented in a draft form), it is fair to say that an important reason for their eventual failure was the vested interests of powerful corporations and their (Western) home states not to see corporate responsibility for human rights extended beyond the 'soft' model of self-regulation through corporate codes of conduct, corporate social responsibility, and the like.[14] A false dichotomy was construed between the UN Norms' attempt to prevent and redress corporate human rights violations (the UN's 'anti-business agenda'[15]) and the positive contributions corporations can make to global economic well-being, technological improvement and international development. Yet another dichotomy – that between 'public' states and 'private' corporations – fuelled contrived concerns that the direct imposition of human rights obligations on corporations would undermine state sovereignty and dilute state responsibility for human rights violations.[16]

Leaving aside partisan politics and political polemics, the imposition of direct human rights obligations on private corporations clearly poses significant structural and normative challenges to the state-centred conception of international law. Although the UN Norms duly recognised the primacy of state obligations to respect, protect and fulfil human rights, their attempt to extend human obligations to corporations *qua* private actors was interpreted by many as an exercise in international law-making at odds with the basic tenets of the international order of states. Notwithstanding the fact that corporations have *de facto* become important participants in international law-making and enforcement,[17] and have been endowed with (partial) international legal personality,[18] international law continues to strive against their formal recognition as its authors on par with the state. Thus, while there is nothing natural or neutral about the distinction between 'public' states and 'private' corporations,[19] it plays a constitutive role in the construction of the collective self-understanding of the international order of states and the global political economy. An important structural role played by the public/private divide in (international) human rights law is the allocation of rights and duties in the triangular relationship between states, corporations and natural persons. Whereas corporations are traditionally treated akin to private (legal) persons, the recognition of direct human rights obligations in international law would appear to align them with public states. Does this entail that other non-state actors (for example, individual consumers that have thus far resisted the fair-trade trend) also have international legal obligations to respect, protect and fulfil human rights within their particular sphere of influence and activity (i.e. shopping)? Or should we rather treat corporations as proto-state entities that are publically accountable to their stakeholders for the realisation of the common good? As Ratner remarks, the challenge is to 'construct a theory both *down* from state responsibility and *up* from individual responsibility' that accommodates the fact that 'a corporation is, as it were, more than an individual and less than a state'.[20]

This problem of re-situating 'private' actors in relation to 'public' states raises broader normative concerns with imposing direct international human rights obligations on corporations. As Fleur Johns notes, the formal recognition of global corporations as authors of international law would 'effectively be sanctioning the exercise of legal authority not conferred by political process'.[21] The state-based national/international law divide institutionalises a bifurcation between, on the one hand, domestic human rights obligations that structure the political relationship between states and non-state actors (including corporations) within the state legal order and, on the other hand, international human rights obligations that structure the political relationship between states *inter se*. An important consequence of this divide is that, as Knox says,

> [a] legal obligation that international law directly places on an individual differs from one that it imposes indirectly, through a duty on governments. In the first case, the international community as a whole exercises prescriptive jurisdiction over individuals in a way that makes them directly subject to international law apart from the mediating intervention of domestic law. In the second, domestic jurisdiction over individuals is left intact. For this reason, the political and practical pressures against regulation of private conduct by international human rights law greatly increase in strength when the regulation is direct rather than filtered through domestic law ... [Whereas] individuals acknowledge that their governments have jurisdiction to determine and enforce their rights and duties, they are less likely to accept that international bodies controlled by foreign governments have such jurisdiction.[22]

There is thus a direct correlation between the legal sequestration of global business entities into 'multi-national' corporations subject to one or more states' public authority and public international law's distinction between direct human rights obligations (imposed on states) and indirect human rights obligations (imposed on corporations via domestic state legislation). It is because corporations are treated as subjects of the state that they appear in international law as mere 'objects' whose interests are to be represented, and whose obligations are to be determined, by that very state.

None of this is to suggest that states lack the competence or capacity to establish an international mechanism that considers and settles disputes involving cross-border corporate human rights violations,[23] or to agree upon an international treaty that directly imposes human rights obligations on corporations.[24] Indeed, as the SRSG made clear early on in his mandate, there are 'no inherent conceptual barriers to states deciding to hold corporations directly responsible [for violations of international law] ... by establishing some form of international jurisdiction'.[25] All we seek to argue here is that the direct imposition of international human rights obligations on corporations is likely to entail a more radical departure from international law's state-centred heritage, including its distinction between 'public' states and 'private' corporations, than many proponents of the UN Norms may have recognised or acknowledged.

3. 'Territorial' *versus* 'extraterritorial': the indirect imposition of human rights obligations on corporations via positive state obligations

Whereas international law presently does not directly impose human rights obligations on corporations, it requires states to take positive steps to prevent and redress corporate human rights 'abuses'.[26] Such positive human rights obligations entail duties of conduct on the part of the state to take all reasonable and appropriate measures to protect human rights in relationships between non-state actors. While, for instance, the human rights obligations imposed by the International Covenant on Civil and Political Rights 'are binding on states parties and do not, as such, have direct horizontal effect as a matter of international law', they nevertheless require states to 'take appropriate measures or to exercise due diligence to prevent, punish, investigate or redress the harm caused by ... private persons or entities'.[27] Similarly, according to the Inter-American Court of Human Rights 'an illegal act which violates human rights and which is initially not directly imputable to a state (for example, because it is the act of a private person) can lead to international responsibility of the state, not because of the act itself, but because of the lack of due diligence to prevent the violation or to respond to it as required by the convention.[28] Or, as in *Fadeyeva* v. *Russia* – a case concerning environmental pollution emitting from a Russian steel plant owned and operated by a private corporation – the European Court of Human Rights (ECtHR) considered that 'the state's responsibility in environmental cases may arise from a failure to regulate private industry. Accordingly, the applicant's complaints fall to be analysed in terms of a positive duty on the state to take reasonable and appropriate measures to secure the applicant's rights under Article 8(1) of the Convention.'[29] As the SRSG puts it, international law imposes obligations on states not only to 'refrain from violating' human rights, but also 'to "ensure" (or some functionally equivalent verb) the enjoyment or realization of those rights by the rights holders'.[30] The latter obligation 'requires protection by states against other social actors, including business, who impede or negate those rights. Guidance from international human rights bodies suggests that the state duty to protect applies to all recognized rights that private parties are capable of impairing and to all types of business enterprises'.[31]

The recognition of positive state obligations mitigates the practical relevance of the distinction between 'public' states and 'private' corporations that has thus far hampered the recognition of direct corporate human rights obligations under international law. As de Schutter says:

> Although we may be trained, as international lawyers, to think that the international responsibility of a state may not be engaged by the conduct of actors not belonging to the state apparatus unless they are in fact acting under the instructions of, or under the direction or control of, that state in carrying out the conduct, the private-public distinction on which this rule of attribution

> is based is mooted (though not contradicted) by the imposition of positive state obligations … : once a situation is found to fall under [its] 'jurisdiction' … the state must accept responsibility not only for the acts its organs have adopted, but also for the omissions of these organs, where such omissions result in an insufficient protection of private persons whose rights or freedoms are violated by acts of other non-state actors.[32]

However, the public/private divide resurfaces in cases of human rights violations committed outside the state's territory. While it is widely accepted that states have negative obligations to respect (that is, to refrain from violating) the human rights of individuals outside their borders, international law has been slow in recognising positive extraterritorial state obligations to protect individuals against violations by private actors. Positive state obligations have traditionally been premised on state control over territory with the consequence that – apart from situations of extraterritorial (military) occupation – they are confined to individuals within the state's territorial jurisdiction. Accordingly, international human rights law has generally not been thought to impose obligations on states to control the activities of their (corporate) nationals abroad even where these activities impair the human rights of third-country victims: 'although, under the active personality principle, the state could impose a liability, in particular a criminal liability, on its nationals wherever they conduct their activities, a failure by a state … to exercise this power would not engage its responsibility [under international human rights law], even though certain individuals' human rights could be affected by this failure to act'.[33]

One important rationale behind this limitation is a concern with the effectiveness of international human rights law, namely that the realisation of positive obligations requires states to be in full and effective control of the territory where the putative violation takes place. As Milanović puts it:

> In order to be realistically complied with, the obligation to respect human rights requires the state to have nothing more than control over the conduct of its own agents. It is the positive obligation to secure or ensure human rights which requires a far greater degree of control over the area in question, control which allows the state to create institutions and mechanisms of government, to impose its laws, and punish violations thereof.[34]

Relatedly, whereas negative extraterritorial obligations are merely predicated on states exercising power over individuals outside their borders, whether lawfully or unlawfully,[35] positive extraterritorial obligations require states to take active measures in relation to individuals located on another state's territory. Accordingly, it has been argued with some force that the scope of positive extraterritorial obligations, *qua* duties of conduct, is delimited by what states are legally permitted to do in relation to other states as it cannot be considered 'reasonable' or 'appropriate' to require them to take steps to protect human rights in violation of general international law.[36] This relates to broader concerns that extraterritorial human rights protection may interfere with the sovereign rights that third states claim over their territory and private actors therein. As the ECtHR held in its (much critiqued) admissibility decision in *Banković*, 'while international law does not exclude a state's exercise of jurisdiction extra-territorially, the suggested bases of such jurisdiction … are, as a general rule, defined and limited by the sovereign territorial rights of other relevant states'.[37] Particularly in the area of social, economic and cultural rights that often involve questions of distributive justice, what is considered a human rights violation in one (developed) country may be considered a legitimate exercise of state authority in another (developing) country, with the consequence that the latter may claim an overriding interest in the non-regulation of corporations operating on its territory.

In such cases, the recognition of extraterritorial positive obligations to regulate and control global corporate power is likely to result in normative competency conflicts between home and host states of 'multi-national' corporations.[38]

Both the difficulties with directly imposing human rights obligations on corporations and the territorial confinement of positive state obligations can be plausibly explained by virtue of the resilience of the international order of states. However, such an approach that reifies the state-centred worldview in the face of global corporate power proves unsatisfactory for three main reasons. By construing international human rights law from the vantage point of (public/private) perpetrators of human rights violations, it fails to acknowledge that from the perspective of the victims, it is immaterial whether their human rights are violated or abused by a public state or a private corporation. Concurrently, by assimilating universal human rights and global business operations to state territory, it disarms international human rights law where it is most needed: for the benefit of individuals in weak (developing) host states which lack the capacity (and at times also the willingness) to protect human rights in relation to business operations conducted with the active support or passive connivance of strong (developed) home state governments. Finally, or so we shall argue in what follows, this lacuna of protection contributes to further undermining the state-centred conception of international law in relation to global corporate power.

4. From international human rights law to global human rights governance

Following the burial of the UN Norms, John Ruggie was appointed SRSG on business and human rights in 2005. In a series of reports over the coming years, he developed his 'Protect, Respect and Remedy' Framework that culminated in a set of Guiding Principles on Business and Human Rights (UNGPs) endorsed by the UN Human Rights Council in June 2011.[39] The UNGPs build on three pillars: the state duty to protect human rights against violations by third parties (including corporations) through appropriate policies, regulation, adjudication and enforcement; the corporate responsibility to respect human rights, meaning to act with due diligence to avoid infringing the rights of others; and greater access to effective remedies, both judicial and non-judicial, for victims of corporate-related human rights abuses. The SRSG was not tasked to develop a new legally binding instrument (but merely to restate the law 'as it is'),[40] and accordingly, his approach to legal obligations governing corporate human rights violations remained firmly rooted in the state-centred conception of international law. The 'corporate responsibility to respect' human rights lacks binding legal effect as 'respecting rights is not an obligation that current international human rights law generally imposes directly on companies'.[41] Relatedly, while the 'state duty to protect' requires states to secure human rights against 'abuses' by corporations, this duty is confined to violations committed on the state's territory as its extraterritorial application remains 'unsettled' in international law.[42] Thus, rather than directly addressing the *legal* protection gaps resulting from the exposure of the international order of states to the human impacts of global corporate power, the SRSG reframed them as 'governance gaps created by globalisation':

> The root cause of the business and human rights predicament today lies in the governance gaps created by globalisation – between the scope and impact of economic forces and actors, and the capacity of societies to manage their adverse consequences. These governance gaps provide the permissive environment for wrongful acts by companies of all kinds without adequate sanctioning or reparation. How to narrow and ultimately bridge the gaps in relation to human rights is our fundamental challenge.[43]

While the language of closing 'governance gaps' may be a useful vehicle to mainstream human rights concerns into business-related law and policies, it risks concealing how today's 'business and human rights predicament' is rooted in the very structure of the state-centred conception of international law. Such language engenders a transition from obligations imposed on states by virtue of international human rights law, to appeals to states' policy rationales to protect human rights in their external relations. This is perhaps most visible in the UNGPs' treatment of human rights violations in the 'state-business nexus' that concurrently implicate public and territorial states and private and globally operating corporations. According to the SRSG, 'states should take additional steps to protect against human rights abuses by business enterprises that are owned or controlled by the state, or that receive substantial support and services from state agencies such as export credit agencies and official investment insurance or guarantee agencies, including, where appropriate, by requiring human rights due diligence'.[44] The commentary appended to this provision recognises that 'where a business enterprise is controlled by the state, or where its acts can be attributed otherwise to the state, an abuse of human rights by the business enterprise may entail a violation of the state's own international law obligations'.[45] This tentative language of legal obligations is bolstered by an appeal to states' reputational, prudential, and business-related 'policy rationales' for ensuring that corporations respect human rights. Moreover, the UNGPs stress that a failure of home states to prevent and redress corporate harm outside their territory may 'add to the human rights challenges faced by the recipient state' (i.e., the host state of corporate investment).[46] Yet, crucially, these human rights challenges faced by the host state are not met with corresponding human rights obligations of the home state to protect third-country victims against corporate violations. There are, as advanced by the UNGPs, 'strong policy reasons for home states to set out clearly the expectation that businesses respect human rights abroad, especially when the State itself is involved in or supports those businesses. The reasons include ensuring predictability for business enterprises by providing coherent and consistent messages, and preserving the State's own reputation.'[47] However, home states are 'not generally required under international law to regulate the extraterritorial activities of businesses domiciled in their territory and/or jurisdiction. Nor are they generally prohibited from doing so, provided there is a recognised jurisdictional basis.'[48]

The assertion that states are neither 'generally required' nor 'generally prohibited' to regulate business operations outside their territories shapes the SRSG's approach to extraterritorial human rights protection against global corporate power. The UNGPs focus on the permissibility of extraterritorial assertions of state authority in accordance with a recognised basis of jurisdiction under general international law. What is at issue is the competence of states, as delimited by general international law, to assert authority over conduct not exclusively of domestic concern. Relatedly, the UNGPs are primarily concerned with the territorial location and/or nationality of the business entity as the perpetrator of human rights violations. The inquiry thus turns on whether a state can exercise jurisdiction over corporate actors violating human rights abroad because they reside within the state's territory (the territoriality principle) and/or because they can be considered 'corporate nationals' of that state (the nationality principle).[49] This twofold focus is perpetuated in a further distinction the SRSG introduces, namely between instances of 'direct extra-territorial jurisdiction' and 'domestic measures with extra-territorial implications':

> In the heated debates about extra-territoriality regarding business and human rights, a critical distinction between two very different phenomena is usually obscured. One is jurisdiction exercised directly in relation to actors or activities overseas, such as criminal regimes governing

> child sex tourism, which rely on the nationality of the perpetrator no matter where the offence occurs. The other is domestic measures with extraterritorial implications; for example, requiring corporate parents to report on the company's overall human rights policy and impacts, including those of its overseas subsidiaries. The latter phenomenon relies on territory as the jurisdictional basis, even though it may have extraterritorial implications.[50]

The SRSG's 'critical distinction' between 'direct extraterritorial jurisdiction' and 'domestic measures with extraterritorial implications' obscures another critical distinction, namely that between extraterritorial obligations imposed on states by virtue of international human rights law and states' domestic policy rationales to protect human rights against extra-territorial corporate violations. While the UNGP's marginalisation of the former is the upshot of the SRSG's (negative) assertion that states 'are not generally required ... to regulate the extraterritorial activities of businesses', their championing of the latter relates to his (positive) assertion that states are not 'prohibited from doing so, provided there is a recognized jurisdictional basis'.[51] However, the question whether states are permitted to assert extraterritorial authority over corporate perpetrators of human rights violations is *not reducible to* the question whether they are obligated to protect third-country victims against corporate violations. Whereas extraterritorial jurisdiction in general international law is a function of state sovereignty and concerns the state's entitlement to exercise jurisdiction abroad,[52] extraterritorial jurisdiction under international human rights treaties is a function of protecting the rights of the individual and concerns the state's obligations when exercising jurisdiction abroad. Put differently, whereas the former establishes whether the state has jurisdiction to act extraterritorially, the latter establishes whether an extraterritorial act brings the individual within the state's jurisdiction for the purpose of the state's extra-territorial obligations under international human rights law.[53]

The UNGPs' appeal to states' policy rationales to prevent and redress human rights violations committed in the course of global business operations is certainly to be welcomed. However, it is equally the expression of a persistent failure of the state-centred conception of international human rights law to account for the human rights impacts of global corporate power. It is one question whether states are *permitted* to adjust their policies and regulation to better promote and protect human rights in relation to extraterritorial corporate violations. It is quite a different question whether states are *obliged* to do so as a matter of international human rights law. Absent a clear recognition of international legal obligations to regulate and control the human rights impacts of their corporate nationals abroad, states will have little incentive to adopt so-called 'home-state' or 'parent-based' regulation to protect third-country victims against human rights violations committed in the course of global business operations.[54] Whereas the profits of corporate undertakings largely accrue on the home state's territory, the prevention and redress of corporate human rights violations falls within the legal and political responsibility of the host state. Below the surface of 'governance gaps created by globalisation' thus lies another 'business and human rights predicament' that is rooted in the interrelation between the international order of states and global corporate power that unleashes the human rights impacts of global business operations from the constraints of narrowly construed international human rights law.

5. From a territory-based to a subject-based approach to international human rights law

The described transition from state obligations imposed by international human rights law to states' policy rationales to protect human rights (through domestic law) is but an attempt to respond to the discrepancy between the global human rights impacts of corporate power and the territorial limitations of the state-centred conception of international law. As our above analysis demonstrates, there are three different ways in which 'territory' determines the allocation of human rights obligations to states under international law. First, the location of the putative victim in relation to the state that holds the obligation determines whether human rights protection is considered territorial or extraterritorial. Second, the way in which states operate on foreign soil determines the type of obligation owed to the individual rights holder: whereas negative extraterritorial obligations only require state agents asserting power and control over individuals abroad, positive extraterritorial obligations are traditionally premised on a state exercising effective control over the territory of another state. Third, the territorial location of a non-state actor (corporation) 'abusing' human rights determines whether, in the terminology of the SRSG, state regulation of that corporate perpetrator is considered 'direct extraterritorial jurisdiction' or merely a 'domestic measure with extraterritorial implications'.[55] The cumulative effect of this threefold legal territorialisation of human rights is that international law has traditionally been primarily concerned with *restraining* states from exercising extraterritorial authority to regulate and control the human rights impacts of their 'corporate nationals' abroad. The state-centred conception of international law privileges the sovereign territorial rights that states claim over their territory and (corporate) persons therein over the claims of third-country victims to have their human rights protected against violations committed in the course of global business operations.

However, in so far as the operations of powerful non-state actors that penetrate territorial borders challenge the legal compartmentalisation of universal human rights in the international order of states, they have also led to a gradual de-centring of international human rights law from the public and territorial state.[56] One important ramification of this development is the destabilisation of the constitutive relationship between control over territory and positive human rights obligations. In *Ilaşcu and Others* v. *Moldova and Russia*, for instance, the ECtHR considered that the Moldovan government had positive obligations to protect the human rights of individuals located on parts of its territory occupied by Russia (the 'Moldovan Republic of Transdniestria') despite the fact that Moldova did not exercise effective control over the area in question: 'Even in absence of effective control over the Transdniestrian region, Moldova still had positive obligations under Article 1 of the Convention to take the diplomatic, economic, judicial or other measures that were in its power to take and are in accordance with international law to secure to the applicants the rights guaranteed by the Convention'.[57] Moreover, in one of the Cyprus cases the same court held that Turkey's human rights obligations in Northern Cyprus extended not only to acts of its own soldiers and officials as well as acts of the local administration (the Turkish Republic of Northern Cyprus, TRNC), but also to acts of private parties violating the rights of Greek and Turkish Cypriots.[58] It remains somewhat unclear in this case whether the court thought that acts of the TRNC could be directly attributed to Turkey with the consequence that the latter could be said to exercise effective control over the territory in question. This notwithstanding, the ECtHR was affirmative on the question of Turkey's extraterritorial positive human rights obligations: 'the acquiescence or connivance of the authorities of a Contracting State in the acts of private individuals which violate the Convention rights of other individuals within its jurisdiction may engage that State's responsibility under the Convention. Any different conclusion would be at variance with the obligation contained in Article 1 of the Convention.'[59] The same point was reiterated in the more recent Cyprus case of *Isaak* concerning a demonstration in the neutral UN buffer zone established between the Turkish and the Greek Cypriot ceasefire lines, in the course of which one participant was beaten to death by TRNC policemen and private actors (the 'Turkish mob').[60] The circumstances of the case precluded any finding of Turkey exercising effective territorial control over the area in question. Nevertheless, having established that 'despite the presence of the Turkish armed forces and other "TRNC" police officers in the area, nothing was done to prevent or stop the attack [by civilian demonstrators] or to help the victim', the court reiterated its earlier dictum that 'the acquiescence or connivance of the authorities of a Contracting State in the acts of private individuals which violate Convention rights of other individuals within its jurisdiction may engage that State's responsibility under the Convention'.[61] Absent effective control over territory, Turkey's extraterritorial positive obligations are apparently directly grounded in the state's acquiescence in the human rights violations committed by private actors outside its territory.[62]

While at variance with the court's traditional approach to 'jurisdiction' under Article 1 of the European Convention on Human Rights (ECHR),[63] the dissociation of positive obligations from control over territory may be indicative of a transition in its jurisprudence from a territory-based to a subject-based approach to (extra-) territorial human rights obligations. Such an approach pays tribute to the fact that in cases of human rights violations committed by non-state actors across territorial borders, the territorial nexus between the state, the perpetrator and the victim will often be tenuous. In the relationship between the state and the victim, a subject-based approach to international human rights law focuses on the power the state wields over circumstances of the individual rights holder and treats control over territory as a mere presumption of control over persons.[64] Grounding human rights obligations in state power over individuals finds support in the interpretation of (extra-) territorial human rights jurisdiction adopted by various other international courts and treaty bodies. In this vein, the ECtHR considers that the 'essential question' to be examined is 'whether the applicants ... were, as a result of [the] extra-territorial act, capable of falling within the jurisdiction of the respondent States'.[65] According to the Inter-American Commission of Human Rights, whether a person is subject to the state's jurisdiction under Article 1 of the American Convention on Human Rights does not depend 'on the presumed victim's nationality or presence within a particular geographic area but on whether, under the specific circumstances, the State observed the rights of a person subject to its authority and control'.[66] And for the UN Human Rights Committee, the International Covenant on Civil and Political Rights' reference to individuals subject to a state's jurisdiction 'is not to the place where the violation occurred, but rather to the relationship between the individual and the State in relation to a violation of any of the rights set forth in the Covenant'.[67]

In the relationship between the state and the corporate perpetrator of human rights violations, the subject-based approach to international human rights law entails a relaxation of the state-based distinction between, on the one hand, the direct attribution of private conduct to public authority (which triggers negative extraterritorial state obligations) and, on the other hand, state control over the foreign territory in which the private conduct takes place (which triggers positive extraterritorial state obligations). As Hakimi points out, both the questions of attribution and third-party responsibility ultimately turn on a 'normative judgment about the nature of the state's relationship [with the human rights abuser]: should international law require the state to exercise governmental authority over – and thereby to influence – the particular third party at issue?'[68] This places the binary distinction between negative and positive state obligations on a continuum of measures that states are required to take to respect and protect human rights in relation to violations by non-state actors. Instead of an 'all or nothing' approach to positive state obligations premised on (extra-) territorial control, the subject-based approach imposes (extra-) territorial obligations to protect against corporate violations that are commensurate with the state's control over the corporate perpetrator.[69] This entails that, absent the degree of control over the perpetrator required for direct attribution and absent control over the territory in which the victim resides, a state's influence over the non-state actor violating human rights can still trigger corresponding human rights obligations towards the victim of human rights violations.[70]

6. Taming corporate power overseas

The subject-based approach to international human rights law disentangles the triangular relationship between states, corporate human rights abusers and victims of human rights violations mediated by state territory into de-territorialised relationships between the state and the victim and the state and the perpetrator constituted by state power and control. By de-centring human rights obligations from state territory, this approach is instrumental in addressing a constellation of human rights violations of particular concern to 'business and human rights', namely where the corporate perpetrator (or a constituent part of it), is located on the state's territory while the victim resides on the territory of another state.[71] In these cases, the influence and control a state asserts over a corporate human rights abuser within its territorial borders constitutes an assertion of state power in relation to third-country victims that attracts a corresponding human rights obligation to protect against extraterritorial corporate violations. The territorial location of the corporate perpetrator thus not only determines whether states are permitted to protect human rights against extraterritorial corporate abuse (the SRSG's distinction between 'direct extraterritorial jurisdiction' and 'domestic measures with extraterritorial implications'). It is also decisive for *establishing a state's human rights obligations* under international law to protect third-country victims against corporate-related human rights violations. Moreover, the territorial location of the corporate perpetrator influences the *scope* of such positive extraterritorial human rights obligations. With regard to corporate actors residing outside the state's territory, that state's positive human rights obligations are delimited by its legal competence to exercise extraterritorial jurisdiction as it cannot be considered 'reasonable' or 'appropriate' to require states to take positive steps to protect human rights in violation of general international law.[72] Such concerns are mitigated by corporate presence within the state's territorial jurisdiction, which entails that its extra-territorial positive human rights obligations to protect third-country victims against corporate violations will be both more stringent and encompassing.

In this vein, the ECtHR distinguishes acts of state agents performed outside the state's territory from acts performed inside the state's territory that merely produce effects outside the state's territory: the 'real connection between the applicants and the respondent states [for the purpose of Article 1 ECHR] is the impugned act which, wherever decided, was performed, or had effects, outside the territory of those States ("the extra-territorial act")'.[73] In extraterritorial effects cases, the influence and control a state asserts, or fails to assert, over a non-state actor on its territory can constitute human rights obligations towards third-country victims. The case of *Kovaĉić*, for example, concerned the domestic regulation of business activities that allegedly violated human rights outside the state's territory.[74] The Croatian applicants complained that they were prevented by a Slovenian law from withdrawing funds from their accounts in the Croatian branch of a Slovenian bank. The Slovenian government submitted that its obligation to secure property rights under Article 1 of Protocol 1 of the ECHR was confined to property within its jurisdiction, and that none of the instances of extraterritorial jurisdiction recognised by the ECtHR was applicable in the present case. Nevertheless, the ECtHR, after reiterating that 'the responsibility of [the High] Contracting

Parties can be involved by acts and omissions of their authorities which produce effects outside their own territory', accepted that the banking legislation introduced by the Slovenian National Assembly 'affected' the applicants' property rights in Croatia. 'This being so', the ECtHR found that 'the acts of the Slovenian authorities continue to produce effects, albeit outside Slovenian territory, such that Slovenia's responsibility under the Convention could be engaged'.[75] Similarly, the Maastricht Principles on Extraterritorial Obligations of States in the Area of Economic, Social and Cultural Rights define extraterritorial human rights obligations as 'obligations relating to the acts and omissions of a state, within or beyond its territory, that have effects on the enjoyment of human rights outside of that State's territory'.[76] In relation to business entities this entails that 'states must adopt and enforce measures to protect economic, social and cultural rights through legal and other means ... where the corporation, or its parent or controlling company, has its centre of activity, is registered or domiciled, or has its main place of business or substantial business activities, in the state concerned'.[77]

A cognate approach to state obligations to prevent and redress corporate human rights violations in extraterritorial effects cases can also be discerned in a series of General Comments, Statements and Concluding Observations issued by UN human rights treaty bodies over the past decade. Thus, for example, in its well-known General Comment No. 14 concerning the right to health, the Committee on Economic, Social and Cultural Rights noted:

> To comply with their international obligations in relation to article 12, States parties have to respect the enjoyment of the right to health in other countries, and to prevent third parties from violating the right in other countries, if they are able to influence these third parties by way of legal or political means, in accordance with the Charter of the United Nations and applicable international law.[78]

With regard to the right to water, the same committee has called upon states parties 'to prevent their own citizens and companies from violating the right to water of individuals and communities in other countries. Where states parties can take steps to influence other third parties to respect the right, through legal or political means, such steps should be taken in accordance with the Charter of the United Nations and applicable international law.'[79] The committee's general comment on social security also provides that 'State parties should extraterritorially protect the right to social security by preventing their own citizens and national entities from violating this right in other countries'.[80] In 2011, the committee further adopted a 'Statement of the obligations of states parties regarding the corporate sector and economic, social and cultural rights' in which it called upon states to 'take steps to prevent human rights contraventions abroad by corporations which have their main seat under their jurisdiction, without infringing the sovereignty or diminishing the obligations of the host states under the Covenant'.[81] In a similar vein, the recent General Comment No. 16 from the Committee on the Rights of the Child provides that home states 'have obligations ... to respect, protect and fulfil children's rights in the context of businesses' extraterritorial activities and operations, provided that there is a reasonable link between the State and the conduct concerned'.[82] What is more, in both these particular statements, the respective committees recognise the part played by the extraterritorial obligations of states regarding corporate human rights abuses, in fulfilling their wider (and still ill-defined) responsibilities to engage in international assistance and cooperation in the realisation of the relevant treaty rights.[83]

The UN treaty bodies have also been active on this issue in respect of their Concluding Observations on individual states' reports. For example, the Committee on the Elimination of Racial Discrimination has called upon the United Kingdom 'to take appropriate legislative and administrative measures to ensure that acts of transnational corporations registered in the State party comply with the provisions of the Convention'.[84] With regard to Australia, the committee recently noted 'with concern the absence of a legal framework regulating the obligation of Australian corporations at home and overseas whose activities, notably in the extractive sector, when carried out on the traditional territories of Indigenous peoples, have had a negative impact on Indigenous peoples' rights to land, health, living environment and livelihoods'.[85] Accordingly, the committee encouraged the state party to 'regulate the extra-territorial activities of Australian corporations abroad'.[86] The same committee has made similar observations with regard to Canada and the United States, and most recently, China, including recommendations that state parties should explore ways to hold business entities incorporated within their jurisdiction accountable for extra-territorial violations of the convention.[87] Finally, noting with concern reported participation and complicity of Australian mining companies in serious human rights violations in third countries, the Committee on the Rights of the Child has called upon the state party to 'examine and adapt its legislative framework (civil, criminal and administrative) ... regarding abuses to human rights, especially child rights, committed in the territory of the State party or overseas and establish monitoring mechanisms, investigation, and redress of such abuses, with a view towards improved accountability, transparency and prevention of violations'.[88]

7. Beyond the 100 Acre Wood

There is now a substantial and growing body of authoritative interpretation of international human rights by leading international human rights courts, commissions, committees and commentators, suggesting that states' hitherto latent extraterritorial obligations are now recognised as material and operative. This expanding body of jurisprudence and commentary illustrates clearly that there is nothing preordained about the nature of a state's jurisdictional territory, the manner by which it structures relations between legal actors, and the form in which it allocates rights and responsibilities. Certainly, the texts of international human rights law themselves accommodate – indeed prescribe – a state's scope of responsibility that stretches beyond purely territorial boundaries, and an allocation of duties (whether direct or indirect) that encompass private as well as public actors. What this means in cases of alleged human rights abuses by corporations operating overseas, is that home states (as well as, or even instead of, host states) may find that they are bound under international human rights laws to provide a forum in which to entertain the dispute, and – where the allegations are upheld – to discipline the corporation and provide remedies for the victims.

The recognition of extraterritorial state obligations to protect human rights against corporate-related violations presents a formidable challenge to international law's state-centred heritage. Yet it also uncovers the epistemic biases of a positivist legal doctrine that has long treated the compartmentalisation of the globe into territorial state entities as a matter of fact, thus insulating it from normative critique. The global human rights impacts of business operations undermine the very normativity of a state-centred conception of international law that assimilates universal human rights *and* global business entities to state territory. Such tendencies of the legal mind to compartmentalisation seldom troubled AA Milne's writings, and his 100 Acre Wood offers an agreeable metaphor for the complications one faces when straying into the borderlands. The 100 Acre Wood did not comprise the extent of the world known to Winnie-the-Pooh and friends. It was in fact just one, specific part of a larger forest, throughout which the writ of Milne's pen freely roamed.[89] Moreover, what sets the 100 Acre Wood apart from the rest of the forest is not a 'natural' territorial border but the stories and practices of its inhabitants through which they claim it as their own. And while the tremendous and sometimes terrible prospects that Milne had his characters believe would accompany their ventures through foreign and strange parts of the forest never quite materialised, through these ventures they were confronted with the challenge of encountering the 'beyond' from within their own domain, including through the appropriate distribution of responsibilities (for plans, promises and making amends),[90] dealing with external threats and dangers (environmental and existential),[91] and the reception and treatment of individuals new to their jurisdiction.[92] In a similar vein, there is nothing preordained or immutable about a state's jurisdictional territory and the way in which it structures relations between spaces, events and people, including the allocation of rights and responsibilities. In the area of international human rights law, this is reflected in the growing body of case-law and commentary suggesting that the state-based distinction between the 'territorial' and the 'extraterritorial' is of decreasing significance in allocating human rights obligations to states. We have argued that from a doctrinal perspective, this development may be indicative of a transition to a subject-based approach to international human rights law that de-centres human rights obligations from the public and territorial state. From a normative perspective, it contributes to recovering human rights' universal aspirations in the face of global corporate power.

Disclosure statement

No potential conflict of interest was reported by the author.

Notes

1. See, for example, J. Donnelly, *Universal Human Rights in Theory & Practice*, 2nd ed. (Ithaca, NY: Cornell University Press, 2003), Chapter 1.
2. See, for example, G. Teubner, 'The Anonymous Matrix: Human Rights Violations by "Private" Transnational Actors', *Modern Law Review* 69, no. 3 (2006): 327–46.
3. See A. Grear, 'Challenging Corporate "Humanity": Legal Disembodiment, Embodiment and Human Rights', *Human Rights Law Review* 7, no. 3 (2007): 511–43.
4. Council of Europe Parliamentary Assembly, 'Resolution 1757 (2010) Human Rights and Business', http://www.assembly.coe.int/Main.asp?link=/Documents/AdoptedText/ta10/ERES1757.htm
5. For example, a study dating back to the year 2000 asserts that when comparing corporate sales with states' gross domestic products (GDPs), 51 of the 100 largest economies in the world are corporations, while only 49 are states. Moreover, the largest 200 corporations are estimated to account for 27.5% of the world's economic activity, see S. Anderson and U. Cavanagh, *Top 200: The Rise of Corporate Global Power* (Washington, DC: Institute for Policy Studies, December 2000).

6. L. Catá Backer, 'Governance without Government: An Overview', in *Beyond Territoriality: Transnational Legal Authority in the Age of Globalisation*, ed. G. Handl, J. Zekoll and P. Zumbansen (The Netherlands: Martinus Nijhoff, 2012), 87, 88.
7. C. Thomas, 'International Financial Institutions and Social and Economic Rights: An Exploration', in *Human Rights Fifty Years On: A Reappraisal*, ed. T. Evans (Manchester: Manchester University Press, 1998), 161, 163.
8. K. de Feyter, *Human Rights: Social Justice in the Age of the Market* (London: Zed Books, 2005), 11.
9. UN Human Rights Council (UN HRC), 'Guiding Principles on Business and Human Rights: Implementing the United Nations' "Protect, Respect and Remedy" Framework', A/HRC/17/31 (21 March 2011).
10. See S. Ratner, 'Corporations and Human Rights: A Theory of Legal Responsibility', *Yale Law Journal* 111 (2001): 443–545; D. Kinley and J. Tadaki, 'From Talk to Walk: The Emergence of Human Rights Responsibilities for Corporations at International Law', *Virginia Journal of International Law* 44, no. 4 (2004): 931–1023.
11. On the practical implications of the distinction between obligations imposed by international human rights law and protecting human rights values through international (criminal, economic, etc.) law see D. Augenstein, 'The Crisis of International Human Rights Law in the Global Market Economy', in *Netherlands Yearbook of International Law*, Volume 44, ed. M. Bulterman and W. van Genugten (The Hague: T.M.C. Asser, 2014), 41–64.
12. UN Economic and Social Council, Commission on Human Rights, Sub-Commission on the Promotion and Protection of Human Rights, 'Draft Norms on the Responsibilities of Transnational Corporations and Other Business Enterprises with Regard to Human Rights', UN Doc E/CN.4/Sub.2/2003/12 (26 August 2003).
13. Ibid., para. 1.
14. See 'Report of the United Nations High Commissioner on Human Rights on the Responsibilities of Transnational Corporations and Related Business Enterprises with Regard to Human Rights', E/CN.4/2005/91 (15 February 2005); and D. Kinley and R. Chambers, 'The UN Human Rights Norms for Corporations: The Private Implications of Public International Law', *Human Rights Law Review* 6, no. 3 (2006) 447, 448–51.
15. Statement of the US Government Delegation to the 61st Session of the UNCHR (20 April 2005), cited in Kinley and Chambers, 'The UN Human Rights Norms for Corporations', 448.
16. On which, see the discussion in Kinley and Chambers, 'The UN Human Rights Norms for Corporations', 480–1.
17. See, for example, R. McCorquodale, 'Pluralism, Global Law and Human Rights: Strengthening Corporate for Human Rights Violations', *Global Constitutionalism* 2, no. 2 (2013): 287–315.
18. N. Jägers, *Corporate Human Rights Obligations: In Search of Accountability* (Antwerp: Intersentia, 2002), Chapter 2.
19. For a critique that traces the ideological roots of the public/private divide in modern international law to the co-emergence of state-based legal positivism and free-market liberalism see C. Cutler, *Private Power and Global Authority: Transnational Merchant Law and the Global Political Economy* (Cambridge: Cambridge University Press, 2003), 3. For an analysis of how that divide ought and might be overcome, by way of 'de-closeting' private international law in a way that enables it to 'reclaim its governance potential' by, for example, holding non-state actors accountable for their international human rights abuses, see Horatio Muir Watt, 'Private International Law Beyond the Schism', *Transnational Legal Theory* 2, no. 3 (2011): 347–428, at 427.
20. See Ratner, 'Corporations and Human Rights', 496.
21. F. Johns, 'The Invisibility of the Transnational Corporation: An Analysis of International Law and Legal Theory', *Melbourne University Law Review* 19 (1994): 893, 913.
22. J. Knox, 'Horizontal Human Rights Law', *American Journal of International Law* 102, no. 1 (2008): 1, 29–30.
23. See the recent proposal by C. Cronstedt et al., 'An International Arbitration Tribunal on Business and Human Rights' (February 2014), http://www.l4bb.org/news/IntlArbTribunal25Feb2014.pdf
24. Ecuador, also on behalf of African Group, the Arab Group, Pakistan, Sri Lanka, Kyrgyzstan, Cuba, Nicaragua, Bolivia, Venezuela and Peru, has recently initiated a new initiative towards developing a legally binding international instrument on business and human rights. It delivered

a statement at the September 2013 session of the UN HRC stressing 'the necessity of moving forward toward a legally binding framework to regulate the work of transnational corporations and to provide appropriate protection, justice and remedy to the victims of human rights abuses resulting from or related to the activities of some transnational corporations and other business entities'. To this effect, Ecuador has convened an expert workshop on this issue during the HRC's session in March 2014, see 'Statement on behalf of a Group of Countries at the 24rd Session of the Human Rights Council, General Debate – Item 3: "Transnational Corporations and Human Rights"' (Geneva, September 2013), http://www.business-humanrights.org/Links/Repository/1024755

25. UN HRC, 'Interim Report of the Special Representative of the Secretary-General on the Issue of Human Rights and Transnational Corporations and Other Business Enterprises', E/CN.4/2006/97 (22 February 2006), para. 65.
26. Apart from requiring states to protect human rights against 'abuses' by corporations as third parties, international human rights law also imposes obligations on states to respect human rights in relation to corporations acting as state agents. In the latter case, the corporate act is attributed to the state so that the state is considered thereby to interfere directly with the victim's rights.
27. UN Human Rights Committee, 'General Comment 31, Nature of General Legal Obligation Imposed on States Parties to the Covenant', CCPR/C/21/Rev.1/Add. 13 (24 May 2004), para. 8.
28. Inter-Am. Ct. H. R., *Velasquez Rodriguez* v. *Honduras* (Judgment of 29 July 1988), para. 172.
29. ECtHR, *Fadeyeva* v. *Russia* (Judgment of 9 June 2005), para. 89.
30. UN HRC, 'Mandate Consultation Outline' (October 2010), http://www.reports-and-materials.org/Ruggie-consultations-outline-Oct-2010.pdf
31. UN HRC, 'Business and Human Rights: Towards Operationalising the "Protect, Respect, Remedy" Framework', A/HRC/11/13 (22 April 2009), para. 13.
32. O. de Schutter, 'Globalisation and Jurisdiction: Lessons from the European Convention on Human Rights', *Centre for Human Rights and Global Justice Working Paper* 9 (2005): 22.
33. Ibid., 13.
34. M. Milanović, *Extraterritorial Application of Human Rights Treaties* (Oxford: Oxford University Press, 2011), 210.
35. Paradigmatic ECtHR, *Loizidou* v. *Turkey*, Preliminary Objections (Judgment of 23 February 1995), para. 62.
36. H. King, 'The Extraterritorial Human Rights Obligations of States', *Human Rights Law Review* 9, no. 4 (2009): 521–56. This view finds support in the International Court of Justice's Genocide Judgment, according to which the scope of the state 'obligation of conduct' to prevent genocide 'must also be assessed by legal criteria, since it is clear that every state may only act within the limits permitted by international law', ICJ, *Application of the Convention on the Prevention of the Crime of Genocide (Bosnia and Herzegovina* v. *Serbia and Montenegro*), Judgment of 26 February 2007, para. 430.
37. ECtHR (Grand Chamber), *Banković & Others* v. *Belgium & Others* (Admissibility Decision of 12 December 2001), para. 59. While the bulk of *Banković* has meanwhile been overruled, the court continues to hold fast to the view that extraterritorial human rights protection is exceptional and in need of special justification in the light of the rights of third states, see ECtHR (Grand Chamber), *Al-Skeini and Others* v. *United Kingdom* (Judgment of 7 July 2011), para. 131.
38. C. Ryngaert, 'Jurisdiction: Towards a Reasonableness Test', in *Global Justice, State Duties*, ed. M. Langford et al. (Cambridge: Cambridge University Press, 2013), 192, 207–10. According to Ryngaert, 'the home state might even be prohibited from regulating the overseas conduct of its MNCs [multi-national corporations] when such regulation collides with the sovereign interest of the host state' (ibid., 209).
39. UN HRC, 'Guiding Principles on Business and Human Rights'.
40. The UNGPs are explicit in this regard: 'The Guiding Principles' normative contribution lies not in the creation of new international law obligations but in elaborating the implications of existing standards and practices for states and businesses … ', see ibid., para. 14.
41. UN HRC, 'Business and Human Rights: Further Steps towards the Operationalisation of the "Protect, Respect and Remedy" Framework', A/HRC/14/27 (9 April 2010), para. 55.
42. UN HRC, 'Business and Human Rights', para. 15.
43. UN HRC, 'Protect, Respect and Remedy: A Framework for Business and Human Rights', A/HRC/8/5 (7 April 2008), para. 3.

44. See UN HRC, 'Guiding Principles on Business and Human Rights', para. 4.
45. Ibid.
46. Ibid.
47. Ibid.
48. Ibid., para. 2; the commentary adds that 'some human rights treaty bodies recommend that home states take steps to prevent abuse abroad by business enterprises within their jurisdiction'.
49. In his earlier work, the SRSG also explored other bases of extra-territorial jurisdiction under general international law, including the nationality of the victim (i.e., the passive personality principle), see, for example, UN HRC, 'Corporate Responsibility under International Law and Issues of Extraterritorial Regulation', A/HRC/4/35/Add.2 (15 February 2007).
50. See UN HRC, 'Business and Human Rights: Further Steps', para. 48.
51. See UN HRC, 'Guiding Principles on Business and Human Rights', para. 2.
52. F.A. Mann, 'The Doctrine of Jurisdiction in International Law', *Recueil des Cours* 111 (The Hague: The Hague Academy of International Law, 1994), 1, 15: the concept of jurisdiction fulfils 'one of the fundamental functions of public international law', namely 'the function of regulating and delimiting the respective [legislative, judicial and administrative] competences of States'.
53. We have previously distinguished between these two forms of a state jurisdiction in respect of human rights by characterising the first as the 'permissive question' and the second as 'the prescriptive question', see D. Augenstein and D. Kinley, 'When Human Rights "Responsibilities" Become "Duties": The Extra-territorial Obligations of States that Bind Corporations', in *Obligations of Business: Beyond the Corporate Responsibility to Respect?*, ed. S. Deva and D. Bilchitz (Cambridge: Cambridge University Press, 2013), 271–94.
54. See, for example, S. Joseph, 'Taming the Leviathans: Multinational Enterprises and Human Rights', *Netherlands International Law Review* 46 (1999): 171–203; S. Deva, 'Acting Extraterritorially to Tame Multinational Corporations for Human Rights Violations: Who Should "Bell the Cat"?', *Melbourne Journal of International Law* 46 (2004): 37–65.
55. See UN HRC, 'Business and Human Rights: Further Steps', para. 48.
56. An important example of this trajectory outside 'business and human rights' is the increasing currency of the 'responsibility to protect' (R2P), see for example, A. Peters, 'Humanity as the A and Ω of Sovereignty', *European Journal of International Law* 20, no. 3 (2009): 513–44.
57. ECtHR (Grand Chamber), *Ilaşcu and Others* v. *Moldova and Russia* (Judgment of 8 July 2004), para. 331.
58. ECtHR, *Cyprus* v. *Turkey* (Judgment of 10 May 2001).
59. Ibid., para. 81.
60. ECtHR, *Isaak and Others* v. *Turkey* (Admissibility Decision of 28 September 2006).
61. Ibid., para. 21.
62. As Miltner notes in her discussion of the case, it is unlikely that the court could have established jurisdiction 'without the broadening of the authority and control test via the use of the "acquiescence" device'. B. Miltner, 'Extraterritorial Jurisdiction under the European Convention on Human Rights: An Expansion Under *Isaak v Turkey*?', *European Human Rights Law Review* 2 (2007): 172, 181.
63. See de Schutter, 'Globalisation and Jurisdiction'; and Milanović, *Extraterritorial Application of Human Rights Treaties*.
64. For a discussion of the parallel evolution of the 'control over territory' and the 'control over persons' test in the jurisprudence of the ECtHR see M. Gondek, *The Reach of Human Rights in a Globalising World: Extra-territorial Application of Human Rights Treaties* (Antwerp: Intersentia, 2009). The further specification of the kind and degree of state control necessary to trigger a corresponding human rights obligation is beyond the scope of this article. Propositions to this regard range from (very restrictive) direct physical capture to (very broad) cause-and-effect notions of control. Behind this doctrinal debate lies the normative issue regarding the conditions necessary and appropriate for states to accept positive human rights obligations in cross-border contexts, see also further section 6.
65. ECtHR, *Banković*, para. 54; see further *R (Al-Skeini and Others)* v. *Secretary of State for Defence* [2007] UKHL 26, 34 (HL), para. 64. Having regard to the case law of the ECtHR, Lord Roger remarked: 'It is important therefore to recognise that, when considering the question of jurisdiction under the Convention, the focus has shifted to the victim or, more precisely, to the link between the victim and the contracting state.'

66. Inter-Am. Com. H. R., *Coard et al.* v. *The United States*, Case 10.951, Report No. 109/99 (Judgment of 29 September 1999), para. 37.
67. UN Human Rights Committee, *López Burgos* v. *Uruguay*, Communication No. 52/1979, CCPR/C/OP/1 (Judgment of 29 July 1981), para. 12.2.
68. M. Hakimi, 'State Bystander Responsibility', *European Journal of International Law* 21, no. 2 (2010): 341, 356–7. This approach bears a resemblance to Ryngaert's proposal to tie extraterritorial human rights obligations to a reasonableness requirement, see Ryngaert, 'Jurisdiction'.
69. In a similar vein, Rick Lawson distinguishes between an 'all or nothing' approach and a 'gradual' approach to human rights jurisdiction, see R. Lawson, '"Life After Banković": On the Extraterritorial Application of the European Convention on Human Rights', in *Extraterritorial Application of Human Rights Treaties*, ed. F. Coomans and M.T. Kamminga (Antwerp: Intersentia, 2004), 83–123. Arguably overruling *Banković*, the ECtHR acknowledged in *Al Skeini* that human rights obligations under the ECHR can be 'divided and tailored', see ECtHR, *Al Skeini*, para. 137.
70. Such an approach can be discerned in the ECtHR's holding Russia responsible for human rights violations committed in Transdniestria because it exercised 'decisive influence' over the Moldovan separatists, see ECtHR, *Ilaşcu*, para. 392; and further Hakimi, 'State Bystander Responsibility', 376–9.
71. Indeed, research conducted by the SRSG suggests that today the majority of corporate-related human rights violations are committed in developing countries by business entities that are based in, and remain controlled from, states in the developed world, see UN HRC, 'Interim Report'.
72. See section 3.
73. ECtHR, *Banković*, para. 54.
74. ECtHR, *Kovačič and Others* v. *Slovenia* (Admissibility Decision of 1 April 2004). The case was struck out at the merits stage due to new facts that had come to the court's attention.
75. Ibid.
76. 'Maastricht Principles on Extraterritorial Obligations of States in the Area of Economic, Social and Cultural Rights' (Maastricht, 2011), Principle 8(a), published with extensive commentary in *Human Rights Quarterly* 34 (2012): 1084–169.
77. Ibid., Principle 25.
78. CESCR, 'General Comment No. 14: The Right to the Highest Attainable Standard of Health', E/C.12/2000/4 (11 August 2000), para. 39.
79. CESCR, 'General Comment No. 15: The Right to Water', E/C.12/2002/11 (20 January 2003), para. 33.
80. CESCR, 'General Comment 19: The Right to Social Security', E/C.12/GC/19 (4 February 2008), para. 54.
81. CESCR, 'Statement on the Obligations of States Parties Regarding the Corporate Sector and Economic, Social and Cultural Rights', E/C.12/2011/1 (12 July 2011), para. 5.
82. CRC, 'General Comment 16 on State Obligations Regarding the Impact of the Business Sector on Children's Rights', CRC/C/CG/16 (17 April 2013), para. 43.
83. Respectively, CESCR, 'General Comment 19′, at para. 3, and CRC, 'General Comment 16', at para. 41. In a similar vein, the Maastricht Principles list 'obligations of a global character that are set out in the Charter of the United Nations and human rights instruments to take action, separately, and jointly through international cooperation, to realise human rights universally'. Such 'international assistance and cooperation' stipulations also exist in a number of other principal human rights instruments, including: the Universal Declaration on Human Rights (Preamble) and the Convention on the Rights of Persons with Disabilities (Art 32); and it is implied in the International Convention on the Protection of the Rights of All Migrant Workers and Members of their Families (Art. 7). In addition, the Vienna Declaration and Programme of Action (1993) reiterates (in para. 4) the command in Article 56 of the UN Charter that states 'take joint and separate action' to achieve (inter alia) the UN's human rights goals, which, the Declaration adds, "must be considered a priority objective of the UN"'.
84. CERD, 'Concluding Observations: United Kingdom of Great Britain and Northern Ireland', CERD/C/GBR/CO/18-20 (14 September 2011), para. 29.
85. CERD, 'Concluding Observations: Australia', CERD/C/AUS/CO/15-17 (13 September 2010), para. 13.
86. Ibid.

87. See CERD, 'Concluding Observations/Comments: Canada', CERD/C/CAN/CO/18 (25 May 2007), para. 17; CERD, 'Concluding Observations: United States', CERD/C/USA/CO/6 (8 May 2008), para. 30; and CERD, 'Concluding Observations: China', E/C.12/CHN/CO/2 (23 May 2014), para. 13.
88. CRC, 'Concluding Observations: Australia', CRC/C/AUS/CO/4 (19 June 2012), para. 28(a).
89. The existence of places beyond the 100 Acre Wood in both *Winnie-the-Pooh* (1926) and the *House at Pooh Corner* (1928) collected stories is based on the simple fact that Milne himself did not seem to have a fixed idea of its boundaries, such that its coverage and dimensions, as well as those of the forest as a whole, differ between stories; see AA Milne, *The World of Pooh: The Complete Winnie-the-Pooh and The House at Pooh Corner* (1958).
90. For example: 'In which Christopher Robin leads an Expotition (sic) to the North Pole', and 'In which Tigger is unbounced' (*The World of Pooh)*.
91. As to the former – the inclemency of the weather, for example: (i) 'In which Piglet is Entirely surrounded by Water'; (ii) 'In which a House is built at Pooh Corner for Eeyore' (snow); and (iii) 'In which Piglet does a Very Grand Thing' (wind), ibid.; and as to the latter – the spectres of Heffalumps and Woozles ('In which Piglet meets a Heffalump' and 'In which Pooh and Piglet go Hunting and nearly catch a Woozle', ibid.
92. For example: Tigger ('In which Tigger comes to the Forest and has Breakfast'), and Kanga and Roo ('In which Kanga and Baby Roo come to the Forest, and Piglet has a Bath'); ibid.

CSR is dead: long live Pigouvian taxation

Nicholas Connolly

Institute of Commonwealth Studies, School of Advanced Studies, University of London, UK

Within economics there is a philosophical impasse that prevents humanity addressing the ethical quandary that is epitomised by the negative social impacts of the globalised corporation. This impasse has created a void which is being filled by corporate social responsibility even though corporate social responsibility does not exist to, and could not, solve this ethical quandary. Humanity can bridge this impasse by viewing the corporation in sociological terms as a functional system that can be manipulated for the purposes of humanity. Pigouvian taxation is a proven method of manipulating the corporation and may be useful in achieving this objective.

The virtue of capitalism is that society can take advantage of people's greed rather than their benevolence ...[1]

Introduction

When Adam Smith envisaged the invisible hand working for the greater good through the single-minded pursuit of profit he did so from a perspective that could not conceive of the modern industrial nation state and its welfare provision, the untrammelled rise of the corporation[2] to become the dominant economic unit, including its ability to decouple ownership from management of the often grim reality of production, or, modern 'hyper-globalisation' facilitated by technological advances such as the internet and containerisation. His was a conception of a market economy wrought in the mercantile era.

By the time financiers of the late nineteenth/early twentieth century had been labelled 'Robber Barons'[3] who organised corporate structures to maximise personal gain and minimise personal risk, Berle and Means[4] were arguing the corporation should be re-conceived to assume certain responsibilities for the betterment of society; the age of the corporation[5] had arrived.[6] This lively discussion about the future of the corporation was neutered by World War II and the ensuing Cold War, which led to a black and white, good versus evil, capitalist versus socialist/communist narrative – in the United States at least[7] – which broadly forced democratic society to choose between a planned redistributive economy that is managed by government to prevent the tyranny of the wealthy[8] and an unplanned market economy, the freedom of which prevents the tyranny of the political classes.[9]

Simultaneously, profound changes occurred in industrialised societies. The post-war boom, technological and scientific developments combined with universal education, health care (more-or-less), pensions, unemployment support, labour laws, product safety standards, and much more, improved lives dramatically and corporations were fundamental to that transformation.[10] In 1960 it was difficult for an average citizen in Western Europe or North America – at least – not to regularly interact with corporations. In 2014, it is virtually impossible.

It was against this background, in the late 1950s, that Galbraith, once labour became organised and the state asserted control over production through regulation and tax, visualised a pluralistic system of countervailing powers which created an equilibrium that, if well managed, promised reliable economic growth and broad prosperity for all.[11] In contrast, Andrew Hacker asserted ' ... when General Electric [GE], American Telephone and Telegraph [AT&T], and Standard Oil of New Jersey [ESSO] enter the pluralist arena we have elephants dancing among the chickens'.[12] Or, perhaps more presciently:

> [i]n the final analysis the fulcrum of corporate power is the investment decision. The uses of capital for investment purposes are, in the final analysis, decided by small handfuls of corporate managers. They decide how much is to be spent; what products are to be made; where they are to be manufactured; and who is to participate in the processes of production. A single corporation can draw up an investment program calling for the expenditure of several billions of dollars on new plants and products. A decision such as this may well determine the quality of life for a substantial segment of society: men and materials will move across continents; old communities will decay and new ones will prosper; tastes and habits will alter; new skills will be demanded and the education of a nation will adjust itself accordingly; even governments will fall into line; providing public services that corporate developments make necessary.[13]

It was not until the 1960s that Milton Friedman addressed the pre-war debate by arguing that attaching any kind of social responsibility to corporations beyond their focus on profit was misconceived because, amongst other reasons, they did not and should not have the capacity to determine how society should address particular issues, if they wished, through regulation.[14] It is important to stress that Friedman was not arguing businesses should be given freedom to maximise profit at all costs rather, he states, 'the role of government ... is to do something that the market cannot do for itself, namely, to determine, arbitrate and enforce the rules of the game'.[15]

The contemporary narrative surrounding neoliberal economic policy, globalisation and its primary agent, the corporation, has moved on little. On the one hand, authors ranging from Stiglitz to Bakan argue that the corporation can be made responsible by attaching additional legal restrictions on their behaviours or essential new criteria to their decision-making. Implicitly following Berle and Means' logic, these authors suggest corporate leaders should be obliged to consider the well-being of the community and presumably, when operating internationally, these obligations would be human rights oriented.

As outlined above there are a number of fundamental issues with this approach, not least competency and mandate. Additional, more recent concerns are that if corporations were to embed human rights in their operational decision-making they would, most likely, apply human rights using existing assumptions[16] and practices[17] which would materially change the content of those rights for the benefit of the corporation and its employees.[18] Also, within the existing profit-centred formulation,[19] corporate success is relatively easy to assess: either the business is competitively profitable or it is not. Corporate decision-making guided by uncertain politically and culturally sensitive criteria (i.e. human rights) would be far more difficult to monitor and assess, thus muddying the waters and increasing opportunities for managerial malfeasance.[20]

On the other hand, it is argued, billions of people have been lifted out of poverty in recent years[21] directly because of neoliberal – corporation-centred – globalisation. Yes, millions have moved from apparently idyllic rural farmsteads to urban slums[22] but they have – on the whole – done so out of *choice*[23] in an effort to improve their standard of living in the long term. Their lives as subsistence farmers with little access to health care, education or, more esoterically, opportunities to do something different, did not meet their personal aspirations for comfort and their ambitions to provide a better a life for their children.[24] Moreover, access to standardised mass-produced consumables has improved living standards by increasing quality, lowering product costs and increasing leisure time.[25] From that perspective, the pain of neoliberal industrialisation caused by profit-centred corporate activity is a necessary precursor to the relative comfort of living in a consumer society which is, some argue, its inevitable consequence.[26]

The fact that most wealthy industrial nations have not in practice adopted neoliberal free market policies except where they have competitive advantage,[27] or allowed corporations to operate, in the modern era at least, without enforced regulation of operational and product standards,[28] is overlooked. While the fact that those counties that have successfully developed their economies in the late twentieth century (e.g. China and South Korea) have ignored neoliberal free market principles while those developing economies that have had neoliberal policies foisted upon them have often become less economically successful, is plainly ignored.[29]

Beyond theoretical weaknesses and factual inaccuracies, neither of these perspectives is useful simply because their ideological foundations render them mutually exclusive despite the evident reality that there are no entirely free market economies,[30] there are no credible alternatives to organising globalised production than the corporation, and, there is little chance of stuffing the capitalist genie back in its bottle.[31] Consequently, the debate has reached a stalemate while, simultaneously, globalisation has occurred and Hacker's dystopian vision of a world dictated by corporations appears to have become a reality.[32]

Banerjee and Duflo, highlight this issue in their book, *Poor Economics*,[33] which is premised on stepping beyond the often binary and essentially unanswerable 'big questions' such as whether 'poverty traps' exist and whether aid promotes sustainable economic development in order to target their experience and knowledge at specific solvable issues. By chipping away at the solvable, they suggest, we can collectively move forward and discover workable compromises that may, ultimately, render the 'big questions' redundant. In their view:

> [t]he lack of a grand universal answer might sound vaguely disappointing, but in fact it is exactly what a policy maker should want to know – not that there are a million ways that the poor are trapped but that there are a few key factors that create the trap, and that alleviating those particular problems could set them free and point them toward a virtuous cycle of increasing wealth and investment.[34]

The purpose of this article is to harness the practical philosophy outlined by Banerjee and Duflo and dissolve the false dichotomies between unrealised and unrealisable theories. It will attempt to identify one method of synchronising some economic activity with the realisation of some human rights. It will, in effect, seek to humanise[35] an element of the globalised economy without entrusting too much authority to politicians.[36]

Why should wealthy states intervene?

Prior to embarking on the main body of this discussion, it is important to ascertain why humanity should collectively and proactively attend to the problem created by the corporation in poor countries. Without doubt, parallels can be drawn between the experiences of early industrialisation in many now wealthy economies – which was both in-humane and environmentally destructive – and the recent rapid industrialisation of many poorer countries. Why are the governments of those countries not addressing these issues as effectively as governments of early industrialised states eventually did for their citizens through state-sponsored welfare alongside workplace and product safety regulations?

The key differences are, at minimum, threefold. First, in many cases the primary beneficiaries of cost savings facilitated by globalised production (i.e. share-holders, consumers and business leaders) do not reside in the country being industrialised. Consequently, the governments that control the governance of global businesses (i.e. the rich industrialised 'consumer' states[37]) are, on the whole,[38] detached from the social pressures rapid industrialisation creates and are therefore not motivated to address them. That is, those pressures that led to industrial regulation, product regulation, the New Deal in the United States and the Welfare State in Europe have been circumvented by globalised production.[39]

Moreover, the prima facie[40] commitment of many wealthy states to neoliberal economic policy has squandered their capacity to build relationships and guide development. How can European governments effectively insist on reform when their aid budgets are completely dwarfed by the investment and tax revenues offered by global corporations? Or, more pressingly, when the international financial organisations (i.e. the Bretton Woods organisation) these states dominate insist on deregulation and privatisation of utilities to encourage foreign investment without meaningful reference to the human rights implications of that deregulation, privatisation or investment?[41]

Second, the first blush of industrialisation was anarchic. There was no plan or blue print – no one knew what to expect – it was a 'revolution'. The same cannot be said of modern globalised industrialisation. Although it is often argued humanity cannot learn from history, there are certainly patterns of behaviour and outcomes that are essentially predictable. That is, given the previous human experience of market economics we could have confidently predicted that without enforceable regulations and regulations that are enforced, contemporary globalisation was likely to create winners and losers and those losers were likely to be the poor people commoditised within the production process and those reliant on a despoiled environment for life.

And third, building on point two, the industrial revolution transformed society creating both a new wealthy elite, a middle class and a new 'working class', whose needs and wants combined to restructure society. This process of restructure included building theoretical frameworks to ameliorate harm. Specifically, the global community, led by industrialised states, has agreed, almost universally, on minimum standards of life, freedom and governance in the shape of the various human rights instruments – which include an obligation on wealthy states to help poorer states[42] – that *should* provide a definitive guide to what effects on people corporate practices should be allowed to have.[43]

The reality, however, is closer to that described by Earnest and Rosenau in their article published by the *Washington Post* in 2000 – 'The Spy Who Loved Globalisation' – within which they argue that Ian Fleming and the script writers of numerous James Bond films realised the capacity for groups of people with the aid of technology to organise themselves in order to avoid control by state governments and further their own interests long before academics and policymakers did the same. Consequently, there is no systemic check or balance to ensure corporations contribute sufficiently to the communities in which they operate, there is little historic reflection or policy planning to build on the experiences of the industrial revolution in order to humanise the process of industrialisation and, where economic decision-making is concerned, human rights are rarely considered.[44]

Plan A?

In a previous article in this journal series,[45] it was argued that where the challenge of controlling corporate behaviour is concerned, corporate social responsibility (CSR) is the only 'game in town'. Without repeating all the arguments laid out in that article and assuming the ideological stalemate outlined above, it suffices to say that CSR is the dominant approach because it is assumed states and corporations are bound together in a virtual 'death roll'.[46] The corporation can move operations at will to maximise profit while states are obliged to compete with each other to secure the corporate investment necessary to govern their territory. This process has been labelled the 'race-to-the-bottom'.[47]

The argument progressed to assert that a sociological analysis of the corporation suggests CSR cannot possibly achieve an objective of humanising corporate behaviour because the corporation represents an 'intermediate-realm'[48] capable of imposing its own decision-making logic – its own morality – on its employees. That is, a human being working within a corporation does not make decisions that it believes are morally correct. It makes decisions that assume the primacy of the corporation and its objectives over other concerns. Consequently, in the final analysis, all CSR is ever likely to achieve is the appearance of responsible behaviour rather than creating corporations that behave responsibly, from a human perspective, on a consistent basis.

Despite this analysis, the purpose of that article was not to admit defeat or propose revolution. It was not a counsel of despair. Rather, it argued that this 'intermediate realm' with its myopic focus on profit is not the uncontrollable beast described by many commentators. In fact it is a machine with the functional realities that define machines. Like a machine, the corporation operates in a predictable way which, given appropriate policies, could be recalibrated to operate more humanely. More excitingly, perhaps the corporation could be recalibrated to deliver positive rather than negative externalities which, given the physical scale and wealth of many corporations, could embed positive human rights[49] within poor communities at a pace that is currently unimaginable.[50] The challenge is to identify methods of achieving that recalibration and the purpose of this article is to contextualise this challenge by providing one such method.

Plan B

A case study

Economic activity, ultimately, is about acquiring or creating goods and services that some people want to buy so that other people can make a profit and increase their wealth. From the consumer perspective, industrialisation initially, and globalisation more recently, has meant that basic products have become cheaper thus enabling poorer people to become active participants in consumer culture.[51] Given that most people are poor and global mass production is designed to provide goods *en masse* we can reasonably deduce that the majority of global businesses make decisions that lower production costs to ensure they retain or increase their profit margin whilst maintaining or increasing market share. The *average* consumer decision is made on price first and quality second[52] – ethics rarely come into the equation[53] – therefore if we are seeking policies that cause businesses to operate differently it is logical to start by considering policies which effect the price consumers pay for their products.

This is not a new realisation. Academics and policymakers have long understood that if you want to influence consumer habits you cannot rely on the market to challenge the consumer or for the consumer to consistently respond to passive information (e.g. public information broadcasts). Hence, in many states, high taxation on tobacco products combined with a series of increasingly restrictive regulations has lowered significantly the number of smokers where simple messages about personal jeopardy had become ineffective. If someone started and continued smoking once it was generally known that tobacco was deadly, telling that person smoking is deadly is not likely to have much impact: their desire to smoke is paramount. Imposing taxation that substantially increases the price of tobacco impacts the smokers' financial capacity to smoke and changes the equation entirely.

Perhaps more pertinently, over the last decade or so, in many developed economies, environmental taxes targeting cars[54] and fuel have reversed a long-standing trend for heavier cars with bigger engines that produce more emissions to one where engines are becoming smaller, cars are becoming lighter and emissions are being substantially reduced. This is not to suggest that environmental taxes on cars and fuel can solve environmental challenges associated with cars alone – more directive legislation was necessary to introduce catalytic converters and enforce the introduction of unleaded petrol and it is true that a second-hand car is by definition less damaging to the environment than a new car, the manufacture of which will use up additional raw materials and energy – but the data below evidence that the impact on consumer choices and corporate assumptions about those choices has been substantial.

In 2001, the United Kingdom, for example,[55] introduced an emission-based ownership tax (Vehicle Excise Duty (VED)) that gradually increased or decreased the annual cost of owning a new car depending on how polluting it was deemed to be. In March 2014 the least polluting cars (those that produce less than 100 g of carbon per 100 km travelled) were subject to no ownership tax, while the most polluting vehicles were subject to an initial ownership rate of £1,065 and an annual rate of £490. This cost differential combined with the increasing costs of fuel, which occurred both as a result of taxation and market forces,[56] represents a substantial incentive for consumers to choose vehicles that consume less fuel and thereby emit less carbon into the atmosphere.

The United Kingdom government's Department of Transport official statistics on vehicle registrations illustrate the effectiveness of this policy.[57] In 2001 no cars were registered that were officially gauged as producing less than 110 g/km. By 2012, there were more cars registered in emission bands under 110 g/km than there were in any other single emission band. Perhaps more significantly, the most common emission band (i.e. the mode) for a newly registered car was 151–165 g/km in 2001 whereas in 2012 the mode was 121–130 g/km with the lower band of 111–120 g/km following closely behind. Figure 1, drawn directly from the above-quoted official statistics, illustrates in more detail the trend towards registering lower emitting cars since the adoption of emission-based ownership taxes between 2001 and 2012.

First, when analysing Figure 1 it is important to note that the reduction in car registrations overall coincides with the recent economic malaise rather than environmental taxes. Simple[58] manipulation of the source data, however, indicates that mean emission in 2012 is in 133 g/km (i.e. in the 131–140 g/km band) where the mean emission in 2001 was 177.8 g/km (i.e. in the 176–185 g/km band), hence if the same number of cars

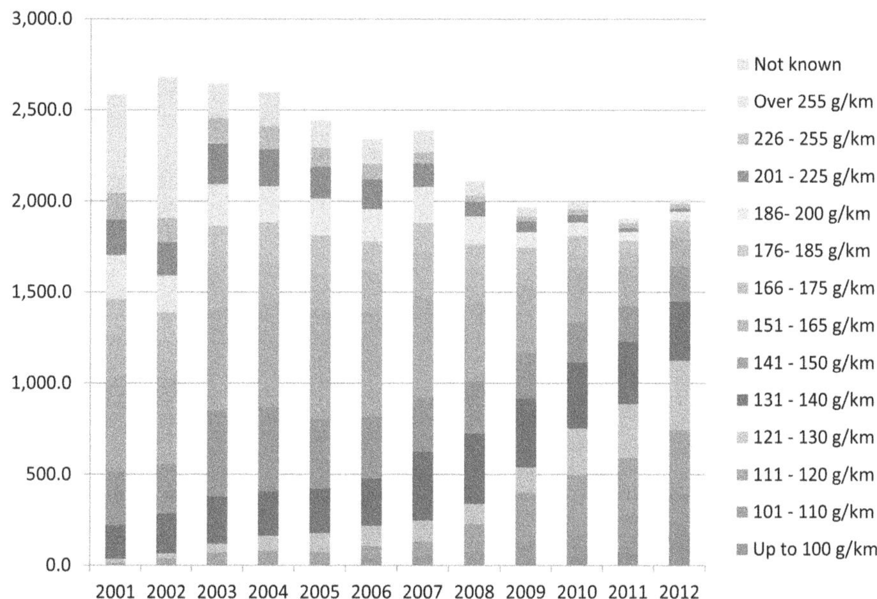

Figure 1.
Source: Vehicle Licensing Statistics, https://www.gov.uk/government/organisations/departmentfor-transport/series/vehicle-licensing-statistics

were sold in 2012 as they were in 2001 the total emission those cars released, on average, would be approximately 25% lower.

Second, we can see from Figure 1 that the total of the most highly polluting cars registered has reduced dramatically. In 2001 those cars emitting more than 201 g/km (i.e. the highest quartile of bands) represented a substantial proportion (c.17%) of the total number of vehicles registered whereas in 2012 those vehicles represented a much smaller proportion of the vehicles registered (c.3%).

Third, it is immediately apparent that in 2012 the lowest quartile of emission band represents more than 50% of the total vehicles registered and if the current trend continues at the current rate it is likely more than 75% of vehicles registered will emit less than 140 g/km in the near future. It is evident, therefore, that in approximately ten years emission rates which were virtually unknown in 2001 (i.e. less than 130 g/km) were, in 2012, the norm.

To summarise, again, it is important to stress that this analysis is not conceived to imply that vehicles are no longer an environmental challenge, that carbon is the appropriate proxy for greenhouse gases, or that man-made global warming should or should not be on the political agenda. Rather, it is utilised simply to evidence that consumer focussed taxes in a number of large consumer markets[59] have forced global corporations to change their products to ensure they can compete effectively. In the words of the Green Fiscal Commission: '[i]t is not clear that there is any other single policy instrument that could have such a large environmental impact at such a low cost'.[60]

The theory

The environmental taxes targeting new cars discussed above are an example of Pigouvian taxation. In Pigou's view, '[Economics] is a positive science of what is and tends to be, not a normative science of what ought to be'[61] and as such, he asserted, economic welfare should not 'serve for a barometer or index of total welfare' if only because 'an economic cause may effect non-economic welfare in ways that cancel its effect on economic welfare'.[62] Pigou goes on to argue that there are examples of decisions or policies that undeniably increase welfare but would have a negative effect on economic welfare (e.g. in his view, it is socially advantageous for mothers to stay at home and focus on parenting rather than going to work).

Where policy is concerned, Pigou stated:

> The free play of self-interest is conceived by [Adam Smith] to be 'confined to certain directions by our general social institutions, especially the family, property and the territorial State' [Cannan, *The History of Local Rates*, 176]. More generally, when one man obtains goods from another man, he is conceived to obtain them by the process, not of seizure, but of exchange in an open market, where the bargainers of both sides are reasonably competent and reasonably cogniscent of the conditions. There is ground, however, for believing that even Adam Smith had not realised fully the extent to which the System of National Liberty needs to be qualified and guarded by special laws, before it will promote the most productive employment of a country's resources. It has been said by a recent writer that 'the working of self-interest is generally beneficent, not because of natural coincidence between the self-interest of each and the good of all, but because human institutions are arranged so as to compel self-interest to work in directions in which it be beneficent' [Cannan, *Economic Review*, July 1913, 133].[63]

Specifically, Pigou suggests that:

> ... whereas a general expenditure tax leaves the relative of expenditure on various commodities unaltered, a tax system, under which different rates of duty are imposed on different things, alters their relative attractiveness, and so modifies the way in which purchasing power, and consequently, productive power is distributed.
>
> Since neither the demand nor the supply of any ordinary product – bread is sometimes an exception – is ever perfectly inelastic, taxes on particular products must, in general, discourage the employment of resources in producing the commodities that are taxed and divert them to producing other untaxed [or less taxed] commodities.[64]

In summary, Pigou's argument is that if society wants to reduce the consumption of a product and consequently reallocate productive resources, for whatever reason, an effective way to achieve this is by organising the tax system[65] to encourage consumers to prefer other products. The example Pigou employs throughout the *Economics of Welfare* is pollution, hence it is not surprising that when his ideas have been analysed, those analyses have predominantly focussed on the issue of pollution and they have been applied to address the issue of pollution. Pigou, however, consistently referred to welfare in the general sense. Pigouvian taxes, in theory at least, could be applied to almost any welfare issue caused by production.

With this in mind, the purpose of this article is to inquire whether Pigouvian taxation could be used to humanise globalised production. A straw man proposal will be outlined in the next section but for the purposes of this section it is useful to state that the proposed model is one of variable sales tax that is calibrated by an assessment of a product's impact on human rights. That is, are human rights likely to have been violated in its production and has the global business that generates the majority of profit from the product actively contributed to the realisation of human rights where the production occurred? The greater the negative 'human rights footprint' a product has, the greater the sales tax burden on that product, while the greater the positive 'human rights footprint' a product has, the lower the sales tax burden.

Although this article does not purport to contribute to the discipline of economics, we should, albeit briefly, assess the credibility of Pigou's thinking. Overshadowed by Keynes, Pigou's ideas do not appear to have benefitted from equally extensive analysis and consideration. Mainstream awareness is certainly low.[66] Within academia, Pigou's thinking has received a variety of criticisms and we will now consider a sample of these criticisms to determine whether they undermine its application in the proposed context.

Buchanan points out that Pigou's approach would not work where a monopoly exists because monopolies tend to restrict output to keep prices artificially high, so we can reasonably assume any firm with a monopoly would be able to avoid incurring the costs necessary to respond to consumer pressure.[67] Similarly, Davis and Whinston argue this approach would not work where production is oligopolistic because they would work in cahoots to manipulate the market.[68] Both criticisms have merit in their own terms but it should be noted most industrialised economies attempt[69] to guard against monopolistic or oligopolistic production because they distort the market and disadvantage consumers and the government in many ways. Consequently, the issue of monopoly or oligopoly in the *majority* of modern production scenarios is not relevant and from a non-economic perspective, these objections would appear to be arguments against monopoly or oligopoly rather than genuine issues with Pigou's thinking.

Coase has at least two further objections.[70] The first is that where small numbers of people are involved, the parties would tend to negotiate a happy compromise which would be undermined by taxation designed to force alternative resource allocation. Again, it is difficult to argue that in this specific case Coase is not correct but this case is not typical and when we are considering applying Pigou's thinking to issues of global concern this criticism can reasonably be overlooked.

The second of Coase's objections relates specifically to the nature of externalities. Coase argues that the cost of an externality should be attributed to the polluter and those affected by the pollution. That is, pollution is only a problem because there are people in the vicinity to be effected by that pollution, hence the associated costs should not be absorbed by one party. Regardless of the strength of this argument in the 1960s, to a substantial extent it has been undermined by the contemporary global pollution debate. Using the vehicle emission issue addressed in the previous section and assuming carbon from internal combustion engines is a major contributor the current phase of global warming, it is impossible for anyone to avoid the impact of that pollution. Whilst it is certainly true the majority of people benefit in some way from the internal combustion engine (e.g. the supply or goods or public transport) the majority of people globally do not own their own vehicles and they have not contributed to decisions to purchase vehicles, whether they benefit from them or not. In this context it would seem grossly unfair to argue that a poor Mauritian farmer whose land is inundated by rising sea levels should incur a portion of the costs associated with the externalities that are assumed to have caused the rising sea levels when they have played no active role in or received significant benefit from the creation of that pollution.

Others adopt a more positive perspective. Baumol, for example, states that 'taken on its own grounds, the conclusions of the Pigouvian tradition are, in fact, impeccable'.[71] Nevertheless Baumol identifies two issues. First, for Pigou's ideas to be effective, society needs to have standards it wants to meet. In the context of pollution, Baumol suggests the application of arbitrary standards is sufficient.[72] In the context of humanising globalised production, such standards although arbitrary would be based on human rights and, for the sake of argument, the ratio of welfare costs as a proportion of production costs that would be absorbed by the business had the production occurred in a wealthy democratic country.

Second, again in the context of pollution, Baumol addresses the issue of setting appropriate tax rates[73] to achieve the desired goal. This is undoubtedly a complex calculation which, to an extent, relies on trial and error but also on principled decisions around whether or not such taxes should be, for example, income generating or simply designed to engender more environmentally friendly production. Given this article is not a contribution to the discipline of economics, it is not necessary to address this issue at length. It suffices to say, that in the proposed context of humanising globalised production, the scale of its application would suggest such tax would necessarily be income generating.

Moving the discussion into the present, there have been a number recent journal articles that revisit Pigou's thinking. Some, like Turgeon,[74] in the context of pollution and the United States, argue that not only does Pigouvian taxation make sense from an environmental perspective, it may offer a triple bottom line of benefits. That is, in addition to its environmental purpose, such taxes would encourage the alternative fuels industry in the United States to grow and become more competitive internationally and it would discourage reliance on external sources of oil and thereby improve national security. In the context of globalised production, the similar advantage could be that where the benefits of globalised production are marginal corporations may choose to maintain production in the wealthy country and thereby slow the race-to-the-bottom. From a politian's perspective, such a policy could even be considered a vote winner because it could retain jobs in the community they are responsible for.

In contrast to Turgeon's positivity, Yandle[75] has expressed substantial doubts as to the effectiveness of Pigouvian taxation. These doubts are based on a number of issues, not least the argument made by Pigou himself that politicians cannot be trusted to tax the right thing at the right rate to achieve the appropriate result. As stated above, few would doubt that such equations are incredibly difficult, especially when an individual's position of power is reliant on keeping a specific constituency happy, but to argue that we should not adopt an approach to policy because it will never be exactly right is to argue we should give up on policy. Given the general thrust of Pigou's thinking it seems unlikely he would agree with Yandle's interpretation of his views on this matter.

Second, Yandle is concerned that such taxes have opaque purposes – that they are about increasing government income as much as improving the environment – and as such are problematic. Again, as mentioned previously, in the context of humanising global production through influencing consumer choice of products, the proposed application of Pigouvian taxes will almost inevitably be used to generate income and therefore this concern is, in this analysis, irrelevant.

The final analysis we shall consider is that of Kaplow in his text book, *The Theory of Taxation and Public Economics*.[76] First, Kaplow makes very clear that, in his view, when one crunches the numbers, income taxation is more efficient than sales or commodity taxation, not least because income taxation is relatively easy to recover and harder to evade than sales or commodity taxation. In relation to Pigouvian taxation specifically Kaplow states:

> By some estimates, government regulation, such as of the environment and of workplace safety, involves costs of a similar order of magnitude to government expenditure on goods and services. A primary difference is that, under regulation, the costs are often borne in the first instance by private actors who respond to government incentives (such as from Pigouvian taxation) or comply with government edicts (such as command and control regulation). These costs as well as the resulting benefits (such as cleaner air, a public good) will have distributive incidence, presenting many of the questions considered with respect to government

> expenditures. [....] Accordingly, regulation (especially environmental regulation in recent times) has been a substantial subject of study regarding redistributive effects and labor supply distortion. Regarding the latter, some have raised the possibility of a double dividend – a Pigouvian tax may both correct an externality and raise revenue without distortion, permitting reduction in distortionary income taxation – and a substantial literature has suggested instead that environmental policies may exacerbate the pre-existing labor supply distortion due to income taxation.[77]

The issue from this perspective is one of distortion of the market and whether or not such taxes will contribute to such distortion and therefore make production less efficient. Again, from a non-economic perspective, distortion of the market is not intrinsically negative. In fact, the purpose of these taxes would be to distort the market in order to humanise production, consequently it would be disappointing if such taxes did not achieve that. Either way, Kaplow is eager to assert that he has no ideological axe to grind and argues the jury is out on whether such taxes positively or negatively affect market distortion in relation to other forms of taxation.

In summary, a detailed theoretical economic analysis of Pigouvian taxation is not essential to support the arguments outlined in this article. The brief survey of criticisms above has been included as evidence that the concept is broad enough at root to be applied beyond its current environmental focus, that the concept is still credible within the discipline of economics generally, that the concept has been fine-tuned since it was initially described and that none of the major objections to the theory – in this survey at least – undermine its application in the context of globalised industrial production.

A straw man proposal

As outlined previously, the purpose of this article is to contextualise a new approach to addressing the challenge of humanising corporate activity by providing an example methodology. The proposed example methodology is to apply Pigouvian taxes in the form of sales taxes calibrated by the product's impact on human rights where it is produced. That impact could be negative, in the form of violations, or positive, in the form of service provision. The primary underlying principle is that corporations should be able to save production costs by situating production in the most economically efficient place but not by saving costs associated with corporate contributions to welfare.[78]

This section is entitled 'A straw man proposal' and is situated towards the end of the article because it does not provide a detailed economic or legal analysis nor does it balance competing concepts to deduce the one most likely to succeed. It proffers an idea to be dissected and analysed, supported or discounted, and followed by other ideas that focus on humanising globalised corporate production rather than perfecting grand theories or re-hashing old ideas that have failed repeatedly.

To create an effective straw man proposal, it is useful to develop a case study scenario that applies the idea to a specific context. What could a Pigouvian sales tax calibrated by human rights look like in practice? Given the long-standing controversy surrounding garment manufacture in sweatshops situated primarily in the poorer countries and the fact clothing is a prime example of a product class where consumers and manufacturers have taken advantage of the reduced production facilitated by globalisation, garment manufacture provides an ideal case study.

In this context, Pigouvian taxes could be applied as follows. If a garment is made in a sweatshop on current terms (i.e. those determined predominantly by cost), the value added tax (VAT) on the product would be set at a high rate. Products that were not produced in sweatshops or were produced in scenarios where workers were given meaningful employment contracts and the corporation contributed a specific proportion of production costs to fund welfare measures (e.g. health insurance, school provision for workers' families, and pension plans to guard against penury in old age) would attract much lower VAT rates that were determined by the number of measures utilised and the sum relative to production costs invested in those measures (i.e. how 'humanised' the production was).

This regime would be introduced gradually. Initially the tax increases for status quo production would be minimal but over a period of time an escalator would be applied that ensured those products became increasingly expensive to consumers. Products that were already 'humanised' would, initially, benefit from no or very low taxation to ensure a substantial incentive existed to change production methods from the outset. The VAT on these 'humanised' products would stay low until they became a substantial proportion of the market, at which point the VAT rates would rise to ensure governments were able to generate sufficient income from them. At this point the tax rate on 'non-humanised' products would be exorbitant to price those products out of the market entirely.

Undoubtedly the proposed regime would be a difficult to police,[79] however, corporations are already able to utilise complicated global structures to limit their tax liabilities on, for example, profit, which may prove more difficult if a greater percentage of the total tax take was collected at the point of sale. Also, the firms that audit global businesses for tax purposes are typically global and governments are already bound, to a substantial degree, to trust their analysis and judgement.[80] Additionally, global and grass-roots non-governmental organisations and government development units (e.g. the Department for International Development (DFID) in the UK) – in conjunction with local authorities where manufacturing occurs – could be enlisted to help guide and organise businesses to make the appropriate investments and qualify for reduced VAT rates.

Such a policy may be objected to on the grounds that much of the globalised production has been outsourced to local businesses and is therefore out of the corporations' direct control but most global corporations claim in their current CSR reports to be able to influence the standards adopted by their production partners. Also, health, education and pension programmes could be established on a collaborative basis by global corporations with contributions calibrated on the amount spent on production in a particular area or state, hence tax benefits could be achieved without the cooperation of local suppliers.

Such a policy may be considered infeasible politically because, ultimately, it will increase product costs to consumers, but such objections have been overcome where environmental taxation is concerned. Also, it is important to note that production costs for many high street items, and especially garments, are a relatively small proportion of the product costs, which also incorporate numerous other overheads including research and development, transportation, marketing, and a route to market (e.g. shops/e-commerce facilities). If a t-shirt costs £4 on the high street it is likely that even a relatively high percentage increase in manufacturing costs would cause a minimal percentage increase in the sale price or could even be absorbed by the business by spending proportionally less elsewhere (e.g. CSR).[81]

Additionally, as mentioned in the previous section, it is possible that such a regime would slow the race-to-the-bottom and encourage corporations to keep production in the wealthy country or even to repatriate some production where the cost advantages of globalised production are marginal. Hence, there may be political advantages associated with adopting a policy of this nature beyond the hopefully[82] positive reputational impact of supporting the global realisation of human rights. It is reasonable to assume most consumers would prefer not to buy goods produced in sweatshops if they could avoid it without experiencing substantial personal disadvantage.

Finally, such a policy may be considered unlikely to succeed because vested interests would perceive that it was to their disadvantage. This concern is likely to be overstated simply because no one vested interest is targeted. This new regime would create a level playing field on which firms could compete in the same way they do now and as such some may even consider the new regime an opportunity. For example, where a larger producer benefitted from greater economies of scale a smaller producer may be able to adapt to the new regime more quickly. Similarly, a producer that has spent time and money attempting to implement better practices in recent years for largely reputational reasons may believe they are well placed to adapt and take advantage of this new regime.

Moreover, the business or business leader that implied publically that they inherently believed sweatshop style production was superior and espoused the advantages of avoiding welfare costs may find their good public reputation in tatters. While a corporation's employees would most likely be pleased they were no longer active participants in the race-to-the-bottom and would endeavour to utilise the new regime to their commercial advantage.

More broadly (i.e. beyond garment manufacture), it is true that this policy would not directly affect all products and services simply because many are not consumer facing while others almost inevitably and practically unavoidably violate or undermine human rights. It is difficult to imagine a humanised extractive industry that does not despoil the environment or collaborate with brutal regimes in unstable countries. First, such limitations should not overshadow the positive impacts the policy could have for the millions or billions employed in those industries that would be directly affected. Second, it is feasible that human rights calibrated VAT assessments could take into account the raw materials in a product and where they came from. Indeed, if this approach was to be effective where information technology is concerned it would need to address this issue.[83] Third, and more controversially, perhaps products that unavoidably violate or undermine human rights *should* be more expensive. From this perspective, we can compare these products with tobacco within the existing regime.

Conclusion

There is no doubt that the corporation in the globalised era has both positive and negative effects on the lives of almost every single human being on the planet, yet there is no coherent source of governance that is similarly global . The prevailing economic dogma might suggest a utilitarian assessment of this reality which accepts there will always be some losers. Human rights, in contrast, explicitly assert there are fundamental standards of protection and service provision that ensure no individual or community should pay the price for economic progress.

It is commonly argued that contemporary globalisation has facilitated a race-to-the-bottom which has enabled corporations to circumvent the regulations and taxation imposed by industrial nations to protect their citizens. To-date, despite much hand-wringing, society has struggled to address this challenge. Some commentators have proposed reformulating the corporation to work for society whilst others suggest creating some form of world government, but such ideas have gained little traction and require a degree of unanimity amongst sovereign states that is difficult to imagine. In effect, humanity has reached an intellectual stalemate that has led to a vacuum of purposeful activity.

This stalemate has given corporations the space to develop their own purposeful activity to fill the vacuum – CSR – which dominates the debate but has little or no chance of achieving the scale of change required. Ultimately CSR will not fundamentally alter corporate behaviour because it is a function of the corporation. Success would require the corporation to defeat itself and we can surmise with a substantial degree of confidence that the corporation will not impose commercially disruptive ethical constraints beyond specific circumstances which are commercially advantageous. That is, CSR will enhance a corporation's reputation and in doing so may improve some lives but it will not fundamentally change its underlying philosophy.

This article has argued that we should look beyond grand theories or projects and seek to apply models that have effectively altered corporate behaviour without requiring governments of wealthy states to lower their tax income, expecting governments of poor states to assert authority over corporations or asking consumers to choose ethically. Specifically, it asserts that Pigouvian taxation – as successfully applied to cars for environmental purposes in many wealthy countries – may provide an example of how to alter corporate activity by manipulating consumer preferences. Following that, through the mechanism of a straw man proposal, it has outlined how this could work in practice when applied to garment manufacture.

Whether or not this idea is genuinely applicable is not fundamental to the success of this article. Its success is gauged by whether this idea persuades the reader it is *possible* to address the corporation as a functional system which can be manipulated to meet the needs of humanity.

Adam Smith realised that trade through the market system could lead to positive but essentially unintended consequences. He and many since have been concerned with the negative unintended consequences of distorting markets. Pigou, in contrast, thought we should distort markets to alter consumer behaviours for the greater good and this idea has been applied successfully to address the issue of pollution from the internal combustion engine. If policymakers learn from this we could reassert the primacy of humanity over the corporate bottom-line and realise human rights on a global scale with corporate efficiency.

Disclosure statement

No potential conflict of interest was reported by the author.

Notes

1. Nassim Nicholas Taleb, *Fooled by Randomness* (London: Penguin, 2007), 144.
2. Adam Smith was quite clear that the corporation as understood in the eighteenth century would not become an influential constituent of economic life.
3. Robert Heilbroner, *The Worldly Philosophers*, 7th ed. (London: Penguin, 2000), originally published by Simon & Shuster, 1953.
4. *The Modern Corporation and Private Property*, 9th ed. (New Brunswick, NJ: Transaction, 2007), originally published by Harcourt, Brace & World, 1932.
5. For the sake of clarity this article refers to corporations as businesses, the shares of which are traded freely on various global stock exchanges. These businesses in general have a fiduciary duty to provide profits in a consistent manner to shareholders who, theoretically at least, have the collective power to remove managers and reframe strategy. These businesses are

often trans-national or multi-national and dominate the globalised economy. They not only own the majority of major consumer brands but they also operate substantial proportions of mining and farming operations and the infrastructure that facilitates globalised production. This infrastructure (e.g. containerised shipping lines, communications networking, standardised information technology and much more) is referred to within this article as a necessary superstructure without which globalisation and therefore the modern economy would not exist. The privately owned nature of this superstructure – much like the privately owned toll-roads, telephone, railways or other utilities which developed in the industrialised economies to meet human desires and needs – posits enormous power in corporations. The historical contrast is that the early industrial developments were funded by known individuals whose actions are governed by their own sentiment and moral framework while today this vital infrastructure is owned by consciencеless corporations with a myopic focus on profit.

6. See: Forest Hill, 'Veblen, Berle and the Modern Corporation', *American Journal of Economics and Sociology* 26, no. 3 (1967): 279–95.
7. While European governments have typically seemed comfortable introducing policy with a socialist flavour, the United States has initiated some similar programmes but its focus has typically been on low tax and individual responsibility.
8. Karl Polanyi, *The Great Transformation*, 3rd ed. (Beacon Press, 2001[1944]).
9. Friedrich August von Hayek, *The Road to Serfdom* (London: Routledge, 2001), originally published by George Routledge and Sons, 1944.
10. Robert Reich, *Supercapitalism: The Battle for Democracy in the Age of Big Business* (Cambridge: Icon Books, 2007).
11. John Kenneth Galbraith, *American Capitalism: The Concept of Countervailing Power* (Boston, MA: Houghton Mifflin, 1952).
12. Andrew Hacker, 'Introduction: Corporate America', in *The Corporate Take-Over*, ed. Andrew Hacker (New York: Anchor Books, 1965), 10.
13. Ibid.
14. Milton Friedman, *Capitalism and Freedom* (Chicago: University of Chicago, 1962), 40th Anniversary ed. 2002. More recently Robert Reich, who does not come from the neoliberal economic tradition associated with Friedman, supports this analysis. Reich, *Supercapitalism.*
15. Friedman, *Capitalism and Freedom* (1962), 27.
16. For example, the assumption that jobs are more valuable to communities than cultural practices: Mulligan, 'Globalization and the Environmental Change in Madagascar: The Opportunities and Challenges Faced by Rio Tinto', in *Development and the Challenge of Globalisation*, ed. Peter Newell, Shirin Rai, and Andrew Scott (London: ITDG Publishing, 2002).
17. For example, the application of strict cost/benefit analysis to decision-making.
18. Neil Stammers, 'Social Movements and Social Construction', *Human Rights Quarterly* 21, no. 4 (1999): 980–1008.
19. It should be noted that not all corporate law from a global perspective insists that corporations are entirely profit-centred. In Germany 'Supervisory Boards' (*Aufsichtsrat*) must include 'Worker' (employees and unions) representation which in theory should make them respond to certain stimuli differently. It is not clear whether these principles substantially move the corporate perspective away from profit or what impact they would have on human rights outside of Germany, but it is certainly an interesting angle worth further investigation.
20. Nicholas Connolly, 'Corporate Social Responsibility: A Duplicitous Distraction?', *International Journal of Human Rights* 16, no. 8 (2012): 1228–49.
21. Rhoda Howard-Hassman, *Can Globalization Promote Human Rights?* (Pennsylvannia: Pennsylvania State University Press, 2010); William Meyer, *Human Rights and International Political Economy in Third World Nations* (Westport, CT: Paeger, 1998).
22. Verdana Shiva, *Earth Democracy; Justice, Sustainability and Peace* (South End Press, 2005).
23. Of course, choice is a relative thing. One could credibly argue that globalisation has meant some small-scale farmers are not able to make a decent living and are consequently forced to seek employment within the global supply chain but this would ignore the reality that the vast majority of humans have lived in abject poverty for millennia with little or no opportunity to achieve anything else (William Easterly, *The White Man's Burden* (Oxford: Oxford University Press, 2006)). Equally, one could argue that advertising has created a desire for material goods which has driven people to desire more than their traditional lifestyle can provide and therefore enticed them to seek new lives (Edward Bernays, *Propaganda* (Ig Publishing, 2004[1928]);

Vance Packard, *The Hidden Persuaders* (New York: Ig Publishing, 2007), originally published by Pocket Books, 1957. Again, although this is probably true it fails to recognise that advertising works because people seek the satisfaction advertising attributes to various products. The average person – we can reasonably assume – wants convenience, they want to look and feel good, and they want to live without fear of hunger and disease; and the modern globalised capitalism has helped more people achieve this objective than any other economic system. One could of course argue that no one should live the modern consumer lifestyle but it is reasonable to doubt that social change is likely to occur, certainly on a global scale (Lester Thurrow, *Fortune Favors the Bold* (New York: Harper Collins, 2005)).

24. Easterly, *The White Man's Burden.*
25. Ibid.
26. Thomas Friedman, *The World is Flat* (Muller, 2002).
27. Ha-Joon Chang, *Bad Samaritan* (London: Random House Business Books, 2008).
28. Ibid.; Reich, *Supercapitalism.*
29. Dani Rodick, *One Economics Many Recipes* (Princeton, NJ: Princeton University Press, 2007); Easterly, *The White Man's Burden*; Chang, *Bad Samaritan.*
30. Joseph Stiglitz, *Globalization and its Discontents* (London: Penguin, 2002).
31. Thurrow, *Fortune Favors the Bold.*
32. For general evidence see Naomi Klein, *No Logo* (London: Flamingo, 2001); and Joel Bakan, *The Corporation* (London: Constable, 2004). For more detailed industry or business-specific evidence see John Ghazvinian, *Untapped: The Scramble for Africa's Oil* (Orlando, FL: Harcourt Books, 2007); Gary Greenberg, *Manufacturing Depression: The Secret History of a Modern Disease* (London: Bloomsbury, 2010); Marie-Monique Robin, *The World According to Monsanto: Pollution, Corruption, and the Control of Our Food Supply* (New York: The New Press, 2010).
33. Abhijit Banerjee and Esther Duflo (London: Penguin, 2011).
34. Ibid., 13.
35. Polanyi, *The Great Transformation* (1944).
36. Hayek, *The Road to Serfdom* (1944).
37. Joseph Stiglitz and Andrew Charlton, *Fair Trade for All: How Trade Can Promote Development* (Oxford: Oxford University Press, 2005).
38. The rise of the new economies (e.g. Brazil, Russia, China and India (the BRICs)) is creating a new global power balance but for the purposes of this article the generalised distinction between consumer and producer states suffices.
39. Reich, *Supercapitalism.*
40. Note previous arguments that most wealthy states do not implement neoliberal policies when they do not benefit them or their citizens (Chang, *Bad Samaritan*).
41. Stiglitz and Charlton, *Fair Trade for All.*
42. International Covenant on Economic and Social Rights (ICESCR)] [1966] Article 2(1).
43. Human Rights as outlined by multi-lateral treaties (for example: International Convention on Civil and Political Rights (1966), the International Convention on Economic and Social Rights (1966), and the United Nations Convention on the Rights of the Child (CRC) (1989)) and interpreted by international, regional and national courts, and Treaty Bodies, are universal and indivisible (Michael Freeman, *Human Rights* (Cambridge: Polity, 2002)). They are intended to protect every human being from the excessive use of state power and, where business practice is concerned, to ensure the state protects human beings within their jurisdiction, as far as is reasonably possible, from that which is out of an individual's control (e.g. environmentally destructive business practice (ICESCR Art. 122(b)) and forced labour (ICCPR Art. 8)). They also confer 'positive' rights on people, for example the rights to education (ICESCR Art. 13), health (ICESCR Art. 12), social security (ICESCR Art. 9), freedom of association (ICCPR Art. 22 and ICESCR Art. 8) and more broadly the right to an adequate standard of living (ICESCR Art. 11), and work (ICESCR Art. 6) in a fair and safe manner (ICESCR Art. 7). No multi-lateral human rights treaty has been ratified by every state but almost every state has ratified at least one treaty which recognises that human rights exist (Michael Ignatieff, *Human Rights: a politics and idolatory* (Princeton, NJ: Princeton University Press, 2003); Freeman, *Human Rights*).
44. David Earnest and James Rosenau, 'The Spy Who Loved Globalisation', *Washington Post*, September–October, 2000; Stigltiz and Charlton, *Fair Trade for All.*

45. Connolly, 'Corporate Social Responsibility: A Duplicitous Distraction?'
46. This term is appropriate because many commentators see the corporation as undermining and ultimately destroying the state. Berle and Means (1932) suggested that the corporation would ultimately replace the state in many areas and that this was effectively inevitable; see Adolf A. Berle and Gardiner Means, *The Modern Corporation and Private Property* (9th ed. Transaction, 2007; originally published by Harcourt, Brace & World, 1932).
47. Klein, *No Logo*.
48. Ian Craib, *Modern Social Theory from Parsons to Habermas* (New York: Haverster Wheatsheaf, 1992).
49. That is, those usually associated with economic, cultural and social rights.
50. An idea explored in more detail by Rhoda Howard-Hassmann, 'The Great Transformation II: Human Rights Leap-frogging in the Era of Globalization' (conference paper delivered at the Southern Sociological Society 2004 annual meeting).
51. To use the previous example and to simplify substantially, by making bread cheaper though industrial processing, poorer people were able to afford hire purchase agreements for televisions or cars.
52. Robert Cialdini's book *Influence* (New York: Harper, 1984) investigated the psychology of persuasion in relation to product sales and asserts that the importance of price is not worth investigating because it is fundamental to the success of every persuasion technique. Its central importance to decision-making is a given.
53. For example, a survey of consumers in Canada in 2000 indicated that only 5% would be willing to pay more for ethical products (Rhys Jenkins, 'Corporate Codes of Conduct: Self-Regulation in a Global Economy, in *Voluntary Approaches to Corporate Responsibility* (UN NGLS, 2002), 29).
54. Cars are a more pertinent example because the decision to purchase a car is not usually determined by addiction. Also, cars represent the third type of product on the elastic/inelastic scale because although for many a car is perceived to be a necessary purchase there is little practical requirement for vehicles that can substantially exceed speed limits or have leather seats. Packard (*The Hidden Persuaders*) describes the efforts car manufacturers have made to create demand for vehicles that exceed consumers' practical requirements.
55. For the purposes of this discussion the evidence from the United Kingdom is sufficient because the globalised nature of vehicle manufacture ensures that the products available there are in most respects identical to those sold in the European Union (the largest single consumer market) and similar to those sold in the United States or Japan.
56. Note, because the market price of oil fluctuate substantially and unpredictably, and the lead time of developing new vehicles is comparatively long in relation to other consumer products, car manufacturers historically have not reacted to oil price changes when considering consumer preferences and determining what characteristics new models may have.
57. See: Vehicle Licensing Statistics, https://www.gov.uk/government/organisations/department-for-transport/series/vehicle-licensing-statistics (accessed 18 April 2014).
58. This calculation is indicative rather than accurate because it assumes vehicles sold within a band are distributed evenly across the band.
59. Denmark instigated environmental taxation of a similar kind in the early 1990s but it did not have an effect on the pollution emissions of vehicles sold in Denmark. We can reasonably assume the Danish tax regime was not as effective as the post-Kyoto industrial consensus because the market for new vehicles in Denmark was not sufficiently large to encourage global car manufacturers to commit the necessary research and development to develop high-performing low-emission vehicles.
60. *The Case for Green Fiscal Reform: Final Report of the UK Green Fiscal Commission*, October (2009), 79. Note, the Green Fiscal Commission was a cross-sector independent body established to assess the effectiveness of environmental taxation.
61. Arthur C. Pigou, *The Economics of Welfare*, 4th ed. (Basingstoke: Palgrave Macmillan, 2013 [1920]), 5.
62. Ibid., 1228.
63. Ibid., 1.
64. Arthur C. Pigou, *The Economics of Welfare* (London: Macmillan and Company, 1920), 619.

65. Pigou spends considerable time discussing subsidies ('bounties') and thought they were necessary in specific circumstances but expected they would be less effective change agents than taxation.
66. A Google search for Arthur Cecil Pigou delivers 49,600 results of which none of the results on the first page is from mainstream media. A plain Google search for John Maynard Keynes delivers 4,650,000 results and there are entries from the BBC and the *Guardian* on the first page of results.
67. James M. Buchanan, 'External Diseconomies, Corrective Taxes and Market Structure', *America Economic Review* 59 (March 1969): 174–7.
68. Otto A. David and Andrew Whinston, 'Externalities, Welfare and the Theory of Games', *Political Economy* 70 (June 1962): 241–62.
69. Anti-trust and pro-competition legislation exist in most established industrial economies although these laws work with varying degrees of effectiveness.
70. Ronald H. Coase, 'The Problem of Social Cost', *Journal of Law Economy* 29 (October 1960): 371–84.
71. William J. Baumol, 'On Taxation and the Control of Externalities', *The American Economic Review* 62, no. 3 (1972): 307–22.
72. In contrast, K. William Kapp (*The Social Cost of Business* (Spokesman, 1978), 41) argues that '[a]bove all, there seems to be no indication that ... [Pigou's] ... envisaged system of bounties and taxes can be made to yield theoretically defensible estimates of social costs and gains'. With the experience of environmental taxation behind us, we now know that Baumol's analysis that tax rates need not be theoretically defensible has proven correct.
73. Baumol agrees with Pigou that subsidies are less effective than taxes.
74. Evan N. Turgeon, 'Triple-Dividends: Toward Pigovian Gasoline Taxation', *Land Resources & Environmental Law* 145 (2010).
75. Bruce Yandle, 'Much Ado about Pigou', *Regulation* 33 (2010): 2–4.
76. Louis Kaplow, *The Theory of Taxation and Public Economics* (Princeton, NJ: Princeton University Press, 2008).
77. Ibid., 212.
78. Implicit in this principle is the calculation that any increase in costs would be relative to the wages and related taxes in the country where the productive activity occurs. Hence a pension, education or health plan would be provided at the market rate in that country which would be, in most cases, as comparatively cheap as the labour.
79. 'The centrality of administrative and enforcement concerns is difficult to overstate, especially given the serious problems of avoidance and evasion of income and other taxes and the fact that information limitations determine the feasibility of different tax instruments' (Kaplow, *The Theory of Taxation and Public Economics*, 411).
80. This need to trust professional services firms is a problem, consider the ENRON saga, but is a systemic imperfection that exists within the current regime.
81. See http://www.macleans.ca/economy/business/what-does-that-14-shirt-really-cost/ (accessed 23 August 2014) for a useful summary of production costs and see: http://www.ecouterre.com/infographic-how-much-does-that-14-t-shirt-really-cost/14-t-shirt-2/ (accessed 23 August 2014) for a related infographic. See: http://www.globalresearch.ca/sweatshop-manufacturing-engine-of-poverty/19193 (accessed 23 August 2014) for a more in-depth analysis of production costs and the impact of sweatshop manufacture.
82. Hopeful because human rights have generated negative perceptions in some counties.
83. See: http://www.bbc.co.uk/news/technology-26144981 for recent article on 'conflict minerals' being used in Apple products (accessed 27 April 2014).

Defending corporate social responsibility: Myanmar and the lesser evil

Andrew Fagan

Human Rights Centre, University of Essex, UK

This article examines an enduring issue in human rights scholarship generally, through the perspective of my recent experiences of undertaking corporate social responsibility (CSR) training in Myanmar. The relationship between theory (in the form of conceptual reasoning and analysis) and practice (the legal and political application of human rights principles) is complex and, on occasion, contradictory and paradoxical. Conceptually a strong and critically coherent argument can be made against CSR as being fundamentally incompatible with the moral objectives of human rights. In many ways, I share the view that, conceptually, CSR and human rights are incompatible. The implication of this standpoint is to refrain from undertaking any forms of CSR promotion and training and thereby remain consistent with one's intellectual principles. However, the human rights challenges in Myanmar caused me to suspend my intellectual objections to accepting an offer to provide CSR training there in 2012. Beginning with a conceptual analysis of the relationship between theory and practice within traditions of radical political philosophy, I proceed to evaluate my own apparent intellectual contradiction by reference to the notion of the lesser evil. By analysing a specific empirical instance I aim to outline a perspective upon human rights which seeks to reconcile apparent conflict between conceptual analysis and practical human rights action. In so doing, I aim to generate further discussion on the nature of the complex relationship between human rights theory as embodying a predominantly critical perspective upon existing economic realities and the unavoidably practical dimension of human rights as the ongoing attempt to transform those realities, which necessitates engaging with them.

Introduction

This article aims to contribute to a growing body of interest for the global human rights community: the relationship between human rights and commercial enterprise, by means of an analysis of a newly emerging area of interest: the ongoing attempts to establish respect for human rights in Myanmar.[1] Specifically, I will evaluate the potential value and validity of corporate social responsibility (CSR), primarily in the form of adherence to the so-called Ruggie Guiding Principles, in the context of contemporary Myanmar and the restricted though urgent economic and political choices which confront its people. Some within the human rights community will find my specific argument to be controversial if not objectionable. I argue against two effectively absolutist positions: first, that commercial enterprise is inherently incompatible with respecting human rights and that, by extension, the entire CSR phenomenon may be rejected by human rights advocates; second, that pragmatic considerations of the 'lesser evil' are similarly incompatible with the ethical foundationalism of human rights thinking. Thus, I offer a contextualist justification of my own contribution to promoting the cause of CSR in Myanmar. I argue that, whilst it is entirely legitimate to acknowledge the devastating impact much commercial enterprise has exerted upon people's human rights, CSR and more specifically the Guiding Principles offer an opportunity for constructive engagement between the human rights community and the wider business community in Myanmar. More importantly, I argue that the wider evaluation of the human rights potential of the Guiding Principles must be accompanied by a consideration of the specific context within which they are appealed to. Based upon a reasonable, though un-argued, assumption that no domestic economy can effectively develop in isolation from potentially global trading partners, I seek to defend the value of a constructive engagement with the growing numbers of businesses considering investment into Myanmar by appeal to a 'lesser argument' position which contrasts such forms of potential investment with the existing precedent set by, for example, Chinese investment which has directly resulted in the widespread abuse of human rights. This article argues for the human rights community endorsing the principle that Myanmar's path towards respect for human rights should include critically endorsing what many generally reject: that commercial enterprise can be conducted in ways which respect, rather than systematically abuse, human rights. My thesis intentionally seeks to stimulate discussion upon at least three distinct levels of analysis and argument: current developments within Myanmar and their implications for human rights; the relationship between commercial enterprise and human rights; and finally, a more critically normative engagement with how we may justify attempts at defending human rights within a politically and economically complex world.

Reconciling the irreconcilable?

The publication in 2011 of John Ruggie's so-called Guiding Principles[2] marked a symbolically important moment in the long-standing and often difficult relationship between what many previously considered to be mutually irreconcilable, if not directly competing, objectives: the pursuit of profit by business on the one hand and the ability and willingness to genuinely respect the human rights of those directly and indirectly affected by the actions of globalising businesses on the other. The Guiding Principles, which were unanimously approved by the United Nations (UN) Human Rights Council, present an authoritative prescription of the basis and scope of the global business sector's commitment to respecting human rights and, in so doing, aims to steer the gaze of the human rights community towards a more productive and affirmative relationship with business than has heretofore often been the case. Any analysis of the relationship between business and human rights must be set against the background of the widespread acknowledgement that adhering to human rights principles requires an international and domestic commitment to fiscal and financial mechanisms which require broadly redistributionist-inspired restrictions upon the raw pursuit of profit. This recognition necessarily flows from the broader acknowledgement that human rights is a holistic moral and legal doctrine which encompasses both civil and political rights and their economic, social and cultural counterparts.[3] While it is clearly not a Marxist or anti-capitalist-inspired manifesto, the International Covenant on Economic, Social and Cultural Rights (ICESCR) establishes a broad range of duties and obligations towards the provision of essential resources that are themselves not ultimately reducible to or circumscribed by the logic and processes of commodification. Complying with the

ICESCR requires that duty-holders commit to a normative perspective which views financial expenditure as both a threat to and a potential resource for those human rights most directly concerned with subsistence. It is increasingly argued that the unconstrained pursuit of profit and ever-greater levels of wealth should be set against their effects upon others' human rights in essentially the same way as expressions of hate speech must be set against others' enjoyment of their human right to be free from discrimination, which may require restricting the former in order to adequately protect and respect the latter. Understanding human rights correctly, that is to say holistically, unequivocally establishes the pursuit of profit as a core human rights concern and establishes the prima facie legitimacy of the human rights community securing a voice within the global business sector.[4] The Guiding Principles may be thought of as the specific language through which that voice attempts to be heard.

As is well known, the Guiding Principles were the culmination of a UN-initiated process which first took tangible form with the publication of the so-called UN Norms on Transnational Corporations in 2003 and which manifestly sought to recognise the role which, particularly, transnational corporations (TNCs) can play in positively respecting human rights. Given widespread and recurrent publicity to the effect, few could legitimately claim to be ignorant of the devastatingly harmful impact of many TNCs upon the human rights of many of those exposed to their pursuit of profit. Beyond the state and even inter-governmental organisations, successive campaigners and non-governmental organisations have testified to the sheer extent of human suffering and environmental destruction wreaked by some of the world's largest and most economically powerful businesses which has directly affected an extensive range of human rights, ranging from the all-too typical exploitative rates of remuneration and the practice of exposing employees to unnecessarily dangerous and harmful working conditions to the less typical but still far too prevalent modern-day forms of slavery in the guise of bonded child-labour or the wilful destruction of indigenous peoples' environmental habitats. Particularly during the 1980s and 1990s, a globalised discourse was established which effectively characterised many businesses' pursuit of profit as essentially immoral, to the extent that for many it appeared to entail the widespread and systematic abuse of human rights. Chief executives and the boards of large TNCs could thereby be included, along with dictators and authoritarian leaders, in the rogue's gallery of human rights abusers. What they also appeared to have in common was the relative impunity they enjoyed from punishment or effective redress, particularly in the case of the key representatives of TNCs who generally appeared to do nothing to prevent their culpability in the abuse of others' human rights whilst remaining legally compliant with the particular regulations to which they were subject in a myriad of legally ingenious ways, including the extensive use of subsidiaries and sub-contractors, to establishing head offices in jurisdictions whose 'business-friendly' dispositions were underlined by the lightest of possible regulatory regimes.

While many critics denounced business's apparent lack of concern for, if not wilful abuse of, human rights, many plaudits of free-market capitalism, most notably perhaps Milton Friedman, rejected the very foundation upon which much of this criticism was based. Friedman[5] asserted unequivocally that the raison d'être of any business was to maximise profit and as such business could not be legitimately required to bear purported social or moral responsibilities. He included the distinctly legally positivist proviso that businesses must abide by the legal regulations to which they are subject but was unequivocal that the specific function and fundamental end of any business is to generate profit and secure the maximal return on shareholders' investment. Interestingly Friedman did not concede what he might have without damaging his central claim: that logically at least, businesses could still commit funds and resources to the promotion of particular social causes or interests so long as the objective of doing so was to further maximise profit. Many businesses have and continue to support a vast range of social and charitable causes but do so not in an attempt to replace governmental or charitable bodies but, on an admittedly somewhat sceptical viewpoint, as an exercise in marketing and corporate branding. Friedman's characterisation of capitalism is thereby retained, albeit with a slightly less forbidding demeanour, perhaps. However, the bottom-line is essentially unaffected. Issues directly within the remit of business – remuneration, working conditions and environmental impact – are all determined by the law-abiding pursuit of profit. Other moral issues apparently beyond the remit of any business such as the health care opportunities of employees' families, the provision of primary education for girls in the areas in which they conduct business, or the discrimination suffered by minorities unable to secure employment within a subsidiary of a particular TNC may all be dismissed as ultimately extraneous to business.

On Friedman's highly influential reading, to attribute extraneous moral responsibilities to businesses was simply to mistake business for government or charity, to commit what philosophers typically refer to as a 'category mistake'. Critics' frequent claims that the sheer financial capacity of many TNCs is sufficient cause for attributing non-commercial responsibilities to them are thereby liable to be dismissed as irrelevant to their domain of responsibility.[6] Simply having the means to alleviate suffering does not create an obligation to do so. In this sense the adage that can implies ought, that the mere capacity to financially support the provision of state-neglected human rights within the developing world societies TNCs operate within, is no reason for disregarding the primary legal duty states possess to protect their citizens' human rights. In so far as he may serve as a spokesperson for free-market global capitalism, Friedman thereby appears to confirm what many critics and opponents of free-market capitalism have consistently alleged: that capitalism suffers from, at best, an amoral lack of concern for its harmful if legal by-products. The pursuit of profit is supreme.

Both the reality and the evaluation of global capitalism have progressed from the somewhat polarised debates of the previous century. While crudely doctrinaire supporters and opponents remain, an alternative discourse has emerged which seeks to reconcile the ends of business and respect for human rights. The Guiding Principles are an important component of this alternative discourse but must themselves be situated within the wider phenomenon of CSR, which aims to identify and promote the basis and shape of the ethically responsible pursuit of profit.[7] A commitment to the idea of CSR ultimately challenges both the Friedman and the anti-capitalist characterisations of business through insisting that businesses do not exist only to maximise their own profits and that the pursuit of profit must itself be situated or contextualised within a broader social and moral context. Against supporters and opponents alike, who characterise the pursuit of profit as an end in itself, proponents of CSR seek to develop the historically well-established precedent of capitalist philanthropy in which profit is viewed as a means to promoting morally desirable social goals. It can be argued that CSR significantly extends upon this way of thinking by seeking to establish the principle of respecting well-established moral responsibilities as an integral element of how businesses pursue profit in the first place and not simply as what one does with all that money once it has been accumulated and one's appetite for palatial villas or vintage cars has been satiated.

Numerous supporters of CSR underline this alternative vision of business with the notion of the so-called 'triple bottom-line', which includes economic prosperity, environmental quality and social justice. The European Commission's 2001 Green Paper on the subject defines CSR as 'a concept whereby companies integrate social and environmental concerns in their business operations and in their interaction with their stakeholders on a voluntary basis'.[8] Setting to one side for the moment questions concerning how various businesses have 'operationalised' CSR within their documents and practices, the essential core of the idea of CSR includes a moralisation of business to include substantive commitments which go beyond a merely market-based and purely affirmative morality and establishes a basis upon which business may be constructively criticised for failing to adhere to standards which do not presuppose the revolutionary overthrow of global capitalism. CSR seeks to characterise capitalist enterprise as capable of acting in a morally laudable fashion. Morality is, of course, a highly, if not inherently, contested phenomenon. Commentators on CSR frequently state that the very concept of CSR is itself understood and presented in significantly diverse ways; an observation often construed as undermining any possible objective or universally applicable set of criteria.[9] Herein lies one of the potential strengths of the Guiding Principles since they are an attempt to initiate the establishment of a common framework for specifying the ethical responsibilities of business. The particular universalising morality which they appeal to and derive from is that of human rights. The Guiding Principles seek to define the ethical basis and character of business in the language of human rights. Having established an understanding of the moral context and potential force of the Guiding Principles I turn now to consider my own attempt to disseminate knowledge of the Guiding Principles in what has been for decades one of the world's most oppressive countries: Myanmar.

Spreading the word: CSR in Myanmar

During the summer of 2012 I was requested to contribute to a project funded by the British government and which was led by the Institute for Human Rights and Business (IHRB). The project was entitled '"Burma Principles": Formation of Human Rights Principles for Business Investment into Myanmar (Burma)'.[10] As the title suggests, one of the core objectives of the project was to establish amongst a wide range of relevant stakeholders an understanding of how subsequent foreign investment into Myanmar can adhere to international human rights principles and standards and thereby avoid the fate of many other 'emerging' economies which have succumbed to corruption, bribery and the usual forms of unscrupulous business behaviour that typically enrich a handful of public officials and foreign investors but always at the expense of the wider populace. The project would comprise a multitude of training and assemblies of relevant stakeholders culminating in an agreed set of principles – the Burma Principles – which were intended to provide a normative framework for the establishment of a human rights-respecting environment for foreign investment and business more generally in Myanmar. I was specifically requested to design and lead two eight-day training seminars for a group of grass-roots activists, labour lawyers, trade union officials, small entrepreneurs and environmentalists, all of whom had suffered violations of their human rights, including in several cases serving lengthy prison sentences, as a consequence of their work. They were also assembled from a cross-section of ethnic communities which comprise Myanmar, essential in a country where ethnic identity is so central to political culture and conflict. The objective of my contribution to the wider project was to establish a practically applicable knowledge of both international mechanisms and standards for human rights-compliant business activity at the grass-roots level and an understanding of how the principles of CSR can be appealed to in subsequent negotiations with the predicted growing number of foreign investors and TNCs seeking to establish a foothold in Myanmar. Including a carefully selected representative sample of grass-roots people with direct interests in the relationship between business and human rights was intended to complement the training of 'higher-level' public officials and chief executive officers which the project also involved. The specific participants of my training seminars were finally selected on the 'cascade' principle: that they were able to diffuse and impart the knowledge they had acquired to their particular communities and constituents and thereby significantly amplify the benefits of the training. It was estimated that around 1500–2000 people would thereby have an opportunity to benefit from the training imparted.

I assume that I was asked to contribute to this particular project more on the basis of my interest in and experience of human rights capacity building in Myanmar, than for the relatively modest expertise I possess in the area of business and human rights. In respect of the former, I have been actively involved in promoting human rights education in Myanmar since 2011 beginning with a period of human rights training I conducted on behalf of the British Council in Yangon in 2011 for a broad and diverse group of political activists with the aim of establishing a commitment to human rights principles as providing the basis for a common political platform for an otherwise very divided political opposition. I then subsequently collaborated with various political opposition movements, such as the National League for Democracy and 88 Generation in their attempts to secure an understanding of how adherence to human rights principles can contribute to their participation in the ongoing reform process. Most recently, I accompanied a group of nine former political prisoners from 88 Generation on a United Kingdom government funded study tour of Northern Ireland in the summer of 2013. I consider myself to be genuinely privileged in being afforded an opportunity to contribute to the very fragile and challenging reform process which the diverse peoples of Myanmar are currently engaged in. In my opinion, the establishment of human rights-respecting institutions and the diffusion of a sufficient knowledge of international human rights standards amongst key stakeholders in Myanmar will be crucial in determining whether that country will be able to realise its political and sustainably economic potential. The sheer extent of Myanmar's international isolation for so long has resulted in a nascent political society which is almost entirely ignorant of what human rights are and how they can be protected and respected and this despite the fact that human rights was a key mobilising slogan for many opposition groups during the 1990s and 2000s. In this respect, and in an admittedly slightly perverse kind of way, contemporary Myanmar bears some resemblance to the mythical states of nature envisaged by contractarian liberal philosophers seeking a tabula rasa from which to build legitimate political institutions. My experiences of having previously taught political activists, almost all of whom had suffered extreme forms of discrimination and oppression throughout the greater parts of their lives, left me inspired and hopeful that even the very worst human rights violations can be transcended, notwithstanding some of their uncomfortable references to the 'Bengalis' who the international community recognise as the ethnic Rohingya, a community numbering some 800,000 people who remain stateless and continue to endure severe violations of many of their human rights, references which only confirmed to me the urgency of establishing and embedding a sufficiently informed human rights culture in Myanmar. My commitment to this objective was my principal motivation for agreeing to contribute to the IHRB project and the establishment of the Burma Principles. Having consulted with colleagues with greater expertise than I possess in the area of business and human rights and also having secured the assistance of a highly experienced human rights trainer for the second of the two training seminars I, or rather we, then travelled to Yangon in September and December 2012 to conduct the training.[11]

The content of the overall training programme was carefully selected and was expressly designed to ensure that trainees acquired a practically applicable set of knowledge-based resources. The training focused upon the following topics and subject-matter: international human rights legal instruments and institutions; the role of the International Labour Organisation (ILO) and various regional labour mechanisms; the role of non-state actors in the international and regional protection of human rights; ASEAN and the extent of its commitment to establishing a quasi-legal human rights protective regime; the relationship between human rights principles and economics; a specific focus upon the Extractive Industries Transparency Initiative, which is particularly relevant given Myanmar's rich stock of mineral resources; the role of National Human Rights Institutes (which included a talk by one of the current Human Rights Commissioners in Myanmar); Myanmar's human rights record generally and specifically in respect of economic, social and cultural rights; an introduction to CSR; and finally, a detailed focus upon the Guiding Principles and how they can be used by grass-roots human rights defenders against the abuse of corporate power. Each day comprised formal lectures accompanied by practical exercises and group-based tasks designed to enable the trainees to both acquire and apply the knowledge being imparted. The trainees' subsequent feedback and evaluations of the training were generally highly favourable and appreciative of the opportunities afforded by the training seminars.

The Guiding Principles formed the central spine of the overall training programme. Cognisant of the conceptually contested nature of CSR and the extensive variety of corporate approaches to the implementation of a CSR policy in their documentation, I decided that the Guiding Principles provided us with the most authoritative and 'objective' criteria for identifying what a commitment to a form of 'ethical', that is to say human-rights respecting, business entailed and required. Thus we devoted considerable time to imparting a practicable knowledge and understanding of Ruggie's proposals and precisely what compliance with these albeit non-legally binding criteria would require of companies seeking to do business in Myanmar. We were honest about the implications of the Guiding Principles possessing a non-legally binding status but insistent that all established international human rights law ultimately originated in a similarly non-legally binding set of aspirational standards in the form of the Universal Declaration of Human Rights. Interestingly enough, it is difficult to adopt anything other than a 'glass half-full' approach to the possibility of reform and progress when conducting human rights training in a country with such an appalling human rights record and amongst trainees who have themselves borne the brunt of decades of human rights violations. The training programme successfully completed our contribution to the IHRB project was complete and we returned home satisfied that the appropriate words had been spread amongst people whose need for the effective establishment of a human rights culture is so urgent.

A critical perspective

When required to disseminate knowledge of the international standards and principles of human rights to cohorts who have themselves suffered severe human rights violations it is, I believe, entirely legitimate and appropriate to set to one side the more potentially unsettling, philosophically critical concerns over the ultimate intellectual coherence and rational validity of a commitment to the doctrine of human rights. The need for human rights is urgent and, in the case of contemporary Myanmar, new opportunities to establish and exercise those fundamental rights are slowly and precariously emerging. Calling into question the very foundations of those rights before they have even been secured is, at the very least, churlish and quite possibly thoroughly counter-productive. In such contexts the analogy of human rights as tools designed and required to perform particular tasks seems sound and justified. Perhaps the possibility of critical reflection is itself a kind of privilege for those whose rights are mostly secured. However, as a (privileged) scholar with long-established and distinct interests in the foundational sphere of human rights I have been unable to entirely resist the deconstructive itch. This is compounded by the fact that I have counted myself as one of those who have been suspicious of the claims made by and on behalf of business' ability and willingness to genuinely comply with human rights standards. It is tempting, of course, to suppress my own qualms by playing the 'Myanmar card', i.e. that in a country whose people have suffered such severe and extensive human rights violations any form of human rights-inspired interventions must be justified and above criticism. While this may be the mantra of many a human rights practitioner it fails to dispel my own fundamental conviction that human rights action should always be potentially subject to critical reflection in the aim of ensuring that such action can generally be justified by appeal to sound reasoning. This principle lacks the value of practicable efficiency, of course, but when applied to the dissemination of material which has been as heavily criticised as CSR and the Guiding Principles becomes potentially debilitating. If only retrospectively, I recognised the need to critically reflect upon what I had done. Is there any way in which CSR and the Guiding Principles can be coherently defended, or do the criticisms of both ultimately serve to negate the intended benefits of the Myanmar project?

There is an extensive and growing literature concerned with the normative basis and coherency of CSR. Arguably the deepest level of this critical attention addresses the relationship between the structure and character of global capitalism and the very possibility of evaluating any capitalist enterprise as ethical in the sense understood here as capable of respecting at the very least those human rights standards which are directly affected by the pursuit of profit. Sceptics of CSR include not only those who continue to define capitalism as an inherently exploitative economic system but also those who are unequivocal in their support for economic relations fundamentally constituted around the pursuit of profit. For these, including Milton Friedman who we considered earlier, CSR is ultimately incompatible with the essence and ultimate requirements of profit maximisation. It amounts to a form of what Blowfield and Frynas refer to as 'bad capitalism'.[12] The same line of argument was presented by Clive Crook in an *Economist* article,[13] which also restated the claim that the purpose of corporations is not to be 'good' in the sense typically evoked by advocates of CSR but is rather to maximise financial returns to shareholders. Governments possess principal duties to provide for the human rights of their citizens. Corporations may indirectly contribute to this via the payment of taxes and the other financial benefits associated with creating employment and generating wealth but it simply is not any part of a corporation's legitimate responsibility to directly bear non-commercial ethical responsibilities. This depiction of capitalism appears to contradict the fact that many corporations have developed CSR policies and principles and do commit funds to supporting the provision of services that are typically considered as the preserve of the state. As noted earlier, however, this could be explained as less a deviation from the profit maximising purpose of business and more as a means for promoting a particular image or branding of the corporation which itself is intended to increase market share amongst particular customer demographic groups and thereby improve financial performance. A commitment to CSR can be explained as a more subtle form of capitalism perhaps, but is still ultimately consistent with the principle that the primary purpose and objective of any business is profit maximisation. Interestingly, it has yet to be conclusively demonstrated that CSR does generally enhance the financial performance of those businesses which have adopted CSR codes. One writer has gone so far as to state that there is 'no evidence that behaving more virtuously makes firms more profitable'.[14] A comprehensive review of the available research on the connection between virtue and profit came to a slightly less assured conclusion but similarly failed to establish any clear and unambiguous positive relationship between CSR and profitability.[15]

Critics of global capitalism typically condemn CSR precisely because of the claim that it is compatible with profit maximisation. Thus, Leslie Sklair, an established and long-standing critic of capitalist economic globalisation, has criticised CSR as being incapable of delivering on its ostensive aspirations of promoting social well-being as a consequence of business's prevailing approach to CSR as a means to the desired end of enhancing financial performance.[16] Sklair views a neoliberal-inspired approach to global capitalism as having massively exacerbated global wealth inequality in a way which has not sufficiently increased the relative wealth of the world's poorest and has left several billion people living in absolute poverty with the threat of destitution. Global capitalism has undoubtedly benefitted the world's affluent, but underpins a globalising economic system which is devastating for respecting, let alone protecting, the poor's fundamental human rights. He writes, 'since the 1950s and increasing so-called neo-liberal free trade in recent decades, the rich are getting richer and the poor are still desperately poor while capitalist globalisation marches on triumphantly all over the world. The clarion calls of CSR ring hollow outside the enclaves of the rich in the postcolonial world'.[17] CSR's claim to ethical legitimacy cannot be sustained because of its inherent relationship with an economic system whose effects, if not its intention, are so manifestly unethical. Sklair's more radical perspective upon global capitalism is ultimately unconcerned with whether or not CSR is good for business since he is committed to a view that business, or at least the global capitalist system, is bad for human rights, so CSR is at best largely irrelevant or at worst is part of the problem. Sklair's critique effectively agrees with what Tumin intended as an affirmative statement that the priority of capitalist economic competitiveness over ethical concerns results in capitalism generally subscribing to the principle of least morality.[18]

Beyond careful scholarly critiques of global capitalism there is also widespread scepticism amongst campaigners and human rights defenders concerning the extent to which CSR codes are developed in good faith by those businesses which have established a CSR code. Thus, with TNCs such as Nike, Coca-Cola, British Petroleum, Wal-Mart and many more all having posted a CSR code on company websites and documentation whilst simultaneously pursuing commercial activities with demonstrably adverse effects upon people's human rights and the environments they must inhabit it has been easy to allege that CSR codes are being deployed in thoroughly bad faith for a series of reasons which clearly have little, if anything, to do with actually compelling the corporations' employees, agents and subsidiaries to comply with the appeals to respecting human rights which echo through many corporations' marketing. The perception that CSR codes are all too often worth little more than the (one hopes recycled) paper they have been printed upon is lent further support by the fact that even the Chinese government has developed a CSR code.[19]

As I noted previously, for the Burma Principles project I decided to focus primarily upon the Guiding Principles as providing the most robust and 'impartial' template for presenting what business' genuine commitment to human rights-respecting company policies and practices would entail in Myanmar. The UN's validation of a set of human rights standards will invariably be viewed as more authoritative than various CSR codes drafted by the marketing and public relations departments of TNCs. During the specific training sessions devoted to the Guiding Principles we considered the genesis and development of the Guiding Principles, beginning with the earlier publication of the so-called UN Norms on Transnational Companies which caused such controversy precisely because of their stated objective of achieving a legally binding status manifestly a step too far for many in the global business sector. We also discussed with the trainees how the Guiding Principles seek to elaborate and clarify existing normative and, in some cases, legal standards and thus cannot be understood as aiming at introducing some revolutionary vision of how businesses should adapt to genuinely respect human rights. We also discussed the potential limitations of the Guiding Principles' focus upon the 'respect' component of the UN's wider Protect, Respect and Remedy Framework. Through specific practical exercises we explored what the principle of 'doing no harm', the conventional formulation of what 'respecting' human rights requires from General Comment 15 of the UN Committee on Economic, Social and Cultural Rights, would require in practice.[20] Finally, we considered the voluntary character of the Guiding Principles and compared this with some existing legally-binding international mechanisms such as those found within the ILO or which apply through federal legislation in the United States (US) and various regulations established by the European Commission which aim to impose restrictions upon the terms and conditions of companies investing and trading in Myanmar.

The principal objective of this detailed dissemination of the Guiding Principles was to alert the trainees to the fact that such normative international standards and principles exist in the first place since decades of censorship have prevented many citizens of Myanmar gaining even this degree of knowledge. Even now that censorship restrictions are being relaxed, very few of these kinds of international standards have been translated into any of the principal ethnic languages of Myanmar, including, as I discovered in an earlier human rights training project I conducted, successive reports written by the UN's Special Representative on Myanmar. Beyond this initial consciousness-raising objective it is hoped that trainees' knowledge of these standards will begin to influence their subsequent relations and negotiations with various public and private bodies likely to be heavily involved in the ongoing opening up of Myanmar's economy and natural resources to foreign investment.

We did not, therefore, dwell upon the myriad criticisms which the Guiding Principles and beyond them of course the entire global capitalist system have attracted. We spent some, but little, time considering the criticisms levelled by various international non-governmental organisations, such as FIDH, Human Rights Watch, and Amnesty International,[21] that the Guiding Principles do not go far enough and fail to establish a set of standards which might effectively ensure businesses' respect for human rights. Nor did we discuss in detail that despite the existence of the Guiding Principles, TNCs generally are only required to legally respect the laws which apply within their jurisdiction and that many choose where to site their head offices and regional subsidiaries very carefully so as to ensure they are exposed to jurisdictions with regulatory regimes designed and advertised to reduce costs in the form of absence of minimum wage legislation, undemanding employee health and safety regulations and the like. We discussed the existence of the UN Global Compact which invites various bodies, including business enterprises, to publicly endorse and subscribe to a range of human rights standards and principles, but we did not stress the potential implications of the still very modest take-up by business and TNCs; even an entirely voluntary and mostly self-regulatory initiative has failed to achieve widespread support and endorsement. Thus, as the above discussion illustrates, CSR and the Guiding Principles have attracted extensive criticism, ranging from wholesale denunciations of the very possibility of capitalism being genuinely 'ethical' through to more specific concerns with the implementation of international standards for human rights-respecting business. We chose not to draw undue attention to such criticism, preferring to acknowledge its existence whilst moving on to consider how this knowledge can be practicably realised.

Was this wrong? Does the force of such extensive criticism effectively invalidate any attempt to instil knowledge of standards and principles which appear to be so precarious? Answering these questions requires a response grounded upon an ethical perspective but one which attempts to address a specific context and set of challenges.

Accentuating the positive: Myanmar, the lesser evil and ethical prudence

Few can be under any illusion that corporate abuse of human rights is going to end any time soon and everyone with a genuine interest in the potential influence of CSR and the Guiding Principles must brace themselves for far too many further examples of just how thoroughly harmful for many people's human rights business practice will be. A fundamental question this raises has both conceptual and strategic elements: given the continuing fact of corporate abuse of human rights are we all justified in throwing out the baby of human rights-respecting business with the dirty bath water of businesses' proven abuse of human rights? Someone who considers any and all forms of capitalism to be inherently unethical and specifically incompatible with human rights will argue that this is precisely what should be done if only in the name of conceptual clarity and rigour. I myself would have been inclined towards a very similar claim not so long ago. However, whilst recognising the truly terrible consequences of many forms of global capitalism for particularly the most vulnerable and poorest members of developing world societies, I am going to resist that conclusion and strategy here. My experiences in Myanmar have, in part, influenced my own shifting view on this key question. A significant part of my revised position and argument stems from a recognition of the need to contextualise the question of what can be done to confront systematic human rights violations and abuses to, in this instance, the peculiar circumstances of contemporary Myanmar.

Contextualising an ethical perspective based upon human rights principles will always cause concern and court controversy among many human rights defenders. After all, an appeal to contextualisation has all too often led directly to a relativist conclusion that specific fundamental human rights should not be upheld in some or other setting precisely because of the alleged need to prioritise some allegedly incompatible cultural or religious tradition or practice. Sometimes this argument has, no doubt, been made in good faith, all too often it has been used only to perpetuate relations of domination and oppression. The appeal to contextualisation is also especially worrying where no human rights law effectively exists (as is mostly the case with corporate human rights obligations in Myanmar) and all one has to fall back upon is an appeal to universally valid moral principles. Needless to say my appeal to a contextualised ethical perspective does not intend to perpetuate domination and oppression in Myanmar. What I do intend to achieve however is to argue that support for CSR and the Guiding Principles, despite the myriad criticisms which have been levelled at both, represents at worst a lesser evil gain, at best an ethically prudential strategy, than simply dismissing the entire venture as nothing more than normative window-dressing for a desperate commercial rush to exploit yet another country's resources and people. Supporting the Burma Principles is, in my opinion, the ethically correct thing to do because the alternative, not supporting them and with them the very aspiration of some ethical business in Myanmar, would be so much worse. Perhaps the opportunity we are confronted by is one of damage limitation, rather than establishing a genuinely and thoroughly human rights-respecting commercial environment. Damage limitation is not typically the kind of call to arms which inspires passionate commitment to the cause, but in certain contexts, it really is an improvement upon the alternative. Justifying this proposed disposition will require a brief summary of Myanmar's current economic condition and the kinds of threats it faces. It will also require a reassessment of the criticisms of capitalism, CSR and the Guiding Principles, evidence of how the spirit of CSR and the Guiding Principles are affecting some commercial developments in Myanmar, before concluding with a fuller explanation of the specific ethical resources I lay claim to.

Having once been considered the Asian country most likely to experience the greatest economic growth immediately after it achieved independence from British colonial rule in 1947, Myanmar now stands as the poorest nation in the region, with the lowest gross domestic product and an estimated 2011 per capita income of just $1144; although this was a significant relative increase on the 2010 figure of $880.[22] Many factors may be blamed for Myanmar's economic catastrophe, including incompetence, corruption and lack of investment, but a crucial factor has been the degree of isolation Myanmar has endured from the rest of the world's economies, which is itself in large measure due to the country's political catastrophe in the form of decades-long, brutally-enforced military rule. Wholesale violations of human rights resulted in many potential Western export markets and sources of foreign investment being denied through effective economic sanctions and embargoes. It is reasonable to say that human rights have thereby exercised a significant impact upon Myanmar's economy for many years. Not all trading partners were deterred by Myanmar's appalling human rights record however. Thus, the absence of Western business investors and partners was filled particularly by Chinese state investment into Myanmar's economy. Although economic trading and investment data are still very unreliable, Myanmar's own Directorate of Investment and Companies Administration indicated that China was responsible for over 31% of all foreign investment in Myanmar as of 31 January 2014. Thailand and Hong Kong were next in the list with 22% and 14.9% respectively. In contrast, all of the European Union countries accounted for 8.75% and the US a mere 0.54%.[23] The biggest investors in Myanmar's economy have been and continue to be countries with poor or very poor human rights records of their own. Anecdotally I have even heard it expressed on several occasions that a desire to reduce Myanmar's growing economic exposure to China was an important motive in initiating the political reform process since Myanmar's human rights record was the single greatest obstacle to attracting many other countries' investment into the country. One commentator on Myanmar has argued that 'since 1988, Myanmar has become reliant on China, too much so for many. Therefore, balancing with India, ASEAN and now the West is seen as helpful in regaining the independence that Myanmar achieved during the Cold War.'[24] Evidence of the harmful impact of Chinese and other foreign investment upon peoples and their environments is widespread. Arguably the most high profile project involves China National Petroleum Corporation's laying of an oil and gas pipeline which runs from the Bay of Bengal all the way to China's Yunnan province and cuts right across the centre of Myanmar with highly damaging environmental consequences for communities whose homes and livelihoods lie in its path. Reports indicate that this project has resulted in land confiscations and widespread forced labour.[25] There have also been popular protests in Myanmar against the exporting of energy resources to China at the same time as much of Myanmar is subject to blackouts and electricity shortages and only 13% of Myanmar's population had access to electricity in 2010. Thailand has also been accused of commercial activities which are significantly harmful, including the Dawei Deep Seaport and Special Economic Zone project which is in the process of destroying swathes of the existing local communities' environments. Other reported abuses of human rights include inadequate levels of financial compensation for farmers whose land was confiscated for a hotel complex at Chaung Tha Beach; the suppression of widespread protests against land confiscation for an industrial zone near Yangon; the beating and arrests of mine workers from Moethi Moemi gold mine in Mandalay division and Myanmar Oil and Gas Enterprise, a largely military-supported commercial enterprise, being linked to widespread land grabs and confiscations.[26] A great deal of Myanmar's economic potential lies within its soil and waters and it is not surprising perhaps that these are the recurring sites of many continuing abuses and the likeliest sources for future conflict. Needless to say, the greater part of current foreign investment into Myanmar does not comply with the Guiding Principles or the spirit of CSR. This constitutes the overriding context within which critical analyses of the justification for CSR and the Guiding Principles must be based. It is an over-used metaphor, perhaps, but the Myanmar economy is at the very least fast approaching a cross-roads wherein there exists a very real possibility of growing economic dependency upon and exposure to state and private investors who have little or no concern for human rights or environmental sustainability. The alternative is to encourage the growth of a different form of capitalist future within which there exists at least the presence of a normative framework that encourages respect for human rights. Clearly, the dissemination of CSR and the Guiding Principles addresses the latter brand of capitalist enterprise, rather than the former. Accepting that Western businesses have all too often directly or indirectly abused human rights leads to a form of lesser evil scenario in respect of prospective investment into Myanmar.

Critics of capitalism (and others as well no doubt) may dismiss this argument as a naïve form of wishful thinking. While this is no place to initiate a deep analysis of the (un)ethical potential and character of capitalism, suffice it to say that Myanmar faces no alternative to some form of capitalist economic growth as a consequence of the global system it is increasingly opening up to. Seen from an essentially utopian standpoint this may be deeply regrettable. Seen from a far more orthodox Marxist perspective one might conclude that it is only a matter of time before the inherent contradictions of the capitalist system collapse in upon themselves. At the acknowledged risk of ludicrously simplifying a vastly complex body of literature, capitalism clearly is not a monolithic, inflexibly determined collection of relations and modes. The ability of capitalism to adapt itself to changing environments which have not themselves been entirely constructed in the image of capitalist relations is a crucial factor in why 'it' has been able to resist internal collapse for so long. Capitalism is capable of reform. One cannot entirely exclude the possibility that the emergence of the notion of extra or non-commercial responsibilities which have been embraced by some businesses, if only mostly at the level of words rather than actions, represents a new development within capitalist enterprise. At the very least, a wholesale denunciation of such gestures as pure cynicism will exclude the possibility of taking these gestures seriously and, as some consumers have already done on occasion, punishing companies for their failure to respect their own CSR codes. Thus, for example, many retail and manufacturing businesses in particular are vulnerable to so-called reputational costs, in which the identity of the brand is compromised through some ethical faux pas. Within post-industrialised societies many consumers opt for particular products not through any needs-based imperative but rather in an attempt to create and fashion a particular sense of personal identity. In a deeper sense, the fact that many people increasingly define themselves through the commodities they buy may be worthy of regret and condemnation but it also creates an area of potential vulnerability for particular types of company. Witness the embarrassment IKEA suffered in 2013 when it air-brushed the images of women out of its Saudi Arabian catalogue.[27] Some IKEA customers, at least, are not only buying flat-packed furniture but are identifying with a brand which has explicitly sought to represent itself as ethical. When it demonstrably fails to do so, the brand is harmed and sales are likely to be affected.

A similar defence can be articulated for the Guiding Principles. The establishment of a normative framework for forms of ethical business which seek to respect human rights is obviously doomed to failure if the pursuit of profit is ultimately incompatible with respecting human rights. However, the Guiding Principles contribute to the emergence of an alternative discourse which, while it may be cynically deployed by some, indicates that there may be increasing commercial interests in respecting, rather than abusing, human rights. The Guiding Principles do not go far enough in some respects, particularly given the entirely voluntary nature of compliance with them, but they do succeed in articulating a space in which human rights considerations can begin to positively influence commercial activity. Many consumers and shareholders may be unconcerned by the knowledge that their products and dividends are blood-stained but there is clearly an established and growing constituency who are and the Guiding Principles address them and thereby also provide criteria by which activists and campaigners may embarrass TNCs doing business in their territories. This does not, of course, include the Chinese government but it does provide a means by which citizens in Myanmar may demand certain standards from many Western investors and businesses. I am inclined to agree with John Ruggie when he writes that the Guiding Principles 'will not bring business and human rights challenges to an end. But it will mark the end of the beginning by establishing a common global platform for action, on which cumulative progress can be built, step-by-step, without foreclosing any other promising longer-term developments.'[28]

It is reasonable to claim that Myanmar is at the beginning of the beginning in respect of the implementation of an ethical framework and culture for business investment and practices. However, developments for both the Guiding Principles and domestic Myanmar circumstances establish some grounds for optimism. The Guiding Principles have been recognised and assimilated into various important regional institutional mechanisms, such as the Organisation for Economic Co-operation and Development and the European Union, both of which will have a direct bearing upon businesses seeking to invest and trade in Myanmar. More specifically, the US government now references the Guiding Principles as a benchmark for a new reporting requirement for US-based commercial enterprises investing more than $500,000 in Myanmar. In his most recent report presented to the UN General Assembly on 24 October 2013, the UN Special Representative explicitly called upon TNCs to adhere to the Guiding Principles in their business dealings in Myanmar. Domestically, while there is no evidence that the Guiding Principles played any role in this decision, the Myanmar president unexpectedly suspended construction of the Myitsone dam in late 2011. The dam was intended as part of a complex of dams supplying electricity to China in a deal struck between Myanmar's previous military regime and the China Power Investment Corporation. A number of domestic non-governmental organisations (some of which were represented at our training sessions) have subsequently referenced the Guiding Principles in their statements and press releases. These are examples of fragile and tenuous gains which if they had occurred in relation to many other countries we would not be justified in celebrating. However, when viewed as part of the ongoing events in Myanmar they take on far greater significance and provide a, albeit tenuous, platform upon which to build.

Finally I wish to conclude by returning to the ethical perspective which informs this analysis and my evaluation of the value and prospects for CSR and the Guiding Principles in Myanmar. The reform process in countries like Myanmar which are emerging from a truly appalling past will necessarily be a slow, incremental affair. The global human rights community has an indispensable contribution to make towards the establishment of an effective human rights-respecting regime and culture in Myanmar. However, one obstacle to this process could originate from within the human rights doctrine itself: namely, the distinct tendency to analyse political and economic challenges in primarily absolutist terms, what Michael Ignatieff refers to as an ethics of 'first principle'.[29]

Rightly or wrongly, many human rights defenders and organisations have long been accused of unduly ignoring the importance of contextual factors in their resort to apparently hard-and-fast tenets of international human rights law. Adopting this approach in Myanmar, particularly beyond the specific issue here of corporate abuse, may prove counter-productive and has already resulted in popular protests against the UN Special Representative's position on the Rohingya. Setting that particular issue to one side for the time being, it nevertheless underlines how great are the challenges faced by those outsiders seeking to support the reform process in Myanmar. Thus, the ethical perspective I am counselling here amounts to what Ignatieff refers to as an 'ethics of prudence'.[30] Western investors and TNCs amount to the lesser evil in the development of Myanmar's economy and, from a human rights perspective, are clearly preferable to some of their counterparts who do not subscribe to any normative code beyond simply what is best for state or private shareholders with no concern for others' human rights. The Guiding Principles provide a basis for seeking to influence subsequent Western investment into Myanmar and should be welcomed on that basis alone. Some TNCs' CSR codes also provide potential leverage for campaigners, both in Myanmar and beyond, in order to name and shame businesses whose conduct in Myanmar violates their own codes.

The greatest legitimate worry about any appeal to ethical prudence and a departure from an ethics of first principle involves the slippery slope fear that we will no longer be able to define where our unconditional lines are to be drawn. Ethical prudence can all too easily accompany a Realpolitik which prioritises the interests of powerful stakeholders over collective interests. The human rights community's engagement in Myanmar will need to be ever vigilant towards this possibility. However, there is an ethical imperative, which calls for engagement, and this engagement will itself only be effective if we are all prepared to accept that corporations can be influenced to respect human rights far more successfully than they have generally to date. The ICESCR includes the key criterion of parties realising their legal obligations progressively. While this criterion has been abused, of course, I believe that it provides a basis upon which we should hold business accountable, but first we have to believe that the whole notion of human rights-respecting business is not an entire sham. In the case of Myanmar, the price of endorsing this belief will most likely be paid by those who will be exposed to the very worst excesses of global capitalism and I can see no good reason for human rights defenders to wish for this outcome.

Disclosure statement

No potential conflict of interest was reported by the author.

Notes

1. How one refers to 'Myanmar' has long been a politicised issue. I opt for Myanmar throughout this article as this is typically how a wide variety of different ethnic communities who I have spent time with have referred to the country.
2. The full text of the 'Guiding Principles' is available here: http://www.ohchr.org/Documents/Issues/Business/A-HRC-17-31_AEV.pdf

3. An understanding of human rights exemplified by Henry Shue, *Basic Rights: Subsistence, Affluence and U.S. Foreign Policy*, 2nd ed. (Princeton, NJ: Princeton University Press, 1996).
4. Surprisingly little academic attention has been paid to the relationship between human rights as normative principles and various manifestations of capitalism as an economic set of relations. One volume which directly addresses this is Janet Dine and Andrew Fagan, eds, *Human Rights and Capitalism: A Multidisciplinary Perspective upon Human Rights* (Cheltenham, UK: Edward Elgar, 2006).
5. Milton Friedman, 'The Social Responsibility of Business is to Increase its Profits', *New York Times Magazine*, 13 September 1970.
6. A very similar argument was defended by Clive Crook, 'The Good Company', *The Economist*, 20 January 2005, http://www.economist.com/node/3555212
7. For a detailed analysis of the relationship between human rights and CSR see D. Cassel, 'Human Rights Business Responsibilities in the Global Marketplace', *Business Ethics Quarterly* 11, no. 2 (2001): 261–74.
8. European Commission, 'Green Paper – Promoting a European Framework for Corporate Social Responsibility', COM/2001/0366 final, 2001, 6–7.
9. See the introduction to A. Crane, D. Matten and L.J. Spence, eds, *Corporate Social Responsibility: Readings and Cases in a Global Context* (London: Routledge, 2008).
10. For more on this see http://www.ihrb.org/about/programmes/multi-year-project-in-myanmar.html
11. I was accompanied by Ms Tara Van Ho to whom I am indebted for the invaluable contribution she made to this project.
12. M. Blowfield and J.G. Frynas, 'Setting New Agendas: Critical Perspectives on Corporate Social Responsibility in the Developing World', *International Affairs* 81, no. 3 (2005): 499–513, 505.
13. See Crook, 'The Good Company'.
14. D. Vogel, *The Market for Virtue: the Potential and Limits of CSR* (Washington, DC: Brookings Institute Press, 2005), 182.
15. J.D. Margolis and J.P. Walsh, *People and Profits: The Search for a Link Between a Company's Social and Financial Performance* (London: Lawrence Erlbaum Associates, 2001).
16. Leslie Sklair, 'Corporate Social Responsibility in the Era of Capitalist Globalization', in *Corporate Social Responsibility: Comparative Critiques*, ed. K. Ravi Rahman and R.D. Lipschutz (Basingstoke: Palgrave, 2010), 25–41.
17. Ibid., 33.
18. M. Tumin, 'Business as a Social System', *Behavioural Science* 9, no. 2 (1964): 120–30.
19. See Crane, Matten and Spence, *Corporate Social Responsibility*, 6.
20. For full text of the General Comment see United Nations Economic and Social Council, *The Right to Water*, E/C.12/2002/11 (General Comments), 2002, http://www.unhchr.ch/tbs/doc.nsf/0/a5458d1d1bbd713fc1256cc400389e94
21. In particular see Human Rights Watch, *Without Rules: A Failed Approach to Corporate Accountability* (2013), hrw.org/world-report/2013/essays/112459
22. UN data, 2012, http://www. http://data.un.org/CountryProfile.aspx?crName=MYANMAR
23. Myanmar Directorate of Investment and Company Administration, http://www.dica.gov.mm/dicagraph.htm. Suffice it to say that most commentators acknowledge the present limitations to obtaining reliable economic data on Myanmar.
24. R.H. Taylor, 'Myanmar's "Pivot" Toward the Shibboleth of Democracy', *Asian Affairs* 44, no. 3 (2013): 392–400, 399.
25. See *The Irrawaddy*, 'Burma an "Extreme Risk" for Business and Rights Abuse', 19 December 2011.
26. See EarthRights International, 'Chinese Oil Company Linked to Human Rights Abuses in Burma (Myanmar)', 9 December 2011; and Business and Human Rights Resource Centre, 'Shwe Gas Movement Report', September 2011.
27. See *The Independent*, 'IKEA Airbrushes Women From its Saudi Catalogue', 2 October 2012.
28. Report of the Special Representative of the Secretary General on the Issue of Transnational Corporations and Other Business Enterprises, John Ruggie, 21 March 2011, 5.
29. M. Ignatieff, *The Lesser Evil: Political Ethics in an Age of Terror* (Princeton, NJ: Princeton University Press, 2004), 9.
30. Ibid.

Index

Note: Page numbers in **bold** type refer to figures
Page numbers in *italic* type refer to tables
Page numbers followed by 'n' refer to notes

For Product Safety Concerns and Information please contact our EU representative GPSR@taylorandfrancis.com
Taylor & Francis Verlag GmbH, Kaufingerstraße 24, 80331 München, Germany

www.ingramcontent.com/pod-product-compliance
Ingram Content Group UK Ltd.
Pitfield, Milton Keynes, MK11 3LW, UK
UKHW051832180425
457613UK00022B/1216